BEFORE WAR

On Marriage, Hierarchy and Our Matriarchal Origins

Elisha Daeva

True Story Books

For

Marija Gimbutas,

Riane Eisler, and

Martin Prechtel

No doubt, for a while at least, very little will change. Whole fields of knowledge–not to mention university chairs and departments, scientific journals, prestigious research grants, libraries, databases, school curricula and the like–have been designed to fit the old structures and the old questions. Max Planck once remarked that new scientific truths don't replace old ones by convincing established scientists that they were wrong; they do so because proponents of the older theory eventually die, and generations that follow find the new truths and theories to be familiar, obvious even. We are optimists. We like to think it will not take that long.

—David Graeber and David Wengrow,
The Dawn of Everything

TABLE OF CONTENTS

INTRODUCTION

We live in exciting times. A paradigm shift is happening. New stories about the nature of our species and the origins of civilization are coming to light.

In science, which has replaced religion as the official creator of truth, paradigm shifts happen when new data leads to new theories. Most of what we think we know are only theories. The theories about human origins become our identity, our cosmology, our mythology.

What do you believe about our ancient past? The standard narrative that most of us learned in school is that we were killer apes who evolved into violent ape men who dragged ape women around by the hair. Then we invented agriculture, which led inevitably to killer civilizations where some people ruled over others with an iron fist, which led to us now, the most advanced and enlightened humans that have ever lived. Men have always been in charge, while women have done nothing of importance to history except raise children and serve men.

But have you ever examined the evidence for this story? We will be examining evidence from archaeology, anthropology, linguistics, history, genetics, zoology, and mythology. A new narrative is emerging: domination and oppression do not seem to be universal or inevitable.

Instead, the evidence suggests that for long stretches of time, humans lived peaceful, sexy lives. We've enjoyed civilizations with skilled artisans, large populations, and long-distance trade, without war and oppression. Women seem to have been at the center of the development of agriculture and the arts of civilization. The oppression of some groups by others that is ubiquitous today may trace back to just two groups who took over the world.

I've been collecting data for this book for over twenty years. For most of that time, these topics were rarely discussed. But since 2017, with the emergence of the genetics data, there's been a surge of interest. Two popular books, *The Dawn of Everything* and *The Patriarchs: How Men Came to Rule*, have challenged these old stories about our past.

The story of oppression is tangled up with the story of Eurasian origins, though not because any one people were inherently bad. A debate raged in academia for two hundred and fifty years about the homeland of Europeans. Then it became taboo. Then it was discovered once again. And then it became taboo again. Now, suddenly, it's an idea whose time has come, once again. It's a big story that needs to be told.

Who am I to write this book, you ask? My degree in Human Biology from Stanford combined anthropology, animal studies, and psychobiology. I'm a generalist: I seek the truth across academic disciplines.

After a few years working in a neuropsychology lab at UCLA, I was shocked at the bias and politics in academia. The researcher I worked for only mentored his one male grad student while treating the female ones like secretaries, advising them to flirt with the computer geek who programmed the experiments if they wanted anything done. I was asked to remove data points that didn't fit my boss' theories.

So I dropped out to become a computer programmer. Since then, I've studied the human animal on my own. I've pored over research papers in archaeology, anthropology, genetics and linguistics.

Since dropping out of academia, I've been studying how politics influences science and how scientific paradigms shift. I've become a scientific heretic, challenging dogmas that limit new ideas. I still believe in the scientific method, but I don't believe that all scientists are objective and unbiased.

Still, I learned a lot from my academic studies. But no one has taught me so much about the human past as Martín Prechtel, brilliant author and teacher of indigenous ways whose school I attended for four years. Martín grew up bilingual on a Pueblo Indian reservation in New Mexico, and later became a medicine man among the highland Maya people of Guatemala. This enables him to understand ancient perspectives in ways that modern academics do not. He speaks many languages and is the most intelligent thinker about ancient cultures I have ever encountered. At the school, he lectured on ancient cultures, led us in ritual, and taught us to create things with our hands as offerings to the divine. He transmitted to us a small inkling of the indigenous way of thinking, as contrasted with what he calls the "gringo mind," the modern mentality. Without this understanding, we've little hope of interpreting the past.

Our first assignment at Martín's school was to research our origins. If you have some ancestors who came from Europe, India, or the Middle East, this book may get you thinking about it. We all deserve to know where we came from.

With the benefit of Martín's unique education along with my Western education, my scientific training, and my travel around the world focusing on ancient sites and museums, I have a broad perspective on the past. I am so focused on, and fascinated by, the ancient world that it sometimes feels more real to me than the modern one.

Ever since I could remember, I had a feeling there was something wrong with the world.

As a teenager in Washington DC in the eighties, I didn't see anybody that I wanted to grow up to be. I lived in fear of nuclear war. I resented the fact that, as a girl, I was expected to clean up after dinner instead of joining the men's conversations.

Most of the boys I knew were cruel to girls. Not in the way girls are to each other, or in the joking, sparring way they were with boys, but in a crude, demeaning, condescending way. In high school, I was date-raped by a college wrestler. Growing up in DC, I was saddened by the fact that rich white people lived in the affluent Northwest area while poor black people lived in the other parts of the city.

I couldn't see the connection between all these things wrong with the world yet, but I knew sex was involved somehow … and nuclear war. That was big back then.

I fell in love for the first time during my freshman year at Stanford. Jim was the one of the first gentle young guys I had met in my short life. He introduced me to environmentalism. When the famous Exxon Valdez oil tanker spilled oil all over the ocean, I was horrified. I went door-to-door, raising awareness. I concluded that the destruction of the planet was something else wrong with the world.

Jim taught me how to have sex that I actually liked. But I still didn't know women could have orgasms, too. How had I gone so long without knowing this? Then, when I was 22, I finally figured out what was wrong with the world, that tied all these terrible things together: bad sex, no orgasms for women, mean boys who hate girls, women who feel obligated to serve men, nuclear war, and environmental destruction.

The book that connected all these dots for me was *The Chalice and the Blade* by Riane Eisler. She presents archaeological evidence that before 3500 BCE, many human societies did just fine without war and without some groups of people oppressing others. The original split of humanity into males and females, in which males are better, paved the way for the racism and classism that came later.

Eisler's book changed my life. One reviewer called it the most important book since Darwin's *Origin of Species*. While no one had ever explicitly taught me that war and dominance are universal parts of human nature, I, like most people, took it for granted. Now I had a name for what was wrong with the world: the "dominator paradigm," as Eisler called it; also known as patriarchy.

The term "patriarchy" triggers some people, because they think it's about blaming men. There was a concerted campaign by the Men's Rights Activists (who advocate for men's rights to continue to dominate women) to convince people that the conversation about patriarchy is about hating men. It's not! *Patriarchy is an institution that oppresses everybody, and which is perpetuated by women as well as by men.* But "dominator paradigm", the term invented by Riane Eisler, doesn't exactly roll off the tongue. The term "patriarchy" has been demonized, and overworked, but it's concise and well-recognized. It doesn't imply that men are to blame, just that most societies are still governed by men, and many women still take men's names. I'm reclaiming it. Some people who mock it claim no one can define it. I can.

Patriarchy is defined as a society where some groups of people dominate others due to accidents of birth: being born male, or into a dominant class or ethnic group. This is distinct from hierarchies of skill or talent.

I'll also use the terms "patrist" and "matrist." A patrist society revolves around male competition: wars and armies. It's basically synonymous with patriarchy. A matrist society revolves around female cooperation. It's synonymous with "partnership" because in matrist societies, men and women are more equal. Having men in charge is associated with patrism, which leads to a lower standard of living for the average person and a higher standard for the elites. But not because men are bad; testosterone and aggression can be channeled in positive ways. Male-dominated societies lead to oppression because the necessity of tracing descent through the father means keeping track of paternity, which means controlling sexuality, which leads to psychopathology and coercion. More about that later.

All societies nowadays are a blend of those two basic polarities, patrism and matrism. Matrist and patrist traits are handed down by cultural tradition. Culture is the transmission of a set of beliefs that we come to consider normal when we're too young to question whether they really *are* normal. A culture can be a civilization, subculture, family, or even a group of friends. It's like a cult, except people usually join cults as adults, which requires more extreme conditioning than with children.

Once we've been conditioned into a set of cultural beliefs, we will often cling to them and angrily defend them if challenged. This is our truth, our cosmology, our foundation. Our lives revolve around it. No one wants to think that our families, friends, religions, and institutions are wrong. So we're subconsciously motivated to notice only those things that align with our beliefs. Beliefs perpetuate themselves with this confirmation bias. As such, this book may bother those attached to beliefs such as Christianity, monogamy, marriage, the nuclear family, or male leadership. In sharing this information for decades I've received a lot of anger. Please excuse me if I come off as defensive or embattled.

Patriarchy is a cult that believes that sex is shameful, while violence is inevitable or even glorious; that some people are born better than others; that only what men do matters. As long as you're seeing the world through this lens, you're missing half the story. The female half. It's not an accurate view of the past or the present.

My hope is that in reading this book, you'll join me in seeing the world through this lens of matrist and patrist, dominator vs egalitarian. You'll see that not only is oppression *not* inevitable, but represents a distortion of human nature. This new worldview is less of a new lens, and more like removing the blinders that block out the female half of the world. The only cultures you learn about in school are the male dominated ones: Sumer, classical Greece, Rome. You never hear about the Minoans, the Cucuteni culture of Ukraine, or Çatalhöyük in Turkey, for example. So the new lens of matrism vs. patrism will enable you to see history more accurately.

As we will see, both matrism and patrism are possibilities for our species, but matrism may be the default, while patrism may be a trauma response. Interestingly, these two poles are mirrored by our closest relatives, the two subspecies of chimps. Common chimps are male dominated and violent, with social hierarchies (alpha and beta males). With bonobos, on the other hand, cooperation between females keeps male dominance in check. Given that bonobos have more in common with us, since we both have extended mating beyond the estrus (heat) period, you'd think that they would be more often studied as our model. As we will see, that's not the case. In the chapter on animals, we'll examine the factors that affect how egalitarian a species is — and see that humans can go either way.

The discovery that oppression is not universal and inevitable sent me on a thirty-year journey. I've been traveling the world collecting data across academic disciplines about how social inequality started, and what was happening before. It's changed my perspective on our species. *Once you see the paradigm, you can't unsee it.*

I advocate for women to be given the opportunity to prove their merit, so that humanity doesn't miss out on their contributions to science and the arts and culture. There have been female physicists, mathematicians, sculptors, carpenters, engineers, biologists, astronauts, chemists, and so on, who have been as successful in their chosen fields as men. Queens and female prime ministers and mayors have led at least as well as men, disproving the notion that women's biology makes them unfit for positions of power. This is all feminism is: the radical notion that women are human beings and should be given the same opportunities as men. There is no good reason to exclude women from playing important roles in society.

Groups wanting to undermine feminism have spread the idea that feminists hate men. There are, of course, women who hate men, who have had terrible experiences, but you won't find any serious feminist literature based around man-hating. There are plenty of men who hate women, though, judging by comments online, the misogynist beliefs that all mass shooters share, and the hate mail received by female celebrities.

Sure, there are plenty of damaged women who throw around feminism and patriarchy when they're angry at their partners. Some of those partners may deserve it, and patriarchy may be relevant. Some may not. Women are not always right. But angry women are not what feminism is about. It's a testament to how much women *love* men that most don't give in to man-hating despite centuries of being sex slaves and domestic servants; being raped, murdered, traded in marriage alignments, and burned at the stake; and nowadays, raped, belittled, talked over, denied promotions, physically beaten, and expected to do most of the childcare and housework even when they work outside the home.

Of course ... that may be partly because this history hasn't been taught. Or they assumed that these situations are normal, natural and inevitable. This book will change that.

If you read historical fiction with female protagonists, you know how terrible things were for women for millennia. They were prevented from being independent beings, travelling alone, working, or studying. A pregnancy without a contract with a man, even if they had been raped, meant their lives were ruined. They bore all the consequences of sex, whether consensual or not, but had no rights over their children. They had no choice whether to bear children. They were entirely dependent on the whims of men. Women who were too smart or independent were imprisoned for life in a convent. That was the fate of others whose family didn't want to pay their dowries.

Those centuries of suffering, and the echoes that remain in our modern lives, is what the story of patriarchy is about. Hating men is what the story of patriarchy is *not*. I for one appreciate men's contributions. There are so many male heroes.

And feminism also doesn't mean that women can't make the choice to dedicate themselves to raising the next generation. That is a beautiful choice. *Feminism means that women have a choice of how to spend their lives!*

I would never consider women to be the victims here, or men to be victimizers. Both men and women are negatively affected by this system. Men are discouraged from seeking support, which leads to high levels of suicide. Women, oftentimes, perpetuate patriarchy even more than men, because they have been even more heavily conditioned, so that they go against their better interests. Personally, I can say that more women in my life have been agents of patriarchy than men. Some women uphold patriarchy to enhance their personal power. Some because they feel insecure about other women's success, or who want to justify their choices. Women as well as men try to silence this important conversation about patriarchy, often by pretending it's saying that men are all bad and women are all good. Nothing is that simple.

This is not a story of victimization. It's a story of empowerment, of knowing our true history, knowing what we are capable of. It can help us understand why women may still feel inferior to men in some ways. This is the telling of a new story.

As for men … partnership culture is better for you, too. Because as the saying goes, unless you're the lead dog, the view never changes. Patrism may bring some advantages, but overall, you're better off with equality, since you won't get bullied by bosses or other guys. That's why men fought for partnership cultures, as we will see. And in fact, many of the things that men are angry about nowadays, that they sometimes blame women or feminism for, are actually due to patriarchy. More on that later.

The personal is political, as the famous feminist slogan goes, so back to my personal story.

Graduating from Stanford with honors, I had a bright future ahead of me in academia. Had I gone straight to graduate school, I would likely have entered my academic career convincing myself that we, the objective academic experts, are the only ones entitled to an opinion, and that the scientific method always uncovers unbiased truth. I would have had so much time and money invested in my career that I would have *had* to believe in the integrity of the scientific system. Instead, by working in the field with nothing invested, I was able to see the way politics informs scientific paradigms.

I had straight A's in school. My boss at the neuroscience lab had to grudgingly admit that the research paper I had presented was brilliant. But I just couldn't deal with academia. I really didn't like the way they treated the lab rats, both the actual rats and the unfortunate human split-brain patients they were using to learn about the brain.

Besides. When I saw how the professors treated the female graduate students, and how only the men got mentored and invited to co-author papers, I knew the deck was stacked against me getting a tenured position somewhere I wanted to be. I would be lucky to get a 20,000 dollar a year assistant position in some backwater. So I became a software engineer making a hundred dollars an hour, helping to create the brand-new internet in San Francisco with a bunch of burners and ravers. That was much more fun.

I don't knock all academics. Most are well-intentioned. They're doing painstaking work, for which I'm very grateful. But it's human nature to subconsciously focus on things that win approval while avoiding things that make others uncomfortable or are unlikely to get funding. That's how dogmas persist despite lack of evidence. In fields that don't affect ordinary lives much, politics plays less of a role. But it plays a huge role in archaeology and history, because the story of our past is about our true nature and potential. Those who control the narrative about our past control our future. Anyway, even without politics, most scientific truths will be revised in the future when the evidence is overwhelming, as they have in the past … so we should be open-minded to new theories. Unfortunately, some academics are not.

After *The Chalice and the Blade* changed my life at the age of 22, I discovered feminism. I'd never heard of it before. I found Gloria Steinem's book *The Revolution Within*, about how patriarchy teaches women to base their self-worth on meeting unrealistic beauty standards. For the first time in my young life I could accept my physical form. Like most girls, I had been critical of my appearance since puberty, when we start comparing ourselves to the images of models we're bombarded with.

On that note: I learned later that Steinem was funded by the CIA. Perhaps governments have a financial interest in collecting taxes from two households instead of one, so benefit from single motherhood, which is a natural result of feminism encouraging women to leave abusive or stagnant relationships. I don't advocate for single parenting, but for conscious, committed co-parenting, ideally in community. The nuclear family has not worked for many, but there are other options other than nuclear families and single parents. More on that in the final chapter.

Newly empowered from my discovery of feminism, I wanted to share the good news that prehistoric people lived in peace. If we had lived in peace before, we could do it again. We weren't doomed! I shared the news with my college friends, in the world's first internet forum, the Well.

My progressive, rebellious friends were triggered by this news. They may have been the first people in history to type in all caps to indicate online anger. WE HAVE ALWAYS BEEN MALE DOMINATED AND VIOLENT!! QUIT LIVING IN A DREAM WORLD!!!

I couldn't believe it. This was *good* news. Why were they so attached to this system? Twenty-five years later, things have changed some: "patriarchy" has become a household word. For example, the *Game of Thrones* series *House of the Dragon* revolves around themes of patriarchy, according to the writers' post-episode commentary. Many people have slowly acclimated to the idea that we live in a patriarchal culture, though a reformed one. Some even have a vague idea that we didn't always. But we're never taught about it in school. We're not taught that there are times when we lived without war and oppression.

If we tell ourselves this is the best that we can do, that all this genocide, rape and torture is our nature, nothing will ever change. If we tell ourselves that blowing up innocent people is the only way to solve conflict, we will keep doing that. If war is inevitable, we might as well be the ones dropping those bombs, or someone else will, right? Why bother protesting it? It's just the way it has always been. Right?

No. There is another way to be. If we tell ourselves that, we have a chance of saving the world. That's why I've been obsessed with this topic for decades. Information is power. This information can help us individually to unpack the neuroses that come with the patriarchy distortion, so we don't have to suffer from those anymore. But more importantly … it's time for society as a whole to wake up from this nightmare.

CHAPTER ONE

THE PATRIARCHY PACKAGE

Once upon a time, before there was war, men and women had equal importance. Civilization arose under these conditions and flourished for longer periods than our Western culture has existed. Our civilization is built upon the foundation of these earlier cultures.

It sounds like a fairy tale. But the evidence is undeniable.

Patriarchy is a system in which some people dominate others based on birth, not merit. Around 5000 years ago, it took over the world, in what Engel's classic book *The Origin of the Family* referred to as "the world-historic defeat of the female sex."

I call it "the Patriarchy Package." It's a package of terrible things that go together: war, rape, racism, social classes, ethnic hatred, and dominance hierarchies. In patriarchy, half of humanity enjoys more freedom, self-confidence, money, and orgasms than the other half.

ORIGINS OF PATRIARCHY

Until recently, the institution of patriarchy was never spoken about, unconsciously assumed to be natural and inevitable. Now there *is* a conversation about it, but few talk about how it came to be, and what came before.

In fact, some people actively deny it exists, or dismiss it entirely. They think it's natural — just the way of the world. This book is for them. It's for people who roll their eyes at the idea that all our problems stem from patriarchy. The thing is … it just may be true. It just may *be* the cause of all societal woes.

As Bruce Gerrard, author of *The Ancient Problem of Men*, put it: "Patriarchy is a modern aberration rather than the natural order of things."[1]

Prehistorians tell us that cultures in prehistory were far more egalitarian and peaceful than those in historical times. Archaeological evidence for violence and status hierarchies is extremely sparse before 4000 BCE, while after that date, it was everywhere. It got more predominant as the years went on, as I will show.

Some scholars believe that while mobile hunter-gatherers were relatively egalitarian, the shift to agricultural settlements led to inequality, with the ability to hoard resources. The evidence does not support this. People lived in egalitarian farming settlements for more millennia than Western culture has existed.

Other scholars believe that inequality arose with increasing population size, which led to "social complexity" — a word academics use which is really a euphemism for class oppression. The evidence that I present in the following chapters does not reflect this either. There were settlements that included tens of thousands of people, with little to no signs of violence or inequality.

I've read every single book and research paper I could find on the origins of patriarchy. No one else was talking about it. Then, around 2017, the new field of genetics created a huge resurgence of interest in it. The DNA evidence confirms there was an enormous transformation of human life that began around 4000 BCE when nomadic herders from the Russian steppe (a huge area of dry grasslands that extends from Ukraine to Manchuria) overran Eurasia. These events created the world as we still know it today.

The nomads spread male dominance, class oppression, war, and marriage around the world by means of the horse. They destroyed the indigenous male genes of western Eurasia. Whether they killed the local men or just monopolized the women, we don't know, but it was successful; genes don't lie. *The local men did not pass on their genes at all.* The indigenous male DNA went from dozens of lineages to just two!

My hypothesis is that when the nomads first arrived in an area, they killed the men; they did not yet know how to keep a permanently enslaved population of men, until they figured out how to *psychologically* enslave them. Future generations were hybrids between the two cultures.

This is a really big story. *Europeans are descended from barbaric steppe nomads and the women whose civilization they destroyed and appropriated.* It's a story of rape and genocide and colonization. Our paternal DNA comes from the invaders, and our maternal DNA from the indigenous Eurasians who developed civilization. The genetic evidence has proved archaeologist Marija Gimbutas right about this.

The scientists who are lecturing and writing books on these topics today are acting like it's a new story that they've uncovered. But it's an old story. It just got silenced with a smear campaign. Some of these academics are only telling half the story, from an unbalanced perspective. They reiterate the evidence for violence, male dominance, inequality, and inheritance through the male line among the steppe nomads, almost with a sort of glee.

What they *don't* talk about is the evidence for the peaceful, egalitarian people who were indigenous to Eurasia, before the invasions. Shouldn't *that* be the big story, given that war and male dominance are the defaults today?

THE LINK BETWEEN PATRIARCHY AND TRAUMA

Some people believe that this package of patriarchal traits only arose once in the world, among the steppe nomads, and spread to everyone from there. However, I lean more toward the hypothesis that patriarchy is a basic pattern in the world that has arisen more than once. There are male-dominant cultures, such as some Australian aborigines and Papua New Guineans and Amazonians, who seem to have had no contact with steppe nomads. Or perhaps they did, and it's been forgotten. (One Papuan language uses the word "*appa*" for "father" like some Semitic

3

and Indian languages, but that one data point alone is insufficient to draw conclusions.) Also, patriarchy existed in the Neolithic in Central Europe: a group in France has been found in 2023 that traced kinship through the male line.

But many cultures trace kinship through both male and female lines. The very ancient cultures of Göbekli Tepe in Turkey and Motza in the Middle East, both from around the 9th century BCE, had mostly male representations in art instead of female. Perhaps this distant age was a previous cycle of male importance. However, there has been no violence found there.

Humans have taken on so many diverse forms of culture. Some may even shift between male-focused and female-focused seasonally. We are a plastic species.

What I *can* say with a high degree of confidence, however, is that before 4000 BCE, in the areas where civilization arose, there is little evidence for violence, status hierarchies, or male dominance.

This book will focus on that region where civilization arose, the agricultural cultures of southern and eastern Europe, the Middle East, Mesopotamia, and India. The focus will be much more on gender inequality than on class or race oppression. I touch only briefly on evidence from hunter-gatherers, and on issues of race or class. Also, the focus is on male-female relationships. Please use whatever terms for men and women you prefer.

OUTLINE OF THIS BOOK

This book will present thousands of data points. You may find some points hard to believe. As I will show, there is a strong bias to believe that violence and hierarchy are universal. Please reserve your judgment until the end. Some parts of this book may not be for everyone. Some science-lovers may delight in the geeky technical details about linguistics and genetics. Some readers, more interested in the basic concepts and how they apply to our lives today, may prefer to skim over some academic details.

The first two chapters will summarize these basic concepts. You won't see many citations, as this is a summary based on twenty years of research. In many cases, it's impossible to trace an argument to a single source. The arguments will be backed up in future chapters, with abundant citations. The following summary comes from hundreds of sources but mostly from the work of archaeologist Marija Gimbutas, Riane Eisler's *The Chalice and the Blade*, Graber and Wengrow's *The Dawn of Everything*, James DeMeo's *Saharasia*, David Anthony's *The Horse, The Wheel, and Language*, Robert Briffault's *The Mothers*, and Gerda Lerner's *The Creation of Patriarchy*.

Bruce Garrard's *The Problem with Men* is another book about this enormous shift from a society based in balance between women and men, to one all about violent men and the destruction of the environment. He says:

> For modern men, there is a tendency to either deny all this outright, or to partake in some form of collective guilt. Neither is helpful. […] this change has affected everyone, both male and female, in negative and harmful ways.
>
> The problem is not entirely with men, but with people. Men may have gained some apparent advantages by way of political control, property rights and so on, but to imagine that this has made them intrinsically happier than women would be to entertain a complete illusion. Sexism […] harms everyone on both sides of the equation, since we all end up being (and being treated as) less than human.[2]

As he says: the problem isn't men. The problem is paternity: the institution of fatherhood, tracing descent through the male line. That's right: needing to know who your daddy is, is the root of all evil.

It's counterintuitive. Fatherhood is a progressive, feminist thing, right? I'm not suggesting you *shouldn't* know who your daddy is, if possible; it's useful information. Personally, I adore my Dad and I'm infinitely grateful that for all he's given me. I'm *not* suggesting men should take no responsibility for children. Anyone who takes responsibility for raising a child is a hero. If it's your dream to father your biological child, that's great too. If you brought a child into being and the mother needs help, of course you should be responsible.

I'm not knocking fatherhood; I'm advocating for doing it consciously, and for being aware of the dynamics of it. *I'm suggesting we restructure society so that children aren't dependent on any one man or on a fragile sexual bond.*

The evidence does not favor monogamy in our ancestral environment. You may think that women benefit from monogamy and paternity — and of course, they're much better off than under polygamy or as abandoned single mothers — yet these things go hand in hand with patriarchy. But some of our ancestors were promiscuous and perhaps even orgiastic. The evidence for this appears in Chapter 7 on Sexology.

IT'S AN INSTITUTION

It would seem that the Patriarchy Package arose sometime around 4000 BCE when men seized control of the world. It's curious that this date corresponds to the creation of the world in the Bible, and the start of the modern era in the Hindu Rig Veda. Gilda Lerner in her book *The Creation of Patriarchy* documents how this original domination of men over women became a template for the domination of men, too: some ethnic groups over others, and some classes over others.

The word "patriarchy" reflects the fact that men still hold most of the positions of power. Most men are good people and are also oppressed under patriarchy. The deal offered to men under patriarchy is: submit to more powerful men, and you can dominate women. The deal offered to women with class privilege is: submit to men, and you can dominate the lower classes. Until recently, most women could not survive without a man. It's a raw deal for everyone, except the tiny number of men at the top. But even *they* suffer, with suppressed guilt and the fear that the oppressed will revolt.

Many people believe it's impossible to have a complex human society where some people don't lord over others. For example, the Canadian professor Jordan Peterson claims dominance hierarchies are universal.

6

(My goal in life is to debate him on YouTube, because the evidence is on my side.) Other people dismiss the idea that our modern western culture is still a patriarchy, but admit that it *used* to be one, and that other societies in the world still are. If this is true, then when exactly did we cease to be one?

As Ralph Metzner, psychedelic psychologist, says: we're taught that since Sumer (what we're told is the first civilization), it's always been killing, and before that, we were killer apes. We went straight from killer apes to killer guys: a very depressing view of history. But Metzner disputes this. And most prehistorians know better.

Some may be thinking, okay, maybe it was egalitarian, but that was back when we were primitive! In order to be organized, complex, and civilized, we need male dominance and hierarchy. But the evidence reveals that every aspect of civilized life arose during the pre-patriarchal era. Riane Eisler says that *"one of the best-kept historical secrets is that practically all the material and social technologies fundamental to civilization were developed before the imposition of a dominator society."*

Eisler compiled this list of things that predate patriarchy: agriculture, construction, fiber, leather, metals, law, government, dance, ritual drama, oral literature, art, architecture, town planning, long-distance trade, administration, education, and forecasting the future.[3]

The 2021 book *The Dawn of Everything,* by Graeber and Wengrow, an instant classic that validates the premise of this book, states: "women, their work, their concerns and innovations are at the core of this more accurate understanding of civilization [...] What until now has passed for 'civilization' might in fact be nothing more than a gendered appropriation—by men, etching their claims in stone—of some earlier system of knowledge that had women at its centre."[4]

There are two basic ways to organize social animals (mammals that live in groups): male-centered, or female-centered. That is, do the related males of the group remain together and bring in unrelated females as mates, or vice-versa? This seems like a small thing, but it makes a huge difference in our quality of life.

Human groups where related males remain together is referred to as *patrilocal:* women leave home to join their mates' families. Patrilocal marriage goes hand in hand with *patrilineal* inheritance — tracing your lineage through your father and passing most property from father to son. Even in modern Western culture, which is no longer an extreme patriarchy thanks to modernization and feminism, we still take the surnames of our fathers. Patrilocal marriage and patrilineal inheritance usually mean higher status for men than women, competition over cooperation, oppression of some groups over others, war, sadistic violence, psychopathology, sexual repression, sex-shaming, body-shaming, environmental destruction, and other undesirable phenomena. The links between these cultural traits will become clear in future chapters.

In patriarchy, until very recently, male choice has been the norm: men have had control over who gets to have sex with whom, because whoever controls reproduction controls society. Marriage was arranged for economic and political reasons, usually by the father. Men have usually been the ones to court, ask and choose, with the father giving permission. In extreme patriarchies, women have no say in their choice of partners at all. Isn't it rape when someone doesn't get a say over who they have sex with? In that sense, patriarchy is also about rape.

It's also all about colonialism, where one group imposes itself as overlords over another. That has been the fate of humanity for the last 5000 years or so. The horrific re-education of indigenous children that happened in North America and Australia not so long ago continues to this day in Indonesia and Africa. According to the wise teacher Martín Prechtel, empires must tame free people to get taxes out of them, and so crush the indigenous spirit.

Ecstatic, orgiastic natural beings are difficult to control. So empires must shame feminine mystical consciousness. They stamp out shamanic trance, ecstatic dance, drumming, psychedelic ritual, free sexuality. They commit violence, which causes trauma, which makes people easier to control.

Colonizers are envious of the natural belonging, bodily integrity, groove and joy of the natural man, and in lust with the natural woman.[5] So, they commit cultural genocide against the indigenous, partly out of jealousy for their own birthright that they have been denied. We are all so deeply indoctrinated into this system that it's practically invisible; it's like water to a fish. None of us are to blame, but it would serve us to collectively to figure out how to stop it, before it destroys the world.

This system, like all systems, becomes self-perpetuating. Many men have worked to subvert it with kindness and love. Many women perpetuate it even more than men, because women must be even more strongly conditioned to internalize the values and impose them on others if they are to go against their own self-interests.

In my life, more women than men have enforced gender norms on me. They've punished me for being too free and independent. *We like to punish others for the freedoms we don't allow ourselves.* That's why it's a cultural norm in some countries for women to mutilate their daughters' genitals, and stone them to death for having consensual sex.

Men are profoundly oppressed by the system as well. They're raised to ignore their emotions and weaknesses to be tough all the time. They're forced to go to war. They're pressured to be strong providers, to be successful, to jockey for status. They're not encouraged to forge deep bonds and be vulnerable. Due to all this, they tend to die younger and may be more likely to end up in mental institutions. Healing from patriarchy will save men's lives, too.

Almost all men under patriarchy have had to answer to their masters: bosses, bullies, kings. But as I said, their core bargain is to rule over women, in exchange for serving their male masters.

The Bible specifically promises this to men: dominion over women, children, animals, and the Earth itself. So while patriarchy ruins men's lives, too, it would be disingenuous to suggest that women haven't gotten screwed even worse, and I mean that literally.

9

Every society expresses patriarchal values in different ways and to different degrees. All these societies also contain deep, beautiful customs and well-meaning people.

WE'VE COME A LONG WAY, BUT WE HAVE A LONG WAY TO GO

In the last century, in the Western world, we've come a long way. Women are no longer considered property, and breasts no longer get sliced off as punishment for adultery like in ancient Persia. Although the Equal Rights Amendment never passed, so women are still not equal in the United States Constitution, feminists have won the right to vote, to divorce, to own property, and to have credit cards. They won rights over their children, which used to belong only to the fathers. Now, a pregnancy without a father attached no longer means a woman's life is ruined.

It's astonishing what feminism has accomplished since the seventies; it's changed the world in a very short time. But we can't take these rights for granted. Evolution doesn't always move forward. Sometimes we move backwards, as we shall see.

Here are some of the rights women have won only since 1970, the year of my birth: to have their own credit cards, to serve on a jury, to fight on the front lines, to get an Ivy League education, to take legal action against workplace sexual harassment, to say no to sex with their husbands, to get health insurance at the same rate as men, and to use birth control to make their own choices about creating new life.

So, we've come a long way since the seventies, but we still have a long way to go. According to the UN, women make up the majority of trafficked people.[6] Prostitutes are prosecuted in the U.S. instead of their clients. In the U.S., an average of three women a day are murdered by their intimate partners. Most women will endure sexual assault at some point in their lives.

As of 2019, men head 477 out of the 500 Fortune 500 companies. They make up 80% of the United States Congress and 71% of senior management positions, and that's a huge increase from any time in the past.[7] Every American president and most other world leaders have been men. Every time you open your wallet and pull out a dollar bill, you look at a man's face.

Women accounted for only 38 percent of major characters in films in 2022, and that figure has remained the same from year to year. Almost all women onscreen are in their 20's and 30s's, while men in their 40's are common. Men talk three times as much as women in films.[8] Sexual scenes are almost always filmed from the male perspective, the camera lingering on women's sexualized body parts, even if the women are dead.[9]

Women are policed constantly by society: judged for being too sexual, for not being sexual enough, for being too assertive, for being too smart. The internet is awash in hideous misogyny, violent porn, and vicious sex-shaming. Female politicians and celebrities are ruthlessly attacked and dismissed in ways that men aren't.

Mothers are expected to sacrifice their lives for their children in ways men aren't. According to a recent study of 2000 parents, 48 percent of moms say they feel judged by strangers, versus only 24 percent of dads.[10] Men are considered independent beings who have identities outside of their families, while women still have a hard time creating an independent life at all. 42% of women say they have experienced gender discrimination on the job.[11] Male voices are listened to much more closely than female voices, while women are interrupted much more frequently.[12] Misogynist influencers like Andrew Tate, who openly says men should own women as slaves, are popular with young people.

Raising a family still consists of unpaid work that's done mostly by women. Women still do most of the housework even when they work outside the home for as many hours as their partners. On the average day, over half of women, and only a fifth of men, do housework. Men spend less than half as much time with children as women do. In one study, men judged job applicants with female names as lower in competence than with male names.[13] Yet, there is no robust evidence for increased intelligence in men; it's out of the scope of this book to prove that, but please read Angela Saini's book *Inferior* and Cordelia Fine's

11

book *Delusions of Gender* for research into sex differences, and the pervasive bias in science to prove them.

Men have said to me, ok, so women are underrepresented in politics, but that's no big deal, they have other kinds of power. My answer to that is, would you be okay with that? Are there many men who would be satisfied if the vast majority of positions of power were held by women? Nope.

I could go on and on, but the bottom line is that women are still treated as inferior by much of society, judged to have little value beyond youth and beauty, and their willingness to serve. They are particularly dismissed, ignored, and condescended to as they age. Young women sometimes look down on feminism, because they aren't aware of how recently the rights they take for granted were won, and how much of a struggle it was. They also don't realize that the attention they receive has everything to do with their youth. If they knew how invisible they may become as they age, they might have more interest in feminism, and more empathy for older women. But the division between older and younger women is a crucial way that patriarchy is maintained.

Are there *institutional* prejudices against women? Probably not. At this point, the prejudice operates at individual levels, and both men and women hold these prejudices, as they are ingrained in us since childhood. A recent book calls it the "authority gap: the way women are belittled, undermined, questioned, mocked, talked over and generally not taken seriously in public and professional life." Boys are given eight times as much attention by teachers. The author Mary Ann Sieghart believes we can close this gap if men expose themselves to women's voices.[14]

Minor disrespect may seem like a small thing, compared to what women suffered in the past, but it adds up. That's why books like *The Authority Gap*, and this one, are one way of changing the world one mind at a time.

Also, a backlash is happening against women and feminism. Our rights are being eroded all over the world. There's a rise in anti-feminist

12

rhetoric. Oversexualized young girls raised on pornography seem less confident than their mothers. There's a movement to restore the patriarchal role of women as domestic servants, known as the "trad wife" trend. Not that there's anything wrong with the patriarchal wife role, but these young girls need to understand the ramifications of being dependent on someone else and on a sexual bond. "5th wave feminism" is calling for a return to society being the exclusive domain of men. We can't abandon real feminism yet.

Ironically, we're seeing a decline in male achievement at the same time. Richard Reeves in his book *Boys and Men* claims that boys have fallen way behind girls in education, with a gap even greater than it used to be in the other direction. Girls are almost a grade level ahead in English, and have caught up in math. There's a 10 percent gap in college graduation.[15]

So what's going on here? Were females smarter all along, and just held back by patriarchy? No, sex differences in IQ are inconclusive. Richard Reeves believes a big factor is the difference in maturation: girls mature about a year sooner than boys, which sets them up for success in school, and boys never catch up. The solution is to start boys a year later in school.

But my theory is that girls are outpacing boys because after thousands of years of being held back, girls are making up for lost time. Boys, on the other hand, are transitioning from being dominant to equal. They still have lingering patriarchal conditioning that they should be smarter than girls, but now that girls are less oppressed, that's often not the case. So they may develop a complex about it and lose interest in competing with girls.

Reeves also discusses the rise in depression among men. Men cite feeling "useless" as the main factor. I believe this could be due to the transition from patriarchy. For thousands of years, men were taught that their purpose was to rule over women, and to protect and provide for them. Most women don't need or want that anymore, but it takes a long time to change such ingrained ideas.

13

The growing anti-feminist movement likes to suggest that feminism is to blame. They scream about how feminists "don't care" that men are struggling, which is ridiculous because women are engaging with these issues with men in a way that men never did with women's oppression. Anti-feminists try to claim it's the conversation about patriarchy that is oppressing men and boys. Women who want to seem pro-men, or who are concerned for their sons, parrot this idea that feminism is oppressing men. But some women have always stumped for the patriarchy.

But is there evidence for this? I've been on the front lines of feminism for decades and while I've seen talk of toxic masculinity, as well as toxic femininity, I've never seen anyone say masculinity *itself* was toxic, or attack men. The only evidence I see is the way men are portrayed as idiots in some shows and movies. But these are still made by men, so we can't blame feminism for that. In any case, the answer is for men to come forward to support their brothers, the way women have done with women's circles and movements. The more men can put aside patriarchal conditioning that they don't need support, the more they will thrive. It's not a zero-sum game. Men and women can support each other to thrive.

THE OTHER TYPE OF SOCIAL ORGANIZATION

What's the alternative? The other type of social organization is *matrifocal*, meaning that the clan is made up of related females; and *matrilineal*, meaning that you trace your lineage through the female line. You would refer to yourself as the son or daughter of your mother, rather than your father. Matrifocal marriage and matrilineal inheritance go hand in hand with egalitarian social organization, strong mother-child bonds, psychological health, sexual freedom, and peace, as we will see in future chapters.

In matrifocal, matrilineal cultures, men are not oppressed. That's because you always know who your mother is, so the matrilineal lineage does not require control of sexuality. You only need monitor, control, and shame our natural sexual urges in order to keep track of the father. Controlling sexuality leads to coercion and suppression. It means shutting down the body's breath, vitality, and natural expression. This leads to sadism and psychopathology.

It's not easy to force grown men into sex, either. So, the differences in aggression and strength between men and women, plus the basic mechanics of sexual reproduction, mean that matrilineal cultures don't oppress men in the reciprocal way. Also … men are less choosy, since sperm donation is a lot easier than pregnancy; therefore, female partner choice is not likely to require coercion, whereas male choice may.

Since we grew up in this culture, it seems normal that a child born outside of marriage is called a "bastard". But if you think about it, it's ridiculous. How can a human being be illegitimate? Marriage is just a concept. What *does* seem normal is tracing descent through the mother, since you always know who she is.

This book will describe the many human cultures that existed on this planet organized around the matrilineal clan, where grandmothers and aunts stayed together to help raise children. Women inherit the house, which means that children always have a stable home and family. The mother's brother plays the role of father in the children's lives, but the whole clan helps raise the children. Children are not dependent on one male to support them, and their stability is not dependent on a fragile sexual bond. No one is considered "illegitimate". Cooperation is emphasized over competition. There's no shame around sex. We will go into detail about these cultures in the chapter on Anthropology.

As I said, there are some kinship systems which recognize both male and female lines of inheritance, such as Australian aborigines. But in the past, it seems that most groups were organized around one or the other, and that more were matrilineal.

Those organized around female kinship have been called matrist, matristic, gylanic, service-to-other, or "leaver" cultures. The word "matriarchy" implies a culture where women dominate men the way men have dominated women in patriarchies. I have found only one potential matriarchy: Minoan Crete. No culture that we know of has ever dominated men to the same extent as patriarchal ones dominate women. *Since the term seems to apply to something non-existant, I'm reclaiming and redefining it here as a culture where women are more central than men.*

I'll also use "patrism" and "matrism", originally coined in 1954 by Gordon Rattray Taylor in his book *Sex in History*. Bruce Garrard sums these up as follows:

> Matrism ('mother-identification') refers to a form of governance based on the maternal pattern of nurturing all for the benefit of both the whole and each individual within it. Patrism ('father-identification') refers to a form of governance based on the concentration of power and resources in the hands of, and for the benefit of, a single ruler or a small elite group.[16]

So matrism and patrism are the two basic forms of social organization in mammals. Which way a species goes is related to its level of "sexual dimorphism": the ratio of male size to female size. If the male has special features like antlers or tusks, the species has an even higher sexual dimorphism score.

Mammals with a high sexual dimorphism score tend to be competitive hierarchies, with alpha males and beta males, where the alpha males have rights to all or most of the females. The species where the males and females look similar tend to be far less violent. Humans have an average amount of sexual dimorphism, so we can go either way. We're right in the middle. And we've done both.

Figure 1-1: Australians in 1905.[17] Figure 1-2: Matrist Trobriand islanders.[18] Does one group look happier and more relaxed?

The evidence suggests that matrism is more natural for our species, while patrism needs extreme circumstances to develop. Matrism was a very stable and long-lasting condition, but once just one group turns violent, the whole thing collapses. Peaceful societies have three choices:

17

to flee and hide; to be decimated by violence; or to learn to fight, which means they will no longer be peaceful.

Today, of course, almost all people live in patrist cultures. Therefore, it's easy to believe that it's inevitable. But it took thousands of years of brainwashing for patriarchy to win, and to rewrite history to erase the past. Men and women fought back, tooth and nail. *Much of the real history of the past five thousand years is the story of the fight against patriarchy, as I will show.*

It's also easy to believe that patrism is the way it's always been because our matrist story, and the thousands of years of transition from matrism to patrism, has not been recorded by history. Cultures with powerful and independent women were destroyed. Perhaps it was done deliberately to maintain the illusion.

But a few remain, either hiding in remote corners of the globe, or bravely struggling to maintain their ancient ways. I have visited some of them. They seem happy and relaxed, including the men. For the men, it's nice to not have to control anyone, or to be controlled. That's why men actively fought in wars to keep their matrist ways. Patriarchy has ignored and censored women's contributions to culture, and even covered them up.

It's critical, especially for women, to understand the dynamics of this system, because though things have gotten much better over the last few decades, these dynamics still affect our lives. Even worse, they're threatening the earth itself through environmental destruction.

Dr Heide Goettner-Abendroth has been studying matrilineal cultures for decades, as I have. She describes how they prevent accumulation of wealth in a few hands by having the wealthiest clans sponsor festivals to enrich the others, and in so doing be honored by the community.[19] Society is created based on non-hierarchical, horizontal, and egalitarian relationships.[20] They have no battle of the sexes, nor generation gap.[21]

History has been written by the most aggressive victors, and women's stories have been ignored and suppressed. We're told that women have had no history, have never done anything that mattered, and have never

18

lived independently from men until recently. Women have been conditioned to accept their inferiority and the assumed inevitability of male dominance. This has wreaked havoc on their self-esteem, which is lower than men's across the globe.[22] This leads to depression and other mental health issues, eating disorders, and becoming victims of abuse. I believe that the more women understand that they haven't always been inferior, the higher their self-esteem will be. It worked for me. That's why I wrote this.

THE DISCOVERY OF OLD EUROPE

In the 1970's, the archaeologist Marija Gimbutas discovered a lost Neolithic matrist civilization that she called Old Europe. She was a genius. She grew up in Lithuania, one of the most remote corners of Europe, where folk customs still held traces of the matrist past. Her family's deep study of these folk customs gave her the context to re-discover our ancient past.

Over decades, Marija worked on hundreds of digs and uncovered thousands of artifacts. Unlike most over-specialized academics, she took an intuitive, multidisciplinary approach. She spoke many languages so was able to read original sources in their original tongues. She incorporated linguistics, mythology and folklore. It's easier to see a picture of the past when you look beyond a single discipline.

Her archaeological digs spanned such wide areas with such similar cultures that she was able to piece together a common system of symbols for a single widespread culture across Eurasia, which she called Old Europe. They had cultural continuity with ancestors as far back as 30,000 BCE. Starting around 4000 BCE, they were colonized, destroyed, and replaced by invaders, but traces of them remain to this day, especially in the most remote corners of the globe.

See the extras tab of my website BeforeWar.com for a map of cultures of Old Europe.

The matrist Old Europeans were peaceful people who lived in beautiful places with access to good soil for farming. Without war, they didn't have to live in inaccessible places or fortify their settlements. They

19

enjoyed a high level of culture, with copper, gold, and ceramic artifacts, and venerated nature and the earth goddess.

We don't learn about these cultures in school; we're taught that civilization began with Sumer in 3100 BCE. But why doesn't Old Europe count as a civilization? Webster defines civilization as "the stage of cultural development at which writing and the keeping of written records is attained." By this definition, the later descendants of Old Europe, the Bronze Age Minoans, were civilized. The Neolithic cultures that preceded them did have an early form of writing, though it wasn't used for record-keeping, only for ritual. They had highly developed arts, large populations, and long-distance trade.

Personally, I don't see why record-keeping needs to be a qualification, so from here on, I'll use the word "civilization" to include groups with large populations, trade networks, and a high level of art and culture. Some examples of civilizations you don't learn about in school are Vinca, Cucuteni, Tripolye, and Çatalhöyük.

THE INVASION

The patrist invaders who destroyed the Old European world spoke languages from two different language groups: Indo-European and Semitic. These two language families are now very widely spoken. Most of the languages we're most familiar with come from these groups. The Semitic language family included some of the earliest ancient Mesopotamian ones such as Akkadian, and Middle Eastern ones such as Phoenician, Hebrew, Aramaic (the language of the Bible), and Arabic. The Indo-European language family includes most of the European languages as well as ones from northern India.

Chapter 4 is about one of the biggest debates that has ever happened in academia: the origin of the Indo-European language family. Where did these people come from? Marija Gimbutas, the discoverer of Old Europe, believed Indo-Europeans originated in the Russian steppe, north of the Black Sea, and that they began to invade the indigenous Old Europeans starting around 4000 BCE. By 2500 BCE they had destroyed and colonized much of Old Europe.

We don't know whether they killed the men or kept them tightly controlled for life. We don't know if they raped the women or if the women were willing to mate with their invaders, but if the recent European colonization of the Americas is a similar model, there was surely a great deal of rape. As documented in detail by Marija Gimbutas, the children that resulted merged the cultures of their mothers and fathers, creating hybrid cultures between the patrist Indo-Europeans and the matrist Old Europeans.

Every city and village had a different destiny. Each resulting merging of cultures was unique. The Old Europeans were superior to the colonizers in metallurgy, art, pottery, building, jewelry, and clothing. In some places these arts were lost, but in others they survived, though they were of inferior quality.

This was an apocalypse for Old Europe. Refugees fled in all directions except east, the direction where the invaders came from.[23] They hid in easily defensible areas or remote places where they would not be found. Other groups learned to fight, eventually becoming more like the invaders. Perhaps some groups made a truce with the invaders, trading with them and slowly becoming more like them as well. Some fled west to the Aegean where their cultures continued for over a thousand years, culminating in the great Minoan civilization.

Jean Manco, author of the 2013 book *Ancestral Journeys: The Peopling of Europe from the First Venturers to the Vikings,* says this of the Indo-European invaders: "So as they advanced there was a fascinating collision of cultures in key zones, out of which sprang the great civilizations of the Classical world. The Indo-European speakers absorbed a great deal from the cultures they eventually overtook."[24]

Some of the captured women must have influenced their captors to soften their ways. Generations later, long-lost cousins of the invaders would arrive and take over the softer hybrid culture,[25] creating a status hierarchy: ranked layers of conquered ethnic groups pressed into subservience to a small invading class. The previous invaders became the new middle class, and the new conquerors became the new upper class. They must have used brainwashing to create an inferiority

21

complex in the underclass. The class system was born. Gerda Lerner tells us that for men, class is based on their relationship to the means of production; for women, it's about their sexual ties to a man who provides resources.[26] (That's why women are defined as either Miss or Mrs., depending on whether they are tied to a man, while men are always just Mr.)

When the invaders subjugated a group, they became civilized by the women they enslaved. The earliest hybrid cultures retained some of their arts, some human rights for women, and their ancient goddess. Women's spiritual role as priestesses and seers of the goddess persisted much longer than their secular power and influence.

For a long time, some European academics tried to ignore the evidence for this invasion. They wanted Indo-Europeans to be the originators of the Eurasian civilizations. That's what led to this epic academic debate about Indo-European origins; it was about not only European origins, but the origins of patriarchy. Of course, those who want to believe that patriarchy is inevitable and natural don't want to know that it *had* a beginning.

The conversation about these topics was silenced by taboos in two different time periods. The Nazis created their Aryan superman fantasy out of the Indo-European debate (Aryan is another world for Indo-European). Besides the Nazis, there were other racists who talked about the Indo-European Aryans to justify white supremacy. Racism was the norm in our past. However, we can't ignore the reality of Indo-Europeans just because some who talked about it were racist. I do not believe the Indo-Europeans were superior. But the subject became untouchable.

For most of the latter half of the 20th century, it was taboo in academia to talk about European *migrations* at all, let alone *invasions*. People wanted to believe that their ancestors were indigenous to the places they now live. Jean Manco says:

> Some prehistorians went into a state of denial, implicitly refusing to accept that population movements had ever been a significant

feature of European prehistory. The anti-migrationist stance reflected the zeitgeist of the post-imperial age. Invasion and colonization were no longer appealing concepts. Gradually a weight of evidence accrued at odds with the prevailing orthodoxy. Eventually any intellectual cage will start to creak if facts won't fit into it.[27]

Decades after Marija's death, DNA evidence proved her theory correct: nomadic bands of Indo-Europeans invaded the indigenous cultures of Eurasia during the Bronze Age. But another taboo shut down the conversation again. She was smeared with misogynistic insults, as we will see, and her theories became unmentionable in academia for twenty years. Only now, a generation later, are people talking about it again.

How did a handful of primitive tribes seize control of the world? The only person to offer a complete and well-researched thesis to answer this question is James DeMeo with his book *Saharasia*. It's not light beach reading. It's heavy. Heavy in both senses of the word: physically weighty, which makes it awkward to hold, but also intensely depressing. The history of patriarchy is the story of sadistic violence.

I promise I won't traumatize you too much. Even in the depressing slog through history where things got more and more violent (until recently when things improved), there have been good moments. The pendulum swings back and forth between authoritarianism and freedom.

HOW THIS HAPPENED

DeMeo argues that patriarchy arose due to drought and famine caused by extreme climate change sometime around 4000 BCE. The region from the Sahara in North Africa through the Middle East, Russia and Central Asia underwent the most significant climatological change on the planet since the end of the Ice Age.

This region, which he calls "Saharasia", changed very rapidly from a lush forest to a desert. Some scientists believe it took only a hundred years! Ancient streams and lakebeds throughout the region offer evidence. Desertification continued over the millennia, worsened by

23

human activity such as overgrazing and burning.[28] In this desert at the heart of the world, there are blazing summers and frigid winters with strong winds. Dust, haze, and sandstorms make life miserable, and ten years can pass without rain.[29] (Use Google Maps to visualize this region. We usually only see the map with north as up, but you can spin the map around to see this sand-colored swath from the Gobi to the Sahara.)

This desertification would also have applied to the Eurasian steppe, which extends five thousand miles through numerous countries, and connects Asia with Europe. These dry grasslands are characterized by extremes in temperature, up to 115 degrees Fahrenheit (45 °C) in summer and −65 °F (−55 °C) in winter.

Trauma from prolonged famine and drought led to violent and sadistic behavior. During times of starvation, sex is forgotten. This set up a pattern of sex repression. The malnutrition caused damage to their brains and to their psyches that was impossible to recover from, especially for the children. Family ties were shattered.

Studies of modern populations devastated by famine show that starving people become aggressive and listless, and lose interest in affection, both between mothers and children, and between men and women. This has been observed in baboons, too; they don't groom each other in dry areas.

DeMeo says: "After living through hell, the child's view of the female would not be a nurturing mother, but a distant, unresponsive, non-protecting figure against a background of parching heat, thirst, dust and flies."[30] Bodily functions such as childbirth, breast feeding, menstruation, intercourse, and defecation would become taboo or the subject of anxious humor. Crying infants would make adults uncomfortable, so children would be rewarded for being quiet and showing no emotion.

Those whose biological functions and maternal bonding are thwarted will hate and fear other cultures who are healthy and intact. Have you ever been sexually shut down, due to heartbreak or sexual trauma or lack of opportunity, and noticed that sexual scenes in movies make you uncomfortable? I think this is why repressed people are so determined to shut down the sexuality of others. DeMeo says: "In patrist religion the chaste male god is at war with the sexual-female devil, and virtue is defined as avoidance of natural sexuality."[31]

This repressed sexual energy blocks us from ecstatic joy, and from having a deep connection with the natural world. We become walled off not only from our own suffering, but from life energy itself. Wilhelm Reich called this energy "orgone". In India, *prana;* in China, *chi.*

Traumatized groups develop customs based around survival, with no focus on pleasure or emotional bonding. Even if times of plenty return, the trauma is passed to children by inflicting pain and withholding pleasure. People who suffer pain are compelled to inflict it on others. These violent behaviors become social institutions that perpetuate themselves, generation after generation. The sadistic and sex-repressive behaviors continue even when food was abundant.

Everyone became subordinate to the will of the male ruler and the male head of the family. Young men were pressed into the new military bands. Male and female children were segregated. The sadistic urges from trauma and repressed sexuality got directed into violence towards infants, children, women, elders, minorities, conquered enemies, enslaved people, and neighboring peoples.[32]

DeMeo used a database of cultural behavior traits, developed by George P Murdock at the University of Pittsburgh, and mapped it to geography. He found that the most extreme patrist peoples lived in, or had contact with, peoples who originated in the harshest environments.[33]

The trauma spread like a virus. The cultural traits that spread far and wide include infant swaddling, infant cranial deformations, virginity taboos, genital mutilations, bride price, concubinage, polygamy, female seclusion, the caste system, slavery, kingship, and human sacrifice. There are many taboos in patrist societies like ours, because patrism goes against our natural instincts to be highly sexual beings. Extreme patrist cultures have heavy taboos around things like childbirth and menstrual blood. (Matrist cultures have only one taboo: incest. That's why they only take mates from other clans. Some of them have a light taboo around eating with a lover, since eating is what you do with your family. Other than that, they have light taboos around arguing and fighting.) According to DeMeo's data which mapped patrist traits onto areas of the world, the greatest preponderance was in the environments with the least rainfall and vegetation, and the most extreme temperatures.[34]

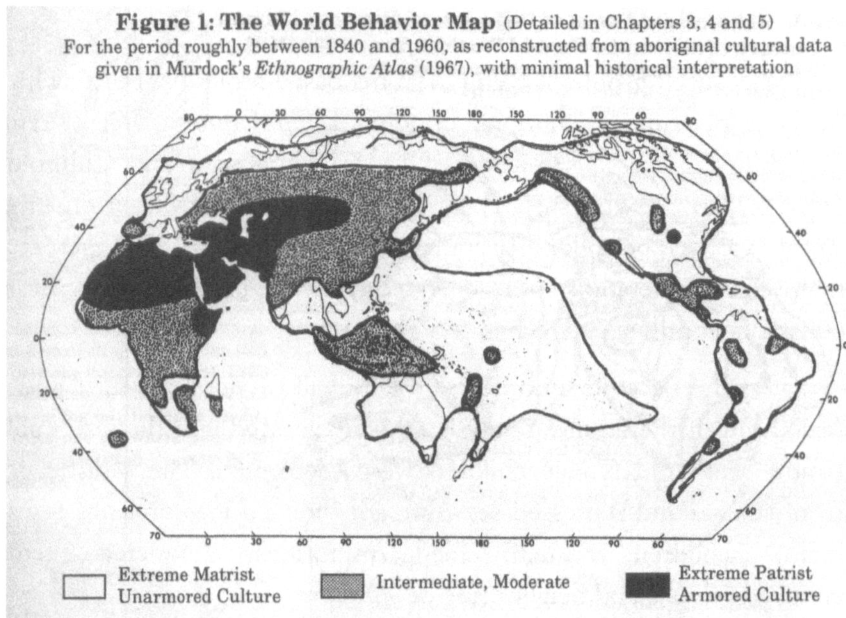

Figure 1-3: Patrist, matrist and intermediate areas.[35]

Before 4000 BCE, there were brief episodes of regional drought. Correspondingly, we see signs of violence in the archaeological record around 5000 BCE at the time of a major drought, but they were brief and sporadic. Serious, widespread desertification began around 4000 BCE, and that is when we see the lasting patrism. As these first patrist tribes migrated outwards, they exported traits even to places that were still lush and abundant, such as Europe, sub-Saharan Africa, India, and eastern China.[36] Hence even rainforests became patrist with contact from the originally traumatized peoples, while semi-arid regions further from Saharasia remained matrist.[37] Historically one of the most important factors determining the intensity of warfare was proximity to

26

dry steppe grasslands inhabited by the horse-riding nomads who spread these traits.[38]

Saharasia spans a huge area that touches several continents and many diverse ethnic groups and language groups. It's tragic that this area turned so violent, because these cultures are some of the most ancient and beautiful on earth. Central Asia, especially the Altai mountains and the Taklamakan Desert, is an ancient cultural seedbed. The trade and migration route known as the Silk Road passed right through these desert lands.

The closer to this desert at the heart of the world, the more violent and sexually repressed you are likely to be. Thousands of years of patriarchy brought military conquests, death camps, institutionalized torture, slavery, genocide, and nuclear weapons. Our culture revolves around financial profit for a tiny elite, through wars and environmental exploitation. Patriarchy threatens life itself.

But there have always been some who managed to resist. The Tuareg of North Africa are a perfect example of a desert people who stayed matrilineal, and whose women stayed free. Among the Tuareg, it's the men who wear the veils. Sadly, in the last few decades, they have started to succumb to patriarchal modernity.

Even during the most patrist times, there were egalitarian cultures everywhere in the fringes of the empires. The brilliant 2021 book *The Dawn of Everything* gives examples of civilizations that never became patriarchal, or who did but then changed course to become egalitarian. The earliest cities of Mesopotamia, of the Cucuteni-Tripolye civilization in the Balkans, and in China, for example, were egalitarian for hundreds of years, with large urban populations.[39] Despots and bureaucracies are optional!

IT'S ABOUT THE TRAUMA, AND THE COWS

Wilhelm Reich, the early 20th century American psychologist, claimed that the cruel way our society treats infants, children and teens leads to the self-destructive behavior of adults. A student of Sigmund Freud, he famously stated that the repression of sexual urges leads to neurotic behavior. In 1896 Freud presented his findings that many children experienced sexual trauma at the hands of fathers, uncles, and family friends. This was so controversial that it was rejected by the establishment, so Freud decided to interpret these experiences as fantasies, at which point it was widely celebrated.

Reich refused to go along with this, having too much experience with sexual assault victims and their symptoms to dismiss their accounts as fantasy.[40] That's when he became a heretic. Worse, he proposed making contraceptives and abortions free, and abolishing the legal distinction between the married and unmarried. He advocated for free sexual education, and for sex offenders to be treated instead of punished. He campaigned for the protection of children from adult seduction. These ideas were extremely unpopular.

In 1933 his book *Mass Psychology of Fascism* got him expelled from The International Psychoanalytic Association and banished from future publishing in journals. This book posited that the male-led nuclear family was the basis of the fascist state. In other words, a family that demands obedience from wife and children is the prerequisite for fascism and authoritarianism. (The authors of *The Dawn of Everything* agree; they point out that across many cultures on all continents, there was a "close connection between the patriarchal household and military might."[41])

Reich believed that people who had been raised in loving, permissive environments would never fall for fascism. He called the communists "red fascists", making little distinction between them and the "black fascists" — Nazis.[42]

Reich noticed that his neurotic patients were shallow breathers, had pelvic tension related to sexual repression, and were unable to express deep emotion. He theorized that emotions that are unacceptable to society get trapped in the nervous system and the muscles of the bodies. This leads to chronic tension in the muscle groups that would be involved in expressing the unacceptable urge. We arm ourselves through muscle tension to protect ourselves from the frustration of our desires not being met. This armoring keeps us from feeling pleasure and joy and makes us vulnerable to authoritarianism.[43]

Reich believed that this repression happened in societies where adults controlled their children's marriages for economic motives. For young people to accept marriages to people they don't love, they must be traumatized and controlled from birth. At birth they are separated from the mother and subjected to inhumane treatment. Then they're circumcised, denied the breast, beaten, and emotionally crushed. They're taught that sex is a shameful and scary event, rather than educated about proper hygiene, contraception, and love. For these heresies, papers that cite Reich are still rejected from academic journals.[44]

This dehumanizing treatment is even worse for girls in extreme patrist cultures. They're greeted with disappointment or even anger just for being female, and are breastfed half as long as boys. They quickly learn they are here to serve, while boys learn that the family is here to serve *them*.[45]

When girls reach puberty in extreme patrist cultures, they become prisoners of the family. A girl's virginity is an economic asset for the family, since a virgin can be sold for a bride price. Men in these cultures prefer unspoiled merchandise; perhaps they also don't want to be compared to another man. Even today in some places, girls are murdered by their brothers or stoned by the whole village if they dare to have consensual sex.[46]

Older women are usually the ones who pass on the traditions. They're the ones who perform female genital mutilation, where they cut the vagina open with no anesthetic, remove the clitoris, then sew it all the way closed, while drummers mask the girl's screams. The girl cannot move for several months and will never experience sexual pleasure or urinate without pain. Perhaps the mother thinks: I went through it, why shouldn't she?[47]

After a lifetime of pain and deprivation, a person comes to believe she doesn't deserve pleasure and freedom, and then may do the same to others. So as patriarchy spread through the world, the trauma

29

compounded itself. Some cultures were far more extreme than others. I rank these cultures based on what I call the "patrist score": the number of generations a culture has been patrist, multiplied by the number of patrist traits.

But not everyone put up with it. There's one example from the 10th century when a harsh form of Christianity came to a remote area of Russia where women had so far retained their sexual freedom. When the new priests put an end to love matches and pre-marital sex, a generation of girls forced into loveless marriages committed suicide. The priests realized they had to raise the next generation of girls with severe obedience training.[48] Perhaps only girls taught from childhood that they have no value will accept lifelong rape.

DeMeo's massive, scholarly work will convince anyone that patriarchy links cultural traits such as patrilineal inheritance, patrilocal marriage, war, male dominance, misogyny, sexual repression, repression of bodily functions, and genital mutilation. Perhaps, as DeMeo believes, it began only once and spread from there all over the world. We may never know. We don't know whether it was imposed by a few men, or if it was a response of both men and women to fear and trauma. His data is convincing: patriarchy arose in response to a harsh environment that led to prolonged trauma and that offered limited resources that were easy to hoard and control. Cows played a huge role in this. As the land became too dry to grow food, peoples' lives depended on their cows. Aggressive men learned how to steal cows and amass herds. Traumatized people may have turned to aggressive male leaders to protect them in times of scarcity.

When aggressive males accumulated wealth in the form of cows, they wanted to pass that wealth on to sons to enhance the success of their line. That created the need to ensure paternity, which meant controlling women's sexuality.

Even in modern times, the rise of cow-herding among matrilineal hunter-gatherers leads to the adoption of patrilineal inheritance. I'll talk more about that in future chapters. You know how working with cows is called animal "husbandry"? It's no coincidence that we use that word.

30

In cow cultures, women became chattel, property to be owned, milked and managed. The word for girl literally means "milk" in some Indo-European languages. The horse played a huge role, too — it enabled the warrior tribes to spread their culture throughout the world.

While DeMeo believes patriarchy evolved once among the early Semites and Indo-Europeans and spread from those populations to everyone else, I lean toward a hypothesis that it has happened more than once. My hunch is that while egalitarianism is our default, natural state, and very stable as long as no oppressors exist, patriarchy can be triggered by prolonged trauma and resource scarcity. After all, there are some groups who seem to have patrilineal inheritance that may never have had contact with Indo-Europeans or Semites, such as Australian aborigines, Papua New Guineans, and the builders of the Neolithic megaliths of western Europe. Unless there was contact I'm not aware of. Contact me with theories!

I see no evidence that patriarchy inevitably and naturally arises as a result of large populations, or agriculture, or the plow, as some believe. It seems to be linked to pastoral lifestyles, dry conditions and prolonged trauma. But any conversation about the rise of inequality that doesn't consider the role of contact with Semitic and Indo-European groups is ignoring the elephant in the room.

WHO GETS TO DECIDE WHO GETS TO HAVE SEX

Patrism is natural, but not as natural as matrism: it requires consistent trauma and brainwashing to maintain it. When men took over, they usurped the spiritual power that had been the realm of the goddess. It was common for priests in the transitional times between matrism and patrism to castrate themselves to appropriate the primal female power. The blood of violence replaced the blood of menstruation as sacred. Menstrual blood, the holiest of holies for at least 100,000 years, became unclean. Anthropologist Chris Knight says that ancient societies all knew that women were made for supernatural power, and their blood was the

31

key. Supernatural power was the most important thing. To seize power, men had to make themselves bleed in imitation, through violence.

The male-headed nuclear family marriage replaced the matrilineal clan. When a woman is separated from her mothers, sisters, brothers and uncles by patrilocal marriage, she's surrounded by strangers, dependent on her husband. This contrasts with the traditional matrilineal clan, where a woman's kin have her back and help her raise her children, in her natal village or household compound. Then she is never forced to stay with a man she doesn't love for the sake of children or security.[49]

It makes sense for women to be the ones to choose their mates. Women are the choosier sex, since they pay a higher biological price to reproduce, and are the ones to take someone else into their body. In matrism, women get to pick, and the men are happy too. In patrism, men get to pick, which for many women has historically meant rape and slavery. For thousands of years in most of the so-called "civilized" world, women had no choice in their mates.

In the hunter-gatherer days, women oversaw gathering, which provided most of the calories, so was equally as valued as hunting. Many hunters were women, too; science is recently discovering this as techniques of bone identification improve. As horticulturists, women would have invented farming. There would have been no concept of man-the-provider; all clan members worked to provide sustenance and to care for all the children. A child could wander the village safely, cared for by everyone. Her mother's sisters were basically her mothers, too; some matrilineal cultures didn't even have separate words for mother and aunt!

The most important male in a child's life was his mother's brother, who always welcomed the child into his home. The uncle usually had a room in the family's group house, which consisted of a grandmother, her children, and *their* children. Siblings remained together for life.

But lovers came and went. A man would spend the night with a woman, then do some work for her family, then take off to be with his own clan. Often men visited more than one woman at a time, and women had multiple visitors. The paternity of a woman's children was unimportant. Her family — mother, sisters, brothers, aunts and uncles — raised her children. Children always had a family. You didn't need to be sexy to be fed and loved. The chapter on Anthropology offers many examples of this societal organization, which occurred on every continent.

There was no need for a man to work his ass off providing for his mate's children, and therefore to obsess over whether they were really his. There was no need to imprison women in the house, cut off their clitorises, lock them in chastity belts, or cover them in burqas to make sure they only mixed their genes with the assigned man.

Men's fear of raising children that aren't theirs is at the root of sex-shaming and misogyny. A man can never really know if a woman has "cheated" on him, which is why society portrays women as untrustworthy. The worst insult for a man is to call him a woman — a "pussy" — or, to call his mother a whore, meaning he's a bastard. That's such a common insult that it's been abbreviated to just "yo' mama."

Without pressure for a man to provide for his children, sex can just be sex, based in mutual respect and desire. Desire doesn't usually last a lifetime, so the brother-sister pair was a much more stable parenting situation.

The groundbreaking bestselling book *Sex at Dawn* by Christopher Ryan and Cacilda Jetha presents evidence that our ancestors lived in groups where people had several ongoing sexual relationships at once. Sexual relationships reinforced social ties. In the chapter on sex, I'll talk about how the human genitals themselves are evidence for a promiscuous evolutionary environment.

But in patriarchy, we went from women deciding who they have sex with, to men deciding. That suddenly changed in the last hundred years. After 5000 years of men having control over sex and reproduction, finally Western women can choose their mates, choose whether to have children and how many, and have rights over those children. For the first time in a long, long time, women in the last century have been able to opt out of motherhood. This change in power dynamics between the sexes happened very quickly, and it left some men feeling shocked. When you're used to control over others, it seems like a right.

There are men's groups now who openly advocate for rape and for women to be allotted to men in need. These so-called "men's rights" groups are fighting for control over women's bodies, while women's rights groups fight for control over their *own* bodies. This explains why societies where men choose who gets to have sex are oppressive and violent: the choice gets forced on women through threat of violence or economic dependency. Where men control all the resources, women must submit to sex they don't want just to be fed and housed.

The bargain for men in patriarchy, if you recall, is that in exchange for being ruled by more powerful men, they can dominate women and nature. But feminism has taken that from them. Women can now support themselves, choose their own partners, divorce, and have rights over their own children. Rape is illegal instead of institutionalized. It's extraordinary how far we've come in such a short time. No wonder some men are taking up assault rifles and blowing women to bits.

The media never mentions the one thing that *all* mass shooters in America have in common: a virulent hatred for women. Isn't it interesting how feminists are accused of being man-haters, but nobody asks why some *men* hate *women* so much? The internet is awash in violently misogynistic articles, posts, and comments. Female celebrities hire people to remove the disturbing threats and insults they routinely receive from male stalkers and harassers. Male celebrities don't.

So in Western culture, we've transitioned from male choice to female choice in a very short time. Women have gone from being dependent on males, to independent, in a few generations.

In 2019, I spent two months in Egypt, where I fell in love with the people and the culture. One man asked me, "When you come back to Egypt?"

I answered, "Never. I don't like how men can marry more than one woman while women can only marry one man."

He answered, "That's to protect women! If her husband dies, his brothers must marry her and take care of her."

That's a common justification for polygamy, but most of the time a man takes a second wife against his wife's wishes. Still, this made me think: this is a safety net for women that we don't have in the West. How did Western women come to be independent in such a short time?

These freedoms can be taken away at any time. We need to understand the dynamics of patriarchy in order to protect our basic human rights. This book will focus on the core dynamics that arose in ancient times between men and women, which set the stage for later oppression based on race, ethnicity, and class. It's a huge topic, so I will focus mainly on gender in Western culture; I won't spend much time on more recent manifestations of patriarchy such as racism, white supremacy, or homophobia, to keep this book as short as possible.

Only through understanding our past can we transcend it. Gilda Lerner says, "Women had no history, they were told. It was men's hegemony over the symbol system which most decisively disadvantaged women: educational deprivation of women and male monopoly on definition. Without history, they had no future alternatives."[50]

To summarize this chapter: there is a very strong correlation between egalitarianism, matrilineal inheritance, matrifocal marriage, and peacefulness on one hand, and between social hierarchy, patrilineal inheritance, patrifocal marriage, and war on the other. These traits tend to be seen together in cultures. This doesn't mean there aren't hybrids between the two who have mixes of these traits, such as egalitarian societies who trace descent through the male line. Nowadays, after thousands of years of mixing, most cultures are hybrids between the two. Our modern global culture is a mild, reformed hybrid patriarchy, largely thanks to the work of feminists.

But my assumption (based on research) is that those two societal organizations used to be more distinct in the distant past, and that most cultures were matrist. Even as recently as 150 years ago, most distinct cultures still were matrist, though highly hybridized, with patrist traits mixed in, such as mostly male leadership. When dealing with male-dominated neighbors it's better to have a male figurehead, even if he's chosen by a council of women as in many native American groups. That change happened quickly in the Americas and in Africa when the Europeans showed up there.

But 5000 years ago, most were matrist aside from Indo-European and Semitic speaking peoples. This book will focus on agrarian Neolithic cultures, with only minimal discussion of Paleolithic hunter-gatherers, aka foragers. We can't make assumptions about ancient forager societies based on current ones, since all the current ones that we know of have been in contact with patrism.

Since male voices carry a lot of weight, let's end the chapter with an eloquent quote from Michael Sky in his book *Beyond the Dominator Virus*:

> This book can be disturbing, especially for men […] I stress that this system tends to favor men in fundamental ways and that our world has indeed been "a man's world" for several thousands of years. […] It may seem at times as if I am indicting men for all the world's problems while casting women as history's poor and pathetic victims. This is not my actual belief […] This is not to say that individual women are never abusive and domineering nor that individual men are never victimized by women. Moreover, there are certain clear benefits to being a woman in a patriarchal world, just as there are specific burdens typically thrust upon a man. […]
>
> As a man, I have found that coming to a place of sexual peace with the women in my life has required that I at least attempt a visceral understand of what it means to grow up female in a male-favoring culture.[51]

This book restores the pieces of our history that have been omitted: the feminine, the earth, the body, and the unconscious. In the next chapter we'll take a journey through our true history.

CHAPTER TWO

THE REAL HISTORY OF WESTERN CIVILIZATION

I n the 80s when I attended Stanford University, the only required course was one year of Western Civ. I loathed it. I had not yet discovered feminism, so I didn't understand *why* I loathed it, but I did.

I suffered through a year of Aristotle's misogynistic musings, Medieval Christians calculating how many angels can dance on the head of a pin, and saints who flogged themselves when they thought about women.

As you might imagine, it's no longer politically correct: it was Patriarchy 101. It was replaced with a course on non-Western cultures. That didn't work either, so it's been scrapped. Here's the real story:

THE STONE AGE

Humans have been burying our dead and making jewelry since at least 40,000 BCE. Those things, perhaps, make us truly human, along with, as some have suggested, carrying stuff around in shoulder bags. Apes don't do that.

There were many kinds of humans, back then. We intermixed: Neanderthals and Denisovans, who were different subspecies, and Cro-

Magnons, who were *Homo sapiens* like us. Some believe this intermixing gave rise to a hybrid culture known as the Gravettian, from whom many of us are descended. This epic meeting created a new breed of modern humans, and a shamanic cultural seedbed that venerated the stars (especially the Pleiades), the spiral, and the magical number seven. This seed would grow into all the major religions.

This culture created extraordinary artwork, such as the paintings in the caves of France and Spain. The three-dimensional shading can barely be reproduced today. They made female figurines that emphasized the breasts and buttocks. The shamans were female. Wherever the Neanderthals lived were centers of art, culture, and mysticism, and later became the home of Old Europe, the Neolithic agricultural civilization that venerated an earth goddess.[52]

Some believe that around 9600 BCE, a massive global catastrophe drove the mega-mammals extinct and killed off a lot of people. A few groups survived on high mountains or underground. These groups diverged from each other in their isolation, their languages changing into new ones.

The group that emerged in Anatolia (modern Turkey) built an enormous monument re-discovered in the last 20 years, that changed our notion of history: Gobleki Tepi. It was deliberately buried in 8000 BCE. Perhaps this culture was going through a very ancient, earlier cycle of patriarchy, because they did have more phallic than feminine iconography. They can be linked, through artistic styles, to two nearby cities in Turkey: Hacılar and Çatalhöyük. These were some of the largest settlements in the agricultural civilization that spread all over Western Eurasia in the Neolithic era, from 9000 to 3500 BCE. This was Old Europe, the agricultural trading route that stretched from western Europe east to India, and from Malta north to the Scottish islands.

THE FIRST FARMERS

The migration of these first farmers transformed the world with agriculture. It wasn't necessarily a step forward. Grain isn't healthy for us, so it led to a decline in human health and an increase in diseases. It also led to more labor. Some people, after trying it for a few millennia, went back to foraging. But it allowed for larger, settled populations.

Many people assume that this dawn of agriculture led to the unequal distribution of wealth, since the storage of food makes this possible. However, this inequality only happened millennia after. It was in the upland groups who were dependent on herding where stratification and violence later happened. The lowland groups who farmed remained egalitarian. According to the book *The Dawn of Everything*, "much of this egalitarianism relates to an increase in the economic and social visibility of women, reflected in their art and ritual."[53]

Old Europe was a mixture of two main genetic types: Western Hunter-gatherers and Anatolian Neolithic farmers (Anatolia is the large peninsula of modern Turkey. The farmers were the ancestors of Southern European and Mediterranean people such as Greeks, Arabs, Berbers, Jews, Italians and possibly South Indians as well.

When Old Europe transitioned from hunting and gathering to agriculture, many things changed, but they maintained some cultural continuity. The same symbols from cave art in 30,000 BCE are seen in Neolithic art tens of thousands of years later!

In Gimbutas' book *Civilization of the Goddess* there is an image from 17000-14000 BCE found in Ukraine, and one from 5200 BCE found in Serbia, both of which use the same chevron, a "V" which represents the vulva. 12,000 years is a long time to still be using the chevron![54] These squiggles would become V, X, Y in the Vinca script used in the Neolithic.[55] Yes, they had an early form of writing. This Vinca script would evolve into Minoan Linear A. Why don't we learn that in school?Many other traditions remained the same over millennia. It seems likely that society was still organized around matrilineal clans. The veneration of nature and the earth goddess must have permeated every aspect of their lives. Art depicted animals and curvy females. Their dead were sprinkled with red ochre, a pigment associated with menstrual blood, going back at least 60,000 years![56] By the time of the second artifact in the photo, they had moved from caves into houses. All houses

were the same size in this egalitarian society. Burial was communal, after
bodies had been exposed to vultures to be cleaned.

NEOLITHIC OLD EUROPE

Figure 2-1: A reconstructed house at the archaeological site of Çatalhöyük. Picture by
author.

Old Europeans lived in wattle-and-daub houses in villages and cities
of up to 45,000 inhabitants, built on sites with good farmland and views.
They made beautiful ceramics, and jewelry out of copper and gold.
According to Gimbutas, their lives revolved around worship of the
goddess, creating offerings for the temple. Their walls were covered in
light-hearted frescos of animals and the female form.

Besides Anatolia, another major area where this Neolithic Old
European civilization flourished was in the Danube River valley in
40

Eastern Europe. The Cucuteni-Tripolye civilization that extended across what is now Ukraine, Romania, and Moldova included mega-sites of tens of thousands of people. The trading route of Old Europe extended even to Pakistan, where excavations of the ancient town of Mehrgarh revealed yet another female-centered, egalitarian society. They sailed the Mediterranean, hopping from coast to coast and island to island.

While violence and hierarchy were scarce across Neolithic Europe, not everyone were as fervent in their goddess worship as they were in Anatolia, the Balkans, the Levant, Mesopotamia, Iran, India and Pakistan, and Greece. Some female figurines have been found in Arabia, England, Italy, Spain, France, and Germany, but not nearly as many as in the goddess hotspots listed above.[57] Sardinia, for example, had a large Neolithic population but comparatively few female figurines.

THE INDO-EUROPEANS

Meanwhile, on the other side of the Black Sea from Old Europe, lived the ancestors of the Indo-Europeans. Indo-European language groups include most of the ones most widely spoken today: Germanic ones like German and English; Latin ones like Spanish and French; Slavic ones like Russian; Baltic ones like Lithuanian; Scandinavian ones like Swedish; Greek; and the languages of North India and Iran. The Indo-Europeans inhabited the Russian steppe, a vast expanse of grassy plains that stretched from the Black Sea all the way to Mongolia. Sometime between the 6th millennium and 4th millennium BCE, abrupt climate change happened on the steppe: it got much dryer and much colder, a climate that encourages patrism.

Some believe that caused the steppe-dwelling Indo-Europeans, also known as "Kurgans" after their burial mounds, to turn violent and hierarchical. These pastoral nomads relied upon their herds for survival. They were much taller than Old Europeans, with longer skulls, and some had blond or red hair. They worshiped storm and sun gods. The wolf and horse were sacred to them.

They would eventually take over the world and erase evidence of the previous civilization. I know it sounds dramatic. It kinda was. How did a

41

group of nomadic herders wandering the distant steppes take over the world?

They domesticated the wild horse.

As their own resources became scarce due to frigid winters and drying out, they conducted raids on horseback into Old Europe to steal food. In the 6th and 5th millennia BCE, these raids were infrequent and sporadic. By the 4th millennia BCE, they must have realized that the peaceful, civilized people to the south were sitting ducks without weapons or fortifications. The genetic mutation that enabled them to drink milk as adults made them stronger than Old Europeans. The spoils of these more advanced peoples were theirs for the taking.

THE INDO-EUROPEAN INVASIONS: THE APOCALYPSE OF OLD EUROPE

There were three large waves of Indo-European barbarian invasions into Old Europe: in 4500, in 4000, and in 3500 BCE. At first, perhaps they just stole food and left. But by 3500 BCE it was a holocaust of apocalyptic proportions, and they settled there. They showed up on horses, most likely killing the men and enslaving the women. Villages were burnt to the ground or abandoned. Around 1900 BCE they invented the chariot, enabling efficient and widespread slaughter. The war machine was born.

It was an environmental disaster as well. The nomads burned the forest to create grazing for their herds. It must have been a total dumpster fire.

And so at least 30,000 years of a mostly-peaceful, egalitarian culture came to a sudden end. Some groups fled into the high mountains. Others migrated to the islands of the Aegean, where they continued their way of life undisturbed for millennia. Others taught themselves to fight, but once you learn, you're no longer peaceful.

The culture of Europe is descended from these waves of invasions, from the combination of Old Europeans and Indo-Europeans. This story of rape and pillage is the story of our ancestors. What would it be

42

like to raise children with your rapist when you had never imagined rape or violence?

THE FIRST COLONIZATION: HYBRID CULTURES BETWEEN INDO-EUROPEANS AND OLD EUROPEANS

When tiny groups of Indo-European men set themselves up as the overlords of Old European towns, the class hierarchy was born. The children of the rulers and the women they conquered spoke both languages and combined both cultures.

After the first barbarian invasion, the level of culture declined markedly. The much taller male skeletons with longer skulls appeared in mound graves known as "kurgans". Copper and ceramic crafts-woman-ship all but disappeared. And yet, some Old European women kept the techniques alive. They formed "hybrid" cultures, some of which retained the ways of their mothers more than others.

For example, the Hatti people were an early hybrid in Turkey who still worshiped goddesses alongside the new gods. They were then conquered in the next wave of Indo-European invasions and became the Hittites, who were more violent and male-dominated than the Hatti but still retained some old goddesses and ceramic techniques. The small number of invaders were all male and became the new upper class, pushing the previous invaders into a middle class. The Old Europeans, of course, formed the lower classes. Colonialism was born.

This pattern, where invaders got civilized by the women they enslaved and got soft, only to be conquered by new waves, continued for millennia. The lower classes of Old Europeans were forced to learn the conquerors' harsh, guttural languages, but their native languages survived at least into the classical Greek times.

In the fringes of Eurasia, Old Europe persisted longer. There were peaceful egalitarian societies that flourished on the British Isles until the 2nd millennium BCE. But the Aegean Sea was the largest refuge of Old Europe, where islands were a natural defense against barbarians. Later, they would become the great Minoan civilization. They managed to keep the good times rolling for a few more millennia!

THE MIDDLE EAST AND MESOPOTAMIA

Meanwhile, the Middle East also experienced abrupt climate change, which transformed society as it had in the Russian steppes. The Sahara area of North Africa and Arabia turned from a rainforest into a desert very rapidly, possibly in just 100 years. This desert extended from North Africa, through the Middle East, and into the Gobi in Central Asia. Traumatic famine combined with cows were likely the factors that turned society towards patriliny, patrilocality, inherited status hierarchy, and violent male gods. Perhaps the Indo-Europeans and the Semites were once one people, and patriarchy arose once among them. Perhaps it happened separately among the two groups.

The Semitic tribes that turned patriarchal, such as the Hebrews, Assyrians, Akkadians, and Phoenicians, passed on the traditions to other groups. Customs that created trauma, such as genital mutilation and infant cranial deformation, were passed from one generation to the next until they became sacred traditions. It spread to the Levant — Syria, Lebanon, Jordan and Israel. They raided and raped the goddess-worshiping cultures they found there, converting them to patriarchy. Although there, too, old customs died hard. Goddess figurines survived, now hidden in homes instead of worshipped in temples, for thousands of years, even much later, after the rise of Islam.

While the Indo-Europeans invaded Anatolia, Greece, and Eastern and Central Europe, these Semitic peoples invaded the Middle East and Mesopotamia. Mesopotamia had been home to a peaceful matrilineal culture known as Ubaid. The first Mesopotamian cities of Sumer and Uruk were peaceful for the first few hundred years, until 3200 BCE when the district dedicated to goddess Inanna was razed to make room for ziggurats. Sumer wasn't the first city, as they teach us in school; it was the first *patriarchal* city. Ur, Akkad, and Babylon became more oppressive with time.

Kings ended the traditional matrilineal succession of leadership and passed on their position to their sons. A series of laws degraded women's status step by step, stripping them of the right to choose their mates or to own property. Women became property and pawns in male politics. Rape became a crime against a male owner, not against the woman. Men took control of children as property.

One law in Akkad, near Babylon, for example, made it a crime for high-status women to go in public unveiled, or for low-status women to wear veils. Thus, women's status became a matter of state: high status women were chaste and belonged to one man, while low-status women were harlots and public property. This was the beginning of the madonna-whore split, the good woman vs bad.[58] It was all downhill from there.

NEW LAWS INVENT PATRIARCHY

Author Gerda Lerner in her book *The Creation of Patriarchy* speculates that years of experimenting with making women into slaves taught societies how to control populations through brainwashing them to believe they are inferior. Groups of men became enslaved based on their physical labor, rather than their reproductive labor. It's no accident the word "labor" refers to both.

We see the creation of patriarchal empires in the laws that have been passed down to us in writing. The law codes created by the Hebrew people, as well as the Mesopotamian peoples, enshrined the step-by-step conversion of women into slaves. After a while, the only thing that remained of the Hebrews' matrilineal past was the transmission of Jewishness through the mother.

Some anecdotes in the Bible remind of us of how brutal this time was. Riane Eisler recounts how two men threw their daughters and lovers to an angry mob to be raped to death rather than give the mob their male guests. One of the male guests wakes up to find his concubine's bloody body in the street, tosses it on his donkey and goes about his day. Both men are held up as righteous men for doing this; Lot is saved from the destruction of Gomorrah for this sacrifice of his

45

daughters for a man's sake. There's no grief or outrage at this. These are virtuous acts. Men matter, daughters don't.[59]

EGYPT

Meanwhile, Egypt remained a matrilineal state well into the Bronze Age. In Neolithic times before the Pharaohs, there was a peaceful culture that made female figurines, known as Naqada. Even in later dynastic times, men married princesses to became pharaohs. This stage, in which kings ascended the throne through their marriage to royal women, was an intermediary stage before the full patriarchal custom of kings inheriting from their fathers.

The Old Kingdom seemed to have been a good time of divine kingship, with just kings. There were more female pharaohs than you learn about in school, even as late as Hatshepsut in 1478 BCE. However, after her prosperous and peaceful rule, they tried to erase her from history, including scraping the face off her statues. Soon after, Egypt fell to the Hyksos, a Semitic tribe who ruled for about 100 years and introduced chariots and slavery to Egypt. It became an oppressive state that conquered and subdued the Semites to the north and the Nubians to the south.

This was the Bronze Age, 3500-1200 BCE, when they learned to mix copper with tin to make bronze. With this harder metal came the first metal weapons. As time marched on, society got bloodier and more oppressive, though there were still pockets of peaceful matrilineal people. The Nubians, one of the founding populations of Egypt, stayed matrilineal until recent times. Libya, the huge country to the west of Egypt, was a hotbed of badass queens for a long time.

In fact, most of the indigenous people of North Africa, the *Amazigh* or Berbers who speak Afro-Asiatic languages related to Egyptian, stayed matrilineal for millennia. Still today in Morocco, Amazigh people speak their native tongues and resist Arab colonization, and traces of matrilineal customs remain.

INDIA

A wave of Indo-Europeans that moved east to South Asia brought languages from a branch of Indo-European languages known as Indo-Aryan family. The Indo-Aryan family included the Persians and Indians, warring cousins. The Persians created mighty brutal empires with horrible harems. The word "Aryan" was first used to refer to the Indo-Europeans of India.

These Indo-Aryans colonized the indigenous inhabitants of South Asia, who were dark-skinned, broad-nosed Tamil peoples. The invaders appropriated the Tamil peoples' ancient sciences of Tantra and Ayurveda. The resulting hybrid culture is the extraordinary Vedic culture, who gave us the holy books of the Indians.

GREECE

Another early branch of Indo-Europeans went west to become the ancestors of the Celts and Greeks. This branch was more influenced by the peaceful goddess people they enslaved and assimilated, so created less oppressive societies. Nature and goddess worship lived on among the Celtic Druids even into the Iron Age.

The Indo-European Greeks were a tiny number of overlords subjugating a large population of Old Europeans. Even today the Greek language is only 30% Indo-European, the rest belonging to the lost language of the people they assimilated. After the invasion, these people continued their old ways on Mediterranean islands such as Crete. There they developed the exquisite Minoan civilization, discovered by Sir Arthur Evans in the early 1900s. Evans had faith that the Trojan War was not just a myth as people believed, and figured out where to dig using the ancient Greek epic *The Iliad*!

Minoan cities had gorgeous architecture and even indoor plumbing with hot water and flushing toilets, which wouldn't be seen again for 3000 years. The buildings that have been called "palaces", but were probably used for community ritual, featured multi-story apartments that opened out onto courtyards. Their art revealed a society that revolved around beauty and nature, with imagery of flowers, offerings, and animals, and a bull leaping sport that involved doing somersaults over the bulls. There were no images of warriors or weapons.

All Minoans lived in decent conditions, unlike their counterparts in the ghettos of the patriarchal Bronze Age civilizations that surrounded them. They had writing, a script known now as Linear A, which has not been deciphered. It was in a now-lost language, probably non-Indo-European.

The Minoans may have been a true matriarchy. "Matriarchy" is a society where women oppress men the way men oppress women in patriarchy. I used to think no such society ever existed. But in all the images from Minoan Crete, women are depicted as powerful and elegant in elaborate dress, while the young half-naked men worship the women. This *is* highly suggestive of an oppressive matriarchy. Of course, people weren't getting dragged around in chains, or having their ears and breasts sliced off like in Persia. It was a far cry from the oppression of patrism. But it may have been a society that marginalized men.

Figure 2-2: Copied from a Minoan fresco, painted by the author.

Sometime around 1500 BCE there was a shift: a tiny population of Indo-European Greeks became overlords over the Minoans. We don't know whether it was an invasion, or whether the Minoans decided they needed military aid and so married their queens to Greek men. From this point on, the civilization is known as Mycenaean.

Things remained the same for most people. One change was the appearance of two throne rooms instead of one, as female leaders were joined by male ones. The writing changed to Linear B, written in an archaic form of Greek: Mycenaean, which *has* been deciphered. This is where our historical records begin — at least, until we decipher Linear A, the Minoan's earlier pre-Greek script. But from this point on, we can learn about them from reading Linear B tablets, not just from artifacts.

From these tablets we know that by this point they had a status elite. There were elite burials, and a concern with death and funerary rites, for the first time. The art became less spontaneous, and images of warriors appeared. These guys looked very different from Minoans: goofy guys with pale skin and hooked noses who look like the Beatles, a stark contrast against the Minoans' long black hair, reddish skin, small noses, and proud athletic bodies. Yet still women were depicted as powerful and confident. The tablets describe power as divided between men and women equally, and women had equal rights of land tenure. There is no mention of marriage, whereas their Bronze Age neighbors in Egypt and Mesopotamia speak of it constantly in their tablets.

Then, in 1177 BCE, another apocalypse happened: Bronze Age civilization collapsed. Volcanoes and wars wiped out 90% of the population. The Greek, Hittite, Cypriot, Mycenaean, Assyrian, and Babylonian civilizations came to an end.[60] Egypt was weakened and declined sharply; it would never regain its Old Kingdom glory. Babylon was taken over by Elam. The Bronze Age was over, and the Iron Age would rise from the ashes.

In Greece they endured a few hundred years of dark ages before the first classical city-states emerged. Writing and art were lost during this time of chaos, famine, and violence. A battle raged between male and female power. At the inception of the war, a vase depicts warriors marching away from a commanding female figure. There are myths describing battles where men fought against women. As documented in the book *War of the Gods: The Conflict between Matriarchy and Patriarchy in the*

49

Greek Dark Age, this war between patrilineal and matrilineal succession was a major force behind the collapse of the civilizations of the Bronze Age.[61]

In other words … the battle of the sexes brought down the great Bronze Age empires!

THE COLLAPSE OF THE BRONZE AGE: A WAR BETWEEN MATRIARCHY AND PATRIARCHY

A myth describes how one battle started: a king refused to honor a goddess. Plato describes another succession, when a king refused to allow matrilineal succession through marriage to a priestess or princess. This was a religious war between the conservative goddess tradition and the incipient patriarchy. Temples depicted horrifically gory violence against women.[62]

Female warriors were recruited to fight for their way of life, leaving their strongholds in the Aegean islands, Libya, Scythia, and the south coast of Anatolia (the lands of Lycia and Lydia). This was the age of heroes, the age of Homer's epic *The Odyssey*. The age of the legendary Trojan war was about Helen's right to choose her own partner. Helen was forced into an arranged political marriage with Menelaus, but ran away with the guy she fancied, Paris of Troy. This is the core issue of patriarchy: do women choose their partners, or do men? The Trojans, like most other cultures in Anatolia at the time, retained more rights for women than the Athenians. They fought for Helen's right to stay with Paris instead of being forcibly returned to the Greek husband who claimed rights over her.

The "hero" Perseus was the chief crusader for patriarchy in these Dark Age wars. When he decapitated the icon of female power, the Gorgon Medusa, the Dark Ages came to an end. Patriarchy was, of course, victorious, and the archaic period began. The Olympians replaced the Titans, and goddesses became mere consorts of gods. Property was now traced through male hands.

This, we are told, is the beginning of our Western civilization that arose out of nowhere, like Athena who sprang full-grown from the head

50

of her father Zeus. Perhaps this myth of Athena was propaganda to convince people of the rightness of the new order: a goddess with a father but no mother who was loyal to the male power structure.

Let's talk about Medusa. According to Ovid, she was a beautiful, innocent girl until she was raped by Poseidon in her sister Athena's temple. Athena could have stopped the rape but didn't, jealous of the girl's beauty. Medusa became the serpent-headed monster whose glance turned men to stone, and was beheaded by Perseus.

It's funny how even today they teach us that she is the monster and Perseus the hero. But if you think about it for just a moment, she is the wronged party. She represents female power that must be defeated by the patriarchal crusader, Perseus. Athena betrays the feminine to win points for the patriarchy, as so many women do, throwing her sister under the bus due to jealousy.

Another piece of propaganda for the triumph of paternity over maternity was the play Oresteia: Riane Eisler recounts how Orestes was exonerated of the murder of his mother ... because the court ruled that women were mere empty vessels, not parents.[63]

This play happened 1000 years after the triumph of the new male order; clearly, propaganda was still required to change the old ways that had persisted. But as the curtain rose on the new world of archaic Greece, when writing and art were restored after the Dark Ages, we see the first Olympic games: all-male athletes striding naked for an all-male audience.

CLASSICAL GREECE

Archaic Greece became the first democracy, at least for a tiny number of land-owning males. But the democratic idea of equality, and Western Civilization, didn't arise out of nowhere. It rose from the ashes of the Minoans. All European cultures were built on the substrates of ancient Old European cultures. It took *millennia* of propaganda to erase their memory and their ways, but their love of art, nature and equality made the Greeks who they were, and these came from their Minoan ancestors.

The early Greek philosophers Plato and Socrates believed in equality for women, but Aristotle was an ass who enshrined misogyny into Greek philosophy. Even so, the worship of the goddess, and techniques for achieving higher consciousness, survived in the form of Eleusinian mysteries: a ritual that was celebrated well into the Christian era.

The rites of the mysteries were kept secret on pain of death. Anyone who spoke Greek was welcome. Many believe a psychedelic was involved and ecstatic, erotic practices.

Other threads of feminine, mystical consciousness survived as well. All kings and leaders sought the advice of female oracles, who got high on volcanic vapors at Delphi and other shrines to the goddess. Spartan women retained equal rights of inheritance, unlike their Athenian sisters. Some Greek women managed to become mathematicians and scientists, especially those educated at Pythagoras' school. Women withheld sex to protest war. The library of Alexandria, a repository of ancient wisdom, still allowed women to teach, like the famous Hypatia, mathematician, philosopher and astronomer.

But these good things, too, came to an end. Hypatia was torn apart by a mob that was furious that women dared to teach men. The library of Alexandria was burned along with its precious ancient knowledge. The Romans, an even more barbarous people than the Dorian Greeks, came to prominence. The Romans got civilized by the indigenous inhabitants of Italy, the Etruscans, a matrilineal group that taught them farming and culture.

Even with the Etruscans as teachers, Roman culture was a huge step down from the Greeks, just as the Greeks had been a huge a step down from the Egyptians and Minoans. At least the Greeks had an appreciation for art, philosophy, and male beauty. It's not true that evolution always proceeds forward, as we are told in school. Unlike the symmetrical, harmonious beauty of Egyptian cities, Roman cities were haphazard and devoid of urban planning: the villas of the rich loomed over sprawling slums. Democracy gave way to tyranny. And Christianity was born.

THE DAWN OF CHRISTIANITY

The early sects of Christianity honored women as disciples and teachers and honored the feminine as divine, such as in the Virgin Mary. Yeshua had treated women as equals, and Magdalene took over his teachings. The gnostic sects carried on his principle of equality; women continued to teach, and leaders were chosen by lot. But Paul, a hardcore misogynist ass, decreed that women were to keep silent, so female teachers and priests were condemned as heretics.[64]

The heretical groups that continued ancient mystery traditions of the divine feminine, such as the Cathars, would survive underground until they were exterminated in a bloody genocide a thousand years later in the 12th century.

In the 4th century, the Council of Nicea edited the Bible, removing references to the divine feminine, reincarnation, and ancient mystical teachings. Christianity was now the official religion of patriarchy, and wherever it spread, sacred groves were burned, and women lost what rights they had retained.

That's not to say there isn't some truth behind Christianity, or that there haven't been countless Christians whose faith inspired them to be giving, loving people in service to others. There is divinity in all faiths.

The Iron Age had come to an end, as the next wave of barbarian hordes overran the Roman empire, which had degenerated to petty tyranny. Some of those barbarians, though, retained their matrilineal ways, especially on the fringes of the empire. The Celtic Druids are one example, whose warrior queen Boudica led an uprising against the Romans. The Thracians were another matrilineal tribe from the Old European lands along the Danube River, who retained some ancient ways into the Dark Age. And dark it was.

THE MIDDLE AGES

The next millennia of dark ages in Europe were so bleak, the only innovation was the windmill. Few people could read, and feudal lords raped and oppressed the peasants. One bright light was the mysterious

53

Gothic architecture. They also had stylish outfits. The flame of culture and learning still burned in the Islamic world, which had extraordinary cities unlike anything in Europe, and even some educated and powerful women.

But there, too, things got more patriarchal with time, as Islam spread through the Middle East and Africa by the sword. The Islamic occupation of Spain and Portugal meant diminished rights for women. Their 800-year occupation of India, too, put an end to the sexual expression we see in the orgiastic images on temples like Khajuraho.

As Islam and Christianity spread through the world, destroying cultures, women's rights, ancient traditions, sacred places, and sexual freedom, they folded the ancient pagan traditions into their religions. In Christianity, old gods became saints.

The world had been turned upside down: sex, previously sacred, was now a sin; women's bodies, previously holy, were now shameful; violence, previously a sin, was now glorious. Everything associated with women's power and bodies had become taboo.[65] Especially menstrual blood, which had been the holiest of holy for at least 100,000 years: red ochre is used in burials and associated with menstrual mysteries on all continents dating back to 100,000 BCE. Now it was perceived as gross.

But still, the ancient wisdom survived in secret mystery traditions. Women healers passed on herbal ways of healing, at least until the 16th century when they became a threat to male doctors who knew far less about medicine. Burning women was a convenient way to get rid of doctors' competition and dispose of those pesky independent types. Few people are aware of the extent of this holocaust. There were stakes set up as thick as a forest, and hundreds burned in a single day. In some villages, few women were left alive.[66] But in the fringes of Europe, in the countryside, pagan ways survived in legends, customs, and traditions.

As history unfolded, feminine principles would arise again and again. Permissive periods with more freedom and creativity alternate with periods of authoritarianism.

CYCLES OF AUTHORITARIAN AND FEMININE VALUES UP UNTIL THE MODERN DAY

In the 12th century, there was a resurgence of what Riane Eisler calls "gylanic", or feminine, values, in the courts of Eleanor of Aquitaine. Poets sang the praises of courtly love and the virtues of women; sacred architecture was revived in the new Gothic cathedrals such as the Notre Dame. Eisler describes how periods of gylanic values alternate with more authoritarianism.

Then came the Inquisition torturing people, a lousy time to be alive. The book *Malleus Maleficarum, A Hammer for Witches,* contains detailed instructions on how to torture women, and how to continue torturing them even after a confession. No one was ever declared innocent.[67]

Then came a gylanic cycle: the Renaissance. Europe woke up from 1000 years of Bible dogma and re-discovered classical art and philosophy. In this peaceful Golden Age under Queen Elizabeth I, upper class women obtained a bit more freedom and access to education. Many women ruled in this era: Mary Queen of Scots, Mary Tudor, Isabella of Castile in Spain, Hapsburg women in the Netherlands, and others. Catherine de Medici ruled France for 29 years.[68] Shakespeare's plays feature powerful and educated heroines.

But the backlash to this permissive era was severe; the following Jacobian Era featured a Reign of Terror with 10,000 beheaded, and the launch of colonialism in the Americas. Life was grim until the next golden age in the late 1800s, often known as the Belle Epoque in French. Quality of life improved. This was the age of the Can-Can, that sexy burlesque dance: a relatively liberated sexual age. But again, the backlash was severe when the pendulum swung again: the Victorian era. Sex through a hole in the sheet. World War I.

An example of how war goes hand in hand with authoritarianism and male dominance was expressed by Filippo Marinetti during the world war, who declared: "We are out to glorify War, the only Health Giver of the world! Militarism patriotism! The destructive arm of the anarchist! Contempt for women!"[69]

55

After the war, the pendulum swung again into the roaring 20's, with the introduction of Art Deco styles inspired by ancient Egypt, a resurgence in mystical and mystery traditions, and an interest in the occult. After decades imprisoned in Victorian corsets, women wore flapper dresses, smoked elegant cigarettes, and did the Charleston. Good times! This was the age when first-wave feminists won the vote for women in the United States twenty years after all men could vote, by enduring constant ridicule, insults, harassment, and even death. European countries varied widely in how soon women won this freedom.

All this came crashing down when the stock market crashed in 1929. The Great Depression was world-wide and ushered in the next age of strict male control and authoritarianism. This was the brief period of history that modern right-wingers look back on as "traditional" — father knew best, and mother was a domestic servant who took valium to deal with the boredom.

The 60's revolution, the next gylanic resurgence, was a reaction against all of this. Birth control, psychedelics, and marijuana catalyzed the outbreak of free love, creativity, music, and social reforms. More good times. Out of this movement arose the second wave of feminism which earned women the right to divorce, to have their own credit cards, and to enter the careers of their choice. For the first time, rape and sexual harassment were discussed as male crimes; before, women had been blamed for these things and hid them in shame.

Then came the 80s backlash, according to writers like Susan Faludi who pointed out that violence against women rose, and depictions of women in film and the media put them in their place. The 90s was a golden age, with a revitalization of interest in ancient goddesses, and a revival of interest in, and legal research into, psychedelics. And now, we are living in a time of rampant online misogyny, violent porn, and widespread hatred of feminists.

CHAPTER THREE

ANTHROPOLOGY

nthropology literally means "the study of man". Of course, the word "man" is supposed to refer to humankind in general, except when it's used to refer to *male* humankind. Until Margaret Mead, the first female anthropologist, came along, anthropology was literally the study of men by men.

In the past when racist attitudes were the norm, some anthropologists held dismissive attitudes and colonial intentions toward the people they studied. I believe that has changed with attitudes. It's important to keep in mind when reading an anthropologist's account that it is filtered through her own cultural assumptions. Also, that the people have all been radically changed by colonization or contact with Europeans. Most are more violent and more male dominated than they were before. For example, Margaret Mead's book *Coming of Age in Samoa* mentions that rape was unknown in Samoa before colonization.

In this chapter I'm going to offer some tantalizing details about matrist peoples that survived into modern times. The similarities across distant continents may convince you that matrism was once much more widespread than it is now.

Much of this information, and most of the quotes, come from a massive tome about matrilineal people called *The Mothers* by Robert Briffault, Any information or quotes that are not cited come from this work.

The Mothers makes it clear that matrilineal people are scattered around the globe and share many traits in common, such as the confidence, freedom, and unfettered sexuality enjoyed by the women. There are many stories from explorers and anthropologists of mate-sharing and orgiastic rituals performed without a bit of shame, such as the reports of the French in Tahiti in the 19th century. Accordingly, paternity is not known and unimportant. The mother's brother plays the role of father in children's lives, known to anthropology as the "avunculate".

Matrilineal people raise their children with a great deal of physical affection and allow their teenagers to express their budding sexuality without repression. Many of them, such as the Ghotul people, have a hut for adolescents to do as they please, where adults aren't allowed to enter. An anthropologist named Verrier Elwin in the first half of the 20th century studied the Muria, a Dravidian (southern Indian) people who had survived in the most remote corner of India, and the Batu (Pygmy) people of Africa, as well as other matrilineal groups. He found almost no physical violence, trauma, anxiety, or psychopathology. Elwin believed that these people, with their gentle innocence, are closest to the original nature of humanity.[70]

Children in matrist groups manage themselves democratically and learn about sex by playing with each other. Sexual unions are sweet and respectful. Anthropologists throughout the 20th century noticed that even though they didn't practice *coitus interruptus* — withdrawing before ejaculation — girls never got pregnant.[71] It was only when female anthropologists came along and won the trust of local women that they realized that contraceptive plants were involved.

Some groups that exist today have even managed to maintain their egalitarian social organization, although more of them have maintained their matrilineal inheritance while developing a hierarchy. According to anthropology, all immediate-return hunter-gatherers are egalitarian and believe that hiding or hoarding food is unforgivably shameful.[72] The San Bushmen of the Kalahari Desert, for example, do not tolerate any aggressive behavior, exercise of power, or accumulation of wealth.[73] How did we get from a society where selfishness is a sin, to one where sex is a sin?

Interestingly, new evidence is coming out that some hunter-gatherers had seasonal periods of strong, even slightly authoritarian, leadership, perhaps to make things more efficient during hard times, then let it go during other seasons.[74]

In 1996 I visited several matrilineal societies in Southeast Asia. This meant a lot of long, bumpy bus rides, because these peoples have managed to retain their traditions by living out in the middle of nowhere. My writings from that trip were lost, so I don't remember all of their names, but I remember distinctly that in all of them, the women were bold and happy.

This was a drastic difference from the other people I visited in Southeast Asia, where women were absent, only appearing briefly to serve tea and then scurry away. In contrast, the women in matrilineal groups were front and center, laughing loudly and bawdily. The older women chewed betel nut, a root that turned their mouths red, spitting it out un-self-consciously. The men in these groups seemed relaxed and happy too.

The one culture I remember very distinctly is the Minangkabau, because they are the only matrilineal group with a whole state, and a modern, urban one at that. Their state on the island of Sumatra is very prosperous, with a 98% literacy rate — higher than in the U.S. The bustling women ran restaurants where they served their traditional cuisine, Penang food, for which they charged by the bite. The Minangkabau have tenaciously held on to their matrilineal ways, resisting Islamic invasions that attempted to convert them to patriarchy.

Another place in Southeast Asia where female power has survived is Myanmar, aka Burma. For political and geographical reasons, it was isolated from the rest of the world, hence has survived full assimilation into patriarchy. Women are prominently featured in government, even as leaders of the country. An article in *The Atlantic* from 1958 claims, "In my own research work in the village system of Burma I have even found vestiges of a matriarchal system which must have flourished here at one time."[75]

Burmese women served as chiefs and as queens during the monarchy era. Some other traces of female power mentioned in the article are oil wells owned exclusively by women, inheritance of village headmanship passed through the female line, and the fact that they don't take their husbands' names. All trades such as law and business are open to women, who make up half of universities. They have always had full inheritance rights. Their conditioning in Buddhism, a patriarchal religion, brainwash them to defer to men in many ways, because Buddhism teaches that only a man can become a Buddha. But much more so than many women across the world, they enjoy equal rights and opportunities by law.[76]

THE MOSUO

Figure 3-1: Mosuo girls look so confident and direct compared to so many women in neighboring societies.[77]

Let's go deep into the Mosuo people of the Xiaolianghshan Mountains of Southeast China, about whom a great deal is known, as

60

their traditions have survived into contemporary times. They're closely related to the Tibetans, who were spoken of in Chinese legends as a matriarchal people. This information comes to us from Erche Namu, a Mosuo woman who became a singer in San Francisco in the 1990's. She wrote a book about her childhood called *Leaving Mother Lake.*

In Mosuo society, the mother is the main pillar of the family. Matrilineal clans live together in the same house, often with three generations: grandmother, daughters, granddaughters, sons, nieces, and nephews. There are no taboos around sex, except for incest. A woman receives lovers who visit for the night and leave by the morning. No one asks who the father of a child is. No one gets jealous.

Mosuo consider the idea of being "faithful" to a lover absurd. They laugh at Western ideas of tragic love affairs and wronged lovers. They would think a visitor is joking about someone committing suicide over a heartbreak: "How is it possible to end your precious life for something so banal like sex?" They like to say that love is like the seasons: it comes and goes.[78]

> These family homes have four rectangular buildings connected with an open central courtyard. The main eating, cooking, and visiting area is on the first floor. The second floor has private rooms for the women to receive lovers. The rest of the family sleep in communal rooms. This is a very stable family structure; if the mother dies, the extended family raises the children. They call their aunts "little mother".[79] Uncles are also responsible for the education, care, and discipline of the children, and are cared for by their nephews and nieces in old age.

If a Mosuo woman likes a guy, she invites him to visit her. He may give her gifts of gold, silver, jade, or silk. They go to parties and dance together. The relationship may last a lifetime, or only one night. They may have other relationships at the same time, or just the one.

Mosuo religion is a combination of Tibetan Buddhism and *Daba,* their ancient animistic religion. Their biggest holiday is the Moon New Year, which involves copious amounts of wine and pork.[80]

61

The author Erchu's grandmother was a *Dabu*, the head of the household, who "wore the key of the granary on her belt and a proud expression on her face."[81] She gained this position of responsibility for distributing goods because she was considered the most capable sibling. Decisions were made in council with all the other adults. Her sisters helped run the house; they were hardworking and skillful, like all Mosuo women. They plowed the earth, chopped wood and butchered animals. Her brothers did what Mosuo men have always done: farm, build houses, make furniture, and conduct business with the outside world.[82]

Namu describes the dance around the bonfire:

> [...] the men danced in a group and faced the women, who danced arm in arm, their multicolored belts tied around their waits. Stomping the ground with their leather boots, the men moved toward the women, and soon both groups were dancing in one circle, stepping and swaying their hips in a single rhythm. Then the women pushed my Ama to show off in the center, and while she danced, a young man snatched a belt from her waist. Then he withdrew from the middle back to the men's group, and he threw the belt to one of his friends, who caught it and threw it to another. He would only catch the belt when a man worthy of her songs caught it. Numbu caught it, and stood his ground. She snatched her belt from his hand and ran back to the women, but the women had seen how she looked at him, so pushed her back into the center. His hands on his hips, Numbu began the courtship song: Little sister, you are like moonlight in the middle of the night sky, but the moon needs a star over it.

Then they danced in the middle, arm and arm, until the next song, when another couple took their place. Later in the night, couples disappeared into the shadows.[83]

After that he visited her every night and would spend a few days a week helping with chores, then go home to work for his own family.[84] When she realized she was pregnant, she hung his bag on a nail outside her door. This is the way women break up with their lovers.[85]

Namu describes how harmonious Mosuo lives are. No one shouts or talks shit about each other. No one remembers a single murder, fight, beating, or robbery. Rape and sexual abuse are unknown.

As a child, she roamed the village and could stop at any house for food or care. People used to gather for a week of dancing, singing and praying. At this time the plain was covered with beautiful tents painted with flower designs. The lamas performed ceremony for the goddess, chanting and blowing trumpets. They killed animals for the feast, with respect.[86]

A man from Argentina spent two months among the Mosuo. He reports that the women in charge there never think to amass wealth or power; they just work hard and make sure the family is thriving. Men do better where women are in charge, he says: they get to see different women, and don't have to work as much. Among the Mosuo, like in so many other matrilineal cultures, there is no violence. It would be shameful to fight, and could threaten one's social standing. People constantly make jokes about sex, and consider marriage a fate worse than death, since they know it rarely works out.[87] They have sex for desire or love only, since they don't need each other for anything else. True love still happens, just not heartbreak.

THE NAXI

The neighboring Naxi people are also matrilineal and so have no concern for paternity. What matters to men is that their sisters have children. Naxi girls skip arm in arm in the streets. This is in stark contrast to the Han Chinese (the majority ethnic group of China); the women and girls stay indoors. Naxi Men stay home, playing cards, smoking tobacco and opium, and looking after babies, while women butcher animals, build houses, and go to market.[88]

Naxi society is documented in the book *A Society without Fathers or Husbands*, by Cai Hua. The religious leaders, or *daba*, can be men or women, though in previous generations there were far more women than today.[89] Day-to-day affairs are governed by chiefs who are more

63

often female than male. The female chiefs tend to take more responsibility for the house while the males deal with the outside world.

The Naxi recognize several types of sexual liaisons: *nana sese* (the furtive visit), *ti dzi ji mao the* (cohabitation of a couple without a ritual banquet), and *ji the ti dzi* (cohabitation after a feast). The first is most common.[90]

Cai Hua, the Han Chinese author who studied the Naxi for this book, could not believe his eyes when he observed the young people watching a movie. A young man would take a woman in his arms, caressing her and whispering to her. Then he'd take off and another man would immediately take his place and do the same.[91] This Han Chinese is more similar to us Westerners in his values than he is to his neighbors the Naxi. Because matrism vs patrism is a more fundamental split than any geographic or ethnic one.

Naxi women say they choose men for the following qualities: physical beauty first and foremost, then sense of humor, vivacity, roguishness, courage, and work capability, and then kindness and generosity. Men express a preference for beauty and charm — allure, gift for conversation, good manners, kindness to others.[92] It just goes to show that women being prized for their looks while men are prized as providers is not human nature. When women aren't forced to be dependent on men, they pick men for their looks, too!

Lovers are referred to as *açia*. They're proud of having many lovers, but not belittled if they don't. But they *will* be ridiculed for having the same one for a long time.[93] It's not uncommon for a person to have two or three lovers in a single night.[94] Age doesn't matter; young men visit older women.[95] One man was seeing a woman 20 years older.

Cai Hua asked men how they feel if they get to a woman's house, and she is already busy. They answered: "Well, it happens, I go looking for someone else. There is no shortage of women. There is always one next door … Besides, a woman doesn't owe you anything. There is no reason to be jealous."[96]

He only heard of one case where a couple was so into each other that they vowed to be faithful forever: they were mocked mercilessly. This kind of vow is considered shameful because it's a negotiation, an exchange. They don't consider sexuality as a kind of merchandise. No one should give, trade or sell themselves. There is no reason for constraint.[97] Doesn't that make a lot of sense?

When a woman no longer needs sexual activity, she turns away all visitors. One woman, asked if she thought about the man she had slept with for 30 years, answered, "No, I don't think about him, and he doesn't think about me, either. The Naxi are not like you. We don't need an old companion."[98]

They enjoy love and sex and infatuation. But because their needs for family and belonging are met by their kin, they don't experience the horror of heartbreak. No one grows old alone.

Sometimes Han Chinese men visit Naxi women, but Naxi men never visit Han women. (I bet sexually experienced women are better in bed than women controlled by patriarchal morality). One Han man who really liked dating Naxi chicks said he would never get married, because then you can no longer see other women.[99]

In 1956, the Han Chinese government decided that the Mosuo and the Naxi were a disgrace and did everything they could to reform them; these backwards societies needed nuclear families that would constitute economic units.[100] Authorities ambushed men on their way to see their lovers, strip them naked, and display them in public. They bribed the men with candy and cigarettes to get married.[101]

When this failed, the government passed a law that family land had to be deeded to the men, and offered men free land if they would get married and set up homes for themselves. *Not a single Na man signed up for that.* The government didn't understand why they had no interest in having their own land![102]

One Na man said: "We are closest to our mothers, our maternal uncles, and our brothers and sisters, and they are the most reliable. A wife is just someone to have fun with when you are young. Will you get

65

along in the future? No one knows. To leave your mother and sisters for a wife, that would be shameful."[103]

When you look through the eyes of another society, you realize how culturally determined our deeply held beliefs are: what is virtuous, and what is shameful. And when you think about it logically, the matrilineal way makes way more sense.

Mosuo and Naxi men and women loved their customs so much that they tenaciously resisted all the Chinese attempts to reform them. They clung to their ancient ways. The Chinese gave up, especially when they realized that these people were tourist magnets. People still flock to Mother Lake to see them. Some young Han men come for the wrong reasons; their patriarchal programming makes them think Mosuo women are indiscriminate and can be treated with disrespect. But having so much interest from all over the world helps the young people take pride in their customs. The tourism is mostly a good thing, although it creates economic inequalities in a culture that has always been egalitarian.[104]

But things are changing. The pull of modernity can achieve what the Chinese government failed to do. Cai Hua tells the story of a young Naxi woman who went to a Han college in the city. She got so influenced by the Han ways that surrounded her that she felt ashamed that her siblings had different fathers. She decided to get married. This is how schools assimilate everyone into the dominant culture.[105]

THE MOTHERS

Unless otherwise cited, the examples that follow are from the 1931 book *The Mothers* by Robert Briffault. It's a three-volume leather-bound set with thousands of examples of female-friendly cultures. There are so many shared characteristics among them, such as a positive view of sex, worship of a goddess, absence of violence and sexual abuse, taboos around lovers eating together (since that's considered something you do with your kin), and a special role for the mother's brother for raising the children. (Because this book is now in the public domain, I've loosely paraphrased, and omitted footnote citations.)

66

BERBER PEOPLES

The Berbers are the indigenous people of North Africa. When Arabs first attacked Tunis in 683 AD, the female Berber resistance leader Kosaila defeated them but was killed in a battle three years later. Her successor, a woman of the Jerawa tribe whom the Arabs called Kahina, meaning "sorcerer", lived to be 127! To this day, there are still fortune-telling sorceresses among the Berber.

The independence of Berber women was considered scandalous by medieval travelers. They reported that women married as they pleased, with a ceremony that went something like: "So and so, daughter of So and so, has taken Such a one as her husband."

In one Berber tribe, the Tibbu of the Eastern Sahara, men don't come home without first sending word that they're on their way in case their wives are entertaining another lover. Women oversee all trade. "The women maintain the men as a race of stallions and not from love of them, but to preserve the Tibbu race from extinction."

It was said of the Berber that this was the ancient norm that covered the whole world, until the coming of rulers and conquerors.

THE TUAREG

The Tuareg are another Berber group of North Africa. Lately they've become famous for their music, which has merged with African blues guitar; the Tuareg band Tinariwen is popular around the world. Only women are allowed to read and write among the Tuareg, and the men wear the veil. Men lead the tribal councils but are chosen by women, and women watch the proceedings.

Rape, or even sexual coercion, is unknown among the Tuareg. Women make love to whom they please, entertain male visitors, and keep the children after divorce. They also own the tents, which they can take with them when they want a divorce. Now, of course, things are shifting toward patriarchy; people are moving to cities, where men own the houses. Like the Mosuo, the Tuareg have maintained their ancient ways for millennia, only to be assimilated in the past few decades.

The 14th century traveler Ibn Batuta had this to say about the Tuareg:

> The women are exceedingly beautiful, and they are of more consequence than the men. The character of these people is indeed strange as they are quite impervious to jealousy. None is named after his father, but each derives his descent from his uncle on his mother's side. Only a man's sister's children inherit from him to the exclusion of his own children... As regards the women, they are not timid in the presence of men, nor do they cover their faces with a veil, although they are zealous at their prayers [...] The women do not follow their husbands, and should any of them wish to do so her relatives would prevent it.

Among the Northern Tuareg, what strikes one most, said French explorer Duveyrier, is "the preponderant part played by the women. In all matters their word is law. The culture of the Tuareg is almost exclusively confined to the women; the men are entirely illiterate but the women have artistic and literary tastes, and it is in their hands alone that is preserved the knowledge of the ancient Libyan tongue and of the script which is identical with that of the most ancient inscriptions of North Africa and presents a striking affinity to Minoan scripts."

THE NAYAR

Like the Mosuo, the Nayar of South India have maternal houses and free visiting relationships. Couples perform symbolic marriage ceremonies, but don't live together. The husband is a visitor to the *tarwad*, the house consisting of matrilineal relatives, and so pays his visits after dinner. Recall that lovers don't eat together in typical matrilineal societies.

THE GARO

The Garo from the Meghalaya state in North-eastern India are rice farmers who speak a Tibeto-Burman language. They're seen as mild, good-humored people. They practice matrilineal succession for both property and tribal leadership, from mother to daughter. The Garo usually choose the youngest daughter as leader. She must marry a man chosen by her parents, who ceremonially capture the groom. This man lives with his wife's parents and becomes the clan leader. They live in large longhouses in extended families. If the father-in-law dies, the man must marry his widow, such that he's married to *both* a mother and a daughter!

Aside from the female chief, the other girls choose their own husbands. The girl is the one to initiate a relationship; boys are supposed to be coy and resist. It just goes to show that there's nothing inevitable about our system where the boy makes the moves, and the girl acts shy!

THE CHIANG

The Chiang of Northwest China, thanks to their remote location, have retained more ancient customs than western Tibetans, like the Mosuo and Naxi people. The women enjoy great respect and are consulted in all matters. Older women are preferred as sexual partners for their experience, and often date younger men, as among the Mosuo. This just goes to show that assumption that men preferring young women isn't some biological constant, but a cultural condition. They still engage in earth and water worship.[106]

THE KHASI

The Khasi are a neighbor of the Garo, except that they speak a Mon-Khmer language, like Cambodian. There are 800,000 Khasi remaining. They are also considered mild-mannered and hospitable. They worship the earth goddess. Her earthly representative, the clan mother, acts as chief and priestess, and administers clan property. The high priestess of the village of Smit, the most powerful shaman in Northeast India, selects the dates of important ceremonies and appoints Khasi village chiefs.

Every young Khasi girl takes part in a ceremonial dance where she absorbs the powers of the earth: girls dance in a large square protected by youths who wave yaks' tails to keep evil spirits away. The girls roll their feet from heel to toe to absorb power from the earth, which they channel through the spine into their heads.

69

Figure 3-2: Khasi women.[107]

Khasi are matrilineal and matrifocal. The men act as hunters and warriors in case of attack, and work in government administration. But women own the land and run the businesses, and fathers are not recognized. Some men have started men's rights groups to protest their lot. They say, "We are sick of playing the roles of breeding bulls and baby-sitters. We have no lines of succession. We have no land, no business."

The irony is, that this is the fate of the half-billion women around them in the patriarchal cultures of India, except that they also have no role in government, no say in who they have sex with, and are victims of male violence!

Though they grumble, most Khasi men prefer their culture over those of their neighbors. "The matriarchal system should not be changed, or it will destroy the moral values of the younger generation," said a tribal king in 1999. "We shall see to it that the custom continues."[108]

THE NAGOVISI

The Nagovisi are one of three tribes of South Bougainville, a large tropical island west of New Guinea. Women control food production. They consider sex equally pleasurable for men and women. Nagovisi are divided into land-owning matrilineal clans, which are then subdivided

70

into smaller matrilineages. Marriage is matrifocal. The women share leadership with men, taking part in decision-making and rituals. They like to poke fun at the male chiefs.

The Nagovisi are one of three tribes on their island, each with a different social organization. Among the neighboring Siuai, matrilineal clans regulate marriage and land tenure, but men can also own property. The neighboring Buin, on the other hand, who have the most contact with the outside world, have a hereditary status hierarchy. They have patriarchal polygamous marriage, and their chiefs own slave-girls who serve as prostitutes during feasts. The only consolation is that unlike in most patriarchal societies, there's no stigma attached to prostitution. But the men practice brutal violence against women. As in many other patriarchal societies, their society revolves around war, trading, and giving feasts, like that of the original steppe nomads.[109] It strongly suggests that these traits result from contact with them.

THE MACHIGUENGA

The Machiguenga people of Peru live in the rainforest east of Cuzco and speak an Arawakan language with about 11,000 speakers. They live in marginal areas deep in the jungle, in tiny villages of about 30 people. They practice slash-and burn agriculture, as they lack fish and game in their area. Most likely, that's why they've been able to continue their matrist ways: no one else wants to live there.

Their myths describe men going to live with their wives, but now each couple builds their own house. Women oversee cultivation. Men are discouraged from being violent and aggressive; warfare is rare. Unfortunately, this made them easy targets for the Shining Path guerillas in the 1990s.[110]

MALABAR

Among the Mappellas of Malabar, the bride and bridegroom, after the wedding ceremony, are locked up together in a room of the bride's home "for a few moments." In theory, this is when the marriage is consummated, but nowadays this custom is merely ritual.

Among the neighboring Wends, the bridegroom spends the night at the bride's house; before doing so he bids an unnecessarily solemn farewell to his family. This must be a holdover from the previous matrilocal custom when the man left his family forever to join his wife's. Even our own society contains traces of the earlier matrilocal ways, with the custom of serving wedding breakfast at the bride's house. The bridegroom thus begins his married life as a guest of his wife's family. Of course, most modern people don't practice either matrilocal or patrilocal marriage, as most couples move into their own house.

In other words, the Malabar have a cultural remnant from an earlier time when the man left to live in his partner's village. In those days, he was leaving for good, so he would have said a long farewell. Things have shifted toward patrilocal marriage, but as a respect to the older custom they say a ceremonial goodbye and spend one night with the woman's family.

MALAY OF MALAYSIA

Briffault says: "In various branches of the Malay race and often in the same district, every conceivable transition between 'Motherhood' and the Islamic patriarchal form of marriage of Islam may be observed." In other words, each Malaysian ethnic group had a slightly different version of the transition between matrilocal and patrilocal marriage.

SAHARAWI

The Saharawi from the Western Sahara have a great deal of respect for experienced women. In most Muslim cultures, a divorced woman becomes a social pariah; but to the Saharawi, she's not only more respected than an unmarried virgin, but more alluring. "Clearly, a woman who already has experience is better than a woman who you have to train in matters of relations with men," a newly married third husband explains.

Divorce is not usually acrimonious in the Sahara; the couple agree it's no longer working, and the husband leaves. Three months after the divorce, the ex-wife throws a party to celebrate her new-found single status. But it doesn't last long: a new suitor usually presents himself at the party.

Saharawi culture treats male and female children the same. The women also take an active role in political struggle. In old Saharawi tradition, the women were the ministers and ambassadors.[111]

HAUSA

The Hausa areas of West Africa were ruled by a dynasty of queens, seventeen in all, until around 1050 AD. In the 16th century, conqueror queen Aminatu expanded her state. According to the legend, she took a new lover in every town she conquered, and the man was beheaded the next morning. At present time, Hausa women are subordinate to their husbands.[112]

EGYPTIANS

Diodorus of Sicily, who had visited Egypt sometime between 60 and 56 BCE, writes that the Egyptians had a law "permitting men to marry their sisters" and adds that "it was ordained that the queen should have greater power and honor than the king and that among private persons the wife should enjoy authority over her husband".[113]

NUBIANS

The great Meroë civilization south of Egypt, in what is now known as Sudan but was anciently known as "Kush", was ruled mainly by women from around 300 BCE till the 2nd century CE. Queens Bartare, Kanarta, and Amanitore were buried in tombs and pyramids.

DAHOMEY

The Dahomey are an interesting case of a culture where the women fought more fiercely than the men. They were stocky and strong, and very brave.[114] This was a rare example of a matrilineal group that was militaristic and hierarchical. Dahomey kings were advised by a female counterpart who had a large say in decision-making. The Dahomey were featured in the 2022 movie *The Woman King*.

Figure 3-3: Dahomey warriors c.1890.[115]

VANATINAI

The Vanatinai of Sudest Island in the Coral Sea are an egalitarian society without chiefs. Male and female tasks overlap greatly. Children belong to a matrilineage, and gardens belong to women. You can read more about them in a book by Maria Lepowski called *The Fruit of the Motherland*.[116]

MARQUESAS ISLANDS

On these islands, women often took multiple husbands. Female chiefs were sometimes married in political alliances to infant boys. Two men sometimes jointly offered themselves to a woman, who chose one as *vahana haka'iki* (primary husband) and the other as *pekio* (secondary husband, more like a domestic servant).[117]

TROBRIAND ISLANDERS

The Trobriand islanders live in the Melanesian islands near New Guinea. Women and men are encouraged to have as many lovers as they can, in a special hut called a *bukumatula* where they can make love in privacy. There's no such thing as virginity. Girls take part (topless) in cricket games that are used for conflict resolution instead of violence.[118]

Margaret Mead, the first female anthropologist and the most widely read anthropologist of all time, amazed the world with her description of

74

the Triobriand and other cultures of Oceania. Working in the 1950s, she was concerned with the question of nature vs. nurture: whether traits are due to biology or culture.

Mead used adolescence as a test case. It was widely assumed at the time that adolescence is a painful time in all societies, so she set out to determine whether that was due to culture or to biological changes in puberty. She found that teenagers in the Pacific Islands were happy; without sexual repression and rape and violence, hormonal changes don't have to suck!

In one of my anthropology courses at Stanford, I saw a documentary about Margaret Mead. One scene stuck with me forever: Trobriand children were taking turns playing with a swing. One aggressive boy grabbed the swing when it wasn't his turn. The other children literally fell on the ground, they were laughing so hard, pointing at the boy. He looked ashamed and handed back the swing. One might imagine this boy won't act like an ass again. Selfishness is one possible human trait, but in societies that don't reward it, it eventually falls away.

It was possibly due to her own healthy upbringing that Mead was able to change the dialog around child-rearing. Her mother breastfed her for a long time and was very responsive to her needs. She believes this was the secret to her success. Her observation of Samoan women's affection to their babies led her to influence Dr. Spock, who reformed western child-raising methods.

The Samoans loved Mead. They cried for her when she died. Watching her old footage from the 50s, I wanted to cry too. The people were slim, healthy, fit, and happy; they danced with so much vigor. Just one generation later, young women were interviewed about whether they had boyfriends before marriage. They all said no; the church did not like it. These girls seemed overweight, timid, and unhappy.

In a video from 1967, the girls stand awkwardly in their matching clean white uniforms singing a Western song, the laughter and movement gone from their bodies. Modern patriarchy had domesticated them.

75

HAWAII

Pre-contact Hawaii, like many other places in Oceania, was free of sexual repression. Men and women were initiated into sexuality by an older woman. Young men were instructed in "timing" and in how to help their partners achieve orgasm. Young women were taught how to touch the male and how to move to maximize pleasure by rhythmically contracting the muscles of her vagina.[119]

SAAMI

The Saami, reindeer herders in the frozen northern parts of Scandinavia and Finland, speak a non-Indo-European language from the Finno-Ugric language group. The Saami singer Valkeapää says, "In the traditional Saami society, the way of grandmothers dominates. In the reindeer economy it is very clear that an elderly woman holds the household together and decides what should be done. She decides particularly the marriages and clothing."[120]

ZUNI

The Zuñi of New Mexico believe that men require initiation ceremonies, but women do not, because they're connected with the mysteries of life and death through menstruation and childbearing. Briffault said of them:

> …a Zuñi girl, when she takes a fancy for a young man conveys a present of the hewe-bread to him as a token and becomes affianced; how he sews clothes and moccasins for her and combs her hair out on the terrace in the sun."

Traditional Zuñi men are devoted to raising babies. They live in the ancestral home of their wives, where generations of her family had lived before her.

OTHER PUEBLO NATIVE PEOPLES OF THE AMERICAN SOUTHWEST

The Spanish priests who settled among the Pueblo Indians were astonished at the beauty of the churches and convents the Pueblo women built. They wrote back to their European countrymen: "No man has ever set his hand to the erection of a house. These buildings have been erected solely by the women, the girls, and the young men of the mission; for among these people it is the custom that the women build the houses."[121]

Other matrilineal Pueblo people include Hopi, Hano, Acoma and Laguna. Even in recent times they have retained their land and customs. Brothers and sisters eat together every night.

Briffaut mentions that matrilocal marriage is found among some of the Eskimo, where the young man lives with his maiden's family to work for her parents; it's also found among the Aleuts, the Senecas, the Haidas of the Queen Charlotte Islands, and the Kwakiutl of British Colombia. For women to remain in their own home after marriage was the general rule among all North American Indians. It was the custom among the Inca monarchy of Peru, the Guatos of the Araguay River, all the tribes of the Gran Chaco near the Paraguay River, and many tribes of Southern Argentina.

MISKITU

The Miskitu are a hunter-horticulturalist-fishing people on Central America's Mosquito Coast who center "confederacies of sisters", groups of matrilineally related females. Men join these confederacies as mates.

The Miskitu have been able to resist the influence of outside cultures for the most part. Contact with the English led to the adoption of a king who is seen as the figurehead of the tribes.[122] But they're still matrilocal: girls inherit the land. It is extremely difficult for women to find jobs, and most rely on men and their incomes to support their children. As women become older, they gain status within their community. Female elders known *kukas* are considered local experts and enforcers of correct behavior in their village.[123]

TAINO

The Taino of the Caribbean were matrilineal without any fixed gender roles, except two: women had to handle the corn meal, and men had to build the houses. Where the *caciques*, or chiefs, were male, they came to power through the female line. The mother's brother was, as usual, the most important male in children's lives. Both sexes could have multiple spouses. The Spanish invaders said of them, in 1492: "They were very well built, with very handsome bodies and very good faces … They do not carry arms or know them They should be good servants."[124]

OTHER MATRIFOCAL PEOPLES

I'll just mention a few more matrilineal, matrilocal people that still exist today in the remote corners of the planet: the Seri of Sinaloa in Mexico; the Wayuu who have been hiding out in a very inhospitable desert in Colombia; the Bayaka in the Congo of Africa; the Bunts of Mangalore; The Udupi of South India; the peoples of in the Polama archipelago of Guinea Bissau; the Tobas and Yaruro of Venezuela; the Hadza in Tanzania; the Huaorani and the Cuiva in South America; the Chukchi of Siberia; the Nayaka, the Pandaram, Paliyan, and the Andaman Onge in India; the Agta and Batak in Philippines; the Batek and Palawan in Malaysia; and the Pintupi, Warlpiri and Cape York peoples in Australia. The Mangaia of the Cook Islands and the Kreung of Cambodia encourage the youth to have as much sex as they please. May such cultures build girls "love huts" to entertain boys. In much of pre-contact Malaysia and Polynesia, it was considered rude to ask who the father was, and the chiefly women had higher status than men.

This is just a small sample of the many matrilineal peoples collected by Briffault.

HOW EGALITARIANISM IS MAINTAINED

There are some common techniques observed among modern egalitarian hunter-gatherers from all continents that suggest they are very ancient ways of making sure authoritarian power did not surface. One was to ridicule people who boasted or tried to impose their power. Someone may take charge if they have more expertise in an area, but if they try to continue to tell others what to do, they will be teased.

Another is that parents don't tell their children what to do. They tell the child a supernatural force will intervene if a child is doing something dangerous. This is a subtle distinction that discourages the habit of obeying authority.

Among the Batek people and other southeast Asian egalitarian groups, violence is not tolerated, it's considered to be a form of madness. Some groups practice a ritual form of fighting to settle conflict or to release aggressive energy, that doesn't draw blood.[125]

TRANSITION TO PATRIARCHY

Now let's examine the anthropological evidence for how matrilineal cultures switch to patriliny. In 1884, Lewis Morgan, the American anthropologist who was accepted into an Iroquois tribe, said this:

> How easily it is accomplished, can be seen in a whole series of American Indian tribes, where it has only recently [1884] taken place and is still taking place under the influence, partly of increasing wealth and a changed mode of life and partly of the moral pressure of civilization and missionaries. As wealth increased, it made the man's position in the family more important than the woman's, and created an impulse to exploit this strengthened position in order to overthrow in favour of his children the traditional order of inheritance. This, however, was impossible so long as descent was reckoned according to mother-right. Mother-right, therefore, had to be overthrown.[126]

Modern-day Bantu people in Africa provide a clue to how other societies may have made the switch: as Bantu groups transitioned from farming to cow-herding, they also transitioned to patriliny. Anthropologists Clare Janaki Holden and Ruth Mace observed:

Many societies use livestock as marriage payment from the groom or his family to the bride's family. Wealth from large herds allows men to support multiple wives, and requires defense against raiders, leading to armed conflict. Therefore, livestock is passed on to sons who can mount this defense, promoting patriliny. This holds true for other herding animals such as camels; camel-herding people share with cow-herders the traits of bride-wealth, polygyny, and raiding.[127]

Sara Lowes, who studies groups from this sub-Saharan belt, reports that the children of matrilineal women have healthier and better-educated children. Since they're not economically dependent on their husbands, matrilineal women have better bargaining power than their sisters in patrilineal systems.[128] Both men and women in matrilineal systems have an average of nine years of education compared to seven years for patrilineal ones.[129] Children of matrilineal mothers are much less likely to get sick than those of patrilineal mothers.[130] Finally, matrilineal women report being quite a bit happier than patrilineal women.[131]

The Thonga of South Africa are a good example of a transitional culture between matrilineal and patrilineal. Men had some "rights" over their biological children, but they didn't take these for granted; they earned them through making payments of cows, known as *lobola*. Even so, the mother's brother, or *malume*, officiated at a young man's ceremonies, not the father.[132]

The usual pattern in this transition, a progressive weakening of the brother-sister bond, is the following: 1. A woman's husband takes her away from her natal village, but she is still considered part of that natal tribe. 2. She is considered to belong to her husband and his village, but her children belong to hers. Finally, 3. Both she and her children belong to the husband's group.[133]

But mostly, the transition to patriarchy happens under influence from other cultures. Anthropologist Eva Meyerowitz in the 1940s described how African communities transitioned under British influence. She lived among the Akan of Ghana and described how the

Ohemmaa, or female king, owned the state and appointed the male king, the *Ohene*. She had her own court and took lovers as she pleased. If a man insulted a woman, she could fine him. But when British colonialists ignored the female leader and spoke only with the men, the Akan started ignoring the women as well.[134]

The Trobriand Islanders are another example of a matrilineal group that has declined under Western influence. As Christianity has increased, so has violence.[135]

Another great case study of the effect of patrist Western influence involved the Yanomamo tribe. They might be the most famous tribal group of all time, because the book *The Fierce People* was required reading in Anthropology 101 in my day. The gist of the book is that since this "primitive" Amazonian tribe is brutal and warlike, violence must be natural for our species. The anthropologist who wrote it, Chagnon, earned fame with lurid tales of warfare when he lived among them in 1964.

Ten years later, another anthropologist named Leslie Sponsel spent years among the same tribe, but he only witnessed one single fight. He learned that the tribe had never been violent until that jackass Chagnon showed up with a bag of shotguns and other shiny toys. The Yanomamo had never seen metal things before, so they started to fight over them. In the end, they kicked Chagnon out and told him never to come back.

Suspicious now, Sponsel examined Chagnon's work more closely and learned that not only had he fomented violence by flooding their market with limited-edition goodies and weapons, but he also misrepresented his data by confusing war with violence in his statistics.[136] It's a cautionary tale about how the beliefs and actions of researchers affect what they observe.

It's this concentration of crucial resources in one or a few hands that is the defining aspect of patriarchy. It's tied in with anxiety, violence, and hierarchy, as well as with male dominance, because men dominate in violent situations and want to pass the resources to their sons. Primates

81

also become violent when researchers put out limited stashes of food for them. I'll talk more about that in the next chapter.

Yet, some anthropologists are obsessed with proving that all humans are naturally violent, even if they must hand out the guns themselves, as Chignon did. As they say in *Sex at Dawn*: "Nothing sells newspapers like headlines of war and killer apes."[137] So that's a big part of it: it's sensational. But there may be an unconscious psychological aspect as well, something like: "If I'm an asshole, and I've had a brutal life, I want it to be true for everybody else, because otherwise I really got screwed." Misery loves company.

When I peruse the archaeology news, I frequently see some dude gloating about how we humans are hopelessly drenched in blood, using sneaky statistical tricks and intellectual dishonesty. They cherry-pick the data, as biologist Stephen Pinker once did when giving a talk on violence among hunter-gatherers: he only mentioned the ones who had been missionized. Pinker is "always one to stump for the patriarchy", say the authors of *Sex at Dawn*.[138]

As I said before, science follows politics, not the other way around. Our scientific theories reflect our biases and expectations. We call this "ethnocentrism". The authors of *Sex at Dawn* call it "'Flintstonization' — this tendency to project contemporary cultural proclivities into the past."[139] They say: "our preferences, whether it's for fish and chips over grubs and beetles or our sexual jealousy, are determined by our culture more than nature. We must not mistake our unexamined assumption for the truth."[140]

For example, when anthropologists talk about marriage, and claim it's universal, they're using the term "marriage" very loosely. In some cultures, "marriage" could be for a few hours.[141] It may be a far cry from the way marriage is done in patriarchal cultures. Our modern Western culture, of course, is a mild, reformed patriarchy. Let's look at how it is in some of the harshest patrist areas.

In these cultures, men must come up with a bride price to buy a wife; this makes it very clear that women are a form of property.[142] In Egypt today, most young people can't even afford to marry because of the bride price requirement. Marriages are arranged by the parents, usually between young girls and much older men. Men are limited to four wives. But then, perhaps women prefer polygamy if they don't desire their husband's attention![143]

Still today, in some of the harshest patrist areas nearest Saharasia, girls as young as seven are given to old men. I saw a *National Geographic* magazine from 2011 about child brides in Yemen and in Rajasthan, the western desert state of northern India. Many countries have banned child brides, but it's still part of the culture. Whole communities collude to hide the weddings from authorities. Tiny nine-year-olds are given to fat old men to rape, often as business transactions to pay off a debt.

This entrenched cultural problem is very difficult to solve because of the idiotic patriarchal value around virginity; the husband wants to be the one to take it. When I think about how selfish and ridiculous this is, the bile rises in my throat. A girl's entire childhood is about keeping her from experiencing pleasure, just for the sake of some man feeling so important to be the first man inside her, for a few minutes. Or less.

When I read that article, I suddenly understood why patriarchy arose in harsh desert climates: when resources are scarce, having a child is a big deal. It takes a lot to support each one, so there's a strong need to control sex to make sure a strong man will provide for a child. Conversely, in lush climates with ample resources, every child can easily be supported.

In patrist cultures, virginity is viewed as a precious resource to be protected. If the girl is raped, the family loses a huge amount of wealth in terms of bride price. Instead of harsh punishments for the rapists, patrist cultures punish and blame girls for "tempting" them. The women are seen as impure, and cast into the street to be prostitutes, while the rapists suffer no repercussions. This ensures that men can do as they please, and that women are fearful and easily controlled.

The article on child brides laments: if we, the well-meaning rescuers, could talk her family out of it, or swoop down and grab the girl and run, what then? How can we keep her safe from rape for all those years until she's 18? Of course, the ultimate answer is for people to stop caring about virginity, and for men to be punished for rape. But that will take time. In 2010 a ten-year-old Yemeni child escaped the rapist her family had sold her to for $2000, made it all the way to the big city, and sued for divorce. She won, and made a video in 2013 that went viral. She was featured in a documentary and in 2017 founded an organization to fight for children's rights in the Arab world.

Progress is happening. But as we read this, most likely there is a girl being dumped off at a hospital dead from internal injuries from being raped by her "husband." Not to mention all the girls who will die from female genital mutilation. I can't even imagine the level of hatred and trauma I would have if the people who are supposed to love me the most cut out my clitoris or sold me to an old man to be raped for life. I am haunted by the memory of the screams of the Somali girl getting mutilated in the movie *Desert Flower*, the true story of a girl who escaped her 60-year-old husband at the age of thirteen. She fled through the desert and eventually became an international model.

Male genital circumcision is another horrific patrist practice. While the majority of men can still enjoy sex and don't suffer the extreme pain that female victims of genital cutting do, some men do have complications. In any case, all of them must surely sustain trauma that affects them forever. Still today, routine mutilations are performed on infant boys without anesthesia in the United States (not in Europe). You'd think we *want* boys to turn violent and sadistic! Oh.

Also, the foreskin plays a role in lubricating during lovemaking. Without it, men must pound harder to reach orgasm, and need much more lubrication. This makes sex less pleasurable for most women, and less tender and loving for both.

In polygamous patrist cultures, where a man has many children by many wives, he must keep his adolescent boys away from his younger wives. [144] Thus, boys in these cultures are often separated off into militaristic gangs. What kind of training does a boy need to prepare him for a lifetime of sex with an unwilling woman? What kind of training does a girl need to subordinate her sexual interests to the economic interests of her parents?[145] Hard core obedience training and deprivation, that's what. Hence, the tradition of infant swaddling in patrist cultures of the past. They tied babies' arms to the sides of a wooden cradleboard for long periods of time, letting urine dribble into a receptacle underneath. They only bathed the babies once a week, and sometimes left them on the board the rest of the time.[146]

So, we see how all the patrist traits that DeMeo correlates in his book *Saharasia* are related: infant pain infliction, segregation of adolescent boys, female premarital sex taboos, bride price, polygamy, slavery, and war. We see how matrist traits are correlated: nonviolence, psychological health, sexual freedom, children raised by stable maternal clans, and the importance of the mother's brother. These traits are common to hundreds if not thousands of known groups across different continents, suggesting they are remnants of a more widespread tradition.

Every moment, as we speak, the matrilineal traditions that survived to this day are being lost to missionaries, modernization, modern schooling, and pressure from those who exploit environmental resources. For example, the matrilineal Pomio people of Papua New Guinea are losing their tradition of having the women in charge of land use issues, since the land developers that seek to exploit them only consult with the men, despite their having no experience in the matter. Hopefully, thanks to one powerful matriarch, people are revaluing their traditional customs.[147] One person truly can make a difference!

Another culture from Papua New Guinea, a patriarchal one like most there, is the subject of the book *A Death in the Rainforest* by Don Kulick. is a tragic account of how patriarchal customs combine with modern exploitation to cause the loss of culture, language and nature. Read it and weep. I did.

CHAPTER FOUR

WHERE DO EUROPEANS

COME FROM?

The origins of European people may be the most vicious debate that has ever raged in academia, yet few people today know about it. Technically, it was about the homeland of the Indo-European language group. Indo-European is a family of languages now spoken by most of the people on the planet, having spread all over the world via colonialism. Whoever spoke these languages in antiquity were the ancestors of many Europeans and South Asians. This debate, at its core, attempts to answer the question: where did they come from?

Archaeologist David Anthony says: "The debate, alternately dryly academic, comically absurd, and brutally political, has continued for almost two hundred years."[148]

After following it for 20 years, I was excited when the new science of genetics finally shed some light.

Almost all modern European languages belong to the Indo-European family. The only exceptions are Finnish, Hungarian and Estonian — all members of the Finno-Ugric family — and Basque, which may be a Stone Age European language, now spoken by a grouchy, badass bunch of separatists in Spain and France.

The main European branches of Indo-European are: Germanic (German, English, Dutch), Latin (French, Spanish, Italian, Portuguese,

Romanian, Catalan), Slavic (Russian, Polish), Scandinavian (Swedish, Icelandic), Baltic (Lithuanian and Latvian), Celtic (Irish, Scottish, Welsh), and Greek.

And then there are the eastern languages, the Indo-Iranian group. The Iranian ones include Persian and Afghan. The Indic, such as Hindi and Urdu, are most widely spoken in northern India.

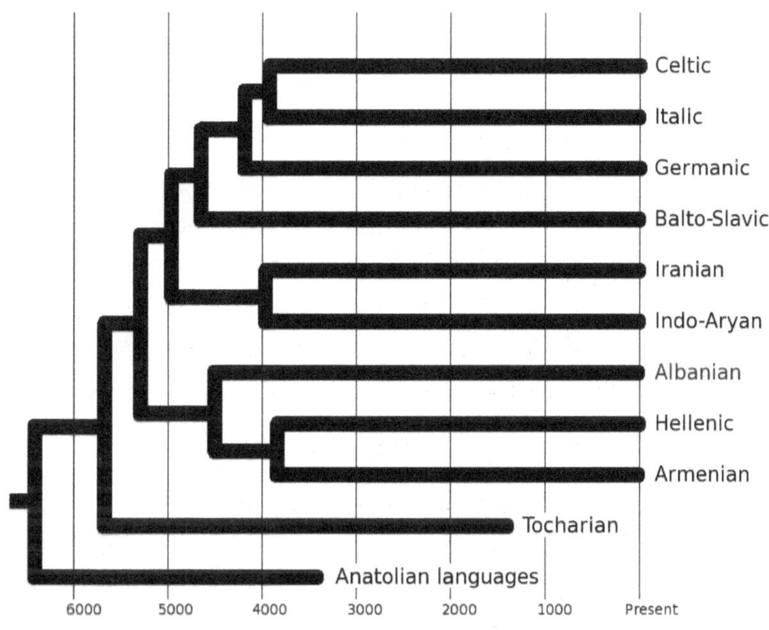

Figure 4-1. Indo-European language family tree.[149]

The family connection between European and Indian languages was discovered in 1785 when William Jones, a linguistic scholar who spoke Greek and Latin, traveled to India. He realized, to his surprise, that he could understand a lot of Sanskrit based on his knowledge of Latin and Greek. Sanskrit, the beautiful ancient Indian language still used in the Hindu religion today, gave birth to many daughter languages such as Hindi. These, like Latin's daughter languages Spanish and French, were simpler and cruder than their ancestor language. That's right. Languages have devolved over the years, like many other things.

87

Languages change over time. When a group splits off to migrate somewhere else, their language will change into a separate dialect and finally into a separate language, especially if they are separated from the mother population by a mountain or a river. That's how a mother language gives rise to daughter languages. (Note: two historical linguists propose more of a wave model than a tree model for language drift, but it has yet to be proven.)

And so, the Indo-European language family was discovered. They found other branches of the family that are now extinct: ancient languages such as Tocharian, and the ones in the Anatolian language family.

This was when the field of linguistics really took off, with an understanding of how languages change over time to reflect our changing reality. This happens unconsciously and somewhat mysteriously across a population that stays in contact. Some languages have a much higher rate of change than others; for example, Japanese changed little over 1000 years, while English has changed so much that we would understand little from 1000 years ago. Even medieval Middle English is barely comprehensible, like the famous Chaucer quote from the 14th century:

> Whan that Aprill with his shoures soote, The droghte of March hath perced to the roote

The shift happens gradually. Words fall out of favor and start to seem old-fashioned until only older generations use them. For example, 'amidst' seems too formal now and is on its way out, like 'betwixt' and 'erst' before them. My spell checker still recognizes 'betwixt' but not 'erst'.

By studying the rate of change within a language, linguists estimate the general time frame of when daughter languages split from the mother. They reconstruct what a now-extinct mother language was like, and when it existed. These mother languages are called "proto" languages; for example, Proto-Germanic was the ancestor of English, German and Dutch; Proto-Indo-European was the ancestor of all the

Indo-European tongues. The latter was never written down and is therefore lost to us. But based on the rate of change, linguists believe it existed around the 4th millennium BCE. They constructed a hypothetical vocabulary based on words found in daughter languages.

Daughter languages have similar words, known as *cognates*. One example is king: *"rex"* in Latin and *"raj"* in Sanskrit. Basic terms such as numbers, pronouns, and kinship words change the least, so are the most likely to be similar in sister languages. One example is "mother", which is *"mater"* in Sanskrit.

So, were the speakers of Proto-Indo-European the ancestors of many Europeans, Indians, and Persians? Most scholars assume so. But how can we link these language groups to ethnic groups? Languages spread differently from cultures or genes, but we can assume some relationship between the two. By combining the data from linguistics and archaeology, we get a fuzzy picture of who these people were. Where were they from? Some said Europe, or India, or Persia, or the Himalayas. And so began the most controversial debate in academic history.

Two competing theories emerged, backed by two very different characters. Although they were both archaeologists, Marija Gimbutas and Sir Colin Renfrew could not have been more different. She was a peasant. He is a baron. His full title is "The Right Honorable the Lord Renfrew of Kaimsthorn". He went to one of those hyper-elite British boarding schools you see in the movies, where one of the houses is named after him, and has degrees from Cambridge in Archaeology and Anthropology. He is the classic blue-blooded, aristocratic, posh-accented, and jocular but condescending Brit. She was elegant, sophisticated, brilliant, and warm, a playful spirit who loved digging in her garden and dancing with her dogs.

Marija came from a peasant family in Lithuania who became revolutionaries. They invited musicians, artists and writers to their home, and founded the first private hospital in Lithuania to help the poor. She grew up surrounded by her traditional culture, as her parents were

Lithuanian folk arts enthusiasts. Her mother was the first female physician in Lithuania.

Marija says that she grew up with "an abundance of love" all around her. Lithuania was the last country in Europe to be Christianized; the religion didn't take root until the 16th century. Things hadn't changed much in millennia, so women were still the center of society. Patriarchy had barely made its way there. So, Marija's upbringing was full of physical affection and a love for mother earth. In her country, in her times, she explained, everything was sacred. Every morning and evening, the men and women kissed the ground. They said prayers to the animals, to the rivers, to the earth. The old women sang long ballads, oral histories that stretched back into prehistory.[150]

Marija was a solid woman with an exotically round face and chestnut brown hair. Capable, brilliant, and cheerful, she worked endlessly and spoke many languages. She had the kind of direct, straightforward manner that is rare for women in our culture. No one could ever win a debate with her.

Figure 4-2: Marija Gimbutas and Sir Colin Renfrew.[151]

During the Second World War, Marija was forced to flee with her husband to Vienna. She boarded the boat by night with a baby under one arm and her PhD dissertation under the other. In Germany, she got PhD's in Archaeology, with minors in Ethnology and the History of Religion. She did this all while raising two young children.

In 1950, she moved to Boston for an unpaid position at Harvard to write a book on the prehistory of Eastern Europe. She was the only person in the US who knew anything about that subject. The unpaid work she produced there established her reputation. Still, as a woman she could not become a full professor at Harvard. Two of the libraries, and the faculty club, were closed to women. She couldn't tolerate that kind of discrimination, so she accepted a position as a professor at the University of California in Los Angeles. She fell in love with California.

In 1965, Marija produced a huge work on the Bronze Age Culture of Central Europe, which brought her international acclaim. For the next 50 years, she excavated sites in Yugoslavia, Greece, and Italy, published 3000 articles and reports, and unearthed *thousands* of artifacts.[152] Since she spoke many languages, she could read primary sources in their original form; this was important, she claimed, since translations can often change the intended meaning of a text.

The settlements Marija studied were separated by thousands of miles. Some were stratified settlements where life had continued for over a thousand years. She described these towns as layer cakes, where the oldest excavation layers are deep under the ground.[153]

Marija was a genius. In addition to archaeology and anthropology, she was also versed in linguistics, mythology, religion, and folklore. It took a truly inter-disciplinary brain to create a coherent picture from this enormous amount of data. Most archaeologists only study the garbage pits of societies' past. She studied all of it.

In deciphering symbols, she saw that these cultures were obsessed with the feminine, and with death and rebirth. She would wake up before dawn to start poring over ancient artifacts. These images and symbols, obviously so central to their lives, were continuous across vast spans of time and space; she had seen them while growing up in Lithuania. She pieced these images together for years, until a narrative emerged from the patterns: Old Europe, the connected culture of Western Eurasia, with shared artistic traditions and a common religion centered on an earth goddess.

Figure 4-3: Female figurines photographed by the author in museums in the Mediterranean, dating from the Neolithic to the Iron age.

After ten years studying the brutal violence of the Bronze Age Indo-Europeans, Marija was thrilled to find that the Old Europeans were peaceful and egalitarian. In a talk she gave in 1991, she nearly wept while describing how comfortably the Old Europeans lived, and in such beautiful locations. She believed that for them, life was a great joy.[154] She theorized that their everyday lives were intertwined with nature, and that they sang while working the earth and doing the chores, as old women still did in her homeland.[155]

In 1987, her work was featured in Riane Eisler's groundbreaking book *The Chalice and the Blade*. This comprehensive and scholarly masterpiece launched an era of feminist scholarship and a revival of the ancient religion of the goddess. Spirituality finally became relevant to women who felt excluded from religions that denigrate the feminine.

Unfortunately for Marija, however, getting adopted by the goddess movement was terrible for her career. Spirituality and academia don't mix. In 1975, she split with her colleagues. Our academic system is based around specialized disciplines, such as archaeology. Those who limited themselves to excavating ancient garbage bins, without any background in mythology or folklore, didn't see the big picture that she saw. They deemed her conclusion that Old Europeans worshipped a goddess "unscientific".

For Marija, a world of empowered women singing while they praised mother earth was easy to imagine: that's how she grew up. Establishment academics such as Renfrew, on the other hand, grew up steeped in the upper echelons of global patriarchy. Her claim that Old Europeans used to worship goddesses, respect women, and live peacefully didn't sit well with those polo-playing Oxford types. She had to be discredited.

Patriarchy, like all institutions, protects itself by suppressing information that doesn't fit its paradigm. Marija's large body of impeccable work proved that war and male dominance were not natural and universal. It attacked the very foundation of Western society. It's not surprising that the academic establishment shut her down.

"She comes to the conclusion that all these images of women represent the goddess, which I think is meaningless," said Renfrew in a video interview, literally lifting his nose in the air.

If she had only done a few archaeological digs, I could see how they could be skeptical about her conclusions, which will be covered in detail in Chapter 10 on Archaeology. But these conclusions were based on an enormous amount of data from many different disciplines.

If the Old European figurines had depicted males, no one would question that they represented male gods. No one doubts that male gods from the historic period, such as Indra of the Indian Vedas, relate to statues from prehistoric times. It's only when the figurines are female that it's controversial. But the evidence for a prehistoric female deity is overwhelming. There were about 1000 female figurines found for every male one from the Neolithic period. They were found in graves and temples, so clearly had a religious function; these were not toys or porn dolls, as some have suggested. Subsequent history from these areas in historical times documents the veneration of goddesses by priestesses.

Brian Swimme, a cosmologist at The California School for Integral Studies, had this to say: "At first, I thought it was all fantasy. I could not conceive of a society free of war. But after a lot of denial, I began to carefully consider what she had written, and it was a deeply religious experience ... to be drawn into a much vaster and deeper sense of the universe."[156]

James Mellaart, the archaeologist who excavated Çatalhöyük, the largest settlement in Old Europe, was asked why the archaeological establishment so roundly dismissed her work. He answered: "Jealousy. I'm afraid archaeology is like that, like most other professions."[157]

Marija and Renfrew used to be friends. They worked on a dig together, and even co-authored a book. But he turned on her when the bra-burning feminists adopted her. In one interview, Marija laughs wryly as she tells of how her close friend "later became my opponent."[158]

In a photo of them together on the archaeological dig, admiration was shining in his eyes as he gazed at her. Maybe unrequited love was part of the reason he turned on her. Or maybe it was just professional jealousy; Marija's warmth inspired great love in people. She got standing ovations when she gave talks. She was one of the most prolific archaeologists of all time. She presented at hundreds of international conferences and wrote several books, plus 350 articles translated into many languages. Until the implications of her work were popularized by feminists, she was one of the most respected archaeologists of all time.

In 1986, Renfrew visited her while she was undergoing painful cancer treatments. He pointed to the manuscript for her next book on the table and said that when his own book came out, "all this will be swept away."[159]

A year later, his book *Archaeology and Language: The Puzzle of Indo-European Origins* came out. Nobody cared. In it, he outlined his hypothesis for the homeland of the Proto-Indo-Europeans, which opposed Marija's widely accepted theory: she placed the homeland in the steppes north of the Black Sea. She called the Proto-Indo-Europeans "Kurgans", a Slavic word referring to their burial mounds. From here, she claimed, they invaded Old Europe, spreading their culture.

By contrast, Renfrew's theory held that Indo-Europeans originated in Anatolia and spread their languages along with agriculture. His 1973 book *Before Civilization* proposed that cultural innovations spread from Europe to the Middle East, rather than the other way around as is usually thought. His "Anatolian hypothesis" held that there were no invasions; the Proto-Indo-Europeans were in Anatolia 2000 years before the Kurgan people arrived, and spread their language and farming techniques by peaceful migration and diffusion.

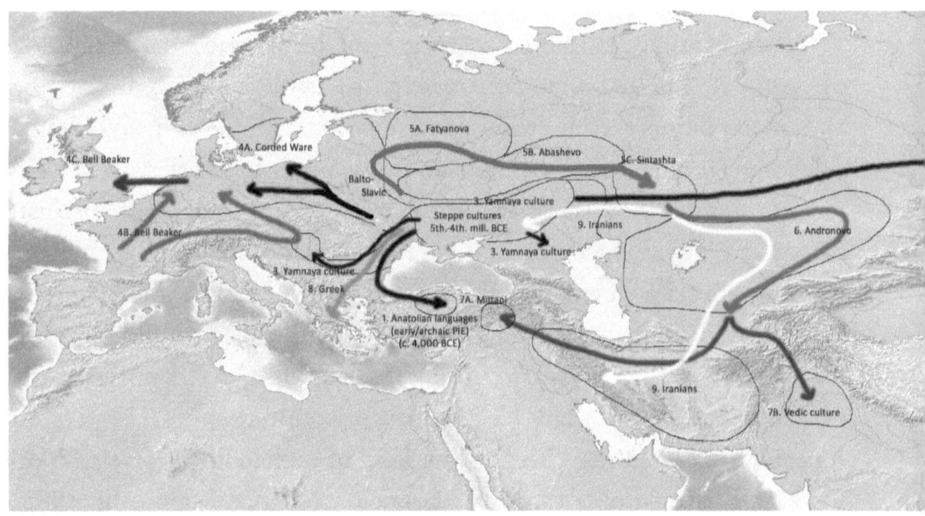

Figure 4-4: Map of Indo-European Kurgan migrations.[160]

But his hypothesis failed to explain why Indo-European languages didn't appear in Europe until thousands of years after the spread of agriculture. And it failed to account for the sudden change in burial patterns and appearance of fortifications around 3500 BCE. At that time, we see burial mounds for elite men who were much taller and with much different skulls than the previous population, buried with treasure. Before, there were communal graves with minimal grave goods. That abrupt change in burial practices coincided with signs of violence and the destruction of villages, all absent from the record before.

Renfrew's theory didn't make sense. Perhaps he badly *wanted* to believe that Indo-Europeans were indigenous to Europe, and that they were the inventors of agriculture and civilization — rather than the primitive barbarians who looted and pillaged it.

His theory held no water, but unlike Marija, he was a tenured professor at Cambridge. He had control over the Cambridge archaeological journal *Antiquity*, and the power to make or break other archaeologists' careers with recommendations or grants. As is so often the case in academia, this political clout kept the critics of his theory silent. He was praised in prestigious journals as the courageous challenger to Marija's mainstream theory.

When Marija was invited to review his book, she mentioned dozens of claims of his that were contradicted by evidence from archaeologists and paleo-linguists. He responded to her critiques by avoiding and sidelining them. He used his clout to publish articles in which he misrepresented her theories, saying that she spoke of a prehistoric matriarchy, meaning cultures where women dominate men, which she did not; she cited evidence for equality between men and women. He hand-picked contributors to journals that he hoped would support his theory, but even *they* had to admit that her Kurgan hypothesis fit the evidence far better than his Anatolian counterhypothesis. Yet Colin repeatedly claimed that "we" in the field of archaeology rejected Marija's work. He pressured others in the field to ignore her.[161] In 1985, an archaeologist presented an unsolicited paper to a conference that was a total hatchet job on Marija, demeaning and contemptuous but empty of any actual facts. He claimed her work was not sufficiently male-oriented. After that, it became a trend to dismiss her as a fad. They misrepresented her work as being about a prehistoric "utopia", which was not what she said; she merely pointed out that there was little evidence of violence. She was accused of "pandering to the Goddess movement," though she did no such thing. And so, other archaeologists,

96

desperate to distance themselves from her, found reasons to denounce her.[162]

In 2000, Cynthia Eller wrote a book called *The Myth of Matriarchal Prehistory* that attacked her and the women's spirituality movement. Reviews of the book pointed out its many inaccuracies, but the damage had been done. At one archaeological conference, Eller mocked Marija with vicious sarcasm and whipped the audience into scornful laughter. One wit joked that she was only obsessed with ancient fertility because she was going through menopause.[163]

The misogynistic lies and slander by people who had not even read her work became more and more exaggerated, showing no regard for intellectual integrity or facts. A guy named Balter wrote a book entitled *The Goddess and the Bull* that mocked her; he had obviously not read her work. The book drones on about the lives of the archaeologists at the dig, without saying anything about the ancient people or their female figurines.

During all this time of crude insults and attacks, Marija never lost her cool. She was unflappable.

The authors of *The Dawn of Everything* have this to say:

> Among academics today, belief in primitive matriarchy is treated as a kind of intellectual offence, almost on a par with "scientific racism", and its exponents have been written out of history [...] Much of this present-day sensitivity stems from a backlash against the legacy of a Lithuanian American archaeologist named Marija Gimbutas. [...] it was near-universal posthumous vilification, or, even worse, becoming an object of dismissive contempt. At least, until quite recently. Over the last few years, the analysis of ancient DNA–unavailable in Gimbutas' time–has led several leading archaeologists to concede that at least one significant part of her reconstruction was probably right.... but either way, after decades of virtual silence, people are suddenly talking about such issues, and hence about Gimbutas' work, again.[164]

97

The orthodox academic establishment also had to discredit archaeologist James Mellaart. After spending years excavating Çatalhöyük, Mellaart had no doubt that the figurines represented goddesses. This was not pleasing to the Turkish government, with their patriarchal god religion; they accused him of smuggling artifacts out of the country. He was fully exonerated of this charge years later.

After his death, he was accused of fraud by archaeologist Eberhard Zangger. Zangger claimed Mellaart had faked images, which were supposedly paintings from Çatalhöyük. Zangger's reasoning was that he found rough sketches of the images hidden among Mellaart's archives, while the finished sketches were in plain sight. Zangger concluded that Mellaart had made these things up, and that the rough sketches were his first prototypes.[165] Why not assume that Mellaart made hasty drafts while on site, and then made neater ones later?

Zangger also accused Mellaart of faking documents in ancient Luwian, an extinct Anatolian language, which seems far-fetched. Luwian had barely been deciphered at the time, so it would have been nearly impossible for him to construct believable fake Luwian sentences. Plus, he never published any of this work or profited from it, so what would have been the point? It's all too easy for a rival archaeologist to create sensational press by making unprovable accusations. *Newsweek* printed this story and failed to mention that Zangger was a controversial figure who had made many debunked claims, and that his claims of Mellaart's fakes were never proven.

To this day, no one has been able to argue with Marija and Mellaart's actual evidence or conclusions. If you aren't familiar with the way things work in academia, you may be shocked, or you may imagine there was truth behind all this slander. Yet, this pattern of ruining academic heretics' reputations, or simply ignoring their research, is incredibly common. They are only exonerated after their death, once their rivals finally die off. Nowadays, we don't literally burn heretics at the stake; we ruin their reputations with snide remarks and keep them from being published in academic journals.

While the merits of her arguments clearly stood for themselves, and Renfrew's were obviously faulty, it still took DNA evidence to finally prove her right. In 2017, analysis of skeletons proved beyond doubt that outsiders from north of the Black Sea entered Europe, bringing Indo-European languages with them.

The two-hundred-year debate over European origins was finally solved. Sadly, Marija had passed away long before, in 1994.

It's rare for academics to admit they are wrong. When evidence disproves a theory, its proponents usually keep quiet about it, never apologizing for ruining their rivals' careers. So it's amazing that Renfrew, to his credit, gave a concession speech admitting that Marija had been "magnificently vindicated" by the DNA evidence.[166] David W Anthony, perhaps the foremost expert on steppe cultures, also vindicated her in a lecture in which he emphatically told his audience "Marija Gimbutas was right."

As I said, the debate between Marija and Renfrew was about much more than just the homeland of the Indo-Europeans. It was about the universality of war and male dominance. It was about interdisciplinary science vs. isolated, over-specialized disciplines. It's an example of how intuition and fresh approaches are crushed by rigid orthodoxy. The orthodox academic establishment suppresses information that doesn't fit its theories; science has replaced religion as the gatekeeper of official truths.

Maybe that's why James Mellaart was ordered to halt excavations at the Neolithic site of Hacılar on grounds that "further work on the site would only yield repetitive results of no great scientific value". Only the top layers had been excavated, with most of the site — the oldest layers — still underground. Mellaart protested, but the dig was halted. It was tragic; with the site no longer protected, it was ravaged by looters, rendering it useless to archaeology.

After Mellaart's death, a guy named Ian Hodder took over the dig at Çatalhöyük, and is still in charge of it today. Hodder and his team distanced themselves from Marija and Mellaart's theories by avoiding drawing any conclusions at all, as if this made them more "scientific" and "objective". They sneered at goddess worshippers. They move at a snail's pace, producing very little data. The dig is effectively on hold.

Hodder dismisses Marija by saying that she was wrong about the existence of a primitive matriarchy at Çatalhöyük. He says, "We are not witnessing a patriarchy or a matriarchy. What we're seeing is perhaps more interesting — a society in which, in many areas, the question of whether you were a man or a woman did not determine the life you could lead."[167] This is his way of discrediting her, except it makes it obvious that he didn't read her work, since that was her conclusion, too.

In the last days of her life, Marija spoke wistfully of the grants she used to get before the backlash against her and feminism. There are few, if any, feminist studies programs left at universities today. Archaeology courses ignore her work. I fear that her books, full of painstaking research and beautiful imagery, will go out of print. It's the most revolutionary and important work imaginable: it proves that civilizations can exist without male dominance, inherited class hierarchy, and war.

I hope that one day, children will learn about Old Europe as well as Sumer. I hope that like all good heretics, Marija will be exonerated and honored after her death, for her huge body of work that changed the world. It gives me hope that there's a library in Santa Barbara, California, dedicated to her. And that in 2021, she was named an eminent personality by UNESCO.

Marija was confident that her work would eventually come back around, even if it took a generation or two. It's happening now! But this is not the first time that evidence of our female-centric past has been uncovered, and then re-covered up...

CHAPTER FIVE

HOW POLITICS TRUMPS TRUTH

Some people think it's impossible that we forgot a whole civilization from 5000 years ago. I don't. We've already forgotten a chapter from 120 years ago, the one where the Marxists discovered the prehistoric "matriarchy", as they called it.

Socialism is making a comeback today, but no one mentions that the first socialists believed that the relationship between the sexes was crucially important and tied in with private property. Karl Marx and Friedrich Engels were certain that all early human cultures were matrilineal.

Nowadays it seems farfetched, since almost all the people alive today live in patrilineal male-dominated societies. But in the late 1800s, there were so many more cultures in the world than there are now. There were thousands of distinct societies which are now extinct. Western culture, which has assimilated so many people on the planet, is really just one culture, like a monocrop. But back in Marx's day, women mattered in most cultures.

I cry about this all the time, how so much human diversity and beauty disappeared so recently, and so rapidly. The only consolation is that we have a record of them in the work of anthropologists.

THE FIRST ANTHROPOLOGISTS DISCOVER THE PREHISTORIC "MATRIARCHY"

Anthropology became an official profession at that time, in the late 1800s. People think academic disciplines are somehow divinely ordained, but they haven't always existed; they got invented at one point. Before the invention of anthropology, ordinary people — usually men of the leisure class — studied culture as a hobby.

Much of the following narrative comes to us from contemporary British anthropologist Chris Knight. This is a summary of his excellent work documenting the discovery (and cover-up) of the prehistoric matriarchy.

Lewis Henry Morgan was the world's first official anthropologist. He was an American lawyer with a fascination for human societies, who got adopted by the Seneca tribe of the Iroquois nation.

In 1858, Morgan noticed that the Native American Ojibway people had the same unusual, elaborate kinship system as the Iroquois. As he studied more societies in North America, he found the same system in all five of the major Native American language groups east of the Rocky Mountains.

The kinship system he had discovered was the matrilineal clan. He came to believe that it was the first stable family institution. People lived in groups descended from ancestral mothers, and shared children in a large clan. Cousins were like sisters and brothers. The children could be fathered by different men, who visited their lovers but went back to their own clan, which was always different from the mother's, as mating within a clan was forbidden.[168]

Clan leaders could be of either sex, but women were responsible for domestic affairs. The clan council comprised of all of the adults in the tribe elected these leaders, and the clan was responsible for aiding all its members.[169] This was a real democracy.

Describing an Iroquois long-house, Morgan wrote of its immense length, its numerous compartments and fires, the "warm, roomy and

102

tidily-kept habitations" and "the matron in each household, who made a division of the food from the kettle to each family according to their needs". "Here", he claimed, "was communism in living carried out in practical life"[170]

When women needed to kick out a free-loading male, they got their brothers to do so. Morgan quotes a missionary who wrote to him: "No matter how many children, or whatever goods he might have in the house, he might at any time be ordered to pack up his blanket and budge […] he must retreat to his own clan; or, as was often done, go and start a new matrimonial alliance in some other. The women were the great power among the clans, as everywhere else."[171]

In early societies, sex was viewed positively. Darwin, Freud and Marx also believed that early societies were promiscuous, but this didn't mean casual sex with random strangers. People would have been deeply intimate with their partners.[172] Lovers came and went, but a woman could always depend on her kin for support.

According to Morgan, it was the domestication of cattle that disempowered women, breaking up their earlier sisterhood. Previously, women cared for their children within a co-operative framework, sharing the burdens with female relatives. Throughout her life, a woman remained living in the same household with her mother and siblings. Children were raised by a confederacy of mothers, daughters and sisters, backed up by male kin and possessing sufficient solidarity and authority to prevent any husband from taking them away. A certain loose kind of "marriage" was consistent with these arrangements, but in-marrying spouses had to agree to visit their brides within these women's communal home.

Morgan believed that this arrangement of "matrilocal residence" — originally prevailed in all human societies across the world. What happened to change such time-honored arrangements? According to Morgan, the key factor was the domestication of animals, notably cattle. A man possessing a herd could bargain with his future bride's kinsfolk, allowing them to keep his cows in exchange for their daughter, whom he could now take away. Under the previous matrilocal system, his bride

103

remained with her kin, benefiting from shared childcare. The introduction of cattle triggered a general shift from matrilocal to patrilocal residence. This change "reversed the position of the wife and the mother in the household". Morgan explains:

She was of a different clan to her children: she had been pulled away to live with her husband. As well as being a different clan from her husband, she was isolated from her kin. Her new condition tended to subvert and destroy the power and influence which descent from the female line that the joint tenement houses had created.[173]

Morgan found it strange that none of the Europeans who had been living among the native people for decades had noticed this. But, unbeknownst to him, some had. The first explorer to describe matrilineal kinship systems was John Lederer in 1672. He wrote about the Tutelo, a Siouan tribe that had four matrilineal clans. He was the first person to describe kinship and kinship systems, which would become the core of the new discipline of anthropology.

Father Lafitau was the next one, fifty-two years later. He described the equality or even superiority of women in Iroquois society:

> Nothing is more real than this superiority of the women. It is essentially the women who embody the Nation, the nobility of blood, the genealogical tree, the sequence of generations and the continuity of families. It is in them that all real authority resides: the land, the fields and all their produce belong to them: they are the soul of the councils, the arbiters of peace and war [...] the children are in their domain and it is in their blood that the order of succession is based.[174]

Then came Adam Ferguson in 1767, a Scottish historian who generalized for the first time about "savage nations.

But historians had written about matrilineal people thousands of years before. Herodotus was a famous ancient Greek historian who wrote about the 'barbarian' peoples around him. The Lycians, Herodotus reported, did not name their children after their fathers like the Greeks, but exclusively after their mothers; in their genealogical

104

records they dealt entirely with the maternal line, and the status of children was defined solely in accordance with that of the mother. Another ancient chronicler, Nicolaus of Damascus, also reports that only the daughters possessed the right of inheritance in these indigenous cultures that surrounded the Greeks.[175] Here is one of his reports:

> The Ethiopians hold their sisters in particular honor. The kings leave their scepter not to their own children but to their sisters. If no heir is available, they choose the most beautiful and belligerent as their leader.' This last observation is confirmed by Herodotus and Strabo. The favoring of the sister's children is a necessary consequence of mother-right and is also to be found elsewhere.[176]

After an analysis of the literature and history of ancient Greece and Rome, Bachofen concluded:

> Mother right is not confined to any particular people but marks a cultural stage. In view of the universal qualities of human nature, this cultural stage cannot be restricted to any particular ethnic family. And consequently what must concern us is not so much the similarities between isolated phenomena as the unity of the basic conception.[177]

Bachofen advanced the following propositions: 1) humanity once lived in a state of sexual promiscuity; 2) there could be no certainty of paternity; 3) kinship was traced through females alone; 4) women's status was correspondingly high; 5) monogamy emerged relatively late in history.[178]

Murdoch, an anthropologist working among the Thonga in Africa, notes that children go to live with their maternal uncle after they are weaned. They can inherit his property and eat his food and use his things. He officiates in the initiations and ceremonies of his nephews.[179]

I have an ex-boyfriend who has now become like family to me, who lives near his mother and sister and helps raise his sister's son. At first he was triggered by this book, but I explained to him that it isn't about blaming men, but about societies like his own family, where men are free

105

from the burden of supporting children that may not related to them, and instead raise their nephews. Now he's all for it!

Like all great discoveries whose time has come, the maternal clan was discovered by more than one person at the same time, independently. Briffault, author of *The Mothers*, had also come to these conclusions on his own, before he read Bachofen or the other theories. The legal historian J. F. McLellan published his book *Primitive Marriage* before reading Bachofen's book, also claiming that "kinship through females" was the "more archaic system".[180]

The matriarchal theory of Bachofen, McLellan, and Morgan was championed by all the scholars of the day, people like E. B. Tylor, Friedrich Engels, W. H. R. Rivers, Emile Durkheim and Sigmund Freud. Marx and Engels, the original communists, believed that the Iroquois lived in a true communist society, with collective ownership and control over their own productive lives.[181] Too bad modern communism never worked like that.

THE MARXISTS' MATRIARCHY

Morgan's work was the basis of Engels' classic socialist book *The Origin of the Family, Private Property and the State*. He believed Morgan's discovery of mother-right was as revolutionary as the theory of evolution. The mother-right clan, he posited, was "the pivot around which the entire science turns."[182]

Engels noted that many societies around the world, such as indigenous Dravidian tribes in India, possessed the same kinship system as the Native American peoples described by Morgan.[183]

Engels described the institutionalization of prostitution as a way for men to endure monogamous marriage, hence indispensable for civilization. He traced the connection between private property, monogamous marriage, and prostitution. He explained the connection between economic and political dominance by men, and their control over female sexuality.[184] On the universality of the earlier custom of mother-right, he said:

> When a system is general throughout America and also exists in
> Asia among peoples of a quite different race, when numerous
> instances of it are found with greater or less variation in every
> part of Africa and Australia, then that system has to be
> historically explained, not talked out of existence [...][185]

It was Marx who first made the connection between patrilineal
inheritance and private property. He wrote in *The German Ideology* that
"the rise of private property caused the switch to patrilocal residence
and patrilineal descent and turned women and children unto slaves of
the husband."[186] He proclaimed:

> The overthrow of mother right was the world-historic defeat of
> the female sex. The man seized the reins in the house also, the
> woman was degraded, enthralled, the slave of the man's lust, a
> mere instrument for breeding children ... The first class
> opposition that appears in history coincides with the
> development of the antagonism between man and woman in
> monogamous marriage, and the first class oppression with that
> of the female sex by the male.[187]

*The discipline of anthropology was founded on this theory of a universal stage of
mother-right: all cultures went through a phase where they were female-centered.* The
theory was expounded on by Murdock who noted that it was a very
plausible for the following reasons: (a) the biological inevitability of the
mother-child bond (b) the intrinsic difficulty in establishing biological
paternity and (c) numerous apparent survivals of matrilineal traditions in
societies with patrilineal descent groups.

"So logical, so closely reasoned, and so apparently in accord with all
known facts was this hypothesis", continued Murdock, "that from its
pioneer formulation by Bachofen in 1861 to nearly the end of the
nineteenth century it was accepted by social scientists practically without
exception."[188]

ONE GUY SHUTS DOWN TO THE STORY, TO SPARE US THE "SHAME"

But then, everything changed. After the Russian Revolution, the West started to associate these ideas with the Bolsheviks. Politicians and clerics preached against it.

Chris Knight, the anthropologist who compiled this history, explains: "A widespread consensus developed on both sides of the Atlantic that regardless of the intellectual merit of Morgan's ideas, 'group motherhood' was in any event too dangerous an idea to be allowed.[189]

The whole "primitive promiscuity" thing was just too much. (Notice how we don't have a single positive English word to describe an active and varied sex life?) Engels commented: "It has become the fashion of late to deny the existence of this initial stage in the sexual life of mankind. The aim is to spare humanity this 'shame.'"[190]

Then, one defender of the patriarchal family, Edward Westermarck, started associating primitive promiscuity with prostitution, to turn people against the theory. In Engel's words: "In my opinion, any understanding of primitive society is impossible to people who only see it as a brothel."[191]

An anthropologist named Bronislaw Malinowsky would become the champion of the nuclear family and would single-handedly bury the entire story of the maternal clan. This guy was triggered by the suffragettes who won the vote for women. It made him feel insecure in his own home. In a radio broadcast in 1956, he said:

> A whole school of anthropologists, from Bachofen on, have maintained that the maternal clan was the primitive domestic institution … In my opinion, as you know, this is entirely incorrect. But an idea like that, once it is taken seriously and applied to modern conditions, becomes positively dangerous. I believe that the most disruptive element in the modern revolutionary tendencies is the idea that parenthood can be made collective. If once we came to the point of doing away with the individual family as the pivotal element of our society, we should

be faced with a social catastrophe compared with which the political upheaval of the French revolution and the economic changes of Bolshevism are insignificant.[192]

Thus, he said, he would "prove to the best of my ability that marriage and the family have been, are, and will remain the foundations of human society". He went to great lengths to show that marriage was universal, even claiming that apes get married![193] In 1931 he debated Briffault, author of the book *The Mothers*, about the matrilineal clan, in a series of broadcasts on the BBC (British Broadcasting Corporation).

At first, the two rivals got along nicely. A guy named Peter Myers introduced them over tea and commented that Malinowsky seemed "much taken by Briffault. In many respects their personalities were not unlike […] they were urbane, witty, and *bon vivants*. Both spoke half a dozen European languages with ease, and they were interested in the same subject. They liked each other."[194]

But with the radio debate, this friendship came to an end. The discussions became more and more acrimonious. Here are some excerpts from the radio debate:

<u>Malinowski</u>: "I shall, however, in the course of these talks, prove to the best of my ability that marriage and the family always have been, are, and will remain the foundations of human society."

<u>Briffault</u>: "The word 'family' covers a variety of meanings, precisely because the conception and constitution of the family have undergone many changes. Family, in Latin *familia*, meant a man's goods and chattels, his man-servant and his maid-servant, his ox, his ass, and his wife. Or, again, when we say that the cat has a family, we are not referring to a group consisting of papa, mama and baby … the primitive human family resembled the animal family more closely than does the civilized family. It consists essentially of mother and children."

<u>Malinowski</u>: "The modern hedonist and misbehaviourist is bent on destroying the home since this is to him the synonym of boredom and repression. You surely don't mean that the clan is really a reproductive group in the same sense as the family?"

109

<u>Briffault</u>: "I most certainly do. The maternal clan is, as I said before, a family group, not a group of families. The assumption that there can be no other form of family, no other reproductive group, than that consisting of papa, mama and baby will no doubt appear very natural to most people, but it is not scientific.

The savage father is, in my experience, considerably fonder of children than is the average English father, but he does not regard them with a possessive feeling, and is equally fond of them whether they are or are not his progeny. Those obligations devolve not on the father, but on the children's uncles.

Civilized man is essentially lonely [...] The savage is never lonely. His social unit, the clan, is a big family. [...] Affection is not concentrated on the man-woman relation; it is diffused in the comradeship of the clan. The savage, as a general rule, is quite kind and tender to his women. But no more so to his wife than to his mother or sisters or his brothers or children of the clan. The dependence of woman in patriarchal society is an economic dependence. That economic advantage of men is not necessarily the outcome of superior ingenuity but is the result of the division of labor between the sexes. One very definite reason why patriarchal society cannot be supposed to represent the primeval condition of the human race is that such an economic dependence of the women and economic monopoly of the men does not exist in the lower phases of culture. Far from the men possessing the advantage of a superior banking account, it is, on the contrary, the women who are the producers of every form of primitive wealth.

One consequence of that organization and that form of marriage, which we call matrilocal, is that there are no illegitimate children. The term illegitimate has no meaning in the lower cultures. All children, being members of their mother's clan, and not of their father's family, are equally legitimate and no legal contract of any kind, no religious ceremony is required to make them so. A legal contract is required to make a child legitimate only where he must inherit his father's name and property. It is only where property is at stake that the legitimacy of marriage, the legitimacy of the children comes to be of importance. [...]

110

Where the men possess considerable wealth, which happens for the first time in pastoral societies, we find that polygamy is universal and extensive."

Malinowski: "Marriage, it is said, 'was ordained for the procreation of children, to be brought up in the fear and nurture of the Lord, and to the praise of His Holy Name.' Now this, in a way, is true of every human community; in most human societies there exists an almost mystical bond of mutual dependence between husband and wife. The notion is universal that the honor and success of the husband depend upon his wife's conduct, while the welfare of the wife is determined by what the husband does. In the traditional ethics of Europe, the wife's misconduct brings dishonor on the husband - a dishonor which, according to the ethics of dueling, can only be washed in blood. To the savages a similar notion says that the wife's adultery may have fatal or, at any rate, dangerous consequences for the husband.

Every society, then, teaches its members the two matrimonial commandments. The one given to the males is: if you want to possess a wife of your choice and have children with her, you will have to shoulder your share of duties and burdens. The one for the woman is: if you want to become a mother you must stick to the lover of your choosing and do your duty by him as your husband as well as by your children."

Thus, Briffault's arguments were based on actual evidence in the world, while Malinowski's were based on religion, and on his view how of things *should* be. Malinowski brushed aside the overwhelming evidence for early mother-right. People today use the same arguments against women working outside the home, or libido drugs for women, or same-sex marriage: we can't destroy the "traditional" family. Some men on social media wave away the evidence for traditional female-centric cultures, confidently opining that it just *couldn't* be true. Wishful thinking has always trumped facts.

That argument of Malinoski's was the last word. Briffault never got to respond, because the BBC shut down the debates. Too many people were triggered by it.

111

IT BECOMES TABOO IN ANTHROPOLOGY TO TALK ABOUT KINSHIP

The damage was done. It was no longer acceptable in academia to raise the topic of the maternal clan, which E. Evans-Pritchard declared "as dead as mutton."[195] Thus, it wasn't possible to talk about kinship at all, because matrilineal kinship is the elephant in the room. Anthropologists were consequently forced to ignore the avunculate, because outside of matrilineal inheritance, it made no sense.

Anthropologist Sir Edmund Leach claimed that this inability to talk about kinship so handicapped the discipline of anthropology as to make it obsolete. They were forced to construct confusing terms and definitions to avoid the taboo of kinship theory. He compared it to Ptolemaic astronomers, who could conceive of the universe only from the standpoint of the centrality of their own Earth.[196]

Chris Knight comments: "Intellectual bankruptcy on this scale is the price paid, I think, when autonomous science is prevented from shaping and informing politics, uninformed politics instead shaping and constraining the revolutionary potential of science."[197]

THINGS SHIFT: WE CAN TALK ABOUT KINSHIP AGAIN!

Finally, the political climate shifted. In 2005, there was a workshop in Wales as part of the prestigious British Academy Centenary Project *From Lucy to Language: The Archaeology of the Human Brain.* Chris Knight gave a talk entitled *Engels Was Right: Early Human Kinship was Matrilineal.* Everyone agreed with him. Anthropologists could now safely talk about kinship again.

Maybe now we can re-visit evolutionary theory without the fetters of dogma. Ever since the mother-right theory was buried, scholars have relied upon patriarchal stereotypes to understand the past. Most people still imagine our ancestors as dull, grunting beasts who dragged women around by the hair.

That's the way it works in academia: rarely does someone admit they're wrong, the way Colin Renfrew did with his Indo-European homeland theory. Usually people just slowly, carefully start talking about a forbidden topic until it quietly becomes the new truth.

As we have seen, one person can have a huge impact, a virtual stranglehold on the truth. Renfrew and Malinoski both single-handedly buried the reality of our ancient past. But the truth can only be suppressed for so long.

It's easier for a non-academic like me to write about taboo topics, with no career to protect. Taboos work the same way in any polite society: there are topics you just don't talk about. You learned what those were when you got punished as a child, or you learned by sensing others' discomfort.

HOW DOGMA CONTROLS WHAT YOU CAN SAY IN ACADEMIA

Here are a few of the topics that are unpopular in academia: women, cyclical history, catastrophic planetary change, and civilizations that haven't yet been discovered. If you broach these topics in academia, you may not get funding.

Time and time again we see a scholar ridiculed for a theory, only to be exonerated later. Troy was thought to be just a legend until the discovery of the Minoans in the early 20th century. Then they wondered how such an advanced, widespread civilization could have possibly been forgotten.

An example of this kind of dogma in action was the "Clovis point" theory that all Native Americans arrived on foot across the Bering Strait when there was a land bridge. This theory was challenged by new discoveries: older and older human remains. What is so ridiculous about the idea that humans sailed to the Americas? Many believe we sailed to Australia 70,000 years ago. Dogmas become entrenched and careers depend on them, so evidence that doesn't fit gets ridiculed or ignored. After decades of lecturing on a theory, an expert will defend it like a religion. It took *decades* before it was finally admitted that some Americans came by boat.

Nowadays, the man-on-social-media responds to a post about ancient peaceful civilizations with a mocking laugh emoji or a quip like, "Where's the peer-reviewed paper??" The thing is, no one writes a peer-reviewed paper about things that are generally known. Few scholars in the field would argue that the Minoans weren't a female-centered society: they just avoid mentioning it. There's cultural amnesia around our feminine past, as well as the mass rape and genocide that followed, and the war between the sexes that followed that. Few people talk about the apocalyptic end of the Bronze Age and the role that the battle of the sexes played in it. Catastrophic events are also buried in this unconscious conspiracy to ignore.

AFTER DECADES OF SILENCE, THE ORIGINS OF SOCIAL INEQUALITY, AND OF EUROPEANS, ARE SUDDENLY HIP AGAIN

As I finish this book in 2022, a new generation of academics and writers are doing the same thing: omitting important truths. The story of the rape of our ancestral mothers by our ancestral fathers is once again finally being told after decades of silence. Lectures are being given and books coming out. But most of them are only telling one half of the story: the genocide, oppression, and male domination that came after the first invasion. They're omitting the more important story of the people who came before, which can give us inspiration to change our ways.

I'll mention several books on the topics of the origins of marriage, hierarchy and Eurasian origins that have come out in the last few years.

YUVAL HARARI

This first came out a while ago in 2011, but is important to mention: Yuval Harari's *Sapiens*. It's based on Jared Diamond's 1997 book *Guns, Germs, and Steel*. Both books are fundamentally biased. They cherry-pick evidence for our species' aggression while omitting the evidence for

114

peace. As I have said, some people have an attachment to the idea that male dominance and oppression are common to every human culture; we like to justify the social structure we are in.[198] Scholars in the fields Harari discusses have been highly critical of his claims, according to Wikipedia. Rightly so: none of it is even cited! The purpose of citing studies is for the reader to interpret data for herself.

Harari's sweeping assertions about the universality of violence and hierarchy are unfounded. He does admit that hunter-gatherers were peaceful. But he claims that inequality increased with the advent of agriculture, showing how little he knows of prehistory. He never even mentions the Indo-European invasions, such a critical part of the story!

Perhaps the book is popular with people who seek validation for their own domineering tendencies. Perhaps the author, despite his lack of academic credentials, became so well-known thanks to his connections at the World Economic Forum. But in general, books about violence and domination are popular. Violence makes better headlines than peace, so news articles on the ancient past focus on the rare violent episodes that occurred before the arrival of the nomads in 4000 BCE, or on the plentiful episodes after their arrival. Harari, Jared Diamond, and Stephen Pinker[199] are the worst culprits of cherry-picking evidence for the universality of violence and inequality.

One example of this cherry-picking can be found in the section in *Sapiens* titled "Peace of War". He chooses four sites from pre-agricultural societies, of which two show violence, and then from those odds claims prehistoric people were as violent as people today. What he doesn't mention is that there aren't just *two* sites that lack evidence of violence, but many more. Violence is the rare anomaly in prehistory, not peace. In the chapter on Archaeology, we will talk about the episodes of violence that we do find, and other evidence that is wrongly interpreted as such.

David Wengrow, co-author of *The Dawn of Everything*, mentions Yuval Harari and Pinker in an interview. He explains how their theories are based on 18th century thinkers like Jean-Jacques Rousseau, whose belief that inequality is inevitable in large populations was pure speculation

115

steeped in the harsh conditions of his time. Over the years, says Wengrow, this theory got taught as objective truth, even as a law of history. It's taught to students as a reason to obey the state, legitimatizing the current status quo.[200]

There is no need to invoke conspiracy to understand the resistance to new ideas in academia. It's merely the reluctance of experts who have been teaching an idea all their lives to admit they were wrong. Theories with politically powerful advocates are adopted, and later enshrined as facts. Generations later, no one remembers that they were just speculation without evidence. Careers are built around them, textbooks are written … and then no one wants to risk their careers to question them.

MORE NEW BOOKS

Two books that have come out recently about Indo-European migrations are *Tracing the Indo-Europeans: New evidence from archaeology and historical linguistics* by Olsen, Olander and Kristiansen, in 2019, and Jean Manco's *Ancestral Journeys: The Peopling of Europe* in 2016. The former is all about Indo-Europeans, so can be forgiven for leaving out the pre-Indo-Europeans. But Manco's book is remiss in leaving out this crucial part of the story.

I have already discussed how *The Dawn of Everything* provides abundant evidence for peaceful, egalitarian societies with large populations, and how rape and the suppression of women go hand in hand with the expansion of empires. The authors explain how the ideas of democracy that radically changed Europe during the Enlightenment came from Native Americans. They offer fascinating examples of how oppressive societies have been abandoned in favor of democratic ones, such as in Teotihuacan where pyramids were demolished to build palaces for everyone; every person lived in lavish dwellings![201] They also abolished human sacrifice at the same time. The authors believe that some of our ancestors carefully kept oppressive tendencies in check in order to create just societies. This should give us hope. Hierarchy can be reversed!

116

Another book on inequality that came in 2022 is *The Journey of Humanity: The Origins of Wealth and Inequality* by Oded Galor et al. With such a sweeping title, you'd think they would mention our egalitarian ancestors, and the massive role that the Indo-Europeans played in bringing inequality to the world. Nope. They don't even mention the Indo-Europeans. They may have interesting things to say about inequality in the later world, but I don't think the book speaks to the origins.

THE BOOK INEQUALITY: A GENETIC HISTORY

And finally, I'll discuss the book *Inequality: A Genetic History,* also from 2022, by Carles Lalueza-Fox, a geneticist who collaborates with well-known geneticist David Reich and with archaeologist Kristian Kristensen. These guys are the biggest voices in this discussion. The good news is that they're combining evidence from genetics and archaeology to tell the story of the Indo-European invasions to the current generation that knows nothing of it, ever since the silencing of Marija Gimbutas. The bad news is that they're leaving out the Old Europeans and focusing only on inequality.

For example, the book mentions a 2017 study in *Nature* that looks at archaeological evidence for inequality in many ancient cultures, assigning each culture a Gini coefficient: a ranking of how egalitarian they are. He does admit that hunter-gatherers had very low inequality numbers. But he then cites two examples that could be evidence for inequality. One is a 10,000 BCE burial of a woman from the Natufian culture with artifacts that seem to have a magical significance. He describes this as organized religion and hence an indicator of inequality.[202] This betrays ignorance of the difference between a medicine woman in an indigenous culture who has earned her position through ability and training, and corrupt religious authorities in later institutionalized religions.

He then goes on to claim that the Gini coefficients of "ancient farming societies" are high. But the society he's looking at is Babylon, well after the arrival of patriarchal Semites in the area. He fails to mention the pre-4000 BCE cultures. If you look at the data, the

117

numbers are low before 4000 BCE (except in China, an area I know nothing about). Çatalhöyük is one of the highest of the Neolithic cultures of the Near East at 28, but the Linear Band Neolithic and Hornstaad-Hornle cultures show only 15 and 17.

After 4000 BCE, high numbers occur in areas after the arrival of the steppe people. One later Bronze Age culture with *low* inequality is BMIII, which stands for the Bactriana-Margiana complex. Despite the later date, they retain matrist characteristics such as fat female figurines, likely because they have no steppe DNA; they descended both from Anatolian farmers and from Neolithic Iranian farmers,[203] who also made female figurines.[204] Somehow the steppe nomads spared them.

The Gini chart shows that some societies in the Americas remained egalitarian well into the common era. Recall that the evidence is mounting that Bronze Age people traveled to the Americas and settled there; this controversial topic is the subject of my next book. It would make sense that hierarchy would have less of a foothold in the Americas if it arrived by boat. The most violent areas were the Mississippi valley and some Mexican cultures.[205] So it makes sense that some American cultures in Gini study with high inequality were Cahokia in the Mississippi and the Mayan culture of Mayapan.[206] (The influence of Bronze Age sailors on the Americas is the answer to Yuval Harari's claim, in *Sapiens*, that the existence of patriarchy in the Americas is proof that it's universal).

In any case ... this Gini coefficient chart is a smoking gun that proves that egalitarian agricultural cultures existed, and that inequality shot up after the Indo-European invasions.

Inequality's author Laleuza-Fox does admit that inequality only appears thousands of years after the advent of agriculture, proposing that the invention of plow oxen is to blame around 4000 BCE. But ... this just happens to be the same time frame as the first wave of Indo-European invasions. Since he spends many chapters talking about the violence, inequality, and male dominance of the Indo-Europeans ... isn't it strange that he doesn't consider the possibility that these traits arrived with them? He discusses the Varna burial as a remarkable example of

118

this "emerging inequality." But he doesn't mention that Varna remains contain steppe DNA, as we will see in the Genetics chapter. Isn't that significant? Wouldn't this suggest that inequality didn't "emerge," but arrived with newcomers?

He does conclude, "Still, such findings are exceptional, and there is a general consensus that Neolithic societies were more egalitarian than later ones." Since that is the case, why doesn't he focus more on the egalitarian cultures, instead of stressing from page one that "ancient history was all about conquerors, dramatic quotes, bloody battles, and deaths?"[207]

Laleuza-Fox mentions in his book, and he and David Reich both lament at length in a lecture,[208] how painful it must have been for the local men of ancient Eurasia to have been prevented from passing on their genes by the Indo-European invaders. But neither of them speculates about what it was like for the *women* who must have had to raise the children of their rapists. Passing on one's genes may leave a record for later geneticists, but it's not what makes a good life. I, for one, would choose death over a lifetime of sex slavery. The tendency for some men (not all!) to see history from an exclusively male perspective is why new ideas enter a field once it opens to women.

Another example from *Inequality* is the ancient city of Jericho. Laleuza-Fox says that by 10,000 years ago it was already fortified with a defensive tower. He does mention that since there was no evidence for invasions back then, many believe the tower had a ritual rather than defensive function. But he goes on to say that since it would have taken so long to build, it was "obviously intended as an imposing demonstration of power and domination. These first farmers then must have already had some degree of social hierarchy."[209]

This claim reveals a bias to see dominance hierarchies. It's pure speculation, but he presents it with certainty. He clearly has no inkling of the ancient indigenous mind. Thanks to my teacher Martín Prechtel, I know that indigenous societies donated enormous time and resources to ritual endeavors. Their societies revolved around cooperative spiritual functions. Domination wasn't required. This is an example of how modern values get projected onto a much different ancient past. Fortunately, this assumption that creating large monuments must involve social hierarchy is being questioned more and more nowadays, as we will see in Chapter 10.

Another example he sites for potential inequality from the deep past is a Russian burial from 34,000 BCE, with fancy clothing decorated with many shell beads. To his credit, he does state that we can't be sure if it's a sign of status or not.[210] The lack of other, less-decorated skeletons from the site suggests it is not. Martín Prechtel taught us how to make these shell beads that were made by ancient peoples around the world as an offering to the divine. It's time-consuming and difficult, but it's not about human status. Academics' lack of understanding of ancient mindsets is one reason they so often get things wrong.

One phrase he used more than once that indicates gaps in his knowledge about prehistory is "military advantage" when applied to the steppe people as compared to the Neolithic farmers. Given that the farmers had no weapons, no warriors, and no military, while the steppe nomads' culture revolved around violent raiding … yeah, I'd say that constitutes an "advantage". Sporadic episodes of violence during times of trauma with hunting tools cannot be compared to a permanent army with weapons that were created for the express purpose of killing people.

I hope these examples have given you some insight into how data can be misinterpreted in accordance with belief systems to distort the past.

I've noticed that those who cite evidence for peaceful and egalitarian cultures are accused of being ideological, while those who wildly speculate that inequality is ubiquitous are not. I get it: inequality is the situation we have today, so therefore the burden of proof is on those who claim it hasn't always been this way.

Those who claim inequality is inevitable, however, receive far more attention and coverage. It reminds me of how studies that show large differences between the sexes receive way more attention than those that do not, according to the book *Inferior: How Science Got Women Wrong, and The New Research That's Writing the Story*. Shouldn't it be the case that revolutionary evidence should attract *more* attention, not less?

THE TIDES ARE TURNING

I'm pleased that a new generation of academics are telling this story again. Even if they act like it's a new story, instead of new evidence for an old story, at least the truth is coming out. But their omission of the happy part of the story is doing more harm than good.

Here's positive new project: a French documentary and video game called *Lady Sapiens* about paleolithic women, overturning stereotypes of the submissive fur-bikini-clad bimbo! It's inspired by the latest research showing that prehistoric women hunted and had great power. It's beautifully rendered and realized. The tides are turning!

That was a lot to take in, so let's summarize the history of these ideas recounted in the past few chapters. In the 19th century, the prehistoric "matriarchy" was independently discovered by several people who were observing matrilineal cultures in North America. Matrilineal kinship became a founding understanding of the new discipline of anthropology. The early Marxists theorized that the male takeover was connected to the inheritance of private property.

One guy in the mid-20th century, threatened by the rise in women's rights, shut down all this talk of promiscuous matriarchies, and it became taboo to talk about it. At around the same time, it became taboo to talk about European origins after the Nazis took that conversation into white supremacist nonsense about the Aryan master race.

So, for a few decades, kinship systems, European origins, and ancient migrations were off-limits. Then, Marija Gimbutas' fifty years of research uncovered the civilization of Old Europe. The debate over Indo-European origins was revived. But when feminists discovered her work, she was discredited with insults. Once again, these topics were silenced by taboo. And now once again, new evidence from genetics has revived this story of our origins.

CHAPTER SIX

ZOOLOGY

Our animal cousins have always been a mirror for ourselves. We use them to justify our own behavior, or to celebrate our uniqueness. We also project our assumptions onto them.

One example is the wolf. We have always assumed that, like us, they have hierarchical societies, with alphas dominating betas. It turns out that this entire belief was based on *one* study observing wolves in captivity who were unknown to each other. In the wild, there are no alphas. Dogs show more dominance behaviors than their wild cousins, perhaps having been bred for submission by humans.[211] It's an example of how our own behavior creates our assumptions. Many animals may be less violent, or less male dominated, than we assume. Elephants and spotted hyenas are both female-dominant. Chinese hamsters, ring-tailed lemurs, and pygmy marmosets all have smaller females that dominate males. Tamarins and titi monkeys, as well as gibbons and siamangs, are pair-bonded primates where neither sex dominates the other.[212] Chimps prefer older females as their mates.[213]

The only two species in the world where males live in groups with their relatives and conduct raids to kill others of their species, are chimpanzees and humans, according to primatologist Richard Wrangham.[214] This is not a normal trait among Earth's creatures!

Primates, of course, are our closest cousins. At Stanford University I had the honor of acting as teaching assistant to the lovable Robert

Sapolsky, biologist and baboon-ologist. His class was extremely popular, and his book *Why Zebras Don't Get Ulcers* is a bestseller. He spends his summers among baboons in Africa, and has a lot to say about violence and male dominance in primates.

In his class we learned that there is *a lot* of variety among primates. Recall the discussion of *sexual dimorphism*, the difference in the size and in the attributes of the male and female of a species. Species in which the male is much larger, and with extra features like antlers, tend to be male-dominated and violent, with status hierarchies. Humans are midway between the most dimorphic and the least. We can go either way. Sapolsky writes:

> And although human males might not be inflexibly polygamous or outfitted with bright red butts and six-inch canines designed for tooth-to-tooth combat, it was clear that our species had at least as much in common with the violent primates as with the gentle ones. "In their nature" thus became "in our nature." This was the humans-as-killer-apes theory popularized by the writer Robert Ardrey, according to which humans have as much chance of becoming intrinsically peaceful as they have of growing prehensile tails. That view always had little more scientific rigor than a *Planet of the Apes* movie, but it took a great deal of field research to figure out just what should supplant it.[215]

Species like gibbons and marmosets, where the males and females are difficult to tell apart, are mellow and peaceful. Monkeys vary widely. Some are adorable and sweet. Others, you would not want to meet in a dark alley. One in India swooped down and took a huge watermelon right out of my hands.

There are two species of macaque that differ greatly from each other. Among rhesus macaques, alpha males eat more than their share of the food. They fight often and never make up. *Stumptail* macaques, on the other hand, despite being genetically nearly identical, are more egalitarian and tend to make up after a fight. When researchers combined the two into one group, something extraordinary happened: the nicer monkeys taught the bullies how to make up. This behavior persisted even when

123

they returned to their own groups. Animals can learn. Cultures can change.

Sapolsky relates an extraordinary story about a gang of baboons that hung out near a dumpster at a tourist safari camp. Baboons are a violent, male-dominated sort of primate, and the alpha males of this troop monopolized all the yummy junk food from the dumpsters. They became tragically obese. Then they all got killed off by some rotten dumpster meat; only females and the less aggressive males were left.

This troop went on to create a peaceful, mellow culture unlike any other baboons ever seen. There was still a hierarchy, but it was loose. The new high-ranking males didn't attack anyone and even shared food. Males and females hung out and even groomed each other, which had never been seen among baboons before.

Years later, there was a new generation of males in the troop, because baboon males leave the troop at puberty and females are joined by males from outside. The new males adjusted to the culture of the troop. Females gave them a warm greeting, grooming them often. The new males got so relaxed with this hippie vibe that they lost their typical aggressiveness and went with the flow!

Now what about apes, our closest relatives? There are five species of ape. The gorilla has high sexual dimorphism, and accordingly, rigid status hierarchies: the silverback gorilla, the alpha male, has access to almost all of the females.

Orangutans, on the other hand, have less sexual dimorphism than gorillas, but still a fair amount. However, they're a solitary species, so you don't see much aggression as do you in gorillas. Gibbons have very little sexual dimorphism, and are peaceful; male and female gibbon pairs raise the young together.

Finally, there's the chimpanzee. Those who are desperate to prove that we are hopelessly violent *love* to talk about killer chimps. (Like they are all talking from the same script.) Chimps have a fair amount of sexual dimorphism, and they *can* be aggressive. This is seized upon, to this day, as proof that human violence is inherent and unavoidable.

Not only does this ignore the peaceful gibbons and monkeys, but also the bonobo chimpanzee, a subspecies of chimp. They're slightly more intelligent than the common chimp and walk more upright. More importantly, they're one of few mammals besides us who are sexually receptive outside of the estrus period. Most female mammals are only interested in sex when they're in heat.

This is an extraordinary thing and rarely mentioned. Because of this rare, significant trait that humans and bonobos share, you would think we would choose bonobos as models for human behavior. While they are definitely not entirely peaceful, we have never observed infanticide, rape, war, or murder among them. So how can rape and extreme violence be universal among primates, as so many claim?[216] Is it possible our view of them is an attempt to justify our current society? The primatologist Frans de Waal opines:

> Just imagine that we had never heard of chimps or baboons and had known bonobos first. We would assume early hominids lived in female-centered societies in which sex served important social functions and in which warfare was rare or absent …The discussion about human evolution might not revolve around violence, warfare, and male dominance, but rather around sexuality, empathy, caring, and cooperation. What a different intellectual landscape we would occupy![217]

Bonobos are female-centered, and much less violent than common chimps. They are extremely sexual, resolving conflicts with sexual play instead of violence. They kiss each other on the lips and hands and feet, and walk arm in arm. Like us, and unlike most primates, they still like to play in adulthood, and like to share even with strangers.[218]

Females do have a sort of hierarchy, but it's based on age, not on inherited status.[219] The matriarchs have a tight sisterhood and like to make love to each other, too; they rub their vulvas together. Females feed first before the males.[220] Male bonobos live longer than male common chimps, as their risk of injury and death is lower.[221] In the end, males too benefit from more peaceful cultures. It's the strong female network that cooperates to keep males more peaceful.[222] The stronger

125

the bonds and cooperation between females, the more peaceful the society. It's no wonder our culture encourages female competition.

De Waal tells a story about how he was lecturing about bonobos when an old male professor stood up and snapped, "What's wrong with those males?"[223] Our patriarchal society is triggered by these apes. While nature documentary cameras love the violence of common chimps, they shy away from bonobo orgies.

De Waal traces this prevailing narrative of the killer ape back to 1924 when Raymond Dart described our hominid ancestor *Australopithecus* as a carnivore that tore its prey apart alive. This was a wild conjecture based on nothing but a juvenile skull.[224] So often, our most intractable dogmas are based on nothing but wishful thinking. As De Waal says: "[…] featuring bonobos could dispel the notion that male dominance is inevitable […] How could the law of the jungle ever have put females in charge? It's just too hard to explain, producers tell me."[225]

Another fun anecdote from De Waal is about how male and female chimps respond to mirrors. Both sexes inspect themselves in the mirror. But females also turn around to inspect their behinds. This body part is significant for females. Males take no interest in their own behinds.[226]

During my years as a research assistant in the Neuropsychology lab at UCLA, I did volunteer research with bonobos at the San Diego Zoo. I spent hours observing them. The matriarch, Lana, came to recognize me, and would run to place her hands on the glass window that separated us. I'd put my own hands up to meet hers. The troop spent a good part of the day in sexual activities: mutual masturbation, copulation, group sex, you name it. You should see the faces of the moms trying to herd their curious offspring away from the orgiastic scene! The increased sexual receptivity means that there's no need for male conflict. Why would you need to fight over something that's plentiful?[227]

Once we discovered bonobos, you'd think people would stop crowing about universal war. Bonobos can be aggressive, but lethal violence is almost unknown. After all, we have so much more in common with bonobos. They stare into each other's eyes during sex, unlike chimps; their vulvas are set forward compared to chimp ones, making face-to-face sex their preference, whereas chimps always do it from behind; they have homosexual play, unlike chimps; and we both use sexual contact as a social activity, whereas for chimps it's only for reproduction.

A male bonobo is tuned into females' facial expressions and vocalizations when they copulate. He adjusts his thrusting speed according to her excitement, and if she seems bored, he will stop. These guys make great lovers.[228]

But even when we take primates as a whole, the most vicious among them included, other primates are far less violent than we are. Overall, they spend only about 1% of their time fighting or competing, usually much less.[229] Bonobos have evolved to favor cooperation, sharing, and negotiation.[230] That is, until they're in captivity with a limited set of food resources.

During Jane Goodall's first four years observing chimps, she represented them as fairly peaceful animals. This agreed with the findings of other primatologists who found peaceful cooperative behaviors far more common than aggressive and competitive ones.

It was when Goodall and her team started leaving a box of bananas near the camp to entice the chimps to come around more, that things turned ugly. The boxes were only unlocked at certain times of day, so the chimps got enraged and frustrated trying to open them. That was when the researchers started seeing much more violence and aggression.[231] Goodall described what seemed like an actual war between two troops. This is when she became famous, and her work began to be widely celebrated. The are still cited as evidence for how we're all killer apes. It's never mentioned that the chimps were peaceful when not tempted with an easy stash of their favorite food. Normally, when food is spread out throughout the forest, chimps cooperate by calling to each other to share what they find.[232]

127

The book *The Egalitarians: Human and Chimpanzee* challenges the view of chimps as dominating, territorial, and violent. In the words of the author Margaret Power:

> [...] all reports from naturalistic (nonfeeding) field studies are of nonaggressive chimpanzees living peacefully on home ranges in fluid, open, nonhierarchical groups. This research has been largely ignored and downgraded by most of the scientific community. By utilizing the data from these studies, the author is able to construct a model of an egalitarian form of social organization, based on a role relationship of mutual dependence among many charismatic chimpanzees of both sexes and other more dependent members. This highly and necessarily positive mutual dependence system is characteristic of both undisturbed chimpanzees and humans who live or lived by the "immediate-return" foraging system.[233]

This tells us a lot about how population density and the availability of resources affect the way we behave.

There's another group of primates that's so similar to us that they act as our space doubles: rhesus monkeys. The rhesus are a violent species, but the females are the more dominant and violent sex. For the longest time, no one seemed to notice or comment on this.[234] I bet it was the first female monkey-ologist to study them that was like, uh, guys? Isn't that a gang of females beating up on that male?

Among rhesus monkeys, status is inherited through a matrilineal line. Females are very promiscuous and hit on the males, placing their butts in the males' faces and slapping them if they don't get on with it.

This brings us right to the next chapter, which is all about sex and monkey balls.

CHAPTER SEVEN

SEXOLOGY

At the end of the last chapter, I dangled the promise of monkey balls in front of you. I won't leave you hanging, so to speak. I'll get right to it.

Human males have big balls (relative to body size) compared to most other primates. Some primates, like gibbons, are monogamous, or at least serially monogamous: they have one mate per season. Others, such as gorillas, are polygamous: the males fight it out and the winner takes all. In both cases, the males have small balls, and penises too. The gorilla penis is an inch long when hard. The testicles are the size of kidney beans and are inside the body. It's their muscles that are large so they can fight over the females.[235]

Bonobos are the only primates with bigger balls than humans. Why? Recall from the last chapter that bonobos are the only other mammal that have sex outside of the estrus season. Sex might break out anytime. They need to keep an army of sperm on hand to attack and outrace all the other sperm that might be swimming around in a reproductive tract. That is only necessary when a female is mating with multiple males during a menstrual cycle.

As I said, bonobo males don't fight much over sex. Promiscuous species don't compete with fists or teeth or claws or antlers. The sperm compete. The fastest, "smartest" sperm gets the egg. This is what's known as "sperm competition". It's a thing. So promiscuity means less violence. Make love not war and all that.

Human balls relative to body size are smaller than bonobos, which makes sense. It seems likely that human balls have gotten smaller over the last few thousand years of monogamy and polygamy. One study with beatles showed their testes size shrank when researchers forced them to be monogamous for 21 generations.[236] One study found sub-Saharan Africans have higher testosterone and smaller testes than Europeans, which is consistent with polygyny.[237] So these things change over time.

A controversial human study suggests that within-population variation in human testes size is due to different male strategies: larger ones for sperm competition, smaller ones for monogamy. In addition, eggs produce sperm chemoattractants that allow for mate choice by the eggs. This all shows that humans have evolved some mechanisms for sperm competition, suggesting multi-male mating in our evolutionary past.

But the balls of modern monogamous males aren't as small as the balls of gibbons, who are truly monogamous. Women have managed to cheat enough to make it necessary for men to keep their balls big. Even under threat of being stoned to death or slut-shamed, many women managed to sneak in shags with square-jawed lovers while their husbands were out fighting infidels or shuffling papers. The urge is strong.

Sperm is even more subject to change with the change in mating habits. A human study that showed that men who engaged in "mate guarding" behaviors had lower equality ejaculate.[238]

Not only is sperm competition a thing, but penis competition too. Humans have long, thick, and flexible penises. One study showed that the unusual flared shape, plus the repeated thrusts, can create a vacuum to pull previously inserted semen out.[239]

The male genitalia and sperm-count suggest that humans evolved in an environment where females regularly had multiple partners. Also, if we were monogamous, men and women would be the same size, like

130

with gibbons. If we were polygamous, men would be *twice* the mass of women, like with gorillas. But our sexual dimorphism is like that of the promiscuous bonobo: in-between.[240]

In polygynous harem species with high sexual dimorphism, everyone's tense because the males fight it out over the females. When everyone's polyamorous, the males can relax and let the sperm fight it out. Less violence and more cooperation allow for larger group sizes. That explains why no multimale primate is monogamous.[241]

Of course, there are millions and millions of people who do make it work! Who stay in love for decades, have eyes only for each other, and support each other in all ways! It can happen. It's worth striving for. But I advocate that we understand the odds, so if it doesn't happen, we don't hate ourselves.

Why haven't you heard of sperm competition, you wonder? Because our culture wants us to believe that we evolved to be good little monogamous male-headed economic family units. Promiscuity is a shameful taboo in sex-negative patriarchy. Remember when talk of promiscuous matriarchies was shut down to "spare us the shame"?

 Before patriarchy, females must have had multiple partners during a single cycle. The female reproductive tract is designed to pick the sperm most compatible with her DNA. It can change its pH to favor some sperm over others, such as choosing X vs Y sperm to favor a male or a female.[242] The female orgasm plays a role in sperm selection, as well.

All this information comes from the incredible book *Sex at Dawn* by Christopher Ryan and Cacilda Jethá, which set a record for time on the bestseller list. It made me laugh and cry so many times.

Men's bodies are evolved to spread their sperm far and wide. They don't need to be as choosy, as they won't be the ones to carry a pregnancy, give birth, and breastfeed. This is the one hypothesis of social anthropology that I believe is universally true, even in a non-patriarchal culture. In a matrilineal clan, where a mother has relatives to help her, it's still more metabolically expensive to breed as a female than a male. Birth is dangerous. Plus, taking someone into your body is more

131

vulnerable than penetrating. It makes sense that women would be pickier. This is confirmed by a study showing that on the dating app Tinder, women are less likely than men to swipe right, indicating willingness to mate.[243]

For this reason, it makes sense to me that women should be the ones to approach men, instead of the current cultural habit of men being the approachers. Most men will be somewhat open to most women. Single women, on the other hand, are overwhelmed at having to rebuff the advances of men that they don't desire — the majority — which can even be dangerous. They're frustrated that when they finally see a man they do desire, they need to play games as so many men are intimidated by a woman who does the approaching. It makes no sense.

They say that hell hath no fury like a woman spurned, but very few have actually hurt the men they desired.

The fact that females are choosier explains why a society based around male dominance and male choice leads to coercion and oppression. Males are usually open to mating with anyone, so when females choose, most males are psyched. Male choice, on the other hand, can lead to rape when females aren't into it.

The best strategy for women in patriarchy is to choose a dependable, faithful provider to take care of her and her kids, while cheating on him with a vigorous bad-boy. Men's strategy in patriarchy is to get their sperm into as many women as they can, while guarding and controlling their official mate to make sure she stays faithful to him. The control part is only true in patrilineal cultures, because the man has to provide for his children.

This can lead to competing strategies between men and women, in patriarchy. Men are programmed to take a young mate with wide hips who will be a good breeder, then guard her from other males, all while cheating on her. Women are programmed to act faithful to score a good provider, then give him the slip while ovulating. A few quotes from *Sex at Dawn*:

The 'mixed strategy' of the standard narrative, is for a man to cheat on his pregnant wife while being insanely — even violently—jealous of her. Charming. [And when having affairs with other women], this investment would be wise for him, given the low costs he incurs (a few drinks and a room at the Shady Grove Motor Lodge — at the hourly rate). The woman's mixed strategy would be to extract a long-term commitment from the man who offers her the best access to resources, status, and protection, while still seeking the occasional fling with rugged dudes in leather jackets who offer genetic advantages her loving, but domesticated, mate lacks. It's hard to decide who comes out looking worse.[244]

And:

At our most basic levels, we're told, heterosexual men and women have evolved to trick one another while selfishly pursuing zero-sum, mutually antagonistic genetic agendas — even though this demands the betrayal of the people we claim to love most sincerely. Original sin indeed.[245]

Furthermore:

According to this theory, women have evolved to unthinkingly and unashamedly exchange erotic pleasure for access to a man's wealth, protection, status, and other treasures likely to benefit her and her children. Darwin says your mother's a whore. Simple as that [...] the bartering of female fertility and fidelity in exchange for goods and services is one of the foundational premises of evolutionary psychology.[246]

Argggh! This made me cry. In other words, patriarchy can make us into liars and cheats. This narrative is often discussed in modern "men's rights" movements. These "Men's Rights Activists", or MRAs, claim to be about men's rights, but are really about men's right to go back to controlling women's sexuality. They lambast women for this pattern of cheating on men, but they're fine with men doing it.

133

Men's groups like the Red Pill divide men into "alpha" and "beta" males; in patriarchy, dominance hierarchies are all-important. They despise women for marrying beta males then cheating on them with alphas. They recommend that men manipulate women by tearing down their self-esteem to conquer and abandon them.

Hence, sex becomes a battlefield, a "bleak design for mutual misery", as they say in *Sex at Dawn*.[247] The sexes can rarely trust each other, with such incompatible interests. It's often tragic.

However, this entire theory, the entire basis of evolutionary biology, sociobiology, and anthropology, is only relevant in patriarchy. It's not universal and inevitable, as the authors of *Sex at Dawn* are well aware: they spend a fourth of the book talking about the rise of patriarchy and how that changed things. However, they blame it on agriculture, which is wrong.

In our ancestral environment, as we saw in the anthropology chapter, women didn't need men to protect and feed them. In matrilineal clans, they gathered and distributed most of the food. Their brothers protected them from wild animals and hunted. We now know women hunted as well. Women didn't need mates to feed and protect them. They had a clan. Mates were for mating.

So, not all ancestral females needed providers. The ones in matrilineal clans didn't need to exchange sex for food, or to pretend to be faithful for protection. They didn't have to "cheat" on anyone or have routine sex. They would have just done it whenever they wanted, with whoever they wanted. The only reason to have sex was because they were turned on. What a concept! How insane that contractual or obligatory sex is considered normal!

Thus, all the assumptions that follow from there are false: why females mate, how they choose mates, how males enter into monogamous contracts, and so on.

The narrative that we learn in anthropology courses, which is entirely theoretical, centers around what's called "paternity certainty," and goes like this: females are helpless when pregnant or nursing young children, so they need males to protect and support them. Males only invest time and energy to support a child if there's a good chance it's his. Otherwise, his efforts will benefit another man's offspring. Therefore, monogamy evolved to get men to stick around and help with the offspring.

The theory makes sense from a patriarchal viewpoint, but the evidence does not support it being common in the ancestral environment. Anthropologists Beckerman and Valentine point out that many lowland South American cultures believe that multiple fathers can create a child. They think a child can inherit different traits from different men that the women have intercourse with.

They also believe that having multiple fathers benefits babies' survival, with more fathers to protect them. This is surely true; all the men who think they might be a baby's father are more likely to help. The baby isn't dependent on one male who might die or be a loser. Some of these cultures live thousands of miles apart, and diverged millennia ago. Thus, it's not an isolated phenomenon, but a belief that was once widespread.[248] Nowadays, after millennia of patriarchy, the men are mostly in charge of sex and that does not go well for women. The point, however, is that if this belief is widespread, then nuclear families were not universal in our past.

The entire core assumption of anthropology is based on anthropomorphic notions of a nuclear family. The first evidence we have for one is from 4,600 years ago in Germany.[249] We can point to several societies which before European colonization had other family organizations, such as the Nayar of India, the Mosuo of China, and the Ik of Africa. The anthropology chapter gave other examples.

Marriage is extremely widespread today, after 5000 years of patriarchy, but we can't assume it was universal in the past. Polyandry was well known and practiced in the age of the Atharva Veda, a holy book of India. Many Pacific Islanders continued to practice unconstrained sexuality despite the shaming of missionaries.[250] One chronicler on the voyage of Magellan in the 16th century, Pigafetta, described public sex and his own adventures in the Phillippines. He knew the church would not approve of these practices he observed, especially the ones that were about the womens' pleasure.[251]

Linear B texts from Mycenean Crete do not mention marriage, except for the overlords. The ancient Greeks observed orgies among the non-Greek "barbarians" that surrounded them, and reported polyandry among Northern European tribes such as Britons, and among Caledonians, Libyrni, Etruscans, Scythians, Lybians and some Arabians. Free sexual behavior permitted to married women in that era were even well-known among male-dominated societies such as Lydia, Macedonia, and Thrace.

Many early researchers were hell-bent on proving humans to be naturally monogamous, but evidence to the contrary has accumulated in recent times as religious morality has waned. Among the matrilineal Himba of Africa, extra-pair paternity (kids not fathered by the husband) is as high as 48%. The husbands know these kids aren't theirs and raise them anyway, knowing their extra-pair kids will be raised by another husband. The authors of this study say, "These data provide a stark contrast to the prevailing opinion in the genetics literature that EPP is negligible in humans.[…] Higher rates of female concurrency have been linked to matrilineal inheritance, reliance on foraging and horticulture, a male-biased adult sex ratio, and prolonged periods of spousal absence."[252]

Another study sampled fifty-three societies outside of the Himalayan and Marquesan areas that are known for polyandrous unions, and found that polyandry "is not as rare as commonly believed, is found worldwide, and is most common in egalitarian societies. We also argue that polyandry likely existed during early human history and should be examined from an evolutionary perspective."[253] One researcher noted that the reason it was assumed to be rare, back in 1957 when it was first discussed, was that most anthropologists back then were men. She says that "there seemed to be a fairly pervasive belief that polyandry didn't make any sense from a male's perspective."[254] Articles that assume that pair bonding is universal tend to look only at modern cultures, long after the rise patriarchy.

Another survey of 186 cultures looked at attitudes toward sex. For extramarital sex for women: 133 had missing data, 6 universal, 23 moderate, 9 occasional, 15 uncommon. For rape: 155 missing data, 8 absent, 10 rare, 13 common. So female fidelity and rape aren't as natural as assumed.[255]

In cultures like the Canela of Brazil, newly married couples were warned not to be jealous of their mates' other lovers.[256] Many cultures have no word or concept for "virginity".[257] The entire concept of virginity and breaking the hymen is a patriarchal myth. Many women don't have a hymen, and most hymens are stretchy and don't break with first penetration by a man. This whole concept of checking the hymen to determine virginity is just more nonsense.[258]

Sex researchers Clellan Ford and Frank Beach found that in societies with no double standards, women are as eager to copulate as men.[259] Anthropologists Berndt and Berndt, who studied the Aborigines of West Arnhem Land in Australia, observed that: "[...] some women are satisfied only after a number of ejaculations — one insertion being 'too quick' for them to enjoy completely. This probably explains why some native women desire the attentions of more than one man during a night...."

And: "Young girls disport themselves with evident enjoyment, while the men to whom they give their attention usually behave shyly..."[260] Our whole story that men push for sex while women resist coyly is not central to human nature. Women are only coy when they're sex-shamed into it because of paternity certainty.

So ... evolutionary theory is basically bullshit. Much of it applies in patriarchy but is not relevant to human evolution or to most of the human story. EO Wilson's book *Sociobiology* in 1975 summed up this theory of paternity certainty: horny males and coy females. It was a defense of the patriarchal status quo and became required reading in biology classes. I had to read that nonsense at Stanford.

Then, feminists came along and pointed out the "circular reasoning, absence of evidence and unscientific assumptions." Anthropologist

137

Kristen Hawkes argued that since there are so many isolated tribes where paternity is unimportant, our evolutionary environment could not have revolved around the exchange of food for fidelity. She also noted a hunter shares meat with the whole tribe, not just his mate.

Anyway, if women are so coy and only have sex to get favors from males and keep them around, then why have patriarchal societies gone to so much trouble to keep the female libido in check? As they put it in *Sex at Dawn*:

> [...] female genital mutilation, head-to-toe chadors, medieval witch burnings, chastity belts, suffocating corsets, muttered insults about 'insatiable' whores, pathologizing, paternalistic medical diagnoses of nymphomania or hysteria, the debilitating scorn heaped on any female who chooses to be generous with her sexuality … all parts of a worldwide campaign to keep the supposedly low-key female libido under control.
>
> Why the electrified high-security razor-wire fence to contain a kitty-cat? Evolutionary psychology's standard narrative contains several clanging contradictions, but one of the most discordant involves the female libido.[261]

Evolutionary psychology, aka sociobiology, is a bunch of unscientific conjectures, assuming that the way things are now is the way things have always been. They claim that female prostitution is the oldest profession, universal in human societies. But the earliest evidence for it is from 2400 BCE, in Uruk — the first patriarchal city. It's not common in societies that don't block young men from easily finding mates, and in which women aren't economically dependent on men. It goes way up during wars, economic depressions, and famines.[262] Even Wikipedia has to admit that farming and hunting are actually the world's oldest professions.

In sex-positive cultures, not only is there no prostitution, but no rape or pedophilia. It's sexual frustration that makes adults rape children.[263]

Sex at Dawn says:

> Today, self-proclaimed [evolutionary psychology] 'realists' argue that it's ancient human nature that leads us to wage war on our neighbors, deceive our spouses, and abuse our stepchildren. They argue that rape is an unfortunate, but largely successful reproductive strategy and that marriage amounts to a no-win struggle of mutually assured disappointment.[264]

Nope. In matrilineal cultures there's no rape, no prostitution, and no battle of the sexes (though it's changing quickly as they "modernize"). There are no alpha and beta males. Males pass on their genes through their sisters. They don't have to compete, or be jealous of their mates. These egalitarian societies represent the triumph of the female reproductive strategy over the males.

As Beckerman and Valentine put it:

> Women's reproductive interests are best served if mate choice is a non-binding, female decision; if there is a network of multiple females to aid or substitute for a woman in mothering responsibilities; if male support for a woman and her children comes from multiple men; and if a woman is shielded from the effects of male sexual jealousy.
>
> Male reproductive interests, contrariwise, are best served by male control over female sexual behavior, promoting paternity certainty and elevated reproductive success for the more powerful males. This profile implies that men choose their own or their sons' wives, and their daughters' husbands; that marriage is a lifetime commitment and extra-marital affairs by women are severely sanctioned; and that this state of affairs is maintained by disallowing women reliable female support networks, or male support other than that of the husband and his primary male consanguines.[265]

In other words, in societies where the female strategy wins, women get to choose who they have sex with. They're surrounded by relatives to help raise the kids, and to protect them from any jealous mate that might try to control them. Women are free, because they have a support network to stand up to jealous, controlling males.

Women in these matrilocal societies have a huge asset in child-raising: their mothers. In traditional patrilocal societies, where women go to live with their husband's kin, a woman's mother is too far away to do much grandmothering. This brings us to the grandmother hypothesis: another piece of evidence that we evolved in matrifocal societies.

The grandmother hypothesis claims that the only evolutionary reason for women to live for a long time after menopause is to ensure the survival of their descendants by serving as grandmothers. Grandmothers must really help their grandkids to survive, if the genes of a grandmother who lives long after her fertility stage are selected for.

However, in a patrilocal culture, an old woman would be separated from her daughters who move to their husbands' tribes after marriage. There's not as much incentive to grandmother your son's kids, because it's not certain whether he's really the father. Therefore, the existence of menopause suggests we evolved in matrilocal societies where the female reproductive strategy predominated.

Where the male reproductive strategy predominates, men get to decide who has sex with whom. Powerful men get more women, and fathers choose mates for their sons. Lifelong monogamy is required for women, and women are isolated from their relatives and from forming coalitions with other women. Slavery and rape become the fate of women in the most extreme patrist societies.

So you see how these two ways of organizing human societies, around the male strategy or around the female, aren't created equal. While the female strategy isn't as ideal for the reproductive interests of powerful aggressive men, it's way better for everybody else.

Where the male strategy wins, evolution revolves around individual competition. Where female strategy wins, evolution operates more at the clan level: children are raised by the clan.

The only taboo in female-centered, sex-positive societies is incest. One must mate outside the clan. However, it's not a taboo that requires much enforcement, because people who grow up together or spend a lot of time together don't want to have sex, anyway. Losing attraction after long overexposure is nature's way of preventing inbreeding. (That explains what happens to long-term couples.)

In these cultures, women import fresh genes from outside the clan by mating with strangers. That could explain why women are more turned on by strangers than by familiar men, despite the narrative that safety is the turn on.[266]

Unfortunately, some women are also turned on by rape. Studies show that rape stories get some women excited. Perhaps it removes the guilt and shame if she has no choice in the matter.[267] Perhaps this arises from millennia of patriarchy, because women who got turned on by it and produced lubrication would have been more likely to survive and pass on their genes, without dying from internal injuries.

Women under patriarchy had to evolve to survive rape, and also to play the patriarchy game. They had to choose between the two reproductive strategies available to them in this system: Madonna or whore. Patriarchal societies force women into these two categories: respectable and non-respectable. Respectable women are the property of one man, and the others are public property, available to any man who can pay. Although even if he can't pay, he can get away with rape, because who will care about a whore? That's why pimps evolved.

A woman with class privilege will choose the Madonna strategy. She will dress demurely, and focus on finding a successful mate and proving to him that she will be faithful. This requires resisting his sexual advances even if she wants him, to prove that she's a prude who won't cheat on him. Patriarchy wants to see these women — mothers, sisters, wives — as pure women who are uninterested in sex, who do it for their husbands or to have children. They "lie back and think of England."

For men to endure these prudish Madonnas, they had "whores" at their service. These women were purely sexualized, never thought of as

141

being someone's mother or sister. It was ok to disrespect them. The "whore" strategy is chosen by attractive women without class privilege. It's more dangerous, but with a lot more economic potential than the other possibilities traditionally open to poor women: seamstress, maid, or dependence on a poor husband.

If a poor woman is very attractive, however, she might climb the class ladder by "marrying up". Interestingly, people in the lower classes naturally give birth to more girl babies, while the opposite is true for upper classes, where boys are needed to carry on their lineage and property. It's amazing that a woman's body is smart enough to know that in a poor family, a girl child is a better bet for the genetic fitness of future generations.

In a rich family, a son is a better bet, because rich men in patriarchy might have a great many children, especially in polygamous cultures. Genghis Kahn sired hundreds of children to the point where he affected the genetics of the whole world: 1 in 200 men in the world today are direct descendants.

So powerful men in patriarchy do extremely well, while poor men have limited opportunities to spread their genes. Women almost always had the opportunity to have some kids, whether they wanted to or not, but the number they can bear is limited compared to male chiefs with harems.[268]

Of course, where paternity is unimportant, there is no Madonna / whore complex. A secure man prefers an experienced woman who knows what she's doing, not a girl who acts clueless so that he feels like a big powerful dude.

Do you see the connection now between patriarchy and preferring youth? As we saw in the Anthropology chapter, men in matrilineal cultures prefer experienced women. In patriarchies, young women are prized as breeders who won't compare a man to someone else, and young men are prized for their strength. Unfortunately, cultures who prefer youth, instead of venerating elder wisdom as older cultures did, are prone to depression. Everyone knows that their best days are already behind them, and it's all downhill from here.

So, in patriarchy, in order for men to be sure they're raising their own biological children, they go to extreme measures to destroy and deny the female libido. In extreme patrist cultures, they tear out the clitoris without anesthetic or even ceremony, just using drums to drown out the hysterical screams.[269] Women are imprisoned in the home and stoned for infidelity.

In our own culture, just a hundred or so years ago, they put carbolic acid on girls' clitorises to keep them from touching themselves.[270] Today, sadistic male surgeons perform unnecessary hysterectomies and breastectomies to "prevent cancer" for the same reasons they do male circumcisions: for money, and, out of unconscious anger toward the natural sexuality they have been denied.[271]

Until recently, girls were given the message that sex is nasty and to just say no. (Nowadays they are being hypersexualized instead, but that's just the other side of the coin). Because women have been told for thousands of years that they have no libido, they're totally disconnected from their own sexual desire.

A recent scientific study set out to learn more about female desire. They designed a device called the plethysmograph, a glass tube which is placed in the vagina to measure blood flow, and thus arousal. With this inside, women subjects were shown videos of various sexy scenes: chimps copulating, group sex, lesbian sex, a couple in missionary position.

When asked which scenes turned them on, the women claimed to be aroused only by the missionary sex. But the device showed that *all* of the scenes aroused them, even the chimps. This proved that women are often completely out of touch with what turns them on. They're so conditioned to be monogamous that they don't even *know* when they're turned on.

However, when they were told that their answers would be anonymous, they admitted to being turned on by way more things. They

143

also admitted to having had more sex partners.[272] So, some female coyness is linked to a fear of being judged.

The revolutionary book *What Women Want: Adventures in the Science of Female Desire* by Daniel Bergner collected scientific research that shows that, contrary to the narrative that women have no sexual desire and just want forever love, they actually have a harder time with monogamy than men. More men can maintain sexual desire in a long-term relationship than women. Maybe it's because men have more desire overall, or maybe because more men allow themselves to cheat, or to fantasize about other women when they're with their partners.

Whatever the case, the failure of sexual desire in marriage, particularly for women, is an epidemic. An Australian study that tracked hundreds of subjects found that hormones weren't the problem: it was the length of time a woman had been with the same partner.[273]

But flagging desire is a huge problem for both sexes. Most couples who have been co-habitating for four-and-a-half years or more report feeling like siblings. Even if they get along and still love each other, they rarely feel motivated to have sex or kiss. Perhaps our bodies figure that if a child hasn't happened after four or five years, we should try someone else. And if we *have* kids together, it's time to mix our genes with other partners for diversity.

After all, only 3% of mammals are monogamous for life. Our fellow primates really like variety in partners, including the females. Put a new male in the enclosure, and females who were tired of sex with the old males will perk up.[274]

Tantra courses teach that living separately, or at least having separate bedrooms, can extend the vitality of a partnership. They recommend couples avoid doing mundane logistical tasks together, like, say, building a house. (This author learned that one the hard way.) But the core tenet of Tantra is *brahmacharya*: the ancient art of cultivating spiritual and vital life energy through minimizing explosive orgasms (ejaculation for men, and clitoral orgasms for women).

144

Tantra teaches that the more you ejaculate as a couple, the quicker you burn out the spark of desire. In the words of this author: most couples have a finite number of ejaculations; they can either blow their wad early, or have the discipline to space them out over decades.

All that being said … everyone knows at least one couple who is still madly in love 30 years later despite living together and raising kids. Perhaps some people are just perfect for each other, destined by fate to walk together for a lifetime. Some are just lucky. The profound beauty of growing old with a soul mate compensates, for some, the potential negative effects of monogamy on their health.

These effects have been studied more in men, of course, since men's bodies are always studied more than women's. Married men show lower levels of testosterone than single men of the same age; low testosterone is linked to heart attacks, cancer, and depression. [275]

Perhaps that's why more than half of people cheat. Powerful men like Bill Clinton risk everything — their careers, reputations, children — to have an affair. The authors of *Sex at Dawn* quote one man who had an affair with his secretary:

> At first the sex was fantastic. I hadn't felt so alive in years. I thought I was in love with Monica [the other woman]. When I was with her, it was like everything was stronger, you know? Food tasted better, colors were richer, I had so much more energy. I felt high all the time.

He got caught, and his wife left him. When the novelty of sex with the new woman faded, he realized that he had traded his soul mate, his best friend, for a woman he didn't even really like. This situation, as the authors say, is "heavy with tragedy." [276] Especially when you have children, or you've built your life around the person.

This need for novelty has nothing to do with the attractiveness of one's partner. Men married to Hollywood starlets get tired of them, too. Novelty seems to be hard wired into our genes. This makes sense, as it's evolutionary advantageous to have offspring with as many diverse partners as possible. Again, some people manage to make it work! Perhaps they are wired differently. Or it's their destiny to work together.

We're told that if we aren't having great sex with our spouses, we should get a therapist or some crotchless panties. Or, that there is something wrong with us.[277] All because we aren't allowed to talk about the truth: most of us aren't evolved for lifelong monogamy. So we shame ourselves, feel inadequate, spend money on strip clubs and porn,[278] waste money on therapists, and lie to each other.

Worse, we uproot children's lives when we tear ourselves away from one partner to jump to the next, instead of creating a stable home for children that's not dependent on their parents' sex life.

While men have always had more leeway for extramarital affairs, female fidelity is considered the cornerstone of our culture, because of the whole paternity-certainty thing. In order to solve the problem of flagging female desire for their husbands, researchers set out to find a female Viagra.

Of course, female desire is more difficult to medicate. Viagra works by increasing blood flow, which doesn't do it for women. The pharmaceutical companies figured it out and created a drug that seemed to work, but the FDA shut it down, realizing that there was no way to restrict female desire to husbands.

One guy in the pharmacology business put it this way: "When you're going to the FDA with this kind of drug, there's the sense that you want your effects to be good but not *too* good." And: "There's a bias, a bias against — a fear of creating the sexually aggressive woman. There's this idea of societal breakdown."[279]

A drawing on the cover of *Time* magazine illustrated what would happen if women all took this drug and became horny: total social collapse. Cars are abandoned as people copulate in freeway medians. This is what the *Time* article imagined if the FDA approved this drug: the world would come to a screeching halt if women were as horny as men. Women are the gatekeepers of society. If they stop sacrificing their desire to keep society on track, all hell will break loose.[280]

146

So what ended up happening? They came up with a different female libido drug. In 2019, it was approved.[281] It's an epi-pen rather than a daily pill like the previous drug. The woman gives herself a shot twenty minutes before having sex.

My hypothesis is this: the FDA were comfortable with this drug because it wouldn't make women indiscriminately horny all the time. It's limited to the moment when she is about to have sex with the one man she's allowed. There will be no orgies raging on car hoods, no societal breakdown.

Think about how awkward this is, though, compared to a pill which boosts your libido all the time. When your husband starts hitting on you, you discreetly retire to the bathroom to take the shot, then hold him off until it takes effect. The pill would be so much more natural and spontaneous; but, as always, what's best for patriarchy is more important than what's best for women. Funny how no one asked whether Viagra would cause men to cheat on their wives.

The same concerns were raised about the birth control pill: it would cause the breakdown of marriage. It's still banned in many Catholic countries. Ironically, abortion rates are higher in countries that ban them, because they also ban contraception.[282]

Before patriarchy, women used natural contraceptives. Anthropology didn't realize this until female anthropologists gained the trust of the women in the cultures they studied. One female student noticed that the Lesu people of the South Pacific chewed the leaves of one special plant and swallowed the juice, in order to keep from getting pregnant.

This knowledge was kept hush-hush. Anthropologist Nicole Maxwell reported that among Peruvian tribes, "Any premature attempt to pry, however delicate, is apt to bring all communication to an abrupt, sullen end." But using a slow, friendly approach, she managed to collect specimens from a sedge called *Piri Piri*. Women grew it in hidden gardens and gave it to their daughters in a tea upon puberty.[283]

One field worker in Dutch New Guinea in 1902 noted: "The worst plant of this kind is called *Lapalet*. The poison of this plant is so

147

destructive that it not only produces sterility but can also kill a 3 or 4-month-old foetus. Why the people wish to produce sterility and even abortion is still unknown to us. Even the men do not know what to say about it. They know neither the secret means of the women, nor the art by which this childlessness is made possible."[284]

After the missionaries arrived and shamed this knowledge, tribal people learned to keep it secret. There are many more examples of native people who had knowledge of natural contraception, most of them located in the matrist areas of the planet.

In patrist areas, they're even more secretive about it. The hill tribes of the Rif in Morocco only sell it in the women's market where men aren't allowed, because if they're caught, it would be grounds for divorce.[285]

Ancient peoples in the "Old World" also knew how to use contraceptive plants. The earliest known mention of them is in the Kahun papyrus in ancient Egypt. After the patriarchal Hyksos people took over Egypt in 1850 BCE, recipes were lost. Chinese texts mentioned them until an invasion from central Asia led to a decline of female healers and midwives.[286]

When Rome became Christianized, there was a crackdown on contraceptive potion drinking, since sex for pleasure became a sin against the Church. But it continued underground, often using a dung recipe. The last mention of contraceptives was in the 1400's, when the Inquisition started.[287] So, contraceptives were driven underground as early as 3000 BCE in the "Old World," but only in the last 200 years in the Americas and the Pacific, thanks to missionaries.[288]

Just as patriarchy put an end to contraception, it has shamed all aspects of female sexuality. The clitoris was re-discovered by a Venetian professor in 1558, for which crime he was accused of Satanism and imprisoned. His drawings were confiscated. During the Inquisition, women with large ones were burned as witches; these clits were called "devil's teats."

Meanwhile, Darwin was obsessed with the red swellings of monkey butts that advertise ovulation. He couldn't talk about it because of the taboo against sex, but it bothered him that if primates were naturally monogamous, such signals should not have been necessary.[289]

In 1850 there was a blitz of propaganda against masturbation. A medical journal declared it public enemy number one. They claimed it would cause blindness and insanity. "Besides," these authorities intoned, "'normal' women had little sexual desire anyway."[290]

In the late 19th century, during the Victorian era when people had sex through a hole in the sheet, "hysteria" was one of the most diagnosed illnesses. The symptoms included anxiety, shortness of breath, fainting, nervousness, sexual desire, insomnia, fluid retention, heaviness in the abdomen, irritability, loss of appetite for food or sex, sexually forward behavior, and a "tendency to cause trouble for others."[291] *Of course* women were hysterical — they didn't even know they could have orgasms. Like I didn't until I was 22. No one bothered to tell me.

Then in the early 20th century, one doctor discovered that if he massaged women until they "spasmed," it cured them of hysteria. Soon there was a line outside the door of his office. He got tendonitis from "treating" so many women every day. That's when he hired an engineer to make the first vibrator, which took up half the room and was steam powered! There's a movie about this called *Hysteria*.

American women needing to be stimulated to orgasm made up the single largest market for therapeutic services at this time. Seventy-five percent of American women needed this treatment. They called it a "nervous paroxysm," pathologizing the normal female response.[292] Soon the vibrator was the number one product sold in catalogues. More people had vibrators than toasters. Some hung from rafters on pulleys, some used high-pressure water.

Then Freud came along and defined women as mutilated, incomplete men whose psyches revolved around "penis envy."[293] He claimed that clitoral orgasms were immature; vaginal orgasms were for *real* women. Clitorectomies were performed as a cure for hysteria and masturbation as late as 1936.[294]

149

The first sex research happened in 1947. Alfred Kinsey published his report based on a wide-ranging survey. He founded the discipline of sexology and finally stated that women were sexual beings, and that the clitoris is the main female sexual organ. He found that suppressing sexuality to wait for marriage is harmful. He also established the Kinsey scale of sexual orientation, liberating same-sex attraction.

Then Masters and Johnson came along. While Kinsey had only surveyed people by asking them anonymous questions, Masters and Johnson actually watched people having sex, which was pretty edgy in the late 50's and early 60's. Even today that would be super weird. They watched 382 women and 312 men copulate while hooked up to wires measuring their responses, wearing paper bags on their heads for the sake of anonymity. A huge rocket-shaped dildo with a camera recorded what was going on inside. It's crazy that this happened!

The next milestone in sexology was the bestselling book *Sex at Dawn*. It changed the world by finally proving that lifelong monogamy is not natural for all human beings, and showing the connection between monogamy and war.

Then came the book *What Do Women Want: Adventures in the Science of Female Desire*, which used scientific evidence to prove that women have strong sexual desire, and that monogamy is harder for them than for men.

Still, after all this progress, we have a long way to go. Still today, of course, 100 million women are circumcised. Midwives are still harassed, and women are encouraged to schedule caesareans so that physicians can manage birth in hospitals instead of midwives using natural means.[295]

Women still feel ashamed to speak of menstruation in front of men, and rarely speak of menopause even among themselves. Sex researcher Monica Chivers reports that when an image of female genitalia was shown to middle schoolers in a sex education class, there was a gasp of horror, whereas the penis just got giggles.[296] She also claims that the best universities never do research into sexuality. "Because there is a kind of taboo. Because we who do this work are second-class citizens."[297]

Plus, there is still an orgasm gap. In Mangaia, a group of islands in the South Pacific that escaped patriarchy until very recently, nearly all women reported having orgasms with every sex act. By contrast, among Americans today, 39 percent of women said that they usually or always experienced orgasm in partnered sex, as compared to 91 percent of men.[298] Relationship sex is better than hookup sex for female orgasm. Not surprisingly, lesbian women do much better than their heterosexual sisters.

All the things that were the most sacred for tens of thousands of years — female sexuality, female bodies, menstrual blood, childbirth — became shameful, disgusting taboos under patriarchy.

Here's a quote from *Sex at Dawn* to sum it all up:

> [...] the seismic shifts that happened a few thousand years ago have made the true story of human sexuality so subversive and threatening that it has been silenced by religious authorities, pathologized by physicians, studiously ignored by scientists, and covered up by moralizing therapists ...The campaign to obscure the true nature of our species' sexuality leaves half our marriages collapsing under an unstoppable tide of stifling sexual frustration, libido-killing boredom, impulsive betrayal, dysfunction, confusion, and shame. Serial monogamy stretches before (and behind) many of us like an archipelago of failure...[299]

Let me just add that we should take *Sex at Dawn*'s conclusions with a pinch of salt. I have researched the details I shared to make sure they have held up the test of time. But still, take *all* science with a grain of salt. Even the most principled researcher is prone to bias.

A rebuttal to *Sex at Dawn* was written, called *Sex at Dusk* by Lynn Saxon. She points out examples of cherry-picking, some of which convinced me. However, she also engages in some serious cherry-picking herself. This was noticed by several Amazon reviews, as were

151

her straw man arguments and obvious vendetta against the book. She pretty much accuses the authors of *Dawn* of advocating for gang rape. My jaw dropped at some of the absurd straw man arguments and accusations.

For example, she claimed that the authors of *Dawn* said our ancestors lived in bands of 150 people, didn't mate outside of that, and mated with everyone inside, finding everyone equally attractive. Nope. They never said that.

She is savagely determined to prove that humans have always been male-dominated and either monogamous or polygynous. And also that all women are whores, not sluts, with no real sex drive outside of procreation or some sort of exchange. I will refrain from speculating about her potential psychological motivation for this, as she does with the authors of *Dawn*. I know for a fact she is wrong about this last point. Because I'm female with no desire to procreate, and have had at some points of my life an overwhelming sex drive. Many female friends say the same.

Saxon, the author of *Sex at Dusk,* confidently declares so many things to be true that the evidence has proven false. "That the Mosuo stand so alone in their replacement of husbands by brothers".[300] I guess she avoids the abundant evidence we've seen for the "avunculate," the uncle system in matrilineal groups that is so common it was given a name by anthropologists.

"It is clear that hunter-gatherers, like all other human societies, all have marriage."[301] Not really, no. Of course there's the Mosuo, who she claims "must have lost it." Talk about circular reasoning. You can call what Trobriand islanders do marriage, but it's basically just moving your stuff into someone's hut for a while. Same for Native Americans. It wasn't formalized or seen as permanent. In pre-contact Hawaii, only chiefs had a marriage that was different from co-habitation, and as we've seen, elites often have separate patriarchal customs, relics of a colonization.

One article cited by Saxon surveyed the wide variety of courtship among modern cultures. It concludes, "The ancestral state of early human marriage is not well known given the lack of conclusive archaeological evidence."[302] I guess Saxon didn't read that part. Talk about cherry-picking.

This was an article she cited as evidence that cross-cousin marriage "arises naturally."[303] But what the article says is that it arises naturally under certain conditions. Which I would describe as extreme patrism. It's seen among extreme patrist groups in Papua New Guinea and the Amazon (there is some evidence to suggest a cross-Pacific journey sometime in antiquity that may have brought these traits to the Amazon.) It's seen among extreme patrist groups in the Middle East, even still today. And there is evidence to suggest it existed among early Indo-Europeans.

She seems to think that hunter-gatherers who had some form of co-habitation despite their remote locations are proof of the universality of marriage. However, hunter-gatherers got around a lot more than we imagine. Over 5000 years of patriarchy, they would have all had contact with patriarchal groups. As we've seen, it spreads very easily to a new group. Saxon mentions that one Mosuo woman said she was embarrassed to not know who her child's father was, as a way of arguing for the universality of paternity insistance. I can only imagine this woman was from very recent times and perhaps went to university, like the Naxi student who became ashamed of her ancestral customs. The Naxi too are male dominated now, though the oldest speak of female leaders in their lifetimes.

She claims all hunter-gatherers were all about paternity and the sexual fidelity of women.[304] Nope. The accounts of Lewis and Clarke's expedition include sex with married women in the area now known as Washington. And others have experienced that with the Inuit. These accounts seem mostly to have been from male-dominated societies where the sex was a form of exchange with the husbands, not examples of empowered women. However, it's still proof that not all husbands are jealous and obsessed with paternity.

153

However, I personally lean toward the belief that jealousy goes deep in us, based on how it feels and how my cat behaves. But in cultures that don't prioritize it, it doesn't predominate.

Saxon says it's "is near-impossible to believe that ancestral males would not use food in exchange for sex."[305] I guess that's a failure of imagination and ignorance of the way women control food in matrilineal cultures.

Saxon herself points out that the Mosuo have fewer children, due to women having full control over their fertility.[306] Hmm. In a world with plenty of people, shouldn't this be an argument *for* a return to matrilineal kinship? And she herself points out that human females' continual sexual receptivity would reduce sperm competition, since mating is spread out. [307] This would help explain why we see less sperm competition than in the bonobo. And, on this note, she quotes anthropologist and primatologist Sarah Hrdy as saying sperm competition is "an unfortunate consequence of polyandrous matings."[308] Doesn't that prove that polyandry was a significant force in our ancestral environment? And finally, she does admit that "no one is arguing that humans had an exclusively sexually monogamous past."[309]

She loves to cherry pick data about the worst aspects of humans, like how the Siriono abandon those too old or sick to travel with the group. This is true of many (patriarchal) cultures, but one archaeologist documented at least thirty cases where severely ill or disabled people only could have survived with help, all in the pre-patriarchal past.[310]

I hope this chapter has convinced you that monogamy and sex-shaming are related to patriarchy. In the final chapter I will offer my suggestions on how we can heal from this and create a better world.

CHAPTER EIGHT

LINGUISTICS

Linguistics is the comparative study of human languages. Some of the basic concepts were covered in Chapter 4, so please read that if you haven't. The core concept is that by examining the evolution of words across time and different cultures, we can learn about ancient cultures before they had written language.

Linguistics is fascinating, but complex and headache-inducing, with complicated terms. My goal is to wrap my head around it and translate it into normal English, because this information should be accessible to everyone.

But this chapter is not for everyone. It's long and technical. There's a lot of background information before we even get to the main points of the chapter: 1. That linguistics offers clues about the location and timing of the origins of patriarchy, and 2. Indo-European languages we speak today are the result of colonization, the imposition of conqueror languages on top of majority languages that were much different. We explore how the structure and terminology of our language may affect our mentality. There seem to be distinctive features in languages spoken by patriarchies.

I have yet to hear anyone else delve into this topic in this way. If the premise interests you, please bear with me while I explain the basics of linguistics. If not, you can skip to future chapters, and they will still make sense.

THE BASICS OF LINGUISTICS

If you think about it, language is weird: we take air from outside into our mouths and use our tongue, cheeks, and teeth to make sounds with it. Vowels are open sounds that can be held or chanted. They're terminated by consonants, which are made by closing the vocal tract.

The language we speak determines not only what kind of sounds we can easily make, but it may affect how we think and perceive the world. We can barely perceive something our language doesn't have a concept for. For example, the Hopi language has no words for distinct chunks of time, such as minutes or seconds. It doesn't make distinctions between past and future the way our language does.[311]

Some linguists will object to this, because the idea that your language affects your thinking (known as "linguistic relativity") was out of favor for a while. I'm not a linguist, so I don't have to conform to that dogma; it seems like common sense. There is evidence for it, and it seems to be coming back into vogue.[312]

HOW LANGUAGES CHANGE AND DIVERGE

Recall from Chapter 4 that all languages change over time, but at different rates. The more unstable the conditions — invasions, famines, changes in leadership — the faster the change.[313]

All languages have their most core, basic terms that change very little over time. Some examples are pronouns, like "he" and "I", and kinship terms, like "sister" and "brother". Other core terms that are conserved over time are body parts, needs (eat and sleep), basic natural features (sun, moon, rain, river), lower numerals, (one, two, and three), and conjunctions (and, or, if).[314]

Languages change at their own pace, naturally by diffusion. Researchers have found that the biggest transmitters of new language usages are teenage girls.[315] (Teenage females are also major agents of change among primates; their innovations spread to their peer group, and eventually to the whole group after one generation.) My theory is that the speed at which you adopt a new meme depends on how social you are and how in-the-loop, or trendy, you are.

Like teenage girls, some groups are more clever innovators than others. African Americans tend to be creative innovators of hip new terms, or "slang." Upper-crust conservatives innovate the least, having the most to gain from the status-quo; think about the stilted, clipped speech of posh British accents which accentuate every syllable so as not to lose any.

The diffusion of new terms usually happens organically, although there may have been times when an authority figure imposed or banned words. One example of deliberate language manipulation was in Italy. When Italy became a unified country, they had to choose a dialect to be their official language. They chose Tuscan because it was the most beautiful, and it was the language of the poet Dante!

As a group splits off from the main population, its language changes so much that it becomes a dialect: different, but still understood by the original population. Then it changes into a distinct language that is no longer understood by the speakers of the original parent language. Some words will be mutually intelligible, especially the basic terms like pronouns or kinship terms, but not much else.

For example, Latin was the language of the Roman Empire. The fall of the empire left groups isolated from each other without written language or trade. Without contact, their languages diverged into French, Occitan, Castilian Spanish, Catalan, Venetian Italian, Tuscan Italian, Romanian, Portuguese, and other lesser-known dialects. The Occitan-speaking people of southern France were later wiped out or forced to speak French by the northerners, so it's not well known, but some diehards still speak it.

A language's rate of change gives us an idea of how much time has elapsed since populations parted ways. For example, ancient Egyptian diverged a great deal from its parent language, proto-Afro-Asiatic. "Proto" refers to the theorized original state of a new language before daughters split off. Knowing the rate of change of these languages, linguists theorize that proto-Afro-Asiatic was likely spoken sometime around 10,000 BCE.

New words arise to explain new concepts in a population. If a daughter language lacks a concept that the mother language has, we assume that it split off before the new term was invented by the mother population. From this we can learn what concepts existed in a group, and when new concepts arose.

If two groups come into contact through trade, migration, or colonization, they learn new concepts from each other. If no word exists for a concept, a foreign word is adopted. For example, many languages borrowed the word "computer" from English and altered it to fit their languages. In Spanish they say "*computador.*" We call this "borrowing", and the words "loanwords". We can learn a lot about a people by the loanwords they received from other languages.

When people migrate to a new place and impose their language, they keep most of the local place-names from the previous occupants. That's why we see so many Native American place-names in North America, such as "Mississippi" and "Massachusetts". The newcomers also borrow the names for flora and fauna that they didn't have in their previous homeland. We can learn a lot about cultures from these clues as well.

THE ORIGINAL WORLD LANGUAGE

The latest research suggests that language evolved only once, and that all of the 6000 or so languages now on earth evolved from that mother tongue.[316] Some believe this mother tongue was associated with the Khoisan people, the San 'Bushmen' of southern Africa who famously speak with clicks. They have more "phonemes" — distinct sounds that can't be broken down further, like "ba" or "cho" — than all other languages. Usually, the older the language, the more phonemes it has; phonemes get lost as small groups drift away from founding populations. The Taa language of Namibia has about 200. English has about 45. Lithuanian has 59. Spanish has 25.

Some linguists believe in the Nostratic superfamily, which includes these groups: Dravidian (south Indian), Semitic-Hamitic (Arabic,

158

Hebrew, Egyptian), Uralic (Finnish, Hungarian), Kartvelian (from the Caucasus Mountains), and Indo-European.

The homeland of a language group is usually at the center of the group's territory, and the place where we see the greatest density of daughter languages. Linguists assume the mother language split from the homeland and spread in all directions from the center. For other clues to the homeland of a language group, we can look at the native words for animals and plants to get an idea of the bioregion where it was spoken.[317]

NOSTRATIC CULTURE RECONSTRUCTED BY COMMON WORDS

Mother languages are reconstructed by linguists based on the words and concepts that are shared in their daughter languages. Nostratic daughter languages have similar words for such terms as "to beat", "to split", "to cut", and "to chop." And "cave", "dark", and "scrape" (they must have scraped a lot of hides). "Lowland", "settlement", and "hoarfroast" (it was the Ice Age).

There were a lot of shared words related to hunting, and none related to economy or construction. From this we gather that Nostratic speakers had no form of money and did not build houses (i.e., were nomadic or lived in caves).[318] One of the oldest Nostratic words is "mother," often a form of *"amma"*, which makes sense, as that's easy for a baby to say while nursing!

INDO-EUROPEAN LANGUAGE FAMILY

You may recall that the Nostratic language family Indo-European (I-E for short) colonized the world, such that more than half of people today speak I-E languages. We refer to the original Indo-European language as Proto-Indo-European, or PIE for short. It's hypothesized that their homeland became a harsh environment around 4000 BCE, turning them towards patrism.

PIE speakers domesticated the horse, which enabled them to spread their culture far and wide. This culture involved male storm and sky

159

gods, the glorification of violence, and feasts hosted by important men. From the words they had, we know they were semi-nomadic, lived in primitive dwellings, wore only wool and leather, and did not have metal work or complex ceramics.

Some linguists have proposed that Pre-Indo-European, the earliest form of the language, began around 7000 BCE in Central Asia, and that these speakers migrated from there to the homeland by about 5000 BCE. It seems likely that the Russian steppes between the Black and Caspian seas was the homeland of the last unified Indo-European language.[319] By 3500 BCE, the languages had begun to split into different dialects as their speakers entered Central Europe, starting with the Danube valley.

KINSHIP TERMS

It's notable that the Nostratic root word "an" for "ancestor", which can mean "mother" or "father" in Proto-Indo-European, only means "mother" in Turkic. Perhaps the concept of "father" didn't exist in Nostratic, but was invented later, before PIE split off from Nostratic? Similarly, the root word "atta" means "father" in PIE, but can mean "mother" in other Nostratic languages. Perhaps the original term meant "mother" and changed to "father" when their culture changed from matrilineal to patrilineal.

There has been much speculation over the word for "grandfather". Many variations have the precise meaning not of "father's father" as we would expect, but "mother's brother." Recall that before fatherhood and paternity, the maternal uncle was the main male figure for children.

To explain this, linguists came up with a desperate long-shot of a theory involving cross-cousin marriages: some Indo-Europeans have a custom of marrying a boy to his father's sister's daughter, thereby making grandfather and uncle the same person. (I might guess they do this to make new wives more obedient to their in-laws. A willful woman would be more likely to obey when her in-laws are her blood kin, and she has no one to escape to. It's still really common in the Middle East). However, this theory does not account for the meaning of "grandfather".[320] The source I'm citing on this point is still not ready to concede the obvious matrilineal roots of Indo-Europeans, even though they point out that the maternal uncle has a strong presence in Indo-European myth and tradition (such as the Irish hero Cu Chulain receiving weapons from his maternal uncle Conchobar).[321] They also point out that there is no common word for "father's brother;"[322] you would expect a patrilineal kinship system to have one.

It's interesting that all I-E languages use a feminine word for the name of the earth, which might be a holdover from the days when they still revered the earth and the feminine.[323]

INDO-EUROPEAN FEATURES

Many I-E languages share features not often seen in other language families. One is the all-important word "to be". When you learn an I-E language, the first thing you learn is how to conjugate the verb "to be": I am, you are, he/she is, we are, y'all are, they are.[324]

First of all, this pattern of "conjugation" — using different verb forms depending on who is the subject of the verb — only exists in I-E. Secondly, the word "to be" doesn't really exist in many other families. You don't say "you are beautiful" or "they are American". You just say "you beautiful". You don't say "how are you?". Actually, even most I-E languages say "how are you *going*", which we can also do in English with "how's it going".

English is also one of the few to say "I *am* hungry" or "I *am* twenty-five"; in most I-E languages you say "I *have* hunger" or "I *have* twenty-five years". Could it make a difference in how you think about it? The verb "to be" leads you to identify strongly with something. And when we say "It is raining", what is this "it"? Other languages just say "raining".

Some non-IE languages don't even have the verb "to have". Welsh is one of those. It's I-E but was on the fringe of I-E territory, so it wasn't fully Indo-Europeanized by the invaders. They retained a large pre-I-E "substrate", meaning a body of words from their original language. In

Welsh, to say "I have a cat", you say "there is a small cat at me." Welsh doesn't allow you to "own" things!

Another unique feature in I-E is called "suppletion": words become irregular and don't match, like "go" and its past tense, "went". Since most I-E languages were imposed by conquerors, they've become irregular with so much mixing: English most of all, since it's a melting pot of Latin, French, Germanic, Old Norse, and Celtic. Only 26% of our words are actually English! Many came from French when William the Conqueror overtook England in 1066. More French words came from a period a few hundred years ago when France was the dominant cultural center of Europe. At that time, England was a backwater, so cultural innovations from France became loanwords and got anglicized. One example is "restaurant"; restaurants must not have existed in England before that.

Besides the verb "to be", there's another major feature that many I-E languages share: "nominative-accusative", as contrasted with "ergative". Bear with me while I explain.

A noun takes its "case" depending on whether it's a subject or an object of a transitive verb. A transitive verb is the kind of verb that involves a subject and object, so somebody is doing something TO someone or something. So, in "I take her", "I" is the subject and "her" is the object. "Her" takes a different form as the object, than "she" as subject. An intransitive verb such as "to go" can't have an object (you can't *go* someone).

In English, "he-him" and "she-her" are the only words that change form between subject and object, but in many I-E languages, all nouns change. This is called "case". In most I-E languages (less so with Indian ones), the subject of a transitive verb takes the same form as the subject of an intransitive verb. So "she takes him" is the same as "she goes"; both use "she" instead of "her".

On the other hand, in ergative languages, the subject of a transitive verb takes the same form as the *object* of an intransitive verb. In other words, the object form is the default. For example, in an ergative language you say "I taken by you" instead of "you take me". If you're just sitting there, or having something done to you, you're the subject. But if you *do* something to someone, you're not the subject!

Nowadays, pure ergative languages are rare. (Though, interestingly, they are widely spread around the world, in isolated regions of the Americas, the Caucasus, Tibet, and Australia, suggesting they could be remnants of a previously widespread pattern. The only one in Europe is Basque). Many today are "split-ergative" where they have features from both types. But at least one researcher believes that back in the time period and region we are talking about, Neolithic Western Eurasia, pure ergative ones were the norm: Hurrian, Urartian, Elamite, and Mesopotamian ones such as Sumerian. He suspects that some Berber (North African) languages have an ergative substrate, as did Harappan (Indus Valley of Pakistan) languages. Finally, he believes that Minoan and another substrate language of Greek were also ergative. In other words, our Anatolian farmer goddess people and their neighbors spoke ergative languages, likely remnants of an ancient, widespread, and now diminished language family.[325]

Some people believe I-E was originally ergative as well, but either way, it seems that western I-E as well as Semitic languages developed in a different direction. Isn't it interesting that these were the patriarchal groups? Could there be a connection? It seems likely that in ancient times languages were more strongly either nominative-accusative or ergative. Perhaps modern languages that show features of both are a result of hybridization of the two types due to colonization?

Could the ancient ergative way of speech, thinking of yourself more as object than subject, be connected with a different mindset than the nominative-accusative? Maybe speakers of these languages conceive of themselves as being acted upon by external forces or gods beyond their control, rather than as actors in control of their fates. Just speculating here.

Some speakers of ergative languages refer to themselves as "me" rather than "I" when they speak English, as in "me Tarzan" or "me good man". Non-native speakers make errors that correspond to the way

163

things are said in their languages, the way a Spanish speaker might say "You no want this?" because in Spanish they use the word "no" before a verb to negate it.

Another related feature that almost all I-E languages have is that the subject of the sentence comes first, like "I'll drive you." In many other languages, the *object* is more prominent than the subject; a word-for-word translation is something like: "people, dogs bite them." Again, I-E seems to center the person doing the action, rather than the receiver of the action.

Then there's the dreaded gender. About one-fourth of the world's languages have gender built into their grammar. Most of these are I-E, Semitic (and its family, Afro-Asiatic) and northern Caucasian, another group from the same area that was affected by the rise of patriarchy. Other than that, there are a smattering of others in Africa and a few South Indian (could these have been influenced by Indo-Aryan conquerors?). Then there are some Australian and Papua New Guinean ones, which lend credence to my hypothesis that these groups are very ancient and descended from a much earlier cycle of patriarchy. Perhaps patriarchy does go in cycles, as does everything else we know of.

But given that I-E and Semitic have the highest number of gendered languages, and are the language families most affected by patriarchy, it's worth asking whether there's a connection. Research suggests that groups with gendered languages have higher than average gender disparity.[326]

In the Semitic language Arabic, all nouns are either masculine or feminine. In Indo-European German, nouns can be feminine, masculine, or neuter. English has lost gendered nouns and only retains gender for pronouns, which is currently wreaking havoc. Gendered nouns and pronouns are more deeply embedded than in some other languages that are considered gendered like Thai, where men and women add a different word to the end of sentences.

It's interesting that the same word can have a different gender even in closely related languages like French or Spanish. For example, milk is masculine in French, "*le lait*", while feminine in Spanish, "*la leche*". For an English speaker learning a gendered language, as most I-E languages are, it's strange that an inanimate object has gender. Some research suggests this affects a native speaker's perception of the thing.[327] Do the French perceive milk as more masculine than the Spanish do? I find it interesting that in both French and Spanish, animals are male by default unless a particular animal is known to be a female. In Hebrew, on the other hand, all animals are female.

All current I-E languages have gender except one, Armenian, which is a very antique language and is an "isolate", meaning that no known languages are related to it. So, language gender must have been invented after Armenian split off from the I-E language family.

The very first daughter language to split off from PIE was the Anatolian branch. Anatolia (Turkey) was a major center of civilization back in the Neolithic and Bronze Ages. Anatolian languages are all extinct and only known from Bronze Age inscriptions. The best known one is Hittite, as the Hittites had a major Bronze Age empire.

The now-extinct Anatolian languages are the only other genderless I-E languages aside from Armenian. This implies that PIE didn't have it either; it must have been a later innovation after Anatolian and Armenian speakers split off. Once patriarchy became entrenched, it was suddenly very important to separate people by sex, and for the listener to know what sex the speaker was talking about.[328] It seems likely that it was unimportant before.

Anatolian verbs have only two tenses: present-future, and past (preterit); they didn't distinguish between present and future. In a way, English doesn't have a real future tense either. We don't conjugate the verb differently, but just put "will" before it: "I will go".

All other I-E languages have past, present and future tense. In contrast, some non-IE languages have no tenses at all. How would that affect your psyche? How would you know if it's *already* happened or if it *will* happen? Usually, it's clear from the context, with words like "yesterday" or "already" or "still". I know this well since I forget my past

and future conjugations in Spanish and say things like, "I go yesterday".
I get my point across, but I sound like a moron.

In summary, we've talked about several features of I-E languages:
gender, a system of verb conjugation, the verb "to be", and irregular
forms. Another unique feature is status syntax: a formal and informal
way to address someone. Other languages have *terms* of respect, but in I-
E languages, there's a whole verb conjugation for this. So,,in French you
say "*tu vas*", meaning "you go", to a friend or a peer, but "*vous allez*" to an
older person or a "superior". This is getting lost in the younger
generations in Spain, and it's already been lost in most Latin American
countries. In Hindi, some wives use the formal to her husband while the
husband uses the informal to the wife!

English used to have it too, and has lost it. Our second-person
informal was similar to French and Spanish "tu": "thou" as in "thou
shalt". The object case of "thou" was "thee" as in "I give thee". All four
of these pronouns are now simplified to one "you".

In English, as in German, Castilian Spanish, and Italian, you used to
have to refer to a noble or royal person in the third person, as in "What
would his lordship like for breakfast?" It's significant that I-E languages,
as the carriers of patriarchal customs of elitism, superiority, and
colonialism, are the only ones to have respect for superiors built into
their core grammar.

Basque, an ancient non-IE European language that is still alive today
in Spain, has a formal pronoun "zu", which is falling out of use. It's the
only verb form in the whole language that makes a gender distinction, so
most likely it came from Arabic (during the 800-year Arab occupation of
Spain). Something similar happened in some Philippine languages which
adopted formal grammar in places that were heavily colonized by the
Spanish.

Another rare feature in I-E languages is their inflected typology.
"Typology" is a core feature of a language by which it's classified. One
typology is "inflected" vs. "agglutinative" (there are some other
possibilities not relevant here).

Most I-E languages are inflected, which means you use a little "morpheme", a chunk of a word, to indicate multiple meanings such as number (singular or plural), actor, and tense. For example, in Spanish, you say "*comí*" ("I ate"); the single suffix (a morpheme you add to the end of a word) "-í" tells you that "I" am the only one who is doing the action, and that the action was done in the past and is now finished. There's a different form of the verb for each tense, to indicate whether the actor is first, second or third person, and to indicate singular or plural; that is, conjugation.

Semitic is also inflected; once again, the other language group of patriarchal customs. In contrast, agglutinative languages convey meanings by stringing together morphemes. The morphemes never change. For example, in Turkish, the word "*evlerinizden*", or "from your houses", consists of the morphemes ev-ler-iniz-den, literally translated morpheme-by-morpheme as "house-plural-your-from".

This results in some very long words, like in Finnish, a non-I-E European language whose longest word is "*lento-kone-suihku-turbiini-moottori-apu-mekaanikko-ali-upseeri-oppilas*", meaning "airplane jet turbine motor assistant mechanic, non-commissioned officer, in training"!

English can do agglutination a little bit, like the word "hope-less-ness". The "less" morpheme indicates "not", and "ness" indicates "the state of", the noun form. We don't know if this is a remnant from older agglutinative languages, or if it got "agglutinized" by a conquered language.

Agglutinative language speakers can sound like they're talking fast or chanting, with a lot of repetition, like the Indonesian food *gado gado*". They often show "vowel harmony", meaning that within a word, the vowels change to be similar to each other. Most of their words have either the kind you make in the front of your mouth — such as "o" or "u" — or, the kind you make in the back of the mouth, like "a" or "ah". For example, "Mississippi": the vowels match. It would be a workout for the mouth to say 'Missossappo" — try saying that 5 times fast.

There *was* one agglutinative I-E language, however: Tocharian, another extinct language whose speakers split off very early on from PIE. If such an early daughter language was agglutinative, PIE itself must have been as well. Perhaps all languages were once agglutinative, and inflection was invented just once in the world: in PIE speakers after the Tocharians left. The Tocharians were six-foot-tall, fabulously dressed people with conical hats and colorful robes. Grave goods indicate little violence or social stratification, so I speculate they branched off before patriarchy. Perhaps the PIE speakers passed inflection to the Semitic speakers along with patriarchal customs?

So, these newer languages are inflected, nominative-accusative, and have the active subject form coming first: "I will give him the book". By contrast, most older languages are agglutinative and ergative, with the *object* coming first: "Him, the book, giving, me". The other language family that shares a lot of these features with I-E is Semitic. I haven't seen anyone else point out the connection between the two patriarchal language families and this set of features that they share, but it seems significant.

Here is a small list of agglutinative languages: Vietnamese, Finnish, Hungarian, Mongolian, Eskimo, Basque, Sumerian, Tibetan, Egyptian, Tamil, Berber, Turkish, Turkic, Kyrgyz, Saami, Tahitian, Samoan; and most south Indian, American, and African languages.[329]

ANATOLIA

It seems likely that the pre-Indo-European languages of Old Europe, including Anatolia, were agglutinative. Anatolia was a hilly region that was home to many diverse groups, including the Hatti. Few people know of them now, but they were a major player in the rise of civilization.

The Hatti were neighbors of the Maikop culture where patriarchy arose. Maybe the Hatti got the concept of a divine ruler from the Maikop. Perhaps because their Maikop neighbors were a good distance away, or because the Hatti were such staunch goddess people, they

168

didn't adopt war or elite burials. They formed peaceful cities with literate bureaucracies led by divine queens.[330]

When the speakers of Indo-European Anatolian languages arrived in Anatolia around 3900 BCE, they co-existed and traded peacefully with the Hatti. Recall that the Anatolians had split off from the PIE group before patriarchy arose, so they were likely peaceful. Later, the Hittites, another group that spoke an I-E Anatolian language, invaded. The Hittites must have left the ancestral group *after* patriarchy arrived, because they were warlike. So perhaps the patriarchy package arrived after some Anatolian speakers had split off, but not others?

The Hittite-speakers were few, so they were more influenced by the Hatti they conquered than vice-versa; the Hatti never got fully Indo-Europeanized.[331] The main goddesses and gods remained Hattic, and Hittite rulers had Hattic names. The Hittites created an empire around 1650 BCE.[332] After that it was warlike and hierarchical.

APPROXIMATING THE LANGUAGE OF THE CONQUERORS

This Hattic majority had what's known as a "substrate effect": the influence the majority language has on that of its conquering minority. The Hattic substrate effect on Anatolian I-E languages was described by Jaan Puhvel as "agglutinative creolization ... What has happened to Anatolian here is reminiscent of what became of French in places like Haiti."[333] Haitian and other Caribbean dialects are more rhythmic and groovy than the original French. That's the substrate effect of Africans making it their own.

A "creole" is a combination of languages, like in Haiti and in Louisiana. Sometimes it's used as a common language for cultures who retain their native ones as well. One example of that is Bahasa Indonesian, a simplified form of Malay that's used as the official language of Indonesia. Most Indonesians speak their own native tongues with their own people and only use the creole to communicate with other language groups.

In other cases, a creole becomes the *only* language. For example, when colonizers brought various African peoples as enslaved people to Jamaica, the Africans formed a language that combined English with their own tongues. The first stage is known as a "pidgin": a crude, bare-bones, makeshift communication bridge with no grammar. Then, the next generation of children creates the creole, a real language, by adding grammar and syntax to the pool of words in the pidgin.

It's truly amazing how this happens. Kids magically formalize the pidgin with grammar, making it into a real living language! They take a random selection of words, add grammar, and poof! A new language is born. They don't talk about it, it just happens. It's as if they're telepathically connected with each other. Human beings are wired for rule creation, especially children with more brain plasticity.

A language usually gets simplified when it's made into a creole, to make it easier to learn. For example, Afrikaans is a South African creole combining Dutch with the native Zulu. Dutch lost its verb tenses when it came to Africa and simplified into Afrikaans.

One of the most difficult things about learning a new language is pronouncing the phonemes that don't exist in your native language. You probably won't ever be able to say them perfectly if you learn as an adult; children's brains are wired to learn phonemes. That's what babies are doing when they babble: they're practicing how to make all the phonemes they hear. The next step is to sort the phonemes into words.

It's hard to imagine how children figure out what abstract words mean; it's kind of a miracle! They pick up languages by osmosis, not needing to memorize words or learn grammar like adults. If you learn a new language after the age of 13 or so, you're too old to acquire new phonemes, and you'll always have a foreign accent unless you have a rare gift for languages. There are some phonemes that are so hard and so foreign that you might not be capable of making them at all. For example, we would sound ridiculous to a Khoisan if we tried to make the clicks they do. (I wonder if Khoisan children are bummed that it's impossible to whisper in that language — you can't whisper a click!)

One phoneme that is difficult to acquire as an adult is "th", a pretty rare sound found in only 7% of languages. French and German speakers can't make it, so they approximate it with a "z": "ze chicken cross ze road". Swedes say "fw" as in "frew" for "through". Irish say "t'ing" for "thing". Spanish speakers tend to use a "d" sound instead: "dee chicken cross dee road"; they don't have a "z" sound really. (Although they *write* the letter "z", it sounds more like "-ss" as in "cerveza"). Spanish has fewer phonemes than almost any language, only 24: 5 vowels and 19 consonants. They don't have an "h", so they just leave it off of English words like "he" and "hands".

Indo-European and Semitic languages have a lot of guttural phonemes. Modern Semitic languages are known for their laryngeal sounds, made in the back of the throat. The Anatolian daughter languages had 3 of those. We don't know how they sounded. Sometime before the next daughters split off from the I-E mother population, those sounds disappeared, because they don't exist in the newer daughters.

This loss of phonemes likely resulted from small bands of colonizers imposing themselves on large populations. The indigenous populations couldn't make those sounds, so the phonemes got dropped. These invaders didn't bring women with them: they mated with the local women. Maybe the children of the foreign conquerors learned those sounds from their fathers, but it's unlikely, given that these warriors probably had little to do with infants. Thus, the sounds got lost.

An example of this from more recent times was the Spanish colonization of Chile. The native people couldn't make that lisping "s" sound as in "Español", which sounds like "eth". Though the Spanish whipped them for it, the Chileans flatly refused to try. Over time the Spanish gave up; no Latin Americans have this lisping "s". It was replaced by the straight "s".

One phoneme that was common in the old I-E languages was the "kW" sound, like English "qu" in "question". It was used in question words such as "who" and "what". The conquered population must not have been able to make this sound, so they approximated it, the way French say "ze" instead of "the".

Just as the French say "ze" and the Spanish say "de", the Indo-European "kW" was approximated differently by different conquered language groups. The ancestors of the Italians must have had a similar phoneme, or they worked hard at it, because Italian has it: "*qui* " (who), pronounced "kwee". Most Latin languages, like French and Spanish, made it into a "k" sound: as in French *qui,,* pronounced "kee", and Spanish *quien,* pronounced "kee-en". Russians use a "k" as well, as in "kavo", but in other places use a "sh" as in "shto", meaning "what". Hindi also uses a "k": "kaun". Germanic languages took a much different route, a fricative (breathy consonant) rather than a hard stop: "w" in Dutch, "v" in German, and "wh" in English as in "who" and "what".

The biggest split that happened in I-E was between the western daughters and the eastern ones. The PIE word for "hundred" had a phoneme other people couldn't pronounce. We don't know how it sounded, something like "dk̂m̥tóm". I-E had way too many consonants and not enough vowels! So, Eastern languages like Slavic (Russian), Baltic (Lithuanian), Iranian, and Indo-Aryan (Indian) made it into an "s" sound. In those languages, "hundred" sounds something like "satem", which was the Sanskrit word, so these are known as the "satem" languages.

In Western languages, like Celtic, Italic (the mother of Latin and the Romance languages), Germanic, Greek, and Anatolian, they used a hard "c" like "k" to approximate the unpronounceable word for "hundred", so these are called the "centum" languages. "Centum" is the Latin word for "hundred", like our word "cent". Oddly, English turned this "k" sound into an "s" like the satem languages! Somehow English and the other Germanic languages got the word "hundred", which goes back to proto-Germanic, and perhaps was not an Indo-European cognate at all. Maybe it came from an indigenous language substrate of the proto-Germanic lands.

Figure 8-1: Centum vs satem languages.[334]

David Anthony says, "Sound changes are rule-governed probably because all humans instinctively search for order in language. This must be a hard-wired part of all human brains."[335] The whole population somehow shifts to a new sound. An example of this is how Chileans swallow the last syllable of words as if they're too lazy to say them. "*Los gatos*" becomes "*lo gato*". "Pesado" becomes "pesa'o". They barely touch that final letter, if at all.

Over time, these final sounds may be forgotten, and the word will start getting spelled without them. This must be what happened when Portuguese and Spanish diverged from their parent language. Portuguese words sound like a Chilean's lazy pronunciation: Spanish "corazón" is "*coração*", pronounced "cor-a-*ssow*". Barely-pronounced syllables or letters, and contractions like "they're", eventually become permanent until the syllable is forgotten.

Losing final or unaccented syllables is a very common "lazy" change. Laziness is a common reason for language drift; we shift to words that are easier and more efficient to pronounce. Another common change is losing consonants between vowels, like saying "a-ite!" (usually spelled aight) instead of "allright". Or dropping vowels between consonants, like "g'nite" instead of "good night". Maybe in 100 years, "g'nite" won't be a contraction anymore; it will just be one word. Old English speakers

173

used to say "May god be with ye" and now it's just "goodbye". Few know where it came from.

There are certain rules that govern these phoneme shifts across all languages, having to do with our mouths. Initial hard consonants like -k and hard -g tend to change toward soft sounds like -s and -sh. A change from -s to -k is unlikely. A consonant pronounced as a stop in the back of the mouth, like –k, is particularly likely to shift when it's followed by a vowel pronounced in the front of the mouth, like -e.[336] That's because these words are hard to wrap your mouth around, so they change to easier sounds.

The way languages become simplified over time is a good example of how we devolve over time. We're taught that evolution always moves forward, but this is untrue: languages have gotten cruder and simpler over time. Three verb tenses simplified to two; three noun genders reduced to two or got lost entirely. Originally, I-E languages had *eight* noun cases! They've been reduced or eliminated in all but the oldest Indo-Iranian languages.

Besides laziness, influences from colonized substrate languages are another huge reason why languages simplify, especially when the substrate was non-I-E. A small group invades a population and forces them to speak their language. The conquered people become the substrate, a permanent underclass. The first generation of children creates a creole language spontaneously out of the two languages. If both languages have a word for a certain concept, the children choose one. The new hybrid culture also drops or transforms the phonemes they can't pronounce.

Let's not forget, when using academic terms like "substrate", that these are real human beings — real women — forced into a life of servitude.

For this reason, the languages of colonizers change and simplify faster than other languages. Change also happens due to cultural influences from another language group. Religious languages are a great example. We got a lot of words from Latin, the religious language of

Europe. Farsi got a lot of words from Arabic, the language of Islam. Educated Muslims learn Arabic everywhere, even in Indonesia, just as educated Christians learned Latin until very recently.

Hence, every language resulting from colonization is a unique blend of the two. If the colonizing population is much smaller than the conquered one, the substrate effect on the colonizer's language will be great. For example, Ossetic, an Iranian language, changed a lot when it was imposed on a Kartvelian language.

Another example is Greek, which is Indo-European but just barely: three-quarters of Greek words don't have Indo-European roots, but belong to a non-I-E substrate. This substrate was most likely the native language of one of the Old European goddess peoples of the Mediterranean or Anatolia. It was possibly the language of the place-names in the Mediterranean, such as Orgyssos, Arabissos, and Mykonos. You'll recall that when new people migrate, they keep the old place-names from the indigenous language. Names ending in -ssos, ssa,or -sa are the most common by far in the Mediterranean. If this ancient language sounded like these place-names, it must have been beautiful. Perhaps it was a very early I-E language, one of the early Anatolian languages with a large indigenous substrate that formed before patriarchy, during the peaceful migration of early Indo-Europeans into Anatolia.

Some of the Old European languages that survived the Indo-European invasions were Ligurian, Pictish, Aquitani, Etruscan, Iberian, Tartessian, Rhaetic, East Italic, Messapic and Sicel.[337] Some of these non-Indo-European languages were recorded in inscriptions in the Mediterranean.[338] All of these were still spoken in Roman times but are now lost to us, with one exception: Etruscan. The Etruscans, mentioned in Chapter 2, taught the ancient Romans everything they knew. The Romans were scandalized that the Etruscans didn't know who their fathers were, were sexually promiscuous, and enjoyed equality between the sexes.

The Etruscan language was re-discovered in the 18th century when a European traveler in Egypt found a mummy and brought it back to

175

Europe to impress his friends. In the accompanying sarcophagus, writings were found in a script that looked similar to the Phoenician alphabet (the predecessor of ours), except it was read right to left, like Hebrew and Arabic. When they flipped it and found a Rosetta stone that combined it with Greek, they were able to read it.

This alphabet had more phonemes than the Etruscans needed for their language. There were letters that didn't match any of their phonemes, because the Phoenicians, who created the alphabet, had more sounds than they did. This is often the case when a language adopts an alphabet that was developed for a much different language. For example, the Vietnamese started using our alphabet, which is a version of the Phoenician one that was adopted for English. Vietnamese had more sounds than there were letters, so they had to add a bunch of accents to make it work.

So aside from Etruscan, all the other indigenous European languages are lost to us. We have many inscriptions from the Minoan language of Crete, but we can't read them because we've never found a Rosetta stone with Minoan next to a language we *can* read. This undeciphered alphabet is called Linear A. It's dated to about 2500 BCE, and many scholars accept Gimbutas' view that it derives from the Old European script of the Danube valley of the Neolithic.[339] It was a written form of the 3rd millennium Cretan language at the time of Troy.[340]

The Greeks regarded these native languages of the eastern Mediterranean as "barbarian", associated with people who knew their mothers instead of their fathers. The oracles who advised Greek leaders, such as the famous oracle at Delphi, spoke these ancient tongues.

Oracles were barefoot women who went into trance by getting high off volcanic vapors. They spoke prophecies in their native tongue, then a translator would translate it to Greek. It was used to decide major questions, like whether to go to war. The Greeks who heard the oracles said their barbarian tongue sounded like the chirping of birds. This bird language was probably the substrate language of Greek, the source of those Greek words that aren't of Indo-European origin. Maybe if we could figure out what language family it came from, we could decipher Linear A.

These ancient bird-like languages were certainly agglutinative, based on the large amount of repetition of short syllables we see in Linear A. They had a lot of vowels. Vowels were considered sacred by the ancient Egyptians, because only vowels can be chanted, and through chanting you can reach an altered state of consciousness. The Hebrews, too, considered them sacred, which is why they don't write them down. Writing was considered profane.

When the Old Europeans got invaded by the Indo-Europeans it must have felt like an invasion of the consonants. Patriarchal languages, whether I-E or Semitic, had a lot of consonants, few vowels, and a lot of guttural sounds. To the Indo-Europeans, the Old Europeans sounded like chattering birds. To the Old Europeans, the Indo-Europeans must have sounded husky and harsh like the Klingons on Star Trek. When forced to speak the language of the conquerors, they simplified the complex consonants, like turning "kW" sounds into "k" and "h".

So Greek was a hybrid language between the indigenous Mediterranean Old Europeans and the invading Indo-Europeans. Greek split off from Proto-Indo-European quite early: after Anatolian, and just before Pre-Indo-Iranian. It shares a lot of traits with the latter. This suggests it was spoken on the eastern border of southeastern Europe, possibly the Catacomb culture.[341] In other words, Greek was the eastern-most branch of the western branches of I-E; right on the border of the western "centum" languages and the eastern "satem" languages. (See Figure 8-1).

The eastern satem groups were more patrist than the western centum ones, since patriarchy arose among the eastern Indo-Iranian branch. The western ones bordered on and absorbed the Old Europeans who made female figurines. The eastern ones, on the other hand, bordered hunter-gatherers who probably honored mother earth, but weren't as staunch goddess worshipers as the Old Europeans. So, it makes sense that the western Indo-Europeans retained stronger feminine influences.

177

In western branches, the spirit of the hearth was female, Hestia, while in the eastern Indo-Iranian it was male, Agni. Western Indo-European mythologies had more strong female deities, such as Queen Magb, while eastern graves contained far more males, up to 80%.[342] To this day, eastern Indo-Europeans such as Russians and Iranians show more patrist traits than the Greeks, Celts, and Italic people who split off to head west.

As the Indo-European warriors went west, leaving a trail of terror in their wake, they picked up more agricultural words. Millet is the only grain word known to Proto-Indo-Europeans, so they must have cultivated wild grass but not done any farming. Common names for rye, barley, and oats are only found in the Western branches. Common names for flax are shared by Latin, Greek, Slavic, Baltic and Germanic, but not in earlier branches, so flax was unknown to the more archaic Indo-Europeans; they would have only worn wool and leather.

The word for hemp, "*kannabis*", is shared between Greek, Albanian, Germanic, Slavic, and Baltic, but not the Indo-Iranian languages.[343] This plant played a huge role in some of these cultures. The Scythians, "barbarians" well known to their neighbors the classical Greeks, were famous for it. The Greeks described how the Scythians threw seeds on the fire and huddled under blankets to huff the vapors, an ancient hotbox. The Scythians spoke an Iranian language, which was a non-cannabis language, but they were a hybrid between Iranian conquerors and the native Thracians, who were descended from Old Europeans from the Danube Valley. The Scythians must have gotten cannabis from their Thracian ancestors on the female side, who not only huffed it (as smoking was unknown), but used it for food and fiber.

The Scythians' ancestors on the male side, the Indo-Iranians, were probably the Sintashta culture known to archaeology. They went east and split into the Proto-Iranians and the Proto-Indo-Aryans of India. The Proto-Iranians would become the Persians: they founded the Zoroastrian religion. The Indo-Aryans would become the Vedic culture with its holy books, the Vedas. These epic texts were written in Sanskrit, an early Indo-Aryan language, still used today in Hinduism. It's considered a very beautiful and grammatically-perfect language; Hindus say it came directly from the gods.

That's the same thing that is said about Hebrew, the holy language of the Jews, and about ancient Egyptian. Ethiopians probably say the same about Ge'ez, the ancient language still used in their religious services the way that Sanskrit, Hebrew, and Latin are used for Hinduism, Judaism, and Christianity.

Sanskrit, like Greek, had a large non-I-E substrate: at least 383 words that don't come from Indo-European roots. There are at least two language families that contributed to it: Dravidian and Austroasiatic, which is an extremely ancient group outside of the Nostratic superfamily. These two groups are still spoken in India.

Some of the words that came from these substrates into Sanskrit (with their English translations) were "bread", "ploughshare", "canal", "brick", "camel", "donkey", "sacrificing priest", and "Indra" (the chief god of the Vedas). The word "*soma*", a very important ritual drink which may have been hallucinogenic, also came from a pre-Indo-European substrate language.[344]

Since the god Indra and the ritual drink Soma are the core aspects of the Vedic religion, it seems obvious that the core of this culture came from the pre-IE people. The obvious candidate is the Dravidian (Tamil) language/culture of South India. They were likely the inhabitants of the Neolithic city Mehrgahr in what is now western Pakistan.

Figure 8-2: Female figurine from Mehrgahr.[345]

Some believe Mehrgahr was the birthplace of the ancient religion of Shaktism, a sect of Tantra that includes sacred sexuality. It was likely the birthplace of dentistry as well. Mehrgahr was peaceful and egalitarian. It's not been proven that Tamil language speakers lived there, but it would make sense, as the Tamil vocabulary is suited to a complex society like at Mehrgahr, with words for upper story and beam, metallurgy, trade, and payment of dues.

The relationship between the Indo-European Aryans and the Tamil people is very controversial among Indians. Tamil languages survive in the south, while I-E languages dominate the north. In the south you find more matrilineal customs, while the north has more harsh patrist customs like female segregation and veiling.

It seems obvious to me that the more advanced and peaceful Tamil people transmitted culture to the violent herders that invaded. Some claim it was cultural diffusion without invasion, but the Vedas talk about slaughtering and enslaving the darker-skinned *dasyus,* so there's little doubt it was oppressive. It was the same story everywhere: small bands of violent nomadic herders imposed their languages on a much larger, peaceful population and assimilated their more advanced culture.

Many scholars believe that the original Tamils were of Mediterranean ethnicity, with olive skin and dark hair, related to the Old Europeans: Minoans, Italians, Greeks, Hebrews, Arabs. Their language has links with Berber, the indigenous language of North Africa. It's likely that the ones who settled in India got darker skin, broader noses, and kinkier hair after thousands of years of intermingling with the Austronesians who had been there for tens of thousands of years. By the time the Indo-Europeans colonized and appropriated their culture, they may have looked much like South Indians today. There are still some die-hard Indo-European supremacists in India who claim Indo-Europeans are native to India and not colonizers, but the genetic evidence has proved them wrong. The next chapter on genetics goes into that story in detail.

The Sanskrit language, with Indo-European grammar on top of a large Tamil substrate, resulted from this colonization. Over time

180

Sanskrit has simplified into Hindi, just as Latin and Greek simplified into *their* modern descendants. French and Spanish have fewer grammatical constructions and a smaller vocabulary than Latin, just as Hindi and Urdu are simplified forms of Sanskrit.

It was these Sanskrit-speaking Indo-Aryans who carried the patriarchy package to China after 2000 BCE. At that time new words appeared in Chinese that correspond to Indo-Aryan words such as "*baga*" (god) and "*bagadur*" (epic hero). The word "*kahn*" also appears at that time, meaning "king" or "high priest". This word also corresponds to the Semitic word "*kohen*" with the same meaning — and survives today in the common Jewish last name "Cohen", connected with the priestly class.

This suggests it was the Indo-Aryans who brought patriarchy (and inflected languages?) to the Semitic peoples of the Middle East. Jewish people may even be an offshoot of Vedic Aryans. The word "Brahmin", the elite caste of Indians, is related to "Abraham", the Hebrew prophet, and "Ibrahim", the Islamic prophet. Wow, right? "Adam" is related to Sanskrit "*Adityam*"; "Christ" to "Krishna"; Abraham's consort Sarah to Sarasvati. There are many other related words between Hebrew and Sanskrit, such as the word for heaven. The word for father "*abba*" in Hebrew came from "*appa*", an Indic word. This borrowing suggests that before contact with the Aryans, the ancient Hebrews had no word for father.

In February 2023, NPR ran a piece about Indo-European languages. It offers a useful summary of how the Indo-European language idea was used in a racist way by the Nazis and others in the past, when racism was the norm. Ironically, the story actually *disproves* the narrative of white supremacy, since the Indo-European language group includes groups such as Indians who are not usually considered white. They mention a historical episode from 1923 about how an Indian named Bhagat Singh Thind argued before the U.S. Supreme Court that, as a Brahmin from the highest caste of Indians, he should be eligible to be a U.S. citizen, since he was descended from the Aryans who invaded India and was therefore white.

The radio show interviews Jim Mallory, author of *In Search of the Indo-Europeans*, who points out that it's a mistake to attribute racial characteristics to ancient people. The modern concept of race did not exist in ancient times.[346]

I would contend that the story of the Indo-Europeans contradicts the racist narrative because it's clear that the I-E conquerors, far from being the master race, were simple barbarians that stole everything from the much more advanced people they conquered. It's time to finally put to rest the lie of whiteness that justified the horrific European conquest. Most of us have the blood of the conquerors *and* the conquered running through our veins. There is only one human race, and thousands of ethnicities, many of which can't be categorized as white or non-white.[347]

INDO-EUROPEAN LOANWORDS AND NEIGHBORING LANGUAGE FAMILIES

In summary, the languages of patriarchy share a distinctive set of features. Caucasian languages like Georgian share some of these. Northwest Caucasian languages also had a gender system. Allan R. Bomhard hypothesizes that PIE is a combination of Northwest Caucasian with Uralic, the Indo-Europeans' other neighboring language family.

I-E and Caucasian languages also probably did a lot of borrowing from each other for a long period of time. Recall that neighbors borrow terms from each other for things that don't exist in their own language.

For example, many words were borrowed from I-E languages by their neighbors to the north and east, the Altaic speakers from Central Asia. Altaic languages include Mongolian, and Turkic languages like Kyrgyz. Some loanwords from I-E into Altaic include one meaning "possessions, property, or power"; "wife"; "to pay"; "building"; and "kurgan". In other words, Altaic people didn't previously have lords, wives, buildings, or funeral mounds before they encountered Indo-Europeans.

Here are some other loanwords from I-E to Altaic: "Army". "Husband". "Loyalty, reverence". "To show respect". "Behest, command", "imperial order, divine decree"; "enclosure, fence"; "warrior"; "power, strength"; "worker"; "glory, fame"; "my, mine"; "money"; "law, prohibition", "blade, sharp"; "slave" and "to fight".

Altaic also borrowed words for "family, household"; "daughter-in-law"; and "a married woman's parent's home". Thus, it's likely that Altaic people didn't previously have nuclear families of the patrilocal type where the woman's parents lived elsewhere, until they encountered the Indo-Europeans.[348]

Let's look at the Uralic languages, from the Ural Mountains of Russia. The Saami are a Uralic people who lived so far out in the frozen north that they remained a tribal reindeer people until very recently. Some look blond, others look Asian, or somewhere between. Looking at pictures of them from just two generations ago, one can imagine Europeans with intact indigenous soul [349] , before millennia of colonization. Their language is the most untouched by I-E of any European one.

But aside from Saami spoken by the most remote people of Europe, most other Uralic languages bordered I-E languages and were heavily affected by them. Here are a few loan words into Uralic from I-E: "to drill, to bore"; "shall, must, have to"; and "merchandise, price".[350] From this, we can surmise that before I-E influence they weren't miners, did what they felt like, and had no money.

Loan-words having to do with patrilocal marriage came from North Caucasian into I-E. I-E got the words "copper" and "weave" from Caucasian, suggesting these innovations spread via the Caucasus. These Old Europeans innovations of copper and weaving spread to the Indo-Europeans via the Caucasus in between them.

"Son-in-law" and "sister-in-law" came into I-E after Anatolian and Tocharian had split off. These two "cognates" (related words across languages) have similar but different meanings in the different languages. Meanings shift as concepts change. The word that meant "sister-in-law" in I-E was related to words that meant "any relation through marriage" in the Uralic language Yukaghir, suggesting that the Yukaghir had the concept of marriage, but it was not necessarily patrilocal.

In Kartvelian and Afro-Asiatic cognates, the word that sounded like "daughter-in-law" simply meant "female", so perhaps they had no marriage at the time of contact. In Semitic, the word meant "bride", so they had patrilocal marriage. It could not have evolved to mean "daughter-in-law" in a Semitic language, because then it would have had a feminine suffix. Therefore, it's not native to a Semitic language; it came to Semitic from either I-E or North Caucasian.

Then there's the word "husband". It doesn't exist in those earliest I-E daughter languages, Anatolian and Tocharian, so the concept came about after those split off. It may have come into Kartvelian from Proto-Indo-Iranian, the eastern branch of PIE. Maybe patrilocal marriage arose among the Proto-Indo-Iranians, who passed it west to the North Caucasians, who in turn passed it back further west to the original PIE population. Then I-E languages lost terms for matrilineal relatives.

I-E languages have a word for "widow", which literally means "to be empty, to be inadequate", but no word for "widower". Words related to a chief paint him as a warrior with the power of life and death over the tribe.[351] The male-headed nuclear family and the male-headed tribe are part of the patriarchy package.

In summary, the words that languages borrow from each other tell us what traditions they had and where they came from. In the next chapter we'll look at the DNA evidence, which finally sheds light on a century of linguistic theories.

CHAPTER NINE

GENETICS

In the last decade, millions of people have tested their DNA, giving us a window into our ancient past. Before, the only clues to the ancients came from archaeology — the material artifacts left behind — or from linguistics — the hints in our languages. Now there's a powerful new tool.

Archaeologists and linguists are not all pleased by this. Theories nursed for centuries were wiped out instantly by the new science. Geneticists have been called "barbarians at the gates of the study of history" (by geneticist David Reich of Harvard) — upstarts untrained in the arcane mysteries of linguistics or archaeology, who have upset the academic apple cart.

As for me, I'm excited. For the first time, we know for sure that major migrations have replaced whole populations very quickly.[352]

In 2010, for the first time, scientists were able to extract a full human genome from ancient bones. That meant they could tell how ancient people were related to each other, what diseases they had, and where they came from.

A startling amount of new evidence for this book has come out since 2017. I'm going to provide genetic evidence for the following main points: 1. matrifocal cultures were common in ancient times; and 2. Indo-Europeans were not native to Europe or to India, but an intrusive force that replaced the indigenous inhabitants (Gimbutas' kurgan hypothesis). I'll also describe the three main groups that combined to create the Europeans of today and talk about a major genetic lineage behind the agricultural revolution.

A QUICK PRIMER ABOUT GENETICS

DNA is short for Deoxyribonucleic acid. This molecule has two chains that coil around each other, known as the double helix. The DNA carries genetic instructions for the growth, development, and reproduction of organisms. Women have two X chromosomes, while men have an X and a Y.

There are three basic types of DNA tested by ancestry DNA tests: mitochondrial DNA, Y-DNA, and autosomal DNA. Mitochondrial DNA, or mtDNA, comes from your female line, passed down from your mother in her egg. Both men and women carry their mother's mtDNA, but only women pass it down to the next generation. Y-DNA is passed from father to son in the Y-chromosome. Autosomal DNA is carried on the other 22 (non-sex) chromosomes, so is inherited from both parents, but the tests can only look back about five generations. Hence, it's useful for an individual to learn about their ancestry, but not useful for ancient populations.

When you test your mitochondrial DNA, you receive your haplogroup. Haplogroup is a group of related people; for example, haplotype J are Mediterranean people. As the mtDNA gets passed down, mutations happen, and that defines a branch. The first branch was J1, then J1b, and so on. Y-DNA haplogroups share the same set of mutations on their Y chromosomes. Most major haplogroups are thousands of years old, going back to Bronze Age, Neolithic, or even Mesolithic.

EVIDENCE FOR MATRIFOCAL GROUPS

First, we'll examine the evidence that some people were matrifocal: related women remained together and mated with men from outside the clan. Since the rapid spread of patriarchy, most cultures today are patrilocal.

The way to determine this is to find groups of skeletons buried together and test them to see if the females are related to each other, or the males. Until recently, we lacked the technology to reliably sample skeletons over 4000 years old, especially in damp areas where samples degrade over time. This time frame was right at the shift to patriarchy. The techniques have only improved in 2015 with the discovery that a high density of DNA could be obtained from the inner ear bone. So I'm excited to see new evidence come to light about the Neolithic over the next few years. Check BeforeWar.com for updates.

A study from November 2022, using the improved technology, sampled 13 individuals in the Upper Tigris region of Mesopotamia from about 8000 BCE. The researchers avoid mentioning it, but their data shows that the females were related, not the males;[353] this Neolithic population was matrifocal. One individual had half her ancestry from the Zagros region of Iran. Skulls showed signs of trepanation. This study is the smoking gun that proves that at least some Neolithic farmers were matrifocal.

Unfortunately, the only genetic sample done thus far on Catalhöyük, the large Neolithic Anatolian site, was from a burial of a bunch of unrelated individuals.[354] This sample was a large number of young girls. Perhaps this site was a school where girls came from around Old Europe to study. So Catalhöyük's matrifocal system has not been confirmed by genetics.

A sample from the Peki'in cave in Israel from about 4500 BCE showed a genetic mixture of locals with Anatolians, Mesopotamians, and even one blue-eyed individual with ancestry from much further north in Iran. There is no information about their relatedness, but they were peaceful with no signs of violence.[355]

Of course, later Bronze Age samples clearly show patrilocal ancestry, with the male skeletons being related to each other and the females coming from elsewhere.

One puzzling case is that of the megalithic people who built stone circles and passage graves along coastal northern Europe around 4500

BCE, such as Newgrange in Ireland. I won't lie: when I found a genetic study of megalith builders, my heart was pounding with anxiety. I'm fascinated with megaliths, and I wanted them to be built by peaceful, matrilineal people.

I was disappointed. A study from 2019 shows these megalithic coastal people knew their paternal line: there were mostly male burials, with unrelated females. It's interesting that the megalith builders were genetically distinct from the non-megalithic cultures that surrounded them, with more male European Mesolithic Hunter-Gatherer ancestry.[356] However, recent genetic studies show they did have steppe DNA.

Another genetic snapshot dating from the dawn of patriarchy was in the Cotswolds in England, dated to 3700 BCE. Thirty-five people were buried in a tomb, including eight who were not related to the others. The majority were males. The related individuals showed clear patrilineal inheritance, and polygamy: one man had four mates. The presence of cattle suggests contact with steppe pastoralists.[357]

One later sample shows matrilineal ancestry. Even though things got more patrilineal as time goes on, it was located in the matriarchal stronghold of the Aegean. It was from a tomb dated to around 800 BCE at Eleutherna on Crete, unearthed in 2010 by Nicholas Stampolidis. Three jar burials contained the remains of a dozen related women. Nearby was a huge funerary building also containing related women. The researchers assumed these were priestesses, based on the religious nature of the rich offerings. This indicates that priestesshood was a hereditary position passed through the female.[358]

We do have evidence of more recent matrifocal cultures in areas of the world where patriarchy penetrated only recently. One example is from Virginia in the 13th century CE. MtDNA analysis of 7 males and 4 females buried there were found to be maternally related.[359]

Another example is from China dated to about 2800 BCE. DNA analysis of 18 individuals from the Fujia site in Shandong Province revealed low DNA diversity from the mtDNA and high diversity from the Y-DNA; hence, the women were related and the males, unrelated.[360]

An example from Mongolia just surfaced recently: the Xiongnu empire from the Iron Age. The higher-status females were the least genetically diverse. This is suggestive of a matrifocal system. Elite graves were disproportionately associated with women, including horse riding gear, which corroborates historical evidence that women had great political power.[361]

Genetic data on sub-Saharan African hunter-gatherers show a long-term pattern of matrilocality. Anthropologist Chris Knight claims, "Embarrassingly for proponents of the patrilocal band model, genetic data on sub-Saharan African hunter-gatherers indicates a long-term historical preference for matrilocal residence. Studies of mitochondrial versus Y-chromosomal dispersal patterns show that over thousands of years, hunter-gatherer women across this vast region have tended to reside close to their mothers following marriage, migration rates for women being lower than those for men."[362]

One recent find that received a lot of press was from Chaco Canyon in the Southwest United States. Chaco was a highly organized, urban Pueblo civilization that thrived from 800 to 1130 AD. An article from Nature journal in 2017 states: "Analyses of nuclear genome data from six samples with the highest DNA preservation demonstrate mother-daughter and grandmother-grandson relationships, evidence for a multigenerational matrilineal descent group. Together, these results demonstrate the persistence of an elite matriline in Chaco for ~330 years."[363]

Y-CHROMOSOME BOTTLENECK

Another recent genetic finding that received a lot of attention since its discovery in 2015, is the Neolithic Y-chromosome bottleneck. Sometime in the Neolithic, the genetic diversity of the Y-chromosome collapsed. Suddenly, there was only one man for every 17 women in the genetic record. The ratio of mating males to females decreased by a factor of 18.

This had researchers scratching their heads. Usually, when DNA bottlenecks show up, it's due to a disaster that kills most people off: an ice age, a famine, a migration gone wrong. In these cases, both mtDNA and Y-DNA are reduced.

When I heard about this, *I* wasn't confused. I believe patriarchy could be to blame for the alarming reduction in Y chromosome diversity. The steppe nomads were killing off local males and taking all the women for the chiefs. In other words, this horrific practice seriously impacted the genetics of the male of the species to this day, in Eurasia. There is far less diversity among males than there was before the steppe nomads took over the world.

Based on this, Angela Saini, in her recent book *The Patriarchs,* speculates that there may have been other factors that contributed to the rise of male dominance besides the steppe nomad invasions.[364] She seems to believe that patriarchy astarted in the Near East independent of the invasions. But, the dates for the Y-chromosome bottleneck are from 4800-6800 years ago. If the younger date of 4800 years ago is right, that's right when the invasions started. If the older date is accurate, that could correspond to the initial rise of patriarchy among the Semitic and Indo-European people. So, this finding is not incompatible with the hypothesis that patriarchy arose only once, among the ancestors of the Semites and Indo-Europeans.

As that hypothesis would predict, areas outside of the spread of patriarchy in the Neolithic, such as Southeast Asia and East Asia, show far less of a bottleneck effect. The researchers looked at the Betsilio people of Madagascar as a recent example of a population going into, and then out of, a Y bottleneck. My guess is that in the 19th century, the Betsilio went into a polygamy bottleneck due to initial contact with patriarchal groups, then came out of it as they modernized and adopted modern monogamy.[365]

Thus, groups of males in the post-Neolithic descend from a much smaller group of males than their Neolithic and hunter-gatherer forebears. A Nature article states: "This pattern is especially pronounced among pastoralists [...] The tendency of pastoralist cultures to show the lowest Y-chromosomal diversity and the shallowest coalescence would also be explained, as they may have experienced the social conditions that characterized cultures of the Central Asian steppes." By "social conditions" they mean brutal patriarchal oppression by chiefs. Steppe pastoralist cultures from the post-Neolithic such as the Bell Beaker and Corded Ware cultures have particularly few male ancestors. In Corded Ware samples from Germany to Estonia, all except one belong to a single clade, subgroup (R1a-M417).[366]

THE THREE GROUPS ANCESTRAL TO EUROPEANS

One of the most important things we can learn from the new science of genetics is that we humans are all mixed up. There is only one human race — and that includes Neanderthals and Denisovans too! We've been interbreeding forever.

Therefore, there is no such thing as a European, strictly speaking. But for the sake of simplification, we can say, based on the new genetic evidence, that three major groups were ancestral to Europeans:

1) The indigenous hunter gatherers, known as WHG — West European Hunter Gatherers. One of their main haplotypes is the I group, one of the most ancient in the world and perhaps the only to originate in Europe. Their genetics persist today mostly in modern Finns, Estonians, and Icelandic people, who, due to their location on the frozen fringes of the civilized world, were less affected by the Indo-European invasions and other migrations. These people likely were short-statured with blue eyes, brown hair, and light brown skin.

2) Early European Farmers, or EEF. These were the Old Europeans who spread agriculture and fertility goddess worship from the Middle East through the Balkans to Greece and Anatolia. We believe they had olive skin, black curly hair, brown eyes, and round heads. Their genetics persist today mostly in Ashkenazi Jews (due to marrying within the group), and Maltese, Sicilians and Sardinians (due to being on remote backwater islands that empires didn't bother to conquer). The main haplogroups would be J, G2, and I2a2.

3) The Indo-Europeans, aka Kurgans or Aryans, were tall, with brown hair and brown eyes, long heads, and white to light-brown skin.

191

Their main haplotypes are R1 and R2, which are now dominant all over the world. They entered Europe only recently, around 3500 BCE, and replaced most of the male lineages alarmingly fast.

In turn, the Indo-Europeans were themselves a mix of three main populations:

1) Eastern European hunter-gatherers (EHG) as opposed to the western European ones (WHG).

2) the hunter-gatherers from the Caucasus Mountains (CHG), a population that weathered the Ice Age isolated in the mountains.

3) the Iranian farmers from the Zagros Mountains. It seems that farming was invented independently, at the same time, both in Iran and in the Middle East and Anatolia.

In summary, Europeans got their pale skin from the Middle Eastern farmers and their blue eyes from the hunter-gatherers. From the steppe nomads, they got their height and their lactose-tolerance. This idea of a white person is a very recent invention. It didn't exist before 500 years ago, when the concept of whiteness was used to justify the horrific European colonization. Even today, it's unclear: are Turkish, Lebanese, Romanian, Georgian, Azerbaijani, and Persian people white?

So the original Indo-European Aryans weren't all what we think of as white. The most typical type was the ancient Persian, with olive to pale skin, black hair, and blue eyes. Light-skinned, blue-eyed people are some of the most ancient groups in the Iranian highlands, which are home to so many fascinating cultures. One is the Kurds, who were originally matrilineal and include many blonds.

Clearly, Indo-Europeans included a spectrum of skin colors across this region from Europe to the Middle East and through Central and South Asia. Their noses were more similar than their colorations. They were all horse nomads who spoke related languages.

It's ironic that the Nazis' vision of an Aryan superman was of the blond type, which only some Indo-Europeans were. What is the origin of blond hair? There is very little to be found about blondness online or in scientific journals. Geneticists theorize that the trait arose among Europeans around 11,000 BCE, at the end of the last Ice Age. But they think it evolved twice, since it occurs among darker-skinned Melanesians.[367]

The 1994 book *The History and Geography of Human Genes* claims blond hair became predominant in Northern Europe beginning about 3000 BCE, in the area now known as Lithuania, once the Indo-Europeans arrived in the area.[368] My hypothesis is that blonds evolved in Baltic area among peaceful Finno-Ugric speakers, and then contact with the Kurgan Indo-Europeans turned them mildly patriarchal, resulting in the culture known to archaeology as Corded Ware. The Kurgans liked blonde women, so the trait spread rapidly as they moved further west into Scandinavia and Germany. Because this area is a long way from the steppes, the invaders were likely few in number: hence the mildness of the cultural impact. They remained relatively egalitarian for millennia, into the common era, compared to groups closer to the steppes and the desert region.

Is skin color only skin deep? Or is pale skin, as some believe, linked to colonization and domination? I don't know. Some believe melanin confers higher states of consciousness. Though, people of all skin colors have committed acts of colonization and genocide. It seems more related to proximity to the harsh desert regions than skin color. Perhaps we will never know the answers to these questions.

What *is* clear is that white supremacy is a recent invention. The Indo-Europeans Aryans, of various shades of skin, were primitive invaders who appropriated the far more advanced civilizations they conquered. There is no genetic evidence for any population being more intelligent than any other. I believe the Indo-Europeans were less advanced than their neighbors because their competitive nature, due to trauma-induced patriarchy, held back their progress. Once they absorbed their neighbors' cultures and women, they progressed technologically.

193

POPULATIONS REPLACED IN THE BLINK OF AN EYE

It is no longer a matter of debate in academia (though Wikipedia has yet to catch up) that a small gaggle of cowherds known as the Yamnaya, Kurgans, or steppe nomads swept through Europe and replaced 75% of the existing human gene pool.[369] The scientific papers politely pretend that this may have been a peaceful migration. But the archaeological record is full of burned villages. The genetics tell us that the indigenous males were replaced by the Yamnaya males.

Not only Gimbutas, but David Anthony, author of the seminal book *The Horse, The Wheel, and Language: How Bronze-Age Riders from the Eurasian Steppes Shaped the Modern World*, has been saying all along that this was an invasion. Anthony is still one of the most respected researchers on the topic. I read the book shortly after its long-awaited release in 2007, and was riveted at his description of the Neolithic farmers and the indigenous hunter-gatherers peacefully co-existing for thousands of years. He states there was no evidence for violence between these two people, but the evidence for violence by the later steppe nomads was everywhere.

In his words: "The domestication of the horse created a steppe bridge into India and Iran on the one side and Europe on the other side." It was the horse that allowed this tiny band of herders to take over all of Europe and much of Asia.

This total re-write of the genetic map of Europe, as well as a new system of family and property, happened over a mere few hundred years. Archaeologist Kristian Kristiansen says that these events were as crucial to the human story as the colonization of the Americas.[370] I would argue that these events were even *more* foundational to the modern world — they were the original model for European colonization. It was genocide for almost all of the indigenous male inhabitants of Western Eurasia.

Of course, even if more male DNA survived the later invasion, words are at a loss to describe the catastrophic impact it had. On top of

194

the genocide of the initial invasion in the 15th and 15th centuries, the rapes of the women and the theft of natural resources, is the effect of the missionaries, NGOs, and other foreign influence that continues *to this day*. They destroy peoples' confidence in themselves, telling them their cultures are demonic, eroding their traditions.

But back to the prehistoric colonization … this is big news. A bunch of herders invaded a much more advanced indigenous civilization of the Near East, killing all the men and enslaving all the women. The mixing (by rape and colonization) of these two populations is the story of the people of Eurasia. All of us had ancestresses who were raped and enslaved by Indo-Europeans. Why has this story never been told?

The answer is obvious: it's political. No one wants to think about these horrible events. Plus, the Aryans, who sat on the thrones of Europe, are still in charge, the privileged upper class who control academia. Perhaps Sir Colin Renfrew (the upper-class Brit whose influence in archaeology allowed him to bury his rival Gimbutas) subconsciously wanted to prove his Indo-European ancestors were indigenous to Europe, and the inventors of agriculture and civilization. This same thing is playing out in India: Aryans manipulating science to try to prove that they are indigenous to India. More about that later.

Let's look at the genetic evidence that Yamnaya steppe herders were outsiders to western Europe. Yamnaya ancestry arrived in the Baltic area around 2700 BCE, in central Europe (Germany) around 2500 BCE, in England in 2400 BCE, and in Spain in 2300 BCE.[371] (See the map.) Gimbutas' Kurgan invasion theory was borne out by the DNA.

Some matrist groups survived intact for a while by retreating to remote areas. In Switzerland, four females were found who lacked steppe ancestry 1000 years after the appearance of steppe nomads in the area, around 2700 BCE. The scientists speculate that their origins lay in more remote valleys, or further south in areas such as Spain, Crete or Sardinia, where steppe ancestry arrived late.[372] Modern Sardinians from mountainous areas show genetic continuity with their Neolithic ancestors, suggesting that remote mountain areas were a haven from invaders.

195

INDIGENOUS EUROPEANS

Genetic data supports the hypothesis that patriarchy in Europe arrived with the steppe invasion in the late Neolithic. Steppe ancestry shows up in the genes at the same time as warfare and status burials appear in the archaeological record.

The early Neolithic shows no sign of steppe ancestry. One study sampled 24 individuals from about 5000 BCE in the Central European Linear Pottery culture. They found only the DNA of Eurasian farmers, such as haplotypes G2a3 and F, rare in Europe today except in the Caucasus Mountains. The researchers note: "Interestingly, we do not find the most common Y chromosome hgs in modern Europe (e.g., R1b, R1a, I, and E1b1)."[373]

A study of the Old European Starcevo culture of the Balkans that lasted from 8000 to 6500 BCE found mostly G2a, plus I, F, and H2. No steppe ancestry was found. The y-DNA was concordant with the mtDNA, meaning that the women and men both grew up in the same areas. This would change dramatically with the arrival of the steppe people.[374]

One genetic heritage of the pre-Indo-European world is Rh negative blood. Found only in Europe, it's the only blood mutation that has ever occurred. It's found in the highest percentage among Basques, those indigenous people of Spain.[375]

Recall from the last chapters that these pre-Indo-European indigenous people of Europe were not a monolithic group. Geneticist David Reich mentions that, genetically, these groups varied widely from each other. Some of them were more closely related to Indo-Europeans than to each other.[376] This suggests that the Indo-Europeans were just one of the many ethnic groups of Neolithic Europe, until they got traumatized and started dominating everybody.

The only place in Europe today where you find significant pre-Indo-European genes is Sardinia. This island was a major crossroads in the seafaring trade routes of Neolithic Old Europe, but became a backwater

196

in later Indo-European empires, which is why it retains Old European genetics.

THE J2 PEOPLE

Sardinians have a high percentage of the pre-Indo-European haplogroup that fascinates me most: J2, a 12,000-year-old group who spread agriculture through Anatolia, Greece, the Middle East, Iran, Afghanistan, Pakistan, and western India. The people of Çatalhöyük, as well as the Hattians, Sumerians, Babylonians, Canaanites, and Minoans had a high percentage of J2. Many Europeans descend from them, and most European religions descend from their religion that honored nature, the Goddess, and the bull. The Minoan tradition of bull-leaping survives today in bull fighting in France and Spain, two places with some percentage of J2. The highest percentage is found in Chechen people of the Caucasus, and in Cyprus, Crete, Iraq, Lebanon, Turkey, Greece, Italy, and Albania, and among Jews.[377]

I believe it to be a major lineage for me, personally. When I researched my ancestry, I found that my favorite folk music happened to come from my ancestral homelands. Maybe some things really are in our blood!

J2 people tend to have long distinctive noses (as compared to Indo-European pointy ones, Asian small ones, and African wide ones). They do a circle dance, two steps forward and one step back, with a leader who flings a cloth around. Many share similar embroidery. You can find similar embroidery and costumes among the Toda, Brahui, Gujarati, Cretan, Romanian, Bedouin, Lebanese, Sardinian, and Romani (gypsy) people. These beautiful fabrics were spread with the Silk Road, along with their music in the Phyrgian scale. See my website BeforeWar.com to see the J2 peoples with their traditional embroidery.

In Biblical times the J2 Canaanites were spoken of in the Bible as wicked and idolatrous. Was this a reference to their customs of worshiping the goddess and her calf, that the Jewish tribes hated so much? The Iron Age descendants of the Canaanites, the Phoenicians, were thoroughly patriarchal.

197

Before patriarchy, the J2 people spread agriculture from northern Africa throughout Eurasia, by boat. They island-hopped from Anatolia, west through the Mediterranean, to the Middle East, the North African coast, the islands of Italy, and all the way to Scotland. (See the Old Europe map). They spread agriculture, fine crafts, and goddess worship as they went. They also traded through the Balkans along the Danube River, through Romania, Serbia, Austria, and Albania.

There is a lot of overlap with the places where Neanderthal remains are found; J2 is a major lineage for Neanderthal hybrids. People today with J2 lineages often have a lot of Neanderthal ancestry. See my website BeforeWar.com for a map of J2 haplogroup distribution.

The DNA of two male Minoan individuals tested in 2020 belonged to J2 as well as G2a.[378] This proves Gimbutas right: the Minoans were descendants of the goddess-worshiping Anatolian farmers, genetics showing at least three-quarters of their ancestry. Their remaining ancestry was from the Caucasus and Iran. They were depicted as having curly black hair and red skin.[379]

What about the Myceneans, the related civilization that replaced the Minoans? There was no sign of an invasion, and things mostly remained the same, except that a second throne appeared in the throne room, and, the first images of warriors appeared, where before it was all bare-breasted women, animals and nature.

Not surprisingly, genetics confirmed that the first steppe ancestry appeared when the culture became Mycenean, at the same time as the warrior imagery. The population's DNA was mostly the same as the Minoans, but with added steppe ancestry.[380] The final wave of invaders to Greece, the barbaric Dorian Greeks, would later bring yet more steppe ancestry, and savagery, to Iron Age Greece.

But the goddess people fought back. They rose up to fight the upstart patriarchal regime. They poured in from their strongholds in the Aegean Islands and the coast of Anatolia. These women warriors raised armies in this great war that killed most people in the Bronze Age empires. History records them as the mysterious "Sea Peoples" who destroyed civilization. It was a coalition of seafaring Amazons. They were associated with the "Pelasgians", the Greeks' name for the indigenous people of their land.

For a long time, the origins of the Sea Peoples were a big mystery. Who were these people who brought the apocalypse of Bronze Age civilization? All we knew was that they were not one ethnicity, but a coalition. Well, a 2019 genetic study determined they were most likely of Aegean and Levantine origin, with J haplotype genetics. [381] This confirmed what I and others suspected: the Sea Peoples were descendants of the goddess-worshiping Anatolian farmers who became warrior women Amazons and brought down civilization as revenge against the patriarchy! This would explain why their identity has been so shrouded in mystery … as is the story of the Bronze Age collapse. History is written by the winners, who erased their enemies, the female-led people they conquered and assimilated, from history. This is such a big story and would make an epic movie!

These Aegean J haplotype people also ended up in Britain, Italy, Spain, Portugal, and southern France, as the DNA evidence shows. That would explain the strong presence of a goddess in southern France. These intrepid travelers also made it to Pakistan to establish the Harappan civilization in the Indus Valley, and to Afghanistan to erect the Oxus civilization, which flourished between 2300 and 1700 BCE. These Neolithic civilizations of South Asia, such as Mehrgarh, featured goddess figurines.

I corresponded with a South Indian scholar who wrote a book about the linguistic correspondences between Crete and India. Cretans were known as "Termiliai", similar to Tamil, the South Indian language group.[382] This corresponds with the genetic data; there are South Asian tribal groups surviving today who have large percentages of J2: the Tamils of South India, as well the Lodha, the Toda, and others. These people tend to have different customs than their neighbors. The Toda religion features a sacred buffalo (like the bull sacred to goddess people of Old Europe and Neolithic India), and they practice polyandry, where women marry multiple men. The Kalash people of Pakistan, far away,

199

worship a mother goddess, and the women have more power than their neighboring sisters. They also practice polyandry and have no history of war. The Brahui of Pakistan still practice a menstruation ritual.

The J2 diaspora is scattered around the world, often in areas associated with goddesses, such as Languedoc France, Malta, southern Portugal, and the parts of Spain where the goddess Ataegina was worshiped. These are pockets of western Europe with significant J2 ancestry.

The J people go way back to the Paleolithic, and are distantly related to the Indo-Europeans. Jones et al. (2015) analyzed genomes from males from western Georgia, in the Caucasus, from the Late Upper Palaeolithic (13,300 years old) and the Mesolithic (9,700 years old). These two males carried Y-DNA haplogroups J and J2a. The mixture between Caucasians and Anatolian farmers happened before 25,000 years ago, at which point the coldest period in the last Ice Age separated them. The Caucasians were probably the source of the farmer-like DNA in the Yamnaya.[383]

In other words, the Yamnaya steppe nomads were raping and colonizing their distant cousins.

THE FIRST STEPPE NOMAD COLONIES

With these colonizations, steppe DNA replaced Anatolian farmer DNA very quickly. The steppe men brought the R1b haplotype along the Danube River through the Balkans.[384] One of the very first colonies they created was in the Balkan site of Varna. This site in Bulgaria, dating to 4569–4340 BCE, is famous for fabulous gold jewelry found in a tomb, including a gold penis ornament at the genitals. Gimbutas claimed that this was the earliest evidence for status hierarchy; the gold-containing tombs were clearly those of elite men.

DNA tests of this man yielded these results:

Anatolia-Aegean Neolithic------------------36%

East European HG--------------------------29%

Iran Neolithic----------------------------15%

Natufian--------------------------------11%

Karitiana-------------------------------8%

In other words, half his DNA is Indo-European (the Eastern European Hunter-Gatherer and Iran Neolithic that make up steppe genetics). The other half is Neolithic farmer (Natufian and Anatolian, probably a lot of J2). This is what you would expect if steppe men mated with local farmer women.

(What about the Karitiana DNA, you ask? Karitiana is a group from the Brazilian Amazon! If you understand how this came to be, contact me.)

Varna is right on the Black Sea coast. It was the first place we see the Yamnaya steppe invaders appear in the archaeological record. From there they made their way through the Balkans along the Danube River through Germany and Switzerland, to Spain and France and Scandinavia, bringing their R1b haplotype with them.

Geneticists Carles Lalueza-Fox and David Reich state in a YouTube lecture that Anatolian farmer DNA in temperate Europe dropped from 60 to 10% very soon after the arrival of steppe DNA. The further south in Europe you go, in modern times as well as ancient, the more Anatolian farmer DNA you will find. These two geneticists stress the decline of male genetic diversity that occurred. For the first generation, males were foreign (based on their diets in childhood), but after that, they were of course locals, having been born there.

The geneticists go on to talk about these hybrid cultures between the Neolithic farmers and the Indo-Europeans, and how the women brought cultural innovations such as pottery. In other words, the genetic evidence has proven everything Marija Gimbutas said. One slide in their lecture even has her name on it (though they never credit her out loud for her discovery, which they are discussing.)[385]

The Indo-Europeans arrived in Ireland right at 3750 BCE, at which point blue eyes, lactose tolerance, and hemochromatosis — a disease where you store excess iron in the body — show up in the population.[386] The original Mediterranean population of Ireland were related to Sardinians, with Middle Eastern features and brown hair and eyes. They were replaced by the steppe newcomers.[387]

In other words, the indigenous inhabitants of Europe and the Near East who created civilization were round-headed Mediterranean people with round heads. The men were replaced with long-headed Indo-Europeans.

The Balkan area of Old Europe, on the frontier of these two groups, was colonized over a long period. In the early fourth millennium, there was about 7% steppe ancestry. A 2022 genetic study of the Verteba cave, in 3935 BCE in Ukraine, shows steppe ancestry at about 20%.[388] Five hundred years later in nearby Moldova, dated to 3500-3100 BCE, genetic testing of four females found a much higher incidence of steppe ancestry. Their male line was steppe-related, and closely related to the males in the Verteba cave. The child had the most steppe ancestry, suggesting an influx of steppe men into the region during that generation. In the Verteba site, there were signs of violence, but not in the later Moldova site.[389] This suggests to me that in the earlier time period, the women were fighting back against outsiders, but by the later time, it was a hybrid culture of indigenous and steppe people.

The indigenous people of England were the same Mediterranean farmers. 90% of both sexes disappeared when the newcomers arrived around 2500 BCE. No signs of genocide have been found, so perhaps they fell to diseases brought by the newcomers for which they had no immunity, due to isolation on these isles. They were almost completely replaced by the culture known as Bell Beaker.[390] The Bell Beaker people had mostly Yamnaya ancestry, though less than the older Corded Ware culture, which suggests extensive mixing with local inhabitants.[391]

The steppe nomads showed up in Spain at about the same time, around 2500 BCE. Here too, they replaced most of the local DNA.[392] These kurgan invasions are finally discussed in mainstream academic journals in recent times (2018).[393] Far to the east, other steppe nomads invaded southern Siberia, almost completely replacing the gene pool. In east Asia, genetic ancestry can be traced to a small number of powerful men, chiefs of the Asian steppe nomads. There were steppe nomads with a related culture to the Indo-Europeans, who were Central Asian and East Asian, such as the Kyrgyz and Mongolians. European genes in Central Asia were replaced by East Asian genes.

Later, around 2000 BCE, the eastern branch of the Indo-Europeans from the Volga basin in Russia rode east to become the Sintashta.[394] They were likely the speakers of proto-Indo-Iranian, the ancestors of the Indians and Iranians, and the inventors of the chariot. There must have been a large population of surviving locals, since they were excellent metalworkers, which was not typical of steppe people. My guess is that these populations had immunity to the diseases of the invaders, unlike the remote, isolated populations of the British Isles and Spain.

In 2019, 50 individuals were sampled from a Sintashta site. The Y-DNA was mostly subclades of R1a and Rb1 — Indo-Europeans. The majority of mtDNA samples were pre-Indo-European: mostly U, and some W, J, T, H and K.[395] So, in South Asia, as in Europe, Aryans were an intrusive, recently arrived group of outsiders who killed the men or prevented them from passing on their genes, and mated with the women.

The parallels between Europe and South Asia are remarkable.

In both places, a tiny number of Aryan Indo-European steppe men became overlords over the local population of matrilineal people who made female figurines, fine pottery and jewelry. In both places, they replaced the local men and bred with the women, appropriating their civilization. These were the first colonies we know of. In many places these high arts of pottery and metalwork did not survive; in others, they survived in a degraded form.

In both places, the culture of the overlords combined with the more advanced culture of the people they colonized. As they were civilized by the local women, they got soft, and were easy prey for later waves of hungrier cousins who replaced them as overlords. This led to a three-tiered system, with the previous overlords as the middle class. In India this caste system was more pronounced than in Europe. In both places, the upper class — the Brahmin caste in India, the nobility in Europe — have a higher percentage of Aryan ancestry than the lower classes. To this day, Aryan ancestry is higher in Northern India than in the South and pre-Indo-European languages are still spoken only in the South.

In both Europe and India, bitter debates have raged for almost 200 years about the origins of the Aryans. Some of their descendants in both Europe and India try to claim they are the indigenous originators of civilization. These Aryan supremacists, who believe themselves to be the "master race", will stop at nothing to force this lie upon the public. For it *is* a lie. The Aryans were herders and killers who preyed upon the civilized, peaceful people around them.

All of this is coming to a head as I write this in 2021, because the genetic evidence finally puts the Aryan question to rest. India has been anxiously awaiting the results of DNA testing from a 4500-year-old skeleton in the Indus Valley, an archaeological site in Pakistan considered to be the first urban civilization of South Asia.

Aryan supremacists claim to have originated the ancient Indus Valley civilization. Since 2016, they've been in charge of the Indian government, imposing their agenda, known as "Hindutva", or Hindu nationalism. Meanwhile, the Tamil people of the south claim to be the indigenous Indians, and rightly so. They claim the Indus Valley was a Dravidian (Tamil) civilization later invaded by Aryans. This "Aryan invasion theory" rankles modern-day Aryans to no end.

You can imagine what happens when you combine the most intense academic debate of all time with internet culture. The Indian forums where Aryan origins and genetics are discussed are rife with vitriol, insults, and ugliness.

As the Indian newspaper *India Today* put it, Aryan supremacists will stop at nothing to establish India as the "native place" of the Indo-European language family. They have a "monomaniacal obsession with refuting the Aryan invasion theory."[396] They create fake news articles hinting that, purportedly based on an interview with the lead scientist, the findings would establish that modern-day Brahmin Hindus were the descendants of the Indus Valley inhabitants. They even threatened to take the samples away from the scientists, if the scientists insisted on using the politically sensitive term "migration", instead of "interaction". Never doubt that politics drives science!

But the truth did prevail. No steppe ancestry was found in the skeleton.[397] The study proved that the chariot-driving, Sanskrit-speaking Aryans did not originate India's first urban civilization; the Indus valley people were multi-ethnic and likely spoke a Tamil language. Quietly, after so much angry debate, scientific journals and media are saying that steppe ancestry "left a particularly strong and 'sex-biased', (i.e., male-driven) imprint on the populations of two geographically distant but linguistically related parts of the world: Northern

Thus, genetic evidence indicates that most groups in India descend from a mixture of two very different ancestral populations: Ancestral North Indians (ANI) related to West Eurasians (people of Central Asia, the Middle East, the Caucasus, and Europe) and Ancestral South Indians (ASI) related to Andaman Islanders.[398]

It was 4000 years ago that this mixing occurred, and soon afterward the caste structure was created. Then the groups were set in stone, since marriages only occurred within castes. This rigid status hierarchy has very negative effects on human life; the genetic bottleneck effect leads to genetic and population-specific diseases.

Today, the system has technically been abolished, but people still usually marry within their historical caste. People who descend from higher castes tend to speak Indo-European languages rather than Tamil or Austroasiatic ones, and have greater amounts of Indo-Aryan ancestry. In other words, some Northern Indians are more closely related to some

Europeans than to some South Indians. It calls into question our ideas and definitions of "white people."

After the Aryan invasion, the ancestral South Indians of the Indus Valley civilization fled east and south to create the city of Keelzadi in the south, which lacked a caste system or any Aryan influence.[399] In 2017, Tamil researchers claimed that the Aryan supremacist Hindutva government was attempting to stall the excavation.[400]

Thus, in both India and Europe, modern Aryans are still trying to claim that Indo-Europeans originated in their own homelands. But the truth needs to be told: they were intruders that appropriated indigenous civilizations. It's finally being discussed again after Gimbutas was silenced, but many academics still beat around the bush.

In a 2022 video discussion between academics entitled "Who were they? Conversations between Genetics and Archaeology" by the Royal Irish Academy, very little of substance is said in the whole hour and a half panel. They avoid topics which they call "politically divisive". They say scientists have the responsibility to be careful with such things. And so, academics never use the words "genocide" or "invasion", to this day. It's good to be sensitive, but we also need to be able to speak the truth and draw conclusions.

In a recent lecture, David Anthony, author of *The Steppe, The Wheel, and Language,* talks about how the bias against the idea of migrations hobbled archaeology for decades.

Those of us outside academia are free to speak the whole truth. The most in-depth internet forum for discussion of European genetics is Eupedia.com. Happily, the intellectual bar is high on this site. Members don't usually disclose whether or not they have degrees, and it doesn't seem to matter; the internet has democratized the discussion of science. I've seen no Aryan supremacists or racists in this forum. This is surprising, since the web is rife with nationalists of every country claiming to be the master race or the origins of some civilization. You find Albanian supremacists, Greek supremacists, Balkan-centrists, Afro-centrists, Hungarian nationalists, and so on. (Don't ask about the genetic results from ancient Egyptian mummies and how everyone has tried to claim them. I'm not going to touch that one.) But Eupedia seems to be a fairly civil, rational corner of the internet for such topics.

In summary, the upstart science of genetics finally proved that the origins of civilization lay with the pre-Indo-European peoples of the Middle East, western Eurasia, and India. The Indo-Europeans were an outside force that arrived starting around the 4th century BCE, displacing and assimilating these locals. The timing of the genetic influx corresponds with archaeological evidence: a new type of mound burial, a new type of physical skeleton, and the degeneration of ceramics. At the same time, we see population displacement in every direction but east — which is where the Indo-Europeans came from. When they arrived, the locals who were not killed or enslaved ran for the hills. From here on, human history is a story of mass migrations and colonization.

CHAPTER TEN

ARCHAEOLOGY

The image most of us have of the Stone Age is of brutish caveman dragging women around by the hair. The record does not reflect this. Archaeological evidence for warfare and male dominance is very scarce before 4500 BCE.

So much of academic theory is created by our own cultural expectations. Especially so in archaeology, where researchers, mostly male until recently, project their biases onto the past. However, thanks to our ever-expanding cultural expectations and an influx of female researchers, evidence continues to surface that even our post-patriarchal past was not as male-centric as we had thought. I stumbled onto an article recently about how the Native American culture that built the mounds of Cahokia was female-centered.[401] Another article in my feed featured an ancient Greek ceramics artist who turned out to be female.[402]

I've also run across several recent articles about how women hunted, too. The new technology of skeleton sex determination has changed everything. One article says, "Essentially, the field has largely resisted theories about ancient female hunters in favor of the existing narrative that ancient women stayed home to have or care for children. The archaeologists partially attribute this oversight to 'contemporary gender bias.' However, remains they discovered in Peru in 2013 may offer too great evidence to the contrary for others to ignore. […]" Randall Haas, anthropologist at UC Davis, said he had to completely change his picture of the basic structure of ancient societies based on these findings.[403]

The more our own assumptions evolve, the more we will be able to see the ancient past as it really was.

CONTINUITY OF CULTURE OVER TENS OF THOUSANDS OF YEARS

Archaeological evidence in all parts of the world show no sign of war in the entire Upper Paleolithic period (40,000 to 10,000 BCE) — no violent death, or damage due to warfare. The many artifacts found, such as 300 stashes of cave art, do not depict warfare or weapons. [404] Archaeologist Bar-Yosef made an extensive evaluation and found no evidence for warfare in the entire Near East region between 12,000 - 6,000 BCE.[405]

The rock art of the Sahara is a great example, as it spans the period from 8000 to 2000 BCE. The earliest art, focused on animal life, was very skilled; it depicted animals in a realistic and sensitive way. Around 5000 BCE the scene changed to nomadic herding, with cattle, and people with dress and hair styles from Central Asia. Around 2000 BCE after the Sahara dried up, the art becomes little more than graffiti: stick figures portraying war, armed males, battles, death, chariots, horses and camels.[406]

The material record shows a continuity of art, symbols, and styles between the Paleolithic (Stone Age), Chalcolithic (copper age), and Neolithic (agricultural age). This is seen most clearly in the cities of Çatalhöyük and Hacilar in Anatolia. Melaart writes: "Çatalhöyük and Hacilar have established a link between these two great schools of art. A continuity in religion can be demonstrated from Çatalhöyük to Hacilar and so on till the great 'Mother-Goddesses' of archaic and classical times."

For example, in the Neolithic period we see Paleolithic symbols such as seeds, dots, eggs, and arrows, along with animal paintings. The "V" symbol for the vulva is found incised on bones going back to 300,000

209

BCE.[407] This became a letter in the first alphabet, the Vinca script. Y's, M's, and P's also have very ancient roots.

Recently it's been discovered that the extraordinary cave art found in France and Spain, dating back tens of thousands of years, was made by women. Dr Dean Snow compared hand size and finger lengths to reach this conclusion.[408] This art, far from being primitive, used sophisticated three-dimensional representations that few artists today could match. In addition, many believe that women made at least as many stone tools as men.[409]

Fast forward to the Neolithic, agricultural age: Old European settlements enjoyed beautiful settings, good water and soil, and good animal pastures.[410] They were not in inaccessible locations, and not surrounded by high walls for defense.

Figure 10-1: 3D Model of the Neolithic city of Maidenetske from the Cucuteni–Trypillia culture.[411]

EVIDENCE OF VIOLENCE WAS RARE

Many people seem keen to prove that we've always been a violent species. They often give a date for the construction of a settlement and imply that violence appeared at that time, when in fact it appeared much later.

We discussed Jericho in a previous chapter. The Ofnet Caves in Bavaria are another famous example often cited as proof of an early massacre: there were 26 skulls detached from their bodies. However, on further examination, they found that the skulls had been detached from

210

the bodies after death. The skulls were also covered in red ochre and accompanied by ornaments, obviously buried with love and ceremony.

On that note, red ochre, a natural clay earth pigment, is found associated with tombs from the Paleolithic through the Neolithic. In every climate and nearly every continent on earth, people coated their deceased with red ochre. The earliest known ochre mine dates to 100,000 BCE. The earliest known ochre burial dates from 46,000 to 80,000 years ago: a small boy in South Africa with a sea-shell pendant and red ochre. Then there was the Red Lady of Paviland in Wales, around 30,000 BCE; and the Fox Lady in the Czech Republic at 23,000 BCE.

Far away, the aboriginals of Australia also used red ochre in burials. Native Americans placed ochre-covered corpses on platforms high in trees.[412] This ancient custom was so widespread and so common — we see it in almost all graves for tens of thousands of years — yet few people talk about it.

It's obvious from these sites that red ochre stands in for menstrual blood, because sometimes actual blood was used in addition to the red ochre. Also, some traditional women speak to this connection. Aboriginal women from Unthippa in Australia claim the ochre deposits came from the vulvas of their ancestors. The fact that we find this in thousands of graves all around the world speaks to an ancient worldwide religion centered around female fertility going back at least 100,000 years!

Another thing often mistaken for prehistoric violence is the widespread custom of trepanation: people drilled a small hole in their skulls while they were alive. More than *half* of all skulls found from the Neolithic period have these holes! People continue to do this even today, claiming that it increases the blood flow to the brain and results in a higher state of consciousness. In the 19th century they used hand drills. In the 1970s, Amanda Fielding in England did it to herself with an electric drill to cure depression, and ran for Parliament on a pro-trepanation platform!

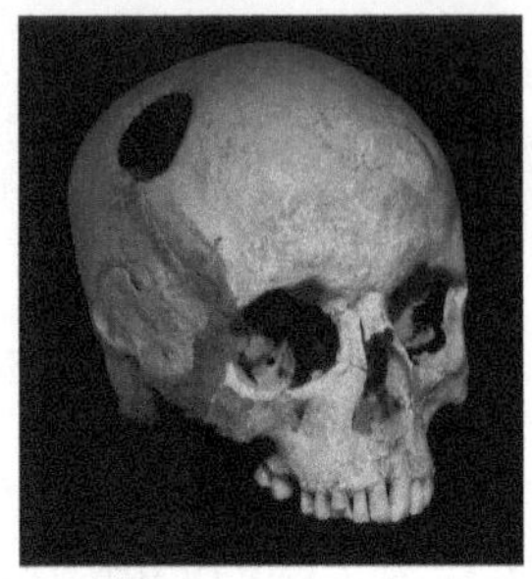

Figure 10-2: Trepanation.[413]

The sort of people who are determined to declare our species hopelessly violent seize on these skulls as evidence for blunt force trauma. But closer examination of the skulls reveals that the holes were made long before death.

One such person is a South African professor named Raymond Dart. He found some fossils that had been broken and stained black by geological processes and misinterpreted this as evidence for cannibalism. The press and academic establishment were quick to spread the word with a sort of glee. He has since been proven wrong, but the episode shows how eager people are to believe we are violent to the core.[414] Perhaps they seek validation for their own violent tendencies.

Another site oft-quoted as evidence for early violence is in China: a skeleton of a man with an arrowhead in his thigh. Given that there are no other signs of violence around there, a hunting accident — which is surprisingly frequent, even today — seems more likely. But few "experts" mention that.

There were a few regional, anomalous signs of violence before 4000 BCE, such as one at Jebel Sahaba. One of the earliest known sites of organized violence was a cluster of massacres around 5000 BCE in Northwestern Europe, mostly Germany, the site of the Talheim death pit and Schletz.[415] DeMeo believes that these were due to early steppe migrants from the areas that dried out first, who committed massacres and then either died off or were assimilated into the peaceful surrounding cultures. With some googling I discovered that during the time period of these massacres, there was an extreme drought.[416] Sporadic violence in times of extreme trauma and scarcity is a much

212

different thing than institutionalized violence at the core of a culture, as we see in the war bands of later Indo-European cultures. In such war cultures there is a permanent class of professional warriors who are then motivated to create war to justify their existance.

Another massacre that is claimed to be the earliest evidence for war in the world is in Kenya around 10,000 BCE, with 27 bodies that show signs of a violent end.[417] If in fact this is the earliest massacre, that still leaves hundreds of thousands of years that we have been anatomically modern humans with big brains and sophisticated too use, without such horrors.

The recent book *Inequality* discussed in detail in Chapter 5 mentions the Talheim death pit as an example of prehistoric violence. It also mentions a skull that received multiple deadly blows in Atapuerca, Spain. I've also come across one instance of rock art in Australia that seems convincing. But over so many millennia, these are rare exceptions to long periods of peace.[418]

Not only do we see no damage from warfare over a timespan of 1500 years in the large Neolithic cities of Çatalhöyük and Hacilar, but also no differences in status between the sexes. We find a division of labor between the sexes, but no superiority for either. A 53-grave cemetery in Vinca in Eastern Europe reveals barely any difference in equipment between male and female graves.[419]

Perhaps that's why we never hear of Neolithic cultures such as Cucuteni-Tripolye, Sesklo, and Vinca: they were peaceful. The Cucuteni-Tripolye settlements of Moldova, Ukraine and Romania, from 5000 to 2700 BCE, stretched over 500 kilometers and were home to up to 46,000 people![420] They were the biggest towns in the world at the time, bigger than later Sumer. (Why are we told that Sumer is the first civilization?)

The only evidence for warfare during the six hundred years that these mega-sites thrived is one archery attack on a small site in Moldova, far from the mega-sites, and a site called Verteba Cave, which shows signs of contact with steppe people.[421] We'll hear more about these cultures later in the chapter.

VENUS FIGURINES

Thousands of female representations have been found going back hundreds of thousands of years, most with exaggerated buttocks and breasts, often referred to as "Venus figurines." [422] Almost no male representations have been found during this period.

Figure 10-3: Venus of Willendorf.[423]

Perhaps the veneration of the female form goes back even further. An artifact known as the Tan Tan from Morocco, a tiny pebble carved into a Venus figurine, was found in a layer from 500,000-300,000 BCE. It's hard to say if it was carved, or just saved because of the resemblance. But one other from slightly more recently, 280,000 BCE, known as the Berekhat Ram Venus, was *definitely* carved, as powder was found in the grooves.[424] So, *a quarter of a million years ago*, our Neanderthal forebears carved curvy females very much like those carved *hundreds of thousands* of years later! A few hundred thousand years later still is the Venus of Hohle Fels, dated to about 40,000 years ago, but with the same exaggerated breasts and buttocks. And so many more. Talk about a continuity of culture over vast spans of time!

Over her career, Marija Gimbutas unearthed 30,000 sculptures, and thousands of ritual vessels, altars, temples, and paintings. In the models

214

of house shrines and temples, females are shown supervising the preparation and performance of rituals. Next to the altar stood a loom and pottery station. Ceramics, weaving, and religious ritual were in the hands of women.[425] One example of evidence for women as potters comes from the cemetery of Basatanya in Hungary, where pottery tools were found in female graves.[426]

Religious ritual was central to all aspects of life, and it centered around worship of a goddess. In Çatalhöyük and on Crete, 40 out of the 139 rooms excavated between 1961 and 1963 were shrines whose art depicted females giving birth and in ritual postures with arms raised. No Neolithic art depicts armies, warriors, or people being dragged around in chains, like certain Egyptian temples. As Eisler says, the core image was not a man dying nailed to a cross, but a goddess giving birth.[427]

These female figurines and images were found in shrines, making it clear that they were religious objects. That is, they were probably not, as some modern dudes have suggested, porn dolls. Renfrew's later excavations in the Cycladic island of Keros confirmed Marija's interpretation of the female icons as religious; this was a holy site.[428] Enormous numbers of them have been found as far back as 20,000 BCE in Mal'ta, Russia.[429] Scholars such as Jeffrey Ashe believe this time and place to be a major cultural seedbed that gave rise to a shamanic religion centered around a goddess, the spiral symbol, and the magical number seven. At that time, most if not all shamans were female.[430]

One interesting burial of what seemed to be a female shaman was found in Germany. An elderly disabled woman was buried with a large collection of unusual artifacts, such as a great many tortoises carefully arranged around the body. They carried her from at least 10 kilometers away, suggesting she was important to them.[431] Offerings were made to her for the next six hundred years![432]

OLD EUROPEAN CULTURE

Marija spent decades studying Old Europe. She described a culture of great beauty and refinement, with a higher quality of life than the later androcratic, classed societies. Old European towns boasted large

215

populations, temples several stories high, spacious houses of four or five rooms, and a sacred script. There were no ramparts for protection from invaders. The tombs and shrines were in the shape of the female.[433] There were professional ceramicists, weavers, copper and gold metallurgists, and other artisans producing a range of sophisticated goods, traded over hundreds of kilometers.[434]

The excavation of Çatalhöyük by James Melaart in 1961 revolutionized our views of prehistory. Of the 150 paintings that survived from this town of at least 10,000 people, none depict conflict. It was situated on a dry plateau on the Konya plain in south central Turkey and composed of two riverside mounds. The larger mound occupies 32 acres, of which only a few acres have been excavated. There are thirteen building levels, each with houses, temples, murals, reliefs, and trade items. In the lower mound are12 levels of an older, pre-ceramic culture, related to finds in Syria and Palestine. The continuity of culture between the 10th to the 8th millennia BCE shows a very stable social organization.[435]

The transition from hunting and gathering to permanent settlements was a gradual development between 9000 and 6500 BCE. Gathering turned to horticulture over time, as gatherers encouraged plants to grow, then figured out how to plant and seed them. After the dramatic rise in sea level after the end of the last ice age, game became scarce, which drove humans into farming. It was not a step forward; it required many more hours of labor, and their health declined. The archaeological record shows the appearance of arthritis with the adoption of agriculture. But it was the only choice in a world of insufficient game. Since women, in their role as gatherers, would have invented farming and herbalism, it's no wonder that they were at the center of the earliest civilizations. The evidence points to gender equality in the Paleolithic Stone Age, but a primacy of women with the transition to agriculture.[436]

The first farmers were likely a people known as the Natufians who lived in caves in the Eastern Mediterranean between 10,000 and 8000 BCE. Most likely the ancestors of the Old Europeans, they slowly transitioned to settled life, and invented ceramics. Old Europeans ate

216

Crab apples, cornelian cherries, strawberries, elder berries, hazelnuts, and acorns. The auroch was their most important game for hunting.

In the agricultural Neolithic, men and women had similar tasks, based on the musculoskeletal stress seen in skeletons. Only later in the Bronze Age did female skeletons show a marked increase in labor compared to males.[437]

OLD EUROPEAN SETTLEMENTS

The neat and tidy houses of Çatalhöyük in Anatolia were timber-framed and built from mud brick, with flat roofs. There were no doors; the entrances were through openings in the roof. Raised mud platforms served for sitting and sleeping. Each house was about 25 square meters and housed up to eight people. There was a kitchen area with an oven, and storage rooms for plaited baskets full of grain, tools, and supplies. The fact that the larger houses contained kitchenware makes it unlikely they were used by "chiefs" as in the patriarchal period. The spaces between houses were left open, perhaps for rituals. (See an artist's rendition on my website BeforeWar.com)

We have some data to suggest the houses of Old Europe were occupied by matrilineal clans. Istvan Zalai-Gaal and Imre Lengyel analyzed the blood type of skeletons and found that the adult women and the children in the same cemetery were related by blood, but the men were unrelated. This is what we would expect for matrifocal groups where men marry into a matrilineal family.[438]

The trade routes for this civilization stretched far and wide. Obsidian used for cutting tools and mirrors came from the Hasan Dag volcano. White marble came from the west. Calcite and alabaster for figurines came from the area of Kayseri in Anatolia. Iron oxides from the hills west of Konya were used for paint pigments: yellow and brown from ochres, bright blues and greens from copper ore, red from hematite, mauve and purple from manganese. Mica dust served as glitter.[439]

Their beautiful paintings were eventually covered with white plaster and then re-painted. The main theme was seemingly regeneration, often depicted as a frog-shaped woman giving birth. Other frequent forms of

217

the feminine were the vulture, representing death, and the bull head, another symbol of regeneration. The bird, snake and nurse goddesses were found in home temples. The pregnant goddess was worshipped in courtyards at platforms with offering pits near bread ovens.

Many symbols were various versions of horns and triangles. We know the triangle represents the vulva, as it often takes the place of female genitals in figurines and paintings. From some paintings that show the horns in the place of a uterus on a woman's body, we see that the bull head looks remarkably like a uterus and fallopian tubes. Horns appear everywhere in the Neolithic, whether bull, ox or cow.

Male divinities occasionally appear, in the shape of a young man or a male animal, often depicted with a hard-on (academics refer to this as "ithyphallic posture"). About 3-5% of total depictions were male. They were not found in temples so perhaps were associated with nature. This role of male spirits as guardians of the forests has survived into the folklore of northern Eurasia.[440]

OLD EUROPEAN FUNERARY RITES

When people died, they were exposed to the elements to be excarnated by vultures. The bones were then buried under platforms in the houses and painted with red ochre. People were rarely buried with valuables as in later patriarchal times, but instead with some of their ornaments or tools, such as antlers or jawbones.

The largest concentration of grave goods — pots, bone and obsidian tools — was found with older women. Men's graves were associated with spondylus jewelry, flint scrapers and arrowheads — mostly jewelry! Women's graves included decorated pottery, ochre, quern stones, palettes, jewelry, and symbolic items. There were no crests or insignias of rank.

Some male graves had distinctly foreign styles, indicating they were buried according to the original customs of their homelands. The richest male graves seemed to represent prominence in hunting, crafts, or trade. There are a few places, such as the Peloponnese in Greece, where only adult women had any grave offerings, suggesting a true matriarchy.

Burials with more goods lay side by side with the others, unlike in later patriarchal times when the upper class had separate cemeteries.[441]

Conversely, on the Black Sea coast of Bulgaria, we see the dominance of adult males in burials in the late Neolithic. This was likely due to trade with the Dnieper-Volga steppe population, patriarchal herders on the other side of the Black Sea. The Varna culture are famous for elaborate grave goods, such as the gold penis sheath mentioned in the last chapter. One female who was about 55 had five beautiful vases, a copper chisel, and a dish with a necklace of spondylus beads. One of the males, about 65, was buried with a stone shaft-hole axe and a copper chisel.[442]

Before Old European bodies were buried, they were exposed to predation. In Sardinia archaeologists found a huge rectangular platform raised high on a stone foundation with a ramp leading to it. A nearby dish depicted a dance scene in which figures with hourglass shapes held hands in a circle. Other finds of dancing figures near excarnation platforms suggest that death was a celebratory ritual. This funerary rite of exposing bodies to vultures was widespread. Some bones found in Scotland were bleached and weathered, so they must have been exposed for a long time before burial.[443]

After excarnation the bones were buried in the homes and covered with slabs on which fires were lit, and ritual deposits of deer and boar jawbones were placed. They were then sealed with stone cairns, and later re-opened for the placement of new bones. Evidence from the site of Isbister suggests they opened the tomb at specific times of year.[444] Skulls were often buried separately. Sometimes males were missing. In Jericho, skulls found underneath floors had shells in the eyes. In Latvia, the eye sockets contained amber disks.

The ritual of collecting the bones and placing them in ossuaries is still practiced in Italy, the Slavic countries, and Greece. The reburial of the dead after five years was recorded in Thessaly, northern Greece, as late as the 1980's. There, the female relatives gathered at the grave for an hour of crying and singing, and sharing a ritual food called *koliva*.

From 6500 BCE on, the same features of culture are found in southeast Europe, and later, most of Europe, until the demise of Old Europe between 4500 and 2500. Old European culture spread from Anatolia throughout Eastern Europe, via the Danube River.

These river valleys that were home to Old European settlements must have been beautiful; lusher and wetter than today, covered in oak and pistachio groves. They reached as far west as eastern France and the Netherlands, and as far north as Germany, a span of 1000 kilometers. Settlements were also found on terraces, slopes and caves, though the caves were mostly used as sanctuaries, not homes.

OLD EUROPEAN STYLE

The art of pottery began around 6300 BCE with lovely vases in the shapes of animals, and tiny replicas of temples. Temples first appeared in the late 7th millennium, inside regular houses, with altars of wood or stone, and a smaller room for the preparation of ritual objects that contained pottery wheels and kilns. After 5500 BCE, temples grew to two stories, and houses grew larger with many rooms. A huge amount of space was dedicated to temples and ritual.

Clay figures sometimes show elaborate hairstyles, turbans, jewelry, hip belts, narrow ankle-length skirts, aprons, fringes, blouses, and footgear. This was an elaborate culture with elegant coiffures. The bird goddess figurine from Achilleion with her hair parted and pulled into a chignon is the best-known example.

Figure 10-4: Modern recreation of the bird goddess of Achilleion, photo by author.

Examples from the Cucuteni culture portray a ritual dance with figures tossing their hair. One figure from the Sesklo culture has luxuriant sausage curls. Some of these hairstyles are similar to ones seen in Africa and the Middle East today. Other figures are shown with tall, elaborate conical caps like the ones worn by Sufis today. Spondylus shells were used to make diadems.[445]

More than half of the figurines were nude above the hips and adorned with beaded necklaces and hip belts. In Vinca they sported ankle length skirts that fall from the knees and seem to invert below, suggesting a draping fabric. Some seemed to wear blouses with front and back panels that left the sides of the body bare. Figurine fragments suggest they wore boots of leather, gathered around the ankle with thongs, painted with symbols.[446] These people were stylish.

Copper metallurgy began around 5500 BCE. Copper was mined in Yugoslavia and Bulgaria and fashioned into jewelry, statuettes, and ritual objects, as well as tools, fishhooks, awls, needles, pins, and wood working tools.[447] Intricate gold items served as jewelry and offerings.

SOME INDIVIDUAL OLD EUROPEAN CULTURES

Here is a sample of some of the connected cultures of Old Europe, with a few evocative details about what made each distinctive.

The Vinca culture in the Central Balkans is now famous for their gold artifacts. At least 650 Vinca settlements have been excavated along rivers, each one occupying up to 100 hectares. These lovely houses were timber framed with clay, and the floors were finished with smooth lime plaster. Marija claimed that the houses were more refined and comfortable than the houses found in the same region today, after millennia of patriarchal misery. Vinca culture lasted for 1000 years. Their artisans produced exquisite, whimsical figures with finely rendered faces, torsos and breasts.

The nearby Tisza people of Yugoslavia painted and carved their houses with designs and decorated them with clay gable ornaments shaped as animal heads.

The Hamangia culture on the Black Sea Coast featured one of the few male clay figures of Old Europe, the famous Thinker.

The Lengyel people of Northern Central Europe, around the Danube River, lived in very large trapezoidal long houses. While many Old European cultures were breast cultures, these were butt people: the figurines rarely showed facial features or breasts, but featured prominent symmetrical buttocks.

The Vepenski Vir people on the Danube built more than 50 shelters over 1000 years in the mid-7th millennium BCE. Floors were made from a mix of red limestone and clay that was still hard when first excavated! Each building had a built-in altar and was shaped like the birth canal. They overlooked a huge whirlpool on the river. These shrines originated in 11,000 BCE, back before agriculture when they were still Paleolithic foragers.

In the Karanovo culture of Eastern Macedonia, every settlement featured a central building that seemed to function as a communal arts and crafts center. Their art has been featured in art books, such as the

Lady of Pazardzik, who has a double spiral for her vulva. Beautiful offering containers were ornamented with deer, dogs, bulls, hedgehogs, and birds. Of the two hundred figures found, all are female. The Karanovo people made masks with huge pubic triangles and perforations for earrings.

The Cucuteni culture of eastern Europe featured the large settlements mentioned earlier, with up to 45,000 people, arranged in ten concentric rings! It must have been a fabulous sight. There were 253 of these sites in an area of 9000 square kilometers (about half the area of New Jersey). The floors were made of clay, and walls of clay-plastered wood, with thatched straw roofs.

Resources were abundant, and there was no division of labor. They had the idea of a wheel, used in models of wagons that may have been children's toys, but no wheeled vehicles. The mega-sites were divided into neighborhoods, each with its own assembly hall. There were concentric circles of houses around a large, open inner space.[448]

Oddly, the settlements and everything in them were deliberately burned every eighty years or so. Some experts think it was an expression of the ancients' belief in the houses as living entities, with a life span like a human being, and a cycle of death and rebirth.[449] The assembly halls were burned differently than the regular houses.

It's interesting that the Cucuteni-Trypillia culture was used as a model for Communist values during the Soviet Union, since they were clearly a classless society. When archaeologists discovered the assembly houses, before they realized that's what they were, they believed them to be larger individual houses and therefore evidence for social classes. These archaeologists were declared enemies of the State and had to flee.[450] It's yet another example of how politics trumps truth. The recent BBC article that talks about this historical anecdote does not mention that the larger houses were actually assembly houses, not dwellings for the elite.

The quality of Cucuteni ceramics was extraordinary: white, red and black with perfectly symmetrical chevrons, spirals, and animals. The female figures found are slimmer than in most other Old European cultures.

Additional Old European cultures flourished in Northern Europe, in the Elbe, Oder, and Vistula river basins, and then spread north to Denmark and southern Sweden. They also sailed along the shorelines to Italy, Greece, Sardinia, and Corsica. Rivers were crucial for trade and diffusion.[451]

In Spain, Portugal, and France cave sites indicate cultural continuity from the Paleolithic to the Neolithic. Open-air settlements on the edge of lagoons extended up to 30 hectares. Rectangular huts with cobbled floors were about six by three square meters in size.

MEGALITHIC SITES

Megalithic sites made of massive stones were created between 5000 and 2000 BCE in the Western British Isles, France, Holland, southern Scandinavia, and Portugal. While the builders had become patrilineal, the feminine roots remain: Megalithic cultures feature passage-grave mounds with tombs aligned north-south. They were shaped at one end like a cervix, while the other side was used for burial, which suggests a "womb to tomb."[452] They were covered with symbols of vultures and snakes. Even today megalithic tombs are seen as caves of the Goddess. The passage grave at Knockmary in Ireland is called Annia's Cave; this is the folkloric name Annia or Anu the "mother of the gods" or "guardian of the dead". In the last chapter we saw these people had become patrilocal, but traces of their feminine roots remain.

The famous Maltese temples, 43 of them, were built of 30-ton blocks of coralline limestone that resemble the shape of their large goddess sculptures. The temples occur in pairs, with one larger, like the later Greek *naos* and *pronaos*. The figures found have long necks, large breasts, and large pubic triangles: they wear a cinch belt and necklaces.

Figure 10-5: Malta underground hypogeum.[453]

Neolithic people arrived in Ireland by at least 4500 BCE, and to the British mainland by 4350. Skara Brae in Scotland is a beautiful example of a large Neolithic village, discovered by accident in the 19th century. The dwellings had furniture, and indoor toilets with drainage away from the building. They were pastoralists rather than farmers, and being megalithic they may well have been patrilocal, but they were peaceful with no weapons found. Human and animal bones were disconnected and carefully placed in the causewayed enclosures, suggesting ritual.

The ellipses of the Neolithic henges of the British Isles, such as Avebury and Stonehenge, were geometrically perfect, suggesting an understanding of the Pythagorean theorem. The people in Ireland who built the large network of villages and passage tombs such as Newgrange, Knowth, and Dowth were known in legend as the Tuatha de Danaan.

THE GODDESSES OF OLD EUROPE

As recounted earlier, once the idea of prehistoric goddesses got adopted by feminists and pagans, Marija's work was discredited in the usual way: by insulting her and ridiculing her, not by disproving her theories.

225

The Çatalhöyük dig was handed over to Ian Hodder in 1993, and little seems to have happened except for speculation about how the Neolithic figurines couldn't possibly be goddesses, because they were sometimes found in areas archaeologists interpreted as "trash heaps". Most people with a modern mindset don't realize that to indigenous minds, compost piles are holy. Hodder's other point is that since he can't think of a way to mount the figurines in a standing position, they must not have been worshiped. This seems a desperate argument. To his credit, however, Hodder did confess that egalitarian traditions, including male-female equality, persisted over a considerable period at Çatalhöyük.[454]

So, it's become fashionable in academic circles to dismiss the thousands of Neolithic figurines as anything-but-goddesses. Yet no one doubts that later statues of Artemis and Apollo from Classical Greek times represent deities. A glance at the photo below, with a statue from Çatalhöyük of a woman on a lion throne compared with Cybele, a mother goddess from the same region who was worshiped in historical times, puts the matter to rest. Prehistoric figurines strongly resembled later historically-attested goddesses.

Figure 10-6: Lion-flanked throned goddess from Çatalhöyük (left) and Classical Greek goddess Cybele (right). Wikipedia made the same connection between these two figures, the prehistoric and historic, as they appear on the same page.[455]

226

The symbols that represented the goddess since the Paleolithic, such as V's, triangles, breasts, swirls, spirals and birds' feet, eventually evolved into a form of writing. Researcher Ben Bacon in 2023 spent hours decoding this 20,000-year-old system of notation that has been found in over 600 Paleolithic sites, such as the "Y" which indicated giving birth. It was used to keep track of time and cycles.[456]

This early system evolved into the Old European script, known as the Vinca script, in east-central Europe 2000 years earlier. It appeared on religious items only, suggesting it was for ritual use.

These signs have been found at nearly 100 sites. It was linear and logographic; each sign expresses a concept, 220 in total.[457] About one-third are universally used throughout Europe. The script disappeared at the time of the invaders but survived in the Aegean region for 2000 years longer than in the Danube, and evolved into the Minoan and Cypriot scripts of the early Bronze age. There are 50 parallels between this script and the later Minoan Linear A.[458] All other non-pictographic scripts were descendants of this Old European one: such as the Crypto-Minoan, and Syro-Palestinian. It was related to the one from the Indus Valley in South Asia.

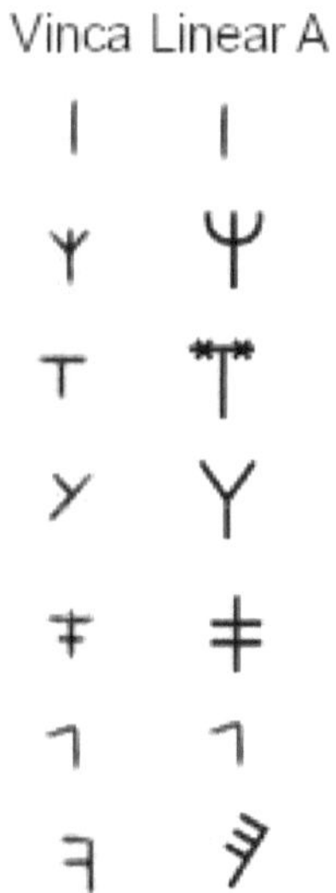

Figure 10-7: Old European Vinca script (left) and Linear A (right). Comparison created by author.

227

THE RISE OF PATRIARCHY AMONG INDO-EUROPEANS

Across the Dnieper River from Old Europe, steppe societies were doing something very different. David Anthony, archaeologist and Indo-European expert, says "The Neolithic and Eneolithic cultures of the Balkans, Carpathians, and middle and lower Danube valley had more productive farming economies in an age when that really mattered, their towns and houses were much more substantial, and their craft techniques, decorative aesthetics, and metallurgy were more sophisticated than those of the steppes. The Early Eneolithic herding cultures of the steppes certainly were aware of the richly ornamented and colorfully decorated people of Old Europe, but some steppe societies developed in a different direction."[459]

Alain De Benoist, in his 2016 book on Indo-Europeans, puts it thus:

> 'Old Europe', particularly due to their 'gynaecocratic' character, has repeatedly underscored their antithetical character in relation to PIE culture. These cultures are characterised by a sedentary and predominantly urban habitat, a high artistic level, and a relatively peaceful way of life. They honour essentially feminine and chthonic divinities (goddesses of fertility and fecundity, the Great Mother, bird and serpent goddesses), and present matrilineal, matrifocal, and matrilocal structures, whose survivals we can observe into the historical period. As egalitarian, theocentric, and matricentric societies, they contrast sharply with the first IE cultures, which are characterised by an above all pastoral economy, combining agriculture and the raising of livestock, a sparse habitat, small villages and fortresses, large rectangular houses, mostly undecorated pottery, horse sacrifice and the cult of fire, a pantheon dominated by celestial divinities and gods of thunder, an endogamy enhanced by marriages among crossed cousins with a network of allegiances and reciprocal dependencies, families gathered into clans and tribes, a system of chiefdoms, a social hierarchy placing a caste of priest-

magicians at the summit and a group of farmers and cattle or horse-breeders at the base, and so on.

How did these steppe cultures develop social hierarchy? As we've seen, James DeMeo's Saharasia theory blames traumatic climate change. The first signs of desertification in the Middle East, Anatolia, Iran, and Central Asia appear in 5000 BCE.[460] We see this not only in the climate records but also in the rock art in the Sahara and in Egypt. Fauna decreased gradually until it disappeared altogether by 2480 BCE.[461]

Anthropologist Susan Vehik studied political change in the deserts and grasslands of the North American Southwest after 1200 CE during a period of desertification. She found that warfare increased sharply during this climatic downturn.[462]

Around 4200 BCE the climate began to shift, an event called the Piora Oscillation. The climate got not only dryer, but colder.[463] People scattered and became more nomadic, relying on herds rather than farming. Perhaps it was the necessity of male strength for herding that led to the rise of male dominance, or the trauma response of seeking a strong leader, or the way that precious resources such as livestock were now able to be hoarded by a few strong men. As we've seen, the adoption of cows in modern hunter-gatherer societies often leads to patrilineal inheritance.

Prehistorian Nicola Di Cosmo describes how warfare may have arisen in the steppe nomads: rival chiefs gained gangs of permanent bodyguards which grew to become armies, which necessitated states to organize, feed, reward and control them.[464]

All of this is speculation. What we do know is that at some point, probably around the fourth millennium BCE based on the linguistic evidence (see Chapter 8), patriarchy came to be, likely due to rapid desertification. Whether it happened once in one population and spread to others from there, or if it's a pattern that arose multiple times in the presence of certain factors — trauma, drying conditions, scarce and easily-hoarded resources — we don't know.

229

It seems likely that the Indo-Europeans who turned patriarchal were culturally connected with other peoples of Eurasia and shared a religious foundation. Ukrainian archaeologist Yuri Shilov presents some evidence of a mother culture in Ukraine dating back to 20,000 BCE that was a precursor to Old Europe, Sumer, the Etruscans, the Tibetans, and the ancient Irish. It's difficult to investigate and peer-review Soviet-era research, but it's suggestive that these cultures had spiritual practices in common such as mound-building.[465]

Recall that since Gimbutas' days, the general consensus was that the Proto-Indo-European homeland was in the Russian steppe. But in 2022, new genetic information surfaced: the DNA of the Anatolian Indo-Europeans contained no steppe DNA. In that case, I-E languages did not come to Anatolia from the steppe as thought. There had to be an older population of Indo-Europeans from somewhere else. The DNA points to the Caucasus, a region of great diversity, as the origin of both the steppe nomads and the Anatolians. Perhaps there's something to this term "Causasian".[466]

However, the linguistics data does not concur, because the I-E lexicon doesn't match the farming lifestyle of the Caucasus. Perhaps a small group of Yamnaya brought their language to Anatolia, then their genetic signal was lost, absorbed into the population without a trace.[467] After hundreds of years, the ultimate Indo-European homeland is still a mystery!

Some are trying to claim that this new genetic data proves Renfrew right with his hypothesis that the I-E homeland was in Anatolia. But the data points to the Caucasus, not Anatolia. This seems like another misogynistic attempt to discredit Gimbutas in favor of the male academic elite establishment. It *would* prove that Gimbutas was slightly wrong about the *ultimate* origins of I-E. However, she would still be correct that the homeland of the people that actually spread the language (and patriarchy) around the world was the Russian steppe.

The archaeological culture of the Caucasus that's the most likely candidate for the homeland of patriarchy, and perhaps for the very first Indo-Europeans as well, is the Maykop culture. It was an interaction zone between local hunter-gatherers, the Yamna steppe nomads, and Mesopotamia to the south.

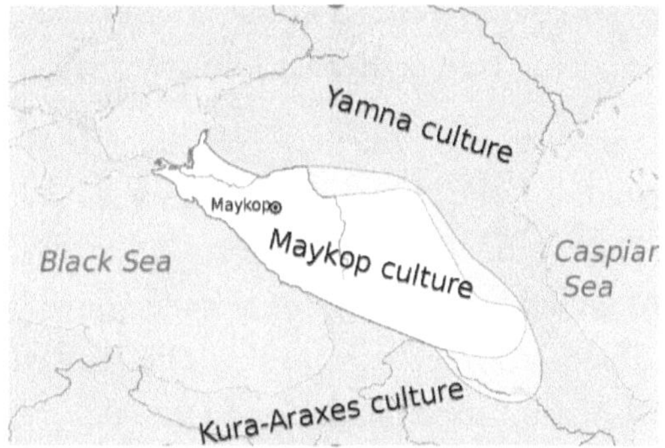

Figure 10-8: Map of archaeological cultures c. 3700 BC–3000 BCE.[468]

The Maykop originated on the Iranian plateau. In the Caucasus, they developed pastoralism and invented the wheeled wagon. These innovations spread to neighboring cultures along with occasional gene flow.[469] The Maykop had learned metallurgy from the Old European farmers, and then used it to make the first metal weapons. (I bet the Old Europeans were bummed they taught them metalworking, only to have it used against them!) This too got passed to their Yamnaya neighbors along with elite graves, as they traded wool and horses.

Perhaps the Maykop got their hierarchical traits from the Mesopotamian Uruk culture to the south, where we see the first oppressive states, ziggurats, and evil-looking reptilian figurines. The Uruk culture abruptly and mysteriously replaced the peaceful, egalitarian Ubaid culture of Mesopotamia that had been stable since 6500 BCE. In contrast, some Russian researchers believe hierarchy arose not first in Uruk, but in Iran and Central Asia.[470] I'm assuming that according to their theory, the Maykop were from Iran where it happened, then moved to the Caucasus and spread it to the Yamnaya, and to Uruk? Whichever it was, the "Uruk expansion" then spread it around Mesopotamia. Like a deadly virus.

The earliest kurgan that we have found is in Azerbaijan, between the Caucasus and Iran. These burial mounds were created to provide an elite dead man with pasture for horses. Recall that kurgans were made by not

231

just Indo-Europeans but by their Central Asian steppe nomad neighbors. Kurgan steppe culture, with its pastoral lifestyle, centrality of the horse, and storm and sky gods, transcended ethnicity, and spanned south-east Anatolia, north-east Syria, and north-west Iran.

The other earliest kurgans were in the Dnieper/Volga region of the Russian steppe in the early half of the 4th millennium BCE, in the Samara culture. The Samara had a transitional, early form of patriarchy: minor differences in wealth, individual graves, one male grave that contained more goods than others, and defensive walls. They still made female figurines, but they were skinny and stilted, not fat and happy like Old European ones.[471] This phase was known as Kurgan period I.

Kurgan period II-III in the latter half of the 4th millennium BCE includes the Caucasian Maykop culture we discussed earlier, and one known as Sredny Stog. These were more strongly patriarchal. It's believed the horse was domesticated in this phase. Finally in Kurgan period IV were the Yamnaya, after they got patriarchal traits from their Maykop neighbors. Evidence suggests the Yamnaya were egalitarian before that contact.[472]

In other words, the earliest Indo-Europeans seem to have been egalitarian. Kurgans were not found among the earliest branches, the Anatolian and Tocharian people who branched off from PIE before contact with the Maykop.

The famous graves of the Tocharian mummies found in China show no sign of status hierarchies or warriors. After the Anatolians and Tocharians branched off from the PIE parent population, they had no further contact, so linguistic changes in I-E languages did not affect them. Maybe the Tocharians split off from their parent culture and went all the way to China because they saw the rise of patriarchy and didn't want any part of it!

But if that's true, they eventually did have a king. There is no native Tocharian word for "king", a key word in most other Indo-European languages; they used the word for "strong" to mean king. Interestingly, Tocharian kings had to have six fingers and toes; if their children did

232

not, they did not get to be kings. There's a deep mystery around polydactyl (six-fingered) people, who are often red heads, and Tocharians had a lot of them. Sadly, the Chinese ordered the Tocharians killed — anyone with a high nose and/or a thick beard. As many as 200,000 were murdered.

THE INDO-EUROPEAN EXPANSION

There were three waves of migration. The first was from Volga Russian steppe around 4400 BCE. This may have predated their conversion to patriarchy by the Maykop. That would explain their peaceful co-existence with their neighbors, the Cucuteni–Trypillia culture, and their contact with the Vinča culture in Serbia and Lengyel culture in Hungary.

The second wave was of the Maykop people from the Caucasus in 3500. This one was definitely post-patriarchy, and definitely an invasion. It resulted in hybrid, kurganized cultures such as the Globular Amphora, Baden, and Corded Ware cultures. The third wave was of the late Yamnaya people from the Volga Russian steppe after 3000. This resulted in the destruction of the Cucuteni–Trypillia culture.[473]

As they came, they imposed their beliefs and customs on the people they conquered. An influx of people and customs continued for two thousand years. Gimbutas called it a marble cake of two cultures, swirled together. Perhaps at first, it was a trading relationship. But when the invasions began, the gentle farmers were no match for fierce warriors with daggers, spears, halberds, and bows and arrows.

Fortifications appeared everywhere, and the population of towns went from hundreds or thousands, to only 30 or 40 people. Layers of destruction appear in the archaeological record: evidence of massive fires and massacres. It was the end of the world.

The most obvious sign of this massive event in the archaeological record is the change in burial practices. The Old European culture known to archaeologists as Funnel Beaker used communal burials with dolmens and passive graves. With the arrival of the Indo-European Corded Ware (Single Grave) culture, we see low burial mounds

233

containing mostly male individuals with stone battle axes and grave goods.

One recent study of the Indo-European migrations states, "Unlike the small and scattered Single Grave households, the Funnel Beaker settlements are often large, holding extensive culture layers indicating a high degree of site continuity, a stable settlement pattern and larger populations." [474] And: "The most characteristic features of the new Corded Ware 'cultural package' included clearly gendered internments of east-west oriented crouched individuals covered by small burial mounds." [475]

After about 3800 BCE the female figurines, copper spiral bracelets, spondylus-shell ornaments, and elaborate pottery disappeared. Stockbreeding replaced farming. Metallurgy, mining, and ceramic technology declined sharply. Female figures either disappeared, or were replaced with ones with cold, asexual faces, no longer the happy and sexy figures of old. [476]

These invasions were able to spread so quickly due to the horse. The earliest evidence for the domesticated horse comes from the forest steppe of the middle Volga basin of Russia. Among the first areas to be contacted was the Danube region of Central Europe, as the Danube River was the route. In this region we find many graves containing a man and woman buried at the same time, suggesting widow sacrifice.

As they crossed into Old Europe they picked up customs from the locals, as well as copper and gold; metal had previously been unknown to them. Elite male graves were provided with thousands of shells, spiral arm rings, and copper pins. The kurgan burial mounds were only for warriors, who were buried with spears and flint daggers. The graves tell us they regarded the horse as divine, but not women; one woman found buried with a man had only a flint scraper for a gift.

The Old European Cucuteni civilization on the Danube survived the first wave of invasions somewhat intact. People survived by relocating to remote areas that were easier to defend. Ramparts were built across the river from a settlement. The Cucuteni ceramic tradition survived, although it picked up Kurgan elements.

It was catastrophic for the Karanovo culture. Some groups in Romania took refuge in Transylvanian caves or on Danubian islands, and were able to maintain their traditions for another four to five hundred years. You can find more detailed, updated information about these waves of invasions in Alan Benoist's 2016 book *The Indo-Europeans: In Search of the Homeland.*

In the first half of the 4th millennium, the Black Sea Varna culture was replaced by a Kurgan one that created low quality, unpainted ceramics. The conquered women may have made the few burnished pieces. Only a few stylized figurines were found. Old European symbolic designs had disappeared. No grains were found, so agriculture must have been abandoned.

These incursions caused a succession of dislocations throughout eastern Europe. Refugees forced others off their land, who in turn became refugees who displaced others. Refugee cultures were found in regions where no humans had lived since Paleolithic times, such as the eastern Alps. The hilly terrain provided protection from invaders, and caves were also occupied.

By the end of the 5th millennium, the Vinca tradition with its temples, figurines, and exquisite pottery had disappeared. One culture in eastern Hungary survived but took on Kurgan influence, such as males buried with status symbols and mace heads.

We find larger male skeletons in graves buried with much smaller indigenous Old European women. Men buried with multiple women suggested polygamy. For example, in the Brailița cemetery, the men had wide Proto-European skulls and faces like the steppe Novodanilovka population, while the females had gracile Mediterranean faces like the Old European Gumelnita population.[477] In the cemetery of Basatanya, of 75 graves, a small group of male burials include mace heads, but the majority are of the Old European style. The invaders must have brought no women with them, as we find no female burials with round skulls.

235

The second wave of invasions brought yet more violent invaders to replace the hybrid Kurgan/Old European cultures from the first wave. These hybrid cultures, with the civilizing influence of the Old European women, would have been no match for pure Kurgans. One example of a second-wave hybrid was the Usatovo culture, an amalgamation of the Kurgans with the Cucuteni culture. By the end of the 4th millennium, all of Europe was disrupted, and Old Europe survived only in isolated pockets such as the culture of Cotofeni. After the third wave, it survived only in Crete and the Cyclades. The Germanic, Slavic, Celtic, and Italic people all descend from the Kurgans via the Corded Ware culture.[478]

Gimbutas' theories still hold up decades later, vindicated by recent archaeology and genetic research. David Anthony and James P Mallory, the two biggest names in Indo-European archaeology, agree with her; Anthony quibbles only with the timelines and intensity of some of the waves of invasion.[479] The latest generation of male researchers who are rediscovering this topic try to distance themselves from her still, with some vague handwaving about her theories needing updating, but never mention a single detail that is inaccurate.

De Benoist, author of *Indo-Europeans: In Search of the Homeland*, believes that early branches of Indo-Europeans were egalitarian. (Ironically, he is an alt-right Indo-European supremacist who is *opposed* to egalitarianism!) The Germanic and Balto-Slavic branches still lacked social stratification around the start of the common era.[480] He talks about how "tripartite" culture, where society was divided into three classes: priest-kings, warriors, and pre-Indo-European commoners, began after the departure of the Anatolian branch. I talk about this too in the linguistics chapter, but unlike me, he sees this as a positive development (cough).

There are many myths of founding wars, such as the Iliad, the war of the Sabines that founded Rome, the one between the Germanic Aesir and the Vanir, or the one between the Aryas and the Dasyus in the Indian *Mahabharata*. In the latter case for certain, and perhaps in all cases, the two sides represent the Indo-European invaders and the indigenous inhabitants they enslaved.[481]

Once warfare became established, it spread like wildfire. At the same time as the fortifications and weapons appeared, we see widespread evidence of contact with steppe cultures: graves with grave goods and sacrificed women and animals; hilltop settlements, horses, pastoral economy, and sun symbols. Primitive pit dwellings replaced the elaborate long houses. Signs of violence appeared: people killed with spears or axes.

In eastern Ireland and central England, single-male burials and signs of warfare began in the middle of the 4th millennium. They transitioned from mostly-agriculture to mostly-husbandry. It seems that the invaders co-existed with the indigenous people for a while, as the new mound tombs with elite males are found near old communal burials. We might speculate that the single graves speak to the personal importance of individual males, while the communal ones honored the return to the ancestors. The Indo-European grave goods indicated prestige and status, while the Old European ones were symbolic and religious.

The first major destruction to appear in the archaeological record was the city of Hacilar, in 5200 BCE. Other major destructions happened from 5000-4300 BCE in Anatolia and Syria along trade routes. Some cities were repeatedly destroyed and rebuilt. After 4000, we see the first royal tombs at Alaca Höyük in Anatolia, with artifacts from Iran and the Indus religion.[482]

After the first wave of invasions, most of the Danube basin was dominated by hill forts. Some indigenous populations survived but were ruled by overlords. What survived was a pale reflection of earlier times. Then the second wave finished most of those off. This period of transformation coincided with a change in metallurgy. Bronze alloys (mixes) of copper with arsenic or tin replaced pure copper. These new arsenical bronze objects were totally different from anything seen in the Neolithic: weapons designed for killing humans, especially daggers.

"We are faced with the complete replacement of a culture," said the foremost expert on Eneolithic metallurgy, E. N. Chernykh. It was "a catastrophe of colossal scope … a complete cultural caesura," wrote Bulgarian archaeologist H. Todorova.[483]

237

The new settlements consisted of rough structures of stone slabs. Walls were engraved with figures of men and male animals, and painted zigzags, crosses, and solar designs in red ochre. After contact with Mesopotamia in the early 3rd millennium, outrageously lavish chiefs suddenly made an appearance among simple farmers.

Steppe culture revolved around the hierarchy of rich over poor, with the three classes or castes: rulers/priests, warriors, and commoners. A major characteristic of these cultures was the sacrifice of cattle, horses, sheep and goats. They burned down the forests of Europe to create open grazing for their herds like in their steppe homeland.[484]

Another central feature of these cultures was the lavish feasts sponsored by wealthy chiefs. These events showcased their wealth and generosity and were a major factor in spreading Indo-European language and culture.[485]

In many places, cultures were an amalgam of old and new, with agriculture of emmer, barley, vetch and pea remaining intact. Metallurgy focused on the axe and dagger, but some Old European traditions persisted: vases of beautiful workmanship, likely made by surviving Old European craftswomen. These exceptional pieces were usually found in the hill forts and rich burial sites, no longer in ordinary villages or graves. This situation was likely similar to Mycenean Greece, where Minoan craftspeople made masterpieces of stone, gold, and ceramic for new lords. Old European symbolism was replaced with solar motifs.

By the end of the 4th millennium, only isolated islands of Old Europe survived, such as the Cotofeni in the Danube who still used copper tools and made bird-shaped vases. One hybrid culture of the period was the Ezero culture of western Anatolia, an amalgam of the Old European Karanovo civilization. They retained the Old European tradition of an open center in the village surrounded with houses, but it was now surrounded by a fortification of huge stones. As the years went on, their copper awls gained more and more arsenic (which made it hard enough for weapons). Pottery declined in shape, make and decoration. It transitioned from liquid vessels used by women for ritual use, to ones used by men for communal eating and drinking. Occasional chevron designs persisted.

The Aegean islands, due to their natural defense from invasion, were a holdout of Old European culture for a much longer time period. There were no visible changes here until 2300 BCE. These shifts are documented in the Cycladic Art Museum in Athens: new pottery styles and a new type of male figurine with a dagger on the waist. Still, most figurines continued to be female, but in different poses. This was finally abandoned around the end of the 3rd millennium BCE. The museum also documents the abrupt change in burial customs, from burials under the floors of houses, to large rock-cut tombs with rich offerings for aristocracy.[486] With the infiltration of Indo-Europeans into Southeastern Europe, the pre-Indo-European population was driven south to the Aegean islands, creating the Cycladic and Minoan cultures.[487]

The Bell Beaker people of Western Europe, a well-known archaeological culture from 2500 BCE, were probably an amalgam of the Yamnaya and the Vucedol, a later hybrid. Their pottery, which was drab and crude compared to Old European pottery, spread quickly across Europe, replacing local styles.

Some early civilizations of Anatolia that were hybrids between Old Europeans and steppe invaders were the Hurrians and the Hattians, who spoke Caucasian languages but had a ruling class of Indo-Aryans. They still honored the goddess; at Nuzi, a Hurrian city, was a temple of Ishtar decorated with lions and naked female figures. Their goddess wielded a battle axe and wore a tall hat with the curly horns of divinity.[488]

These early hybrids were replaced in Anatolia by the Hittites, speakers of an Indo-European language of the Anatolian group. The Hittites married the ancient Anatolian sun goddess to the Indo-European storm god.[489] Ancient documents spoke of powerful Hittite sorceresses.[490] They were replaced in turn by an even more patriarchal wave, the Phrygians, but even *they* managed to hold onto one last goddess, the great Cybele, a mother-earth goddess. Of course, goddesses persisted into classical times, but they were always associated with gods, not solo powers.

239

The later Mitanni people of Syria in 1500 BCE were probably the ones who first wrote down the Indian holy books, the Vedas. They still spoke Hurrian, but kings took Indian Indo-European throne names upon their crowning. This gives us a glimpse of how colonization worked: most people continued to speak the old languages and followed some indigenous customs, while the royal classes spoke the invading language and worshipped the new male gods.

Some hybrid cultures would later grow into large Bronze Age city-states while still preserving some Old European traits, such as Bactria, Margiana, Parthia, and Sogdiana. These lacked steppe DNA, so somehow they were spared. The women wore flounced skirts like the Minoans.[491]

With the incursions, Old European temple-building ceased except in the Mediterranean and Aegean. Not a single temple or altar was found elsewhere. Instead, we see the new symbols: the sun and the breast plate. The newcomers introduced the concept of divine kingship wherever they appeared.[492]

MINOAN CRETE: THE LAST STAND OF OLD EUROPE

In Minoan Crete, Old Europe continued for millennia longer than on the mainland. Sir Leonard Wooley called this later Bronze Age culture "the most complete acceptance of the grace of life the world has ever known." The pottery and metalwork were of very fine quality. People enjoyed ornate games. Lighting was provided by olive oil lamps. Aromatic oils and resins burned in ornate vessels.[493]

Figure 10-9: Minoan seal, taken by author at the Heraklion Archaeological Museum.

Figure 10-10: Minoan vase, taken by author at the Heraklion Archaeological Museum.

The population of Knossos, the capital, was about 18,000 at the time of its demise. It was thought to collapse from a combination of natural catastrophes (especially the eruption of the volcano on Thera), and the gradual incursion of the Indo-European Mycenaeans.

241

The buildings we now call "palaces" were temples for elaborate religious rituals. Huge halls with rows of elegant columns were used for banquets.

Figure 10-11: Artist's rendition of Cretan temple, taken by the author at the Heraklion Archaeological Museum.

When the culture was discovered in the early 20th century, people were impressed by the confident way women were portrayed in the frescoes that covered the walls of the temples and homes, and astonished by the exquisite, bare-breasted costumes.

The frescoes depict women driving chariots and competing as athletes in ritual bull games. Women preside over large crowds at large

242

naval festivals. Men are depicted not as kings but as cup bearers, pages, musicians, harvesters, craftsmen, and sailors. There is not a single man shown seated.[494]

Art historians have used phrases like "the enchantment of a fairy world" to describe this culture's artistic expression.[495] The worship of nature pervaded every aspect of life.[496] There was a relatively equitable sharing of wealth; everyone enjoyed a high standard of living. No one lived in squalor as did the lower classes in the surrounding patriarchal Bronze Age civilizations.[497]

The first bureaucracy on Crete was described in Linear B tablets. Recall that Linear B was written in Indo-European Mycenean Greek, so this was after the arrival of the Mycenean ruling class. Even then, revenues were used to improve living conditions: perfect drainage systems, sanitary installations, viaducts, paved roads, water pipes, fountains, and large-scale irrigation works. Steam vents from volcanoes heated the water in their pipes! They even had steam power and simple electric batteries.[498] One interesting detail is the presence of what appear to be menstrual pits in their shrines. These are also found in patriarchal cultures, but only on the fringe of the village. This indicates that for the Minoans, menstrual blood was still sacred, instead of unclean; valued or revered, not hidden.[499]

Unlike in patriarchal Bronze Age civilizations such as Sumer, the Minoans worshiped nude figures. For these people, religion was sexy. Later, the figures ceased to be naked.

The palaces were beautiful, unlike the monuments to authority and power in the surrounding patriarchal civilizations. Apartments of several stories were arranged symmetrically around a central courtyard, with majestic facades and labyrinths.

Figure 10-12: Model of Knossos palace, taken by the author in the Heraklion Archaeological Museum.

Meticulous decorations and paintings from court life, religious ceremonies, and nature adorned the walls. They must have been aware of the constant warfare in the rest of the region, but did not depict it in art. There is no evidence of warfare between settlements on the island. There are no accounts in Linear B tablets of the deeds of rulers. Only later was there an authoritarian leadership, and even then, it was only in their largest cities.[500]

Minoan Crete proves that humans are capable of technologically advanced yet peaceful civilizations. It's a funny thing that most scholars neglect to mention that the Minoans were peaceful, with women in the most prominent positions. Author James DeMeo calls it a "subtle evasion of the obvious, a reluctance among contemporary scholars to consider that the peaceful matristic Minoans could have been technologically superior to the patristic, war-dominated societies of the region."[501]

The 2021 book *The Dawn of Everything* puts it thus: "Pretty much all the available evidence from Minoan Crete suggests a system of female political rule —effectively a theocracy of some sort, governed by a

244

college of priestesses. We might ask: why are contemporary researchers so resistant to this conclusion?"[502]

When Minoan Crete was discovered in the 19th century, archaeologists could not imagine how such a highly developed civilization could have been so completely lost to history. Perhaps the later Greeks and Romans had deliberately covered up the feminine origins of their own cultures.[503] Did they plaster over the paintings of sexy people on the walls of their villas? By then, accounts of their ancestors had been relegated to myth. Any remaining traces of matrist culture went deep underground, into the mystery schools.

Minoan Crete gradually ceased being egalitarian. They had picked up a status hierarchy over the millennia of living among patriarchal societies. There was an elite class and a queen, all still matrilineal, based on the genetic evidence we saw in the last chapter. But the elite class did not live large while the regular people suffered; public money was used to improve living conditions for all.

As an island, Crete enjoyed natural protection from the warlike hordes of the Bronze Age. But around 1450 BCE, when a small population of Myceneans came to rule as the upper class, art lost its natural character, and elite burials appeared. One theory is that earthquakes weakened the Minoans such that they could not resist the barbarian Achaean Greeks, so Minoan queens were obliged to marry Achaean Greek chieftains. Linear B tablets tell us that both Cretan and Achaean Olympian divinities (Zeus, Hera, etc.) were part of their pantheon.

Every single image we have from this time attests to the primacy of women. One in the British museum depicts a sacred grove where female spectators watch women dancing, seated around a shrine with a symbol of the goddess, wearing elaborate court dress. A woman with a sword faces one with a staff, attended by two much smaller, naked male figures. Females seated on raised platforms converse and gesture vividly to a large crowd.[504]

Not a single image from Minoan Crete shows a man in a position of power. Men were always depicted with no clothes except loincloths, while women sported full skirts and headdresses. By Mycenean times, after the Greek elite was installed, we see men wearing more clothes.[505]

After the Mycenean takeover, Greek names appear on the tablets, while the common people still had pre-Greek names. Terms such as *"wanax"* (king) and *"basileus"* (official) appeared in the records: new political institutions.

Then the Dorian Greeks, even more barbaric than their Mycenean cousins, invaded and burned the whole thing down. That was the end of the world, and the beginning of the Dark Ages.

But in eastern Crete, they continued writing inscriptions in their now-lost pre-Indo-European language, Eteocretan, until the 3rd century - well into the Classical Greek period. Pottery survived, though lower in quality. There is no comparison between colorful Minoan pottery juxtaposed to the drab stuff from the later classical Greek era.

Some groups took refuge on high peaks in Karphi.[506] The culture survived in classical Greek deities such as Britomartis and Dictynna; in the Eleusinian mysteries; and in the representation of female deities as the poppy, snake, and dove.[507] Even Zeus was a later form of the archaic Greek god Kouros, who died yearly as did male gods in the old days.[508]

Mycenaean Crete is the point of transition between the old world and the new. It was the beginning of history: Linear B tablets are the earliest writing we have deciphered. It's the bifurcation point where mythology, literature, history, and archaeology meet, where matrism meets patrism in the historical record, where matrist civilization touches history.

THE FALL OF BRONZE AGE CIVILIZATION, AND THE DARK AGE

As described in previous chapters, the Dark Age after the fall of the Bronze Age was a time of constant warfare between the old matrist order and the upstart patriarchy. Male and female warriors defended the matrist order against the patrist male warriors. Archaeologists have found many graves containing female warriors from this period. One woman was buried with an 18-year-old man at her feet. Her grave contained arrowheads, a quiver, iron knives, a loom weight, and jewelry, while he was only given jewelry.[509] Another burial from the 2nd millennium was of a woman sitting up with a short sword on her knees. She was 4'8" tall and between 30 and 40 years old.[510]

Among the Scythians, an Indo-Iranian tribe from the Black Sea, 25% of tombs containing weapons were female.[511] Many survived into their 60's. Scythian men were often buried along with children, suggesting flexible gender roles.[512] One recent find was of a thirteen-year-old female warrior.[513]

THE TRANSITION TO PATRIARCHY IN OTHER PARTS OF THE WORLD

EGYPT

In Egypt the culture remained matrilineal and relatively peaceful until the people known as the "followers of Horus" appeared, taller with larger skulls. When they came to rule, a sudden centralization of wealth reduced the protein intake of the farmers, and women were reduced to concubines. Graves were suddenly full of status items and sacrificed servants and women.[514]

THE MIDDLE EAST AND MESOPOTAMIA

The Halaf culture of the Levant featured advanced ceramics and abundant female figurines with large thighs, until an invasion by Semitic peoples from the south.[515]

Archaeological evidence for the pre-patriarchal roots of Judaism were hard to find until 1975, when controversial inscriptions were found in the Negev desert of Palestine dating to the 8th century BCE. They refer to Yahweh with "his Asherah", the main mother-goddess of the Middle East. Like the other deities of the era, all male-female couples, Yahweh had a female counterpart.

The second piece of evidence that really floored biblical scholars in the 70's and 80's was the discovery of the Pillar Figurines, hundreds of small clay figurines that depict a woman holding her breasts. They have been found everywhere in ancient Jewish households — hundreds in Jerusalem alone — evidence that the common people continued to worship a female figure long after the official religion was all Yahweh, all the time.[516]

In 2019, routine constructions in Israel unearthed a 9000-year-old city that had been home to 3000 people. No weapons or fortifications have been found. There were public buildings with plaster floors. Under the floors were burials with offerings that came from Anatolia, such as obsidian beads. The news story mentions "figurines whose styles date to the Neolithic" — which I take to mean "sexy female figurines", since most news sources seem to avoid mentioning the ubiquitous sexy female figurines of prehistory.[517]

We keep finding sites that push back our timeline of human civilization further and further, like the site of Göbekli Tepe and Boncuklu Tara in Turkey, dated to 10,000 and 13,000 BCE, respectively. Every time they dig up a sewer line, they find a site that's older than they used to believe was possible! Göbekli Tepe was discovered in 1995, so you would think they would have changed the textbooks by now. Nope.

New discoveries of egalitarian societies are popping up daily in my news feed. For example, a cemetery in Kenya called Lothagan from 4300 years ago was built by an egalitarian community; hunter-gatherers were mixing peacefully with pastoralists and burying their dead together, with no graves receiving more ornaments than any other. This contradicts the narrative that social hierarchy is required for constructing large public monuments.[518] This is consistent with other such finds in Africa and elsewhere. A researcher says, "This finding makes us reconsider how we define social complexity, and the kinds of motives that lead groups of people to create public architecture."[519]

SOUTH ASIA

The site of Mehrgahr in the Saraswati river valley of Pakistan was continuously occupied, and peaceful, from 7000-2600 BCE. It's staggering to think of such a long time span, 4400 years, when our own Western Civilization is only about 2000 years old! They had advanced ceramics and copper metallurgy.

When the Saraswati River dried up due to the climate change happening throughout, the inhabitants must have moved to the Indus Valley, where the Harappan culture appeared suddenly, fully mature, around 3000 BCE. At that time the Indus was a rainforest with elephants, tigers, and rhinos, not the bleak desert it is today. Women still had high status; we find female statues sitting in lotus pose. There were large, unfortified cities and fine fabrics.[520] Houses had toilets on the outer walls, and cities had sewers. There were even trash cans on city streets. They apparently invented dentistry.[521]

But by 1750 the Harappan civilization was destroyed by massacres. The Sanskrit-speaking Indo-Aryans had appeared and pushed the indigenous Tamil people further south, calling them *dasyu*, "slave". The Tamils escaped to the far south and east, and into rainforests. The ancient Vedic scripts speak of drought and famine. Horse sacrifices appear in the record. The goddess Kali arises: a more violent, vengeful form of the mother-goddess.[522]

CENTRAL ASIA AND RUSSIA

In this region there is no record of violence in the archaeological record until 4000 BCE. The goddess figurines that date back to 20,000 BCE persisted in cultures such as the Turkmenian as late as 2000 BCE.[523] By 4000, similar tools, pottery and skeletal types had spread across the Near East and Central Asia, across the Iranian highlands to the Indus Valley, and across Central Asia into the Tarim Basin and northern China. They were still peaceful and female-centered. But by 3500, desertification caused mass migrations.[524] After 2000, we see grave wealth and sacrificed horses around the Altai mountains of central Asia. By 1500, we see human sacrifice, executions, and torture.[525]

249

CHINA

Archaeologists have not studied much of the Chinese Neolithic, so we have only legends which told of noble people such as the Shen Nung: "… people rested at ease and acted with vigor. They cared for their mothers, but not for their fathers. They lived among deer. They ate what they cultivated and wore what they wove. They did not think of harming one another."[526]

Indo-Aryan migrations brought patriarchy to China in the Bronze Age, with the package of slavery, a military caste, polygamy, infant swaddling, and so on. A unique patrist trait developed here: foot-binding.[527]

OCEANIA

This book is focused on Western culture and the Near East, but I'll give a few details about other cultures to give you the big picture. The further from the Saharasia region, the fewer patrist traits. According to DeMeo's data, Africa and Eurasia contain 95% of the world's extreme patrist cultures; that is, cultures with at least 354 out of the 368 patrist traits he identified. Oceania (the Pacific islands between Asia and the Americas) and the Americas contain 88% of the world's extreme matrist cultures; that is, cultures with at least 259 out of 293 matrist traits.[528]

When the European colonists arrived a few hundred years ago, most of these cultures were still polyamorous, free of sexual shame and sexually transmitted disease. French travelers described casual public orgies.

We don't have any archaeological evidence from Oceania, but based on the anthropology, DeMeo believes that some patrist traits were introduced in the distant past by very small bands of invaders who either died out, moved on, or were assimilated by much larger indigenous populations. The large distances made it hard to impose their culture on these areas in a lasting way.[529] Original patrist tendencies of invaders would have been diluted through the generations. Oceanic alphabets contain traces of Phoenician, Libyan, and Anatolian languages, so these cultures were likely the original carriers of patrist traits.[530]

250

Here is one example of how culture change happens. The Trobriand islanders kept their matrist character but had a chief with limited powers, who seemed to exist to protect them from violent neighbors.[531] This seems a likely scenario for many groups in transition to patriarchy; designated warriors and chiefs who allowed the majority to remain peaceful.

THE AMERICAS

In North America, most of the patrist traits seemed to have spread south from the Pacific Northwest. As in Oceania, patrist invaders must have had insufficient numbers to overwhelm indigenous cultures, who retreated to high mountains and canyons and remained intact. The fact that this west coast region was the source of patrist traits in North America suggests that the newcomers came via the Pacific, not via the Bering land bridge.

This brings up another controversial subject: the growing evidence that the Americas were settled by sea, not only overland via the Bering Strait as we are taught in school. Academics cling to the theories they grew up with as long as they can, but this one is finally starting to shift. There is nothing unlikely about Bronze Age people sailing to the Americas. Bronze Age ships were solid enough to make this voyage, borne along by trade winds. One replica of a Phoenician sailing ship made it across in 2019.

I've run across a huge amount of evidence for Bronze Age peoples in the Americas, but that will be the topic for a future book. The evidence points to patrist traits in the Americas having been introduced by Bronze Age sailors. The Pacific Northwest peoples had many cultural similarities with the Shang or Chou period in Asia, such as backpack cradleboards to swaddle infants and flatten their skulls.

Enough about that; my next book will prove this point. Let's look at the Mississippi valley culture. In its heyday in the 1100s, the capital Cahokia would have been one of the largest cities in the world, at about 15,000 people. There are no signs of violence, but they did have a class structure. Leadership seems to have been matrilineal, where the ruler was replaced by his sister's son (an example of the avunculate). But nobles could only marry commoners, which meant that eventually nobles became commoners. Perhaps this was a way to keep power from being hoarded by one family. There were pyramids and mounds, and then, the city suddenly disappeared. Everybody left. It seems the people rejected what was happening there.[532]

Teotihuacan in Mexico had to have been the largest city in the world, at 100,000 at its peak around 700 CE. Most residents lived in luxury, with a better standard of living than in our civilization today. We see no inequality or overlords, and very few signs of violence. Art depicted hallucinogenic mushrooms and people with rainbows coming out of their heads. Good times.[533]

Then there were the Aztecs. Evidence suggests that in early times women had power, and a snake goddess was a central figure. But they turned patrist, and rape as a symbolic act of dominance was a core part of their imperial expansion. In fact, rape of conquered women was the main complaint that led their enemies to align with the Spanish conquistador Cortes against them. This suggests this was a new practice that their neighbors were not down with.[534]

For the Incas, too, rape and changes in gender roles played a central role in the creation and expansion of their empire. Their marriage customs changed to become a method of class domination.[535]

Then there were the Mayans, a highly literate culture. There were wars between Calakmul, a city of 50,000 that was somewhat egalitarian and whose imagery favored the female line and powerful queens, and Tikmal, all about the male rulers.[536] It's interesting that Calakmul had the serpent as their mascot, associated with female power by the Aztecs, Greeks, English, and others. Perhaps this was the ancient Mexican version of the wars between matriarchy and patriarchy that brought down the Bronze Age!

The Olmecs practiced genital mutilation, cranial deformation, and the practice of flaying: peeling off the skin. The same practices were known by the Phoenicians, a Semitic empire based in Lebanon in the 1st millennium BCE. I find it more likely that the Phoenicians, who were excellent sailors, sailed across the ocean, than that the Olmecs just happened to have the same constellation of sadistic habits.

In Peru, on the other hand, the Moche were led by women, with lavish tombs for queens and warrior priestesses.[537] But Peru was also the site of the other major patrist center in the Americas, after Mexico and the Pacific Northwest. DeMeo notes that after 2500 BCE, coastal Peru suddenly became an ocean-oriented, temple-building, irrigating, widow-murdering, caste-stratified society that spread into the highlands.[538] Again, patriarchy appeared fully developed on the coast and spread from there, as in the Pacific Northwest.

Caral in Peru, however, seems to have been peaceful, with no evidence of violence found. They did seem to have social inequality though, based on city layout.[539]

That sums up the evidence from archaeology. With the appearance of writing systems we can decipher, archaeology gives way to history. Now we turn to the historical evidence.

CHAPTER ELEVEN

HISTORY

I never took a single history class. It wasn't taught in my high school, an all-girls school in Washington DC. By the way, the school is now famous as the alma mater of Dr. Blasey-Ford, the woman who accused Supreme Court Justice Brett Kavanaugh of sexual assault. I believe Dr. Blasey-Ford's story, having spent my formative years marinating in the virulent misogyny of the most privileged boys in the country. I was raped by a boy from the same school as Kavanaugh, Georgetown Prep.

His name was Hugh and he was a stocky, dark-haired wrestler. My friend had invited me on a double date. She and her date went off to a separate room in the house. Hugh jumped on me. I did try to fight him off, but I had no chance with a wrestler. If someone had told me to attack his genitals, if I had been educated about this, I might have had a chance. His smell lingered in my nostrils for months.

My friend brushed off my story, saying, "You're so lucky! He's so cute!" I never told a soul after that. Amazing how girls learn to stay quiet, without even being told. Even today, as an extremely empowered "middle-aged" woman, I sometimes go along with abusive situations rather than make a fuss. We are so thoroughly trained.

But I digress. My school had only three males in the building. One was the "headmaster", and when he died, only male candidates were interviewed. (To their credit, nowadays the role is called "head of school" and they only interview women). Another was the Latin teacher, who, I was unsurprised to learn many years later, was having an affair with a student. The third was the geography teacher, who was cool. Geography, which consisted of memorizing the exports of various countries, was the closest we got to history. But I guess they figured girls didn't need to learn history. After all, it's not about us. It doesn't concern us. It's all about kings and armies, which bores me to tears.

When I grew up I discovered a book about history that was actually about the lives of normal people, and the patterns of history that drove their destinies. For example, after the Black Plague decimated the population of Europe in the 1400s, the infected linen sheets and clothing were made into paper, which led to the invention of the printing press. This led to widespread literacy and the Renaissance. Now *that* is interesting!

This chapter is about history as if ordinary women and men matter. It provides historical evidence to back up the thesis that in the early days of the historical world, things were different than they are now: women had more power; inheritance and kingship were matrilineal, and the goddess was the most powerful force there was. All this eroded bit by bit as history marched on, but traces remain in the historical record.

The overall pattern we see in history is a transition from matrilineal and matrifocal, to patrilineal and patrifocal systems; and from egalitarian organization to an elite hierarchy. The new elite classes, the conquerors, adopted patrilineal ways sooner than the regular people. Leadership transitioned from councils, to a queen, to kings who attained power through marrying a princess, and finally, to kings who inherited the throne from their fathers. The laws of new city-states made women into property and slaves, as nuclear families became the basic unit of patrist states.

Women continued to play roles as priestesses, seers, diviners and healers; the goddess continued to be worshipped in private even after male gods became the official deities. Over time, goddesses got demoted from the only great power in the universe, to petty, jealous consorts of male gods, and finally, turned into saints or erased altogether.

255

The standard narrative we learn in school is that humans were beastlike ape-men who eventually invented agriculture, which inevitably led to the rise of oppressive, bureaucratic city-states with slaves. Nope. The 2021 book *The Dawn of Everything* debunks this narrative. They point out that if we exclude the European Iron Age, the rest of the human experience consists of relatively free societies.[540] Even during the most oppressive empires — Roman, Persian, Mongol, Ottoman — a huge number of people existed outside them, organizing their lives in opposition to them. They've been denigrated as "barbarians", but they were really anarchists who did their best to avoid stratified class hierarchies.[541]

This chapter is broken down by region: Anatolia (modern Turkey); Mesopotamia; the Middle East; Europe, Asia and Africa; and finally, the Americas.

ANATOLIA

It's not surprising that you don't learn much about Anatolian cultures in school, even about the patrist empires such as the Hittites. It would be too easy to trace them back to the earliest Anatolian civilizations, which were peaceful. The patrist academic establishment does not want you to do that. Not that it's a conspiracy, but there is a tendency for paradigms and institutions to perpetuate themselves. History is written by the winners.

Before the Hittites were the Hurrians and Hattians, who spoke non-Indo-European languages. The Hatti royals practiced brother-sister marriages like in Egypt. The female leader of the pair was known as "*tawanna*" and had political powers, such as the right to collect taxes. Researcher J.G Macqueen concluded that "the queen must have once ruled in her own right."[542]

The title for king, "*tabarnas*", meant "husband of the queen". The *tawanna* was of equal importance with the king in ceremonies.[543] Later, brother-sister marriage was outlawed and the *tawannanna* became purely a spiritual role, a priestess. Her brother's son inherited the throne.[544]

In the late 3rd millennium BCE a band of Indo-Europeans installed themselves as the ruling class over the Hurrian and Hattian underclasses. This became the Hittite culture that would rule over a large empire. Even still, the old goddesses held sway. Hittitologist Volkert Haas claims that the "Hattian throne goddess Hanwasuit is the personification of the throne."[545] At that time, kings rose to the throne by marrying a princess or priestess.

In the 2nd millennium BCE, the first strong Hittite king, Hattusilis I, challenged this matrilineal succession of the king by appointing his grandson over his son. His decree was: "Should no one ever again raise his sister's son." This tells us that raising one's sister's son was a common practice at this time.[546] His aunt was not happy with this. Then he did away with the office of *tawanna* and proclaimed himself chief priest.

His royal son-in-law, Telepinu, who became king in the old matrilineal custom, passed a law saying that in the absence of sons for succession, the daughter's husband would take the throne. This came after a battle was fought over matrilineal succession. Yes, men were fighting to *keep* the matrilineal kinship system. It would survive for another 150 years, at which point King Tuthaliya accused his sister of witchcraft. There was a compromise, in which the king's son succeeded to the kingship while the daughter served as *tawanna*. These struggles over patrilineal vs. matrilineal succession were so intense that the empire was almost toppled by outside invaders.[547]

The rules kept shifting. In 1380 BCE a strong king, Suppiluluimas I, appointed his wife as *tawanna*. So now the king's wife, not sister or daughter, held this office. In any case, it had become merely ceremonial. He married his daughters to figurehead kings who became his vassals. Powerful men learned they could gain more power by giving daughters to other powerful men. Now women became subject to male decisions, and their power was linked to their sexual connection to a particular male.[548]

A later king, Hattusilis III, elevated his wife priestess-queen Puduhepa to co-ruler. They built the rock shrine of Yazilikaya, inscribed

257

with images of divine couples.[549] Even then, he felt compelled to apologize to the goddess Ishtar for taking power through the male line, and credits her as the source of his power.[550]

One old text describes King Tudhaliya petitioning the throne goddess to support him.[551] Even though queens now only came to power through their husbands, they were still influential in that role. Powerful goddesses were honored in the Zagros mountains, in Nineveh in Assyria, in Carchemish in eastern Anatolia, and in Comana in Cappadocia.[552]

MESOPOTAMIA

The glorious Queen Nana was known as "The Mother who gave birth to heaven and earth." Only later was she The Great Wife, secondary to her husband Humbam.[553]

The city of Uruk in the late fourth millennium boasted a high acropolis and a public district named Eanna, dedicated to the goddess Inanna. It was egalitarian and peaceful. Around 3200 there was a big event: the Eanna sanctuary was trashed, and replaced with gated communities and ziggurats.[554]

Tablets show that the rights of women had not yet declined as of 2000 BCE. A legal document from Elam, a city-state east of Sumer contemporary with Babylon, gave married women the right to pass their property on to their daughters. The Elamite religion, according to one classical Greek writer, was "characterized by uncommon reverence and respect for womanhood." They were into big thigh goddesses holding out their breasts, similar to the ones from the Indus Valley. The rulers at the capital, Susa, practiced kingship by matrilineal descent, being referred to as "son of a sister".[555]

Even in later Babylon, which had become more male dominant, women still managed their own property, especially some priestesses who actively traded.[556] In the first dynasty of the city-state of Ur, one Queen ruled alone, Queen Shubad.[557]

In 2371 King Sargon of Akkad founded a dynasty to rule over Sumer, Assyria, Elam, and the Euphrates valley. He appointed his daughter Enheduanna, a gifted poet and politician, as high priestess of the Moon-God temple. In those days, princesses were influential and wielded economic, legal, and judicial political power. They were highly educated in preparation for their role in diplomatic marriages, to be able to stand in for their husbands.[558]

A tablet in 2300 BCE speaks of a reform declaring that food grown on temple lands would be for those in need rather than for the priests. This was a return to an older custom, and known as "*amargi*", which meant both "freedom" and "return to the mother". Riane Eisler, author of *The Chalice and the Blade*, believes this was a return to the days when female leaders saw power as responsibility, not control.[559]

In Mari, a city-state north of Sumer, women owned and managed property and participated in business and in judicial matters. They also served as scribes, musicians and singers. Bernard Frank Batto, an expert in the ancient Assyrians, explains the position of women in Mari as a holdover from an earlier time.[560]

It was with Akkadian influence that things really went downhill in Mesopotamia. King Urukagina passed a reform in 2350 BCE decreeing "the women of former days used to take two husbands, but the women of today were stoned with stones inscribed with their evil intent". And, "If a woman speaks disrespectfully to a man, that woman's mouth is crushed with a fired brick."[561]

Historical evidence from this period sheds light on how taking female war captives led to the practice of slavery. In the earliest periods most slaves were women, and, like married women, were separated from their kin and had no rights. Only later do smaller numbers of male slaves appear, perhaps only when various cultures discovered how to break peoples' spirits in order to control them without force. Rape has been a tool to express dominance over both sexes since the dawn of patrism. The first female slaves led to social institutions for creating a class of psychologically enslaved people. Later, institutionalized distinctions of

259

class and race arose as well.[562] Oppression of these classes and races was modeled on the oppression of women.

Women were enslaved for their sexual, reproductive, and domestic labor, while men were enslaved for hard work. Female slaves were also at the disposal of the wives, who had the economic privilege to exploit slaves, but no sexual rights. Slaves could also be hired out as prostitutes by their masters, who collected their pay. The law codes became preoccupied with regulating women's sexual behavior.[563]

At this point, the earlier matrifocal form of marriage was known in the Middle East and Mesopotamia as *"beena"* marriage: the woman had her own house or tent, and could divorce as she pleased. In the later form of marriage, known as *"ba'al"* marriage, men were allowed to divorce for any reason, including her failure to produce sons, while adultery for the woman was punishable by death.[564] I find it curious that the name for patrilocal marriage is the same as for their god.

The Code of Hammurabi, one of the first law codes in the world, formalized *ba'al* marriage. Ancient historian Koschaker believes it started out as marriage by purchase but developed into marriage by written contract. The Code of Hammurabi was a disaster for women. It made rape a property crime against a woman's father or husband. If she could not prove that she resisted by shouting, she would be punished for adultery by having her breasts, nose and ears sliced off. The only good news was that the code required an official to do this, not the husband himself. The code also created the first laws against abortion: it was a crime against the state, equal in severity to high treason; punishable by impalement in public. The control of women had become a matter of state.[565]

Even still, women held sway as priestesses. Ishtar was still the main deity, receiving huge quantities of food, animal sacrifices, oil, and wine every day. The Sacred Marriage was still practiced: a sexual act between a priestess as the goddess Inanna, and a priest as the boy-god known as Dumuzi, Tammuz, Attis, Adonis, Baal, or Osiris, depending on where you were.[566] I don't know whether they had intercourse, or just pretended to. They pretended to kill the young god, and he was

260

resurrected through union with the goddess, just as Osiris was. Jesus, the later dying god who was based on this one, would be resurrected too but without any goddess to help.

The first known literary work, *Gilgamesh*, is about a wild man tamed by a prostitute; he follows this wise woman into civilization. Could this be a mythic retelling of the feminine origins of civilization?[567]

At this point a class of temple prostitutes arose to offer sexual services to the gods. Then commercial prostitution was created to meet the sexual needs of men. That's when they needed to divide women into two categories: respectable, and not. The laws of middle Assyria made it a state legal matter: respectable women were forced to be veiled. Prostitutes were forced to be unveiled, or their ears would be cut off. So women were now defined on sight by their use to men: the property of one, or accessible to all. They were divided from each other, and men were prevented from associating with women of different backgrounds. By the 1st millennia BCE, women were barred from receiving education.[568]

THE MIDDLE EAST

In the 1970s, new discoveries unearthed archaeological evidence for the goddess-worshiping roots of Judaism. The Hebrew goddess, Asherah (the Middle Eastern name for the one known as Hathor in Egypt and Astarte in Greece), had been lost to history, because she was usually worshipped as a wooden idol, which would not have survived the ages even if they weren't destroyed by misogynistic Yahweh zealots. But in the early years, Yahweh was mated to Asherah. Priests' invocations were considered worthless unless they were married.

Most Biblical evidence was similarly destroyed when the Bible was edited to remove references to the goddess, except in the context of stamping her out. Hint: when the Bible talks about idolators, it's usually talking about goddess worshipers. Of course, the idolators worshipped male gods by that point too, especially Baal, but the goddess was still the most popular. She was revered in the form of a golden calf, or as a woman with her breasts in her hands.

261

The Bible says: "… and the women knead their dough, to make cakes to the queen of heaven." (Jeremiah 7:18)

The Book of Judges tells the story of Gideon in the 12th century BCE, who cut down the wooden statue of Asherah that the town was worshipping. This tells us that people still worshipped her publicly together, not just in the privacy of their own homes. The town demanded Gideon's death for daring to cut her down.[569]

The Bible also recounts how King Josiah purged the Queen of Heaven from the temple, whatever that meant. He also made it illegal to look up at the stars! Shortly after that, Israel was destroyed. Perhaps some believed this was Israel's punishment for forsaking their ancient mother goddess.

Some Biblical stories offer hints about the transition from matrifocal to patrifocal marriage. Jacob in the book of Genesis did seven years of service for Laban in exchange for Laban's daughter in marriage. This was the old custom, in which men lived with their lover's families and did chores for them. Later, of course, it changed.[570]

By now you understand the connection between father-headed families and the restriction of women's rights. In a system where paternity is all-important, women are imprisoned by their kin to ensure they stay faithful. Their virginity becomes a financial asset of the family, and a matter of family "honor". Adulteresses were stoned by the whole village all over the Middle East, and this continued well into the 20th century in Greece, Albania, and Sicily. It still happens in some countries in the Middle East.

Hebrews started to look down on women and sex due to influence from the Indo-Aryans and Assyrians.[571] But even after Josiah purged the Queen of Heaven, there was some backsliding into the old ways. King Saul got converted back to Asherah worship by some of his slave women, and the Queen of Sheba converted King Solomon to her "wicked ways".[572]

At this point they passed laws to forbid normal, natural stuff. You could be killed for masturbating. It became a sin for a man to look at or speak to an unchaperoned woman. Men could no longer kiss their sons or appear naked in front of them. The biggest crime was for a woman to attack a man's genitals.[573]

This last law got me thinking. I have always wondered why we don't see more women fighting back this way, especially during times when women were taken prisoner and raped. It's so easy to hurt a man that way. I had a vague theory that sometime long ago, women were so horribly punished for doing this that it got buried deep in the subconscious. Besides, a woman who fought off a rapist sanctioned by her family would have suffered terribly. She had nowhere to escape to, nor any way to support herself if she did. So perhaps it was forgotten. I for one did not think to try this when I was being raped.

The Bible contains not a single passage about taking care of children's needs. But it talks all about sacrificing them, stoning them, beating them, and forcing them to carry on the family name.[574] In the book of Genesis, creativity and procreativity become associated with a male God, "Lord" or "king", while female sexuality outside of procreation becomes associated with sin and evil. The only access to God left for women is motherhood.[575]

THE ARAB WORLD

Meanwhile, the Hebrews' Arab cousins continued to worship their goddess, often known as Al-Uzza, into Islamic times, and retained antique customs of respect for women well into Roman times. Pockets of female-centered cultures survived. Among the Nabataeans, the Roman-era people who occupied the astonishing site of Petra in Jordan, women enjoyed equal rights and queens ruled aside kings.[576] The Nabateans worshipped three female deities: Al-'Uzza (the Powerful One), Manat (the Goddess of Fate), and Allat (Goddess).[577] Obviously, Allat got masculinized into Allah.

Before the time of Islam, women could choose their own husbands, even taking more than one. Yemen had female rulers even into Islamic times, such as Malika Asma and her daughter-in-law Malika Urwa.[578]

263

The holy of holies of the Arab world is known as Kubaba or Ka'ba, the big black stone in Mecca, which sounds suspiciously like "Cybele" (the C sounded like K), a goddess worshipped in their lands in the old days. The Ka'ba stone was originally called "the old woman", and contains a mark known as the impression of Aphrodite. The priests that care for the stone are called "Beni Shayba", "the sons of the old women".[579] The Islamic logo with the star and crescent represents the moon and Venus!

So, the goddess is at the root of Islam, and goddess worship survived well into Islamic times, in private. In a museum in Egypt, I saw female figurines from the 5th century AD that looked like Neolithic ones from thousands of years earlier!

Then there are the Sufis, who practice a more feminine, ecstatic form of Islam. Sufi dervishes still wear the double axe, a symbol of the goddess since Minoan times. They do a ritual called the *zikr*, a communal trance practice involving chanting and rhythmic movements.

Arabic cultures were only mildly patrist until 1000 CE, when they fell under the influence of Central Asian empires and became much more puritanical about sex and women. That was when they colonized Northern India. Indian men would kill the women to save them from capture by the Arabs. In the invasion of Jaisalmer, more than 24,000 women died.

Some parts of India were already more patristic than their conquerors though, with their practice of ritual widow murder: the whole crowd took part in stabbing a woman after her husband's death. Independent women without men were a threat to the whole society.[580] DeMeo asks us, what kind of training would a young man need to murder his own mother?[581] The Arabic conquerors, to their credit, attempted to curb this horror.

The widows were usually drugged so that they would not resist. Imagine living your whole life knowing that this is how you'll end up: the people you've known all your life stabbing you to death? When we see the underpinnings of our culture in the most extreme examples of patriarchy, we can see the dynamics behind it, and understand the virulent misogyny that's all over the Internet.

Perhaps the harshest patriarchy of all time was the Sassanid Persian Empire. Kings had harems consisting of thousands of concubines and eunuchs. Ninety percent of eunuchs died while being castrated, but the few who lived fetched such a high price on the slave market that it was still worth doing.[582] These harems were hellish realms of disease, scandal, violence, rape, and boredom. Their holy book blamed the first woman, the "queen of all whore demons", for bringing evil into the world by having intercourse with the devil.[583]

GREECE

In the earliest written records of Europe, the Linear B tablets from Mycenean Crete, women were on equal terms with men. They held land on the same terms.[584] Men and women were segregated into work groups, and young kids stayed with the mother.

The tablets don't mention marriage or family life. More women are mentioned in the tablets than men, and when men are mentioned it's as the sons of women.[585] The only time that men are described as sons of fathers is among the ruling class at Pylos, Crete.[586] Recall that in Minoan Crete, women predominated in social settings.[587] Power was divided between the priestly and political, male and female.

There's a gap of a hundred years between the tablets found in the city of Knossos, and the next ones found in Pylos. During that gap in the historical record, there's a new development: pairs of gods appear in the tablets, such as Zeus and Diwia, Zeus and Hera, Poseidon and Posidaeia. Before that it was only goddesses.

One document from 1000 BCE, during the apocalyptic Dark Age at the dusk of the Bronze Age, gives us a window into that time. *The Journey of Wen-Amon to Phoenicia* chronicles a traveler who petitions a queen for protection in this time of piracy. Obviously, there were still powerful women at that time.[588]

We're told that our Western culture began with the classical Greeks, who invented true culture. But, as *The Chalice and the Blade* points out, we're never taught about the high culture and flushing toilets of Minoan Crete. We're taught that Pythagoras brought us philosophy, mathematics, geometry, and other scientific disciplines. But no one tells us that he learned these things form Themistoclea, a priestess at the goddess temple of Delphi. We're told that Socrates is the father of philosophy, but not that he was taught it by Ditema, a priestess of Mantinea. These priestesses advised the leaders of the Greeks in every major decision.[589]

Yet, in the first epics of Western literature, the most powerful figures are female. In Homer's Odyssey, Odysseus is a prisoner of the nymph Calypso, ruler of the island of Ogygia. He's saved by Athena, and then ends up in the lands of the Phaecians, ruled by the princess Nausicaa. He tangles with female gorgons, sirens, and the queen-sorceress Circe.

When Odysseus finally makes it home, he finds out that his wife has been besieged with suitors who want to marry her to gain control of Ithaca; this tells us that matrilineal succession, through marrying a woman, was the way to power in those days. Anyways, he kills all the suitors, tells the maids to clean up the bloody mess, and then murders the maids for the shame of having been raped by those suitors. That's a hero for you.[590]

In fact, the early Greek histories make it clear that succession to the throne was through marrying a woman. The narratives from the ancient kingdoms of Elis, Aegina, Aetolia, Argos, Lycia, Salamis, Attica, Sparta and Ithaca describe these succession rules.[591]

The Dorian Greeks, our cultural ancestors, were the Indo-Europeans who invaded the indigenous civilization of ancient Greece. They appropriated the culture and pretended it was theirs, and we still believe it today.[592] But the best parts of Greek culture can be traced to earlier epochs before the Dorian invasion.

These cultural threads survived underground in the mystery school traditions that still worshipped the goddess as Demeter and

266

Persephone.[593] Anyone who spoke Greek and had never committed a murder was welcome at the ancient fertility rites, in which a child was conceived in a sacred marriage. These rites were practiced for thousands of years.[594]

The oracles were also remnants of the old ways. These women went barefoot, never washed their feet, and slept on the bare ground: in these ways, they stayed connected to mother earth.[595]

Later, in Roman times, the traveler Pausanias reported that the goddess was still the main deity in the countryside. Throughout the classical Greek period, the ancient fertility religion was still celebrated during the festival of Anthesteria, when the queen performed symbolic copulation with the priest of Dionysus. Perhaps in the good old days of the Neolithic, it wasn't symbolic.[596]

While Plato and Socrates believed in equal rights for women, Aristotle wrote that women were incomplete and inferior beings of a totally different kind than men. His pseudo-scientific reasoning was that semen is the divine essence, and since women are too cold to create semen, they have no souls. This became the founding philosophy of the incipient patriarchy. From then on, the subjugation of women was seen as natural and inevitable in Western civilization.

The early wars of Sparta can be interpreted as a conflict between the conservative matriarchy and incipient patriarchy. Plato tells a story of how Deiphontes became king through the traditional matrilineal succession, via his marriage to Hyrnetho, the princess. But his sons wanted to become king instead of their sister's husband as tradition dictated, so a battle ensued.[597] These battles mirror the ones over matrilineal vs patrilineal succession in Anatolia.

Legends recount battles between armies of women, the Amazons, and armies of men. Paintings depict these, too, with bloody scenes of women being slaughtered.

For a long time, the Amazons were assumed to be a myth. But then they discovered the graves of warrior women. Perhaps there never was a female warrior society that lived without men, but without a doubt, large

267

numbers of women defended themselves fiercely in the Bronze Age. They fought back!

Amazons poured in from the regions that were matrilineal holdouts. These were remote and rugged places where Old European survivors had maintained their ancient goddess and learned to retaliate — Lydia, Lycia and Ephesus in Anatolia; Libya, Scythia, and the River Thermadon in Asia Minor. Art depicts parades to honor women killed in battle, carrying the banner of the matriarchy: a figure-of-8 shield.[598] Pausanias writes that a town called Tegea was a matriarchy with enough female warriors to overpower a huge force of men.[599] It was founded by refugees from the Trojan War; the Trojans were on the side of more freedom for women. The ruins of Tegea were discovered in 2018 by archaeologist Eleni Korka, who found it based on historical accounts of the location.[600]

Amazons appear in legend as the enemies of Hercules, who was the champion of the new patriarchal order. His mission was to steal the Amazon queen Hippolyta's girdle, a symbol of female independent sexual power. When she refused to give it to him, he slaughtered all of her champions, all women with beautiful names. When the last one standing, Melanippe, surrenders, he doesn't kill her but rapes her instead, taking her girdle, knowing this was worse than death for her. This was a landmark moment in the psychology of the Western world: men steal the power from the Great Mother, who had for so long been the ultimate source of power in the universe.[601] This was the turning point where history began. It's been a shitshow ever since.

Homer is the first to describe the Amazons, in about 750 BCE, as women equal to men, when writing about the Trojan War four hundred years before his time.[602] Pliny the historian reports that the Amazons founded the famous city of Ephesus on the west coast of Turkey.

Figure 11-1: The goddess Artemis of Ephesus with many breasts, photo by the author.

The book *On the Trail of the Women Warriors* describes an Amazon depicted on an ancient vase: "a determined-looking beefy girl in a short black tunic who pulls back a sling while showing her noble profile and who conveys a real sense of muscle and athletic power." In addition to the bow and arrow, the Amazons' signature weapon was a spear with a sickle attached.[603] I guess this came in handy for farming when there were no wars.

Some of the defeated Amazons joined a tribe of Scythians and married the men, creating the hybrid tribe of the Sauromatians, whose women had to kill a male enemy before they could marry.[604] The historian Diodorus and others report that Alexander the Great had an Amazon girlfriend who wanted to conceive a superhero girl child. They hunted lions together.[605] That sounds like a romantic date.

Amazons, and women warriors in general, were the stuff of legend until the 70's, when archaeologists noticed that some of the Scythians buried with weapons were female. One grave in Russia contained three generations of women with battle scars in one tomb. (This also proves they were matrilineal, not surprisingly.) More than 300 Scythian warrior women have been unearthed. There were also female warriors among

269

the Mongols in the time of Genghis Khan.[606] Lately I've stumbled across several articles detailing discoveries of female warriors, and hunters, from all around the world. Two were found in Armenia, from the Urartu era.[607]

The Greeks as we knew them were a hybrid culture, an amalgam of Indo-European newcomers and the indigenous peoples who survived into historic times as the Carians, Leleges, Lydians, Lycians, and Pelasgians. These cultures were spoken of by classical Greek historians such as Herodotus and Strabo. The Lydians had a famous Queen, Omphale. Countless other warrior-queens are mentioned, such as Telessilla, the warrior poet who led the women of Argos to defend their city against invaders. Zababi and Sansi were Arabian warrior-queens from 740 BCE whose armies contained many women. Queen Zenobia Septimia defended Syria on horseback, in full armor.[608]

We can infer that Old Europe was matrilineal based on the survival of matrilineal succession into historic times, in the strongholds where matrist culture survived the longest. These societies, described by classical historians, spoke non-Indo-European languages. We also find matrilineal succession in places where Indo-Europeans absorbed Old European traditions, such as the Teutons and the Slavs. It was particularly strong in the Aegean islands, especially Lesbos, Lemos, Naxos, and Kos, where matrilineal succession for property was still the rule at the end of the 18th century. Of those islands, 16th century English traveler John Hawkins wrote: "In the large number of the islands the eldest daughter takes as her inheritance a portion of the family house … the other daughters, when they marry off in succession, are likewise entitled to a portion." He mentioned 13 islands where this was the case.[609]

These traditions persisted longer where the Indo-European presence was weak or where the Old European substratum was strong, such as Greece, and the Etruscan area in Italy. There is a strong correlation between non-Indo-European languages and matrilineal succession in places all over the world.[610]

Strabo's book *Geography*, from the time of Jesus, has many references to powerful women. He referred to the poet Sappho as "an extraordinary person", and praised Queen Amastris of Herakleia and Arete of Kyrene, the head of the Kyrenaian school of philosophy.

Strabo is the only classical historian to focus on the female scholars of the classic Greek period, such as Hestiaia of Alexandria, and Queen Aba of Olbe, who ruled alone in southern Anatolia. Perhaps Strabo was interested in powerful women because he named his ancestors from the female side; he came from a family with strong matrilineal roots. Also, he served a queen, Pythodoris, who sponsored his work.[611]

Herodotus, another classical Greek historian, wrote of the Agathyrsi people, who had group marriage "in order that they should all be blood kin and that their family relationships should prevent them from harboring envy and hostility toward one another."[612] He also mentions the Massagetae under the reign of Queen Tomyris as "promiscuous". Another historian, Damascenus, noticed the same custom among the Galagtophagi, who were "distinguished for righteousness and hold their women and property in common."[613]

Julius Caesar noted yet another example in Roman times, that of the natives of the British Isles: "by tens and by twelves, husbands possessed their wives in common; and especially brothers with brothers and parents with their children."[614] In other words, women had multiple men. Then there were the Garamantians of Libya, who maintained free sexuality and high status for women into modern times.[615]

Of the Termilae tribe, Herodotus says: "they take their names not from their fathers but from their mothers, and when one is asked by his neighbor who he is, he will say that he is the son of such a mother, and rehearse the mothers of his mother. Indeed, if a female citizen marries a slave, her children are considered pure-blooded; but if a male citizen, even the most prominent of them, takes an alien wife or concubine, the children are dishonored."[616] This was also true of the Lycians of western Turkey.

Herodotus tells us that his native Halicarnassus was ruled by a queen, Artemisia, even though she had an adult son. She commanded five warships in battle.[617]

So we see that the classical Greeks had neighbors who were governed by queens and practiced free sexuality and matrilineal succession. But in Athens, women were either actual slaves or confined to the home in dark, unsanitary buildings. Meanwhile men participated in public life in beautiful courtyards, discussing politics and philosophy, exercising, and having sex with courtesans. Women were not permitted to own land. Wives could not attend the theater, although the *hetairai*, the courtesans, could. These beautiful and educated women commanded respect and influence. But in general, women were not considered worthy of love, so the greatest love was between a man and a boy (the boys had no choice but to serve the men sexually).

Girls were usually married off at fourteen to a man of thirty or older. To divorce they needed a male relative to bring the case to court. We know of only three women to divorce during the entire classical era. But unlike women in some civilizations, such as Victorian Europe 1900 years later, women could at least masturbate, and they must have needed it.[618]

The famous play Lysistrata tells us about an anti-war movement started by Athenian women: they refused to have sex until men stopped the war. Men shut this down using ridicule and trivialization, strategies still common today to silence women. We're told that "women's issues" like peace and the human rights of half the world are trivial.[619]

However, Athenian women did have one day of the year when they could let loose and remember the good old days. It was a women's holiday where they sat on beds of willow branches mourning the goddess Persephone, eating pomegranates (an old symbol of the goddess), telling dirty jokes, and making penis-shaped cakes.[620]

Meanwhile, women of the classical era in the Greek city-state of Sparta, Athens's rival, had it a bit better. Here, the pre-Indo-European substrate was larger. Women weren't shamed for speaking their minds and were witty and outspoken. They were allowed to go outside and exercise and were well-fed with strong muscles. (Athenians didn't waste good food on women).

Spartan women enjoyed sexual freedom. Husbands who went to war didn't care what their wives did at home. Paternity wasn't an obsession with the Spartans, you see. As long as Spartan women were raising mighty warriors, it didn't matter whose sperm was involved.[621] So virginity was not required and there were no "illegitimate" children. Marriage was matrilocal, and they practiced fraternal polyandry, meaning a woman married multiple brothers. Their clan names even retain a female linguistic ending, "-idas", from their matrilineal roots.[622]

Paternity didn't used to be a thing in Athens, either, of course. Perhaps all cultures have a matrilineal past if you go back far enough. Greek tradition tells us that the first king of Athens, Kekrops, invented marriage, while before that, intercourse was promiscuous, and children didn't know their fathers. Kekrops himself became king by marrying a princess, during the transitional phase when kingship passed via matrilineal succession.

I'll relate the story as told by the Roman historian Varro, and passed on by Wikipedia, about how this marriage thing came to be:

> The olive-tree suddenly appeared in Attica, and at the same time there was an eruption of water in another part of the country. So king Kekrops sent to inquire of Apollo at Delphi what these portents might signify. The oracle answered that the olive and the water were the symbols of Athena and Poseidon respectively, and that the people of Attica were free to choose which of these deities they would worship.
>
> Accordingly, the question was submitted to a general assembly of the citizens and citizenesses; for in these days women had the vote as well as men. All the men voted for the god, and all the women voted for the goddess; and as there was one more woman than there were men, the goddess appeared at the head of the poll. Chagrined at the loss of the election, the male candidate flooded the country with the water of the sea, and to

appease his wrath it was decided to deprive women of the vote and to forbid children to bear their mother's names for the future.[623]

That auspicious day was deleted from the calendar, and promptly forgotten until now.

EGYPT

In Egypt, as of the 1st millennium, women still had some influence. A high priestess was consulted on all matters in the government at Thebes.[624] Alexander the Great brought back patrist values from the east, which put an end to the high priestess. But even in the following Ptolemy period during which Greece ruled Egypt, matrilineal kinship determined kingship as it had since predynastic times. That is, kings ruled but gained the throne by marrying a princess. It lasted until the Roman invasion in 30 BCE. [625] But new queens who ruled alone continue to be discovered, as I write this in 2022, who were previously unknown.

In 430 BCE, Hypatia, the beloved mathematician and astronomer, was murdered by a mob who dragged her into a church, stripped her naked, and scraped her with oyster shells.[626] I sobbed when I watched the movie version. I guess they didn't like female teachers.

Rome was initially more female-friendly than Athens, because the Etruscans taught them everything they knew. The Etruscans were an old non-Indo-European, matrilineal society from Italy who gave the barbarian Romans culture — writing, the arts, and agriculture.

The Greek historian Theopompus records with alarm that Etruscan women exercised naked along with the men. They did everything along with the men: drinking and toasting, lounging around after dinner. Paternity was not a thing with them either, of course; control and limitation of women is all about paternity. No one cared who fathered the children, and they married multiple men at once. Men, women and children made love in public. In the words of Theopompus: "It is not a disgrace for them to be seen naked. They do not share their couches with their husbands but with the other men who happen to be present,

274

and they propose toasts to anyone they choose. They are expert drinkers and very attractive."[627]

Figure 11-2: Famous life-size statue of an Etruscan couple. Photo by the author in the Etruscan Museum, Rome. Love the dreadlocks.

Etruscan city-states were governed by magistrates. Historical sources mention monarchs, but the word "king" seems to be a later creation. Etruscan texts don't mention public officials. So, with Etruscan tutelage, early Romans had no official institution of marriage, and there was no taboo against sexual pleasure. But later this changed with influences from the east. After that, the poet Ovid was put to death for writing heterosexual love poems! The crime for pre-marital sex was getting molten lead poured down your throat![628]

Even the Etruscans succumbed to patriarchy from the 7th century BCE onward. The nobles had growing power. Funerary practices switched from small pit burials with razors for men and spindle whorls for women to ornate graves for elite warriors with status symbols. According to the Etruscan Museum in Rome, there was a new necessity of proclaiming role and status. Female graves had more and more personal ornaments, as women became more and more ornamental.

275

THE REST OF EUROPE AND AFRICA

Western Europe had less influence from patrist groups than in the east. The areas furthest from the desert maintained higher status for women, and less sexual repression. Spain, Italy, and Eastern Europe were closer to the desert and therefore more patrist.[629]

The Basque people from the highlands of France and Spain are a remnant of indigenous Europeans. Their language is the only non-Indo-European one still spoken in Western Europe. Their religion of the Goddess, use of a lunar calendar, and matrilineal laws of inheritance continued into the early 20th century. In the French Basque area, the law codes dictated total equality between the sexes, and women served as judges in medieval and modern times.[630]

Matrifocal marriage survived in the Scottish Highlands into the 20th century. Matrilineal succession was the rule with other Celtic peoples as well; it survived in Germany and Scandinavia, where even royal titles and property passed through the women. Among Germanic tribes, kings had to marry a queen to attain the throne. Matrilineal succession for kingship also shows up in the ancient Welsh epic the *Mabinogion* and in Irish literature, where a king has sex with a priestess of the goddess to gain the throne.[631]Caesar noted that in Iron Age Britain, women had many husbands.[632]

The Gauls of France also maintained some old ways. According to historian Diodorus Siculus, Gaulish women rivaled their husbands not only in stature but also in strength.[633]

Some of these tribal Europeans persisted into the Christian era, depending on how remote they were from so-called "civilization". Their ancient traditions of honoring nature and the earth goddess were absorbed into Christianity. Eostre, the Anglo-Saxon fertility goddess, gave her name to Easter. The birth of Jesus was assigned to Winter Solstice. The horned deer, a goddess symbol going back tens of thousands of years, ended up in our weird modern Santa myth. Gods became saints.

Early Christians still worshipped the divine feminine, and women served as leaders, starting with Mary Magdalene. Leaders were chosen by lot. Then Christian scholar Clement of Alexandria preached that "every woman should blush at the thought that she is a woman".[634] Paul, the ultimate misogynist, preached, "Let a woman learn in silence with all submissiveness. I permit no woman to teach or to have authority over me: she is to keep silent." So, after the end of the 2nd century, groups with female preachers had become heretics.[635]

Around 900, as a response to ugly papal debauchery, it became illegal for priests to live with any female, even their mothers.[636] Christianity had become a force for spreading patrism. One Christian holiday involved whipping children. Anyone who insulted a priest was subject to sadistic torture.[637]

It got worse with the Crusades. Crusaders brought back patrist customs from the east, such as the chastity belt and the wedding band.[638] When the Crusaders saw how submissive the Muslim women were, they borrowed the custom of wearing wedding bands on the left fourth finger, as we still do today.

It was during the Crusades that the slave trade of African people by Arabic people began. Arabs set up slave trading centers all along the Red Sea Coast and on the island of Zanzibar.[639] Maybe this is when patrist traits spread to the Bantu people in sub-Saharan African, who then subjugated the peaceful Bata (pygmy), Bushmen, and Hottentot people. Those oppressed people didn't become patrist in response, but chose instead to flee into fringe areas that were less desirable to their oppressors. The spread of patrism is traceable in the trait of circumcision, which declines as you go further south into the African continent.[640]

In the 700's, Arab armies invaded Russia, India and China. On the plus side, they tried to abolish ritual murder in India. Their historians recorded that when a big chief died, his female slaves and animals were piled on a boat to be burned alive out at sea.[641] But they were unable to stamp out human sacrifice. It continued in India until the British made it illegal when they, in turn, invaded.[642]

277

It was the Huns — Central Asian nomads — who had carried the patrist customs to India in the first place, such as cranial deformation and infant swaddling. They also transmitted them to Slavic people in Eastern Europe. Slavs had free sexual lives and high status for women before their contact with Central Asian nomads and Christians. [643] Especially in the more isolated areas of Russia and Ukraine, people remained happy until the 900's when they were converted to a harsh form of Christianity. Many girls killed themselves rather than face a life of sex and servitude to a man they didn't like. [644] Unlike their counterparts in the rest of Eurasia, they weren't raised to believe that's normal.

When the even more isolated parts of Russia were converted in the 1500's, girls put up a fight. They threw rocks at the priests and went on choosing their own husbands, divorcing and remarrying.[645] I would *love* to see that made into a movie.

England also remained isolated due to the English Channel, so they lived pretty freely. Women could own land, and premarital sex was allowed. This changed with the Norman invasion in 1066: 20% of their population was slaughtered. The Normans colonized and became the ruling class. Even so, people were still more free than on the mainland. The old horse warrior culture from Central Asia lived on in medieval Europe in the knights, bored young men wandering around looking for trouble and starting wars.[646]

Meanwhile, the Turks had their own style of massacre, torture, and rape-mutilation of women and children. Under the Ottomans in the 1700's, the king's brothers were imprisoned in a cage with a slave until it was their time to rule. One can only imagine how sadistic they would be after that upbringing. As for their harems, as James DeMeo puts it: "a place of murderous intrigues, sadistic cruelties, sexual frustration, pathologies, disease, suicide and misery."[647]

The Christians of that era started a charming new custom, the *auto-da-fe*: popular public mass murders of heretics on special Sundays. In Russia, it was the era of the Tsars, with their special brand of sadistic cruelty and huge royal harems. Any Russian noble could do anything he wanted to any women he saw.[648]

Recall from Chapter 2 that history goes in cycles between permissive times, when some sexual freedom, women's rights, and creativity are allowed, and authoritarian times, when war and male domination re-assert themselves. For more information, read Gordon Rattray Taylor's book *Sex in History*, which, like so many of the most important books, is now out of print. Ilya Prigogine, Isabel Stengers, Edward Lorenz, and mathematician Ralph Abraham are also great sources for further reading on these cycles.[649]

Psychologist David Winter proves the connection between war and repressive attitudes toward women. One example he gives is Spain during wartime: they adopted the Moorish custom of imprisoning women indoors.[650] War is great for authoritarians, as it not only reinforces male dominance but also allows for suspension of civil rights.[651] The reforms of the Enlightenment, when Christianity gave way to Science as the main disseminator of official truth, was catalyzed by the invention of the printing press, which allowed for widespread literacy. Women such as Madame Geoffrin hosted intellectual salons to discuss the new ideas that spread like wildfire, questioning the patriarchal status quo.[652]

In some parts of the Christian world, during the Reformation, there was a call for reform in the treatment of women and children. They stopped infant swaddling, except in Germany, Eastern Europe, and Russia. Russia, with its large population of Central Asian horse warriors, held on to sadistic customs concerning sex and families. But France and Italy put an end to most forms of torture.

The Industrial Revolution was a huge win for patriarchy. Women had previously maintained independence by managing their own income and home economies. But now, goods previously made by women were made in factories. A recent article in *Scientific American* about the financial power of Viking women through the textile trade (only recently acknowledged now that archaeology is starting to pay attention to women), states: "It was in part the Industrial Revolution that sealed the

279

fates of women as second-class citizens and ensured that Western society would become so vehemently patriarchal."[653]

When the pendulum swung, it was time for the witch burnings. Nine million or more women along with millions of men were murdered between 1484 and 1784. Everyone confessed under torture. Sometimes they would kill off the entire female population of a town in one day. For sexual "sins" they got impaled through the vagina and paraded around, or torn apart by flaming tongs.[654]

The witch trials finally destroyed ancient knowledge about healing plants that had persisted since the cavewoman days, since healers were a threat to new male doctors who loved to bleed people with leeches. They also eliminated millions of women just for being too smart, too sexy, or too independent.[655] Children, writers, poets, scientists, Jews and queer people were also persecuted.[656]

And then, of course, was the African slave trade by Arabic and European people, and, the European colonization of the Americas: possibly the most heinous colonialism the world has ever seen ... the pinnacle of patriarchy. White supremacy was invented and became perhaps the most brutal tool for oppression of all time. A great deal has been written about this, so I'll touch on it only briefly, as it's beyond the scope of this book.

The Americas had a different fate than Asia and Africa in the European colonization, for two reasons: one, the isolation of the continents meant people had no resistance to diseases, so the "population replacement", as they say in academia, was greater. Two, the invaders settled in the Americas with their families in huge numbers, as opposed to Africa and Asia where they mostly raped the women, enslaved the men, and destroyed the environment, stealing the resources and bleeding them dry.

I'll discuss just one example of transmissions of traits via the colonization of the Americas: that of female seclusion, the practice of imprisoning women in the home. This first arose in cultures closest to the desert, such as northwestern India and the Middle East. When the

280

Moors of North Africa occupied Spain for 800 years, they passed on their superior civilization to Spain, as they were more culturally advanced than Europe at that time, but also passed on their practice of female seclusion. The Spanish in turn passed it to some cultures in South America, where upper class women were confined to the home until recent times.

Meanwhile, religion was gradually giving way to science. While the post-Enlightenment scientific world was more rational and slightly less brutal than the Christian one, it invented new ways to justify keeping women as second-class citizens. Now it wasn't God, it was women's biological functions that made them unfit for education and public life. They were inferior not because of a magic apple, but because of their "diseases" of menstruation, menopause and pregnancy. Freud made it even worse, by representing women as incomplete humans whose lack of a penis defines their entire psychological makeup. Who *wouldn't* have penis envy when raised to believe you were nothing without one?

The first feminists, tough broads like Sojourner Truth and Florence Nightingale, changed the world with the movement to treat the mentally ill more humanely and the abolitionist movement to free the enslaved people. Suddenly women entered the public world in large numbers, with the emergence of new careers like nursing and social work that were open to women. They flooded into public life and caused huge changes in the world. As Riane Eisler says, "feminism has upgraded the situation of both women and men."[657]

As a response to the 19th century women's movement, there was a huge rise in aggravated assaults on women, bone-breaking beatings, and tortures such as putting out women's eyes. This happened all over the world. There were public executions of women in Iran and torture of women in Latin America. Of course, violence against women has always been one way the patriarchy keeps them in line. Most people know that the phrase "rule of thumb" refers to the custom in England and America where men were allowed to whip their wives as long as the whip was no thicker than a thumb. Thankfully domestic violence is now illegal, but still epidemic. A woman is raped in the United States every thirteen seconds.[658]

ASIA

As I've said, this book is focused on the Western world, since that's where I come from, but here are a few details from Asia.

Most of Southeast Asia, meaning Thailand, Malaysia, and Indonesia, remained matrist until recently. The matrilineal Thai and Malay people are mentioned in the chapter on anthropology. Myanmar retained more rights for women due to its geographical and political isolation.

In eastern Asia, the Ainu of the islands off Japan remained matrist into modern times. They enjoyed a high civilization of lovemaking, poems, and singing and dancing until about 400 AD. Only women served the gods, and menstruation was a cause for celebration. Remnants of these customs persist even today; tourists flock to see them. Meanwhile, in *mainland* Japan, beating women in temples was a popular pastime until World War II.[659]

As I said in the last chapter, China became patriarchal early in the game, with its proximity to the desert. Clearly, they had influence from Indo-Europeans, as Chinese goddesses are similar to Indo-European sun and dawn goddesses.[660] Like everywhere, it got progressively worse over time. Kings had harems of a thousand women who were instructed to go limp during sex, a practice known as *"Cong fou"*. What kind of sick man wants that? One prince had his entire team of attendants buried alive in his tomb. Things got even worse when the red-haired invaders, the Yueh Chi, destroyed the peaceful Andronov and Karasuk cultures.

Of course, there was the famous custom of foot binding, where the bones of the foot were repeatedly crushed to make helpless women with cute little feet. Many died from infections. All were permanently disabled.[661] Sexual repression got even worse during the Confucian era in the 800's: women were spoken of as the root of all evil. Vaginal blood became taboo, and dangerous to the ordinary man, so Buddhist priests had to deflower virgins on their wedding night.[662]

282

But pockets of matrism persisted. The histories of the Tang dynasties in the 6th-9th centuries CE speak of the Country of Women, the Yongning, who were ruled by queens and a council of female ministers. Men took their mothers' names.

The Country of Women disappeared from the historical record after the 9th century. But chroniclers speak of the Quang and other groups as people who knew their mothers but not their fathers. Chinese legends describe the high mountains of the Tibetan borderland as the mythical paradise of the queen mother. The descendants of these people persisted into the modern era: the Naxi and Mosuo described in the Anthropology chapter.[663]

THE AMERICAS

We delved into some archaeological data on the Americas in the previous chapter. There was a vast diversity of different cultures, some extremely patrist, some matrist. It's only starting to come out now, as old paradigms are being toppled, that they were much more advanced than was admitted. There were large cities that were decimated by the germs the Europeans brought. Without the germ advantage, the invasion might have gone very differently.

Accounts of the cultures the Europeans found were all filtered through the minds of men and their prejudices. They spoke only with men in the local cultures, and therefore missed the female perspective: the ways that women held power and influence in their communities, and the goddesses they worshiped.

For example, Heide Goettner-Abendroth wrote volumes on matriarchal societies, discussing how male observers of Hopi culture missed the female kachina doll dances, the life-cycle festivals that were entirely in the hands of the women, name-giving through the matriline, female ownership of houses, great women architects, and so on.[664]

Also, it did not serve the purposes of the invaders to consider how advanced the cultures they destroyed were. So little mention was made, for example, of the democratic decision-making process of the Tlaxcala of Mexico who joined with the Spanish to defeat the Aztec.[665]

283

Plus, the influence of the Europeans caused native American groups to become more male dominated very rapidly. In trading and negotiations, when European men ignored women, the locals learned to do the same.

For example, the anonymous friar-chronicler of the Tarascan culture of 16th century Mexico admits to interpreting the culture through his perspective. The Spanish observers whose accounts of the indigenous have come down to us disproportionately recorded the gender relations that resonated with them. The imposition of European gender customs disrupted existing gender roles, and the Spanish understood that female power was a barrier to colonial rule. The Tarascans responded to humiliation by the Spanish by making male figures central in the stories they recounted to chroniclers, and emphasizing their more assertive and aggressive tendencies.[666] It's the same thing that happened in Africa: people lost respect for their female leaders when the invading English showed them no respect.

But traces of pre-patriarchal Mexico are faint. My visit to the archaeology museum in Mexico City left me depressed; it's all about empires and wars. The figurines are almost all leering, mean-looking males. The only nude female figurines were attributed to the Huaxtecas, with a sign saying their region was predominated by female imagery. The only other female artifact was entitled "Hueca figure". I could find no information anywhere about the Huaxteca or Hueca people.

A visit to the museum in Cholula, near the city of Puebla, lifted my spirits. There were more female figurines, such as one from the Guanajuato people, and far more happy-looking faces and whimsical animal representations.

I don't pretend to know whether patriarchy arrived in Mexico from overseas or if it developed independently there. Perhaps it was always present. It has been strong there for a long time. One trace of female agency that remains is in Juchitan, Oaxaca: women are at the center of the market economy. They make all the decisions at home. Thanks to their management of household funds, there is little malnutrition or abject poverty as seen in other places where the money goes toward the local bar. Women have no pressure to marry, and there is no stigma around single motherhood. They are strong and independent, not seen as inferior.[667]

The people of Juchitan are part of the ancient matrifocal isthmus Zapotec culture, the builders of egalitarian cities such as Monte Alban. The ruins feature no images of rulers, and everyone had the same high standard of living, with well-insulated adobe and high-quality pottery.[668] They were isolated from other cultures by a mountain barrier, like so many other people who have retained more autonomy for women. They are the only linguistic group in Mesoamerica who currently produces literature in their native language. [669] While male historians and anthropologists ignored women's roles and stories, the Zapotecs themselves attach great importance to them, and women fought the colonizers with equal strength as the men.[670]

Zapotec women don't currently hold many formalized political roles, but wield economic and personal power, and are strong and independent. Unlike most other cultures in the region, which tend to be puritanical about bodily functions, fathers support mothers during labor. [671] Body parts and functions are not taboo words in their language.[672] Children are not physically punished.[673] Macho behavior is negatively sanctioned. Women don't critizie each other.[674] These are the kinds of remnants of feminine partnership cultures that remain even when formal female power is a thing of the past.

CHAPTER TWELVE

MYTHOLOGY

I was tempted to leave this chapter out entirely, for the sake of academic credibility. By definition, mythology is the study of made-up stuff. But taken together with the academic disciplines of the other chapters, it adds to the picture: the myths tell the same stories as the written words of the historical period. While many people use the word "myth" to mean "untrue", most myths are true stories that were passed down orally instead of written down. They may have gotten distorted over time, and we can't prove them scientifically, but there are usually kernels of truth worth considering.

I was also tempted to skip this chapter because mythology is so complex that it feels irresponsible to do such a cursory study. My task, as in each of the other chapters, is to show that males supplanted females in importance starting around 3500 BCE, in what had previously been female-centric cultures all over the world. It happened gradually: goddesses got demoted to consorts, then deleted completely. The mythology mirrors the recorded history of the Bronze Age: from queens to kings appointed by women, to kings who attained power through marrying women, to kings passing power to their sons. Women still held power as priestesses even after they lost political influence, but over time lost even that until they were burned at the stake for that mystical power.

We'll touch on a few systems of mythologies, but the main focus will be on Greece, the mythology most well-known to our Western culture.
286

It's very well preserved, as so much of it was recorded in writing and passed down to us. Classical Greece is considered our cultural origin (while the feminine roots of its own origins are not widely known). But most of all, as we've seen in previous chapters, Greece was a hotbed of matriarchy that persisted into historical times. Greek mythology tells the tale of the transition to patriarchy. The main source for this chapter is the classic masterpiece, Robert Graves' *The White Goddess*. Graves did the comprehensive work on the transition to patriarchy in mythology.

Arthur Evans, the archaeologist who unearthed Minoan Crete and discovered the Linear A and B tablets there, declared that the Minoans had only two deities: the goddess and the subordinate boy god. The goddess, whom the Linear B tablets called *"potnia"*— 'Our Lady" — manifested in many forms, such as mountains (Cybele), animals (Artemis), a dove (Aphrodite), barley (Demeter), the protectress (Hera), goddess of the dead (Persephone), goddess of childbirth (Eileithia), and arouser of the lions (Iphimedeia).[675] The great goddess was often known as the "Queen of Heaven", especially by Biblical prophets in the context of stamping out her worship.[676]

The boy god, clearly inferior to the goddess in Bronze Age Crete, was a primal archetype of the male. He manifested as the spirit of vegetation, of animals, and of a single year. Each year he died and was reborn.[677] He was known to the Greeks as Dionysus. In other cultures, he is called Osiris, Tammuz, or Dumuzi. Jesus was based on this archetype.

Another ancient archetype was the mother-child. The ancient Greeks worshiped Ceres and her child. The Romans called them Fortuna and Jupiter. The Assyrians honored Rhea (known as the mother of the gods) and Ninus her son. In Egypt, Isis and Horus. In Canaan, Ashtoreth and Tammuz. In India, Isi and Iswara.

India was all about the goddess in prehistory. Even Wikipedia admits that the goddess had a central role which became subordinate once the Vedic civilization arose. But even Vedic hymns are dedicated to the goddess Usha. The Vedic gods were born from three divine mothers mentioned in the Rig Veda: Aditi, Prithvi and Saraswati. Aditi, depicted as a faceless, lotus-headed goddess in birthing stance, was probably the

287

main ancient mother goddess of prehistoric sites like Harappa. Hindus still pray to Her with this hymn:

> I am the Sovereign Queen; the treasury of all treasures; the chief of all objects of worship; whose all-pervading Self manifests all gods and goddesses; whose birthplace is in the midst of the causal waters; who in breathing forth gives birth to all created worlds, and yet extends beyond them, so vast am I in greatness.[678]

Besides the great goddess, boy god, and mother/son archetypes, another widespread ancient myth is of an earlier time of harmony. The Garden of Eden story is the most familiar example. Perhaps this is a cultural memory of the peaceful Neolithic period.

OLD EUROPEAN GODDESSES

Marija Gimbutas divided goddesses of Old Europe into three categories: 1. protectresses of life energy and health; 2. daily goddesses (the bird, snake, and madonna); and 3. goddesses of death and regeneration. Different symbols were found for each type. She discovered this through studying thousands of symbols and representations. For example, the cow-bull-ox, crescent, and egg belong in the category of regeneration.[679]

In Çatalhöyük the goddess is shown with leopards, dogs, and lions. Later goddesses are often shown on a throne flanked by a winged griffin and a monkey. The deer and the bear are two animals symbolic of her life-giving powers. Deer and bear beliefs persist to this day in folklore; in northern Asia a pregnant deer is seen as a birthing Mother Goddess. Greek Artemis appears as both a deer and bear; and still today in Lithuania they refer to birthing women as bears.[680]

The bird goddess represents both fertility, and, in the guise of the vulture, death. Water birds, such as geese, cranes, and especially swans, have symbolized the goddess since the Upper Paleolithic. On the walls at Çatalhöyük, vultures are shown with headless humans on towers. (To this day in Turkey, you can find rugs with themes of vultures and fat

288

goddess figures.) In western Europe, the owl fills the same niche as the vulture.

The snake is also connected with cycles of death and rebirth. The Cretan Neolithic snake goddess was sometimes depicted sitting in lotus pose. The most widely known snake goddesses were found in Knossos in Crete, with exposed breasts and snakes wound around their arms. Hence in Indo-European, Christian, and Semitic religions the snake is the symbol of evil, used to demonize the ancient goddess religion.

ASSOCIATION OF THE FEMININE WITH WISDOM AND JUSTICE

The association of femininity with wisdom, intelligence and justice is very ancient. The deity of justice in Egypt was female, Maat. The Nabataean (Arabic) goddess al-Kutba was the patroness of writing, education, and intellectuality. A Basque goddess was the guardian of law codes. Celtic Cerridwen was the deity of intelligence and knowledge.[681] Even the invention of writing is associated with the goddess, used as a sacred script long before its use in imperial bureaucracies.

Spirituality was also associated with the feminine. Ishtar of Babylon was the lady of vision; Ua Zit was the Egyptian goddess of mystic insight. And of course, the oracle at Delphi delivered prophecies at a site holy to the goddess.[682] The Basque priestess "the *serora*" inhabited caves with her female helpers, where they were consulted as oracles; they had higher status than the Catholic priests even into the 20th century. An inscription in Gaul mentions a sisterhood of enchantresses called the "*bristia anderon*".

Let's delve into Robert Graves' *White Goddess*. The very ancient Sumerian white goddess who preceded Ishtar was Belili, goddess of trees and the moon. All trees belonged to her, as well as the wells and springs. The Jews made her name into Belial (*Beliy ya'al*) — The Underworld." The Latin "*bellus*" and all the Latin derived words for "beautiful" like "bella" come from her name. In this pantheon the boy-god Du'uzu (Tammuz), god of corn and pomegranates, was her brother and lover.[683]

FERTILITY RITES

Then there was the goddess Cotytto who was worshiped in Thrace (Bulgaria), Corinth (Greece), and Sicily. Strabo described her worship at nocturnal orgies known as "the *Cotyttia*". The fertility rite of Demeter, the *Thesmaphoria,* was celebrated well into historical times as part of the Eleusinian mysteries. Men castrated themselves in honor of Cybele of Phrygia, goddess of lions and bees. The castration of men to serve the goddess was a frequent theme at the dawn of patriarchy, as men assumed the ancient power of the goddess.[684]

Fertility rites (and orgies) survived into the patriarchal era through mystery schools and ecstatic cults. The divine mating of god and goddess to ensure fertility of the crops was known as *"Hieros Gamos"* in Greek, or "sacred marriage". The priestess had public intercourse with the year king, dressed in goatskins, representing Goat-Dionysus. Then the year king was ritually killed and resurrected as his successor, or a goat was sacrificed in his stead. In England, this was the basis of witches' ceremonies. In Sweden it was known as *"Bükkerwise"*. These fertility rites took place in the spring: May in northern Europe, February in Greece (the "Lesser Mysteries" of the Eleusis mystery school).[685]

The *Hieros Gamos* was also featured in erotic hymns of Ancient Sumer. Tribal kings of Ireland were inaugurated by ritual copulation with the local goddess, such as Medb. Beltaine, the marriage of the May King and May Queen, is still celebrated today by neo-pagans.[686] In early Rome, springtime parades featured huge carved phalluses and a sacred ritual where a married noblewoman and a priest did the deed in front of the whole community.[687]

THE PELASGIANS, INDIGENOUS PEOPLE OF GREECE AND THE AEGEAN

The White Goddess focuses on a people known as the "Pelasgians", or *"Pelasgoi",* as the ancient Greeks called them. These were the indigenous people of Greece before the Indo-European Greeks. The ancient historian Strabo speaks of them as one of the five root races of the Greeks. The word is related to "Philistines", a people from the Levant

290

demonized in the Bible for worshiping Astarte. They were also connected with the Danaans, a mysterious people named after the goddess Danae. (Later Greeks appropriated this name).

The ancients spoke of the Pelasgians as *"Dioi"*, "divine", because only they preserved written language after it was lost in the great flood. They were kin to the Lycians from Crete, and to the neighboring Carians, Lydians and Mysians, all coastal people of Turkey like the Trojans.[688] They were all said to speak the same language — perhaps the one spoken by the oracles, who sounded to the Greeks like chattering birds.

These related Pelasgian peoples were almost certainly descended from the matrilineal Neolithic civilization of Old Europe. Herodotus stated that the Lycians were the least Greek of these "barbarian" (i.e., non-Greek) nations, and that they reckoned descent through the mother, not the father. Matrilineal descent, as well as female independence, was shared by all of the Cretan tribes. This was reported as late as the fourth century AD.[689] The genealogy of the Kings of Nisa in Greek mythology shows descent through the female line.[690] Matrifocal marriage even shows up in the Bible; Delilah stayed with her own tribe after marriage to Samson.

When Achaean Greeks invaded the Peloponnese, they repudiated the great goddess, founded a new patriarchal dynasty, and instituted the Olympian pantheon we all know so well, with Zeus at the head of an equal number of gods and goddesses. The myths of Zeus fighting with his nagging wife Hera (a name associated with the great goddess), and with Apollo of Delphi (a god who dates to the goddess times), reflect the resistance of the Pelasgians to this new religion.

The invasion of the Dorians, the most barbaric of the Indo-European Greeks, involved much sacking and pillaging. Refugees fled in all directions; one branch of this Pelasgian diaspora became the Tuatha de Danaan, who worshiped the goddess Danae of Argos. By the time of Homer's *Odyssey*, Danae had gotten masculinized into Danaus, who brought his daughters the Danaids to Greece from Libya, which a hotbed of goddess matriarchy in classical Greek times.

291

In a well-known myth, the Danaids massacred the sons of Aegyptus on their wedding night. Graves believes that the number of Danaids was 50, because that was the number of priestesses in many goddess cults.[691] This myth likely represents the uprising of the goddess people against the new cult of patriarchal marriage.

Danae is also associated with the Aegean Danuna people who invaded Syria in 1200 BCE along with their allies, 64 other Eastern Mediterranean peoples. The Egyptians called all these related people the "Sea Peoples". They had been forced from their homes by the invading Indo-European hordes.[692] They brought Bronze Age civilization to its knees; 90% of the civilized world died in these religious wars. It was truly the revenge of the goddess.

THE VICTORY OF THE PATRIARCHY: GOOD BECAME EVIL, AND EVIL GOOD

But the eventual victory of the patriarchy was inevitable. Goddesses were converted into gods. Sumerian Belili became Bel, Nana became Anu.[693] Some transitional deities were both male and female; Sun goddess Estan became Istanu, meaning the "father and mother of the oppressed." Apollo replaced Artemis, and their island was renamed from Ortygia, associated only with Artemis, to Delos, associated with both.[694]

Now the main deity was the sky god, associated with morning, daylight, grain, oxen and plowing: Indian Mitra, Baltic Dievas, Roman Janus, Celtic Lug, Icelandic Tyr. Second in importance was the thunder god, hunter and warrior, who would later supplant the sun god. These patriarchal gods carried shining weapons. The goddesses still ruled the moon and the springs and wells, but now they were the wives of gods.

Early Indo-European myths involved mortal males and immortal females, like the Swan Maiden and the prince. She is the source of power for the aging king, bestowing power on him through her annual ritual copulation. Over time she becomes more mortal and subservient, the helpless female pining for a visit from the horse god. Her consort ages, and is either emasculated by her insatiable divine appetites, or is

292

restored. This Proto-Indo-European goddess is both maternal and erotic. But over time she splits into two, the mother and the lover.[695]

As the human representations changed, so did the divine animals. Traditional cultures prized bulls, while later patriarchal ones were all about female cows — the docile, fertile female — and male stallions, for strength. So, while the goddess-worshiping Indus Valley culture in Pakistan had seals of women jumping over bull horns, the later Indian cultures venerated the cow.[696]

The new Indo-European overlords appropriated the most important symbols of the goddess — the serpent, the bull, and the spiral. The five-pointed star, which represents the goddess Venus, is in the heart of the Islamic flag. But the snake, sacred to the main deity of Minoan Crete and to the later oracles of Greece and Rome, was the most important symbol to appropriate; the patriarchal takeover is mythologized by the slaying of the serpent or the dragon. The heroes Hercules, Zeus, and Apollo all do that, in Greek mythology, but it also happens in Indic, Hittite, Irish, and German myths.[697] Baal in the Middle East takes one on. Anthropologist Chris Knight says the myth of the many-headed Hydra symbolized the many mothers in a clan, how female kin worked together to raise children and to resist male control.

And, of course, there's Eve, who dares to disobey the male god at the serpent's advice. And so was woman blamed for all the woes of the world, a political masterpiece.

Another important symbol of the goddess, the horned bull, became literally demonized into the devil. Reality was turned on its head: good became evil, evil good. Rape in myth symbolized the defeat of the feminine. Rome was founded on the rape of the Sabines. Sumerian Enlil became a god when he raped Ninlil.[698]

Another Bible story with this reversal of good and evil is that of Cain and Abel. Cain was the pastoralist, Abel the farmer. This was a conflict between two lifestyles: the Semitic pastoral steppe nomads (J1 haplogroup), vs. the Anatolian farmers (J2 haplogroup). The Semites were of course the chosen people of their jealous, vengeful, violent god.

293

Abel was framed as the murderer in this propaganda piece, while in reality it was the pastoralists murdering the farmers. The followers of Yahweh could murder anyone they wanted, anyone who didn't follow their god, as when Elijah the prophet tricked and murdered 850 followers of Astarte and Baal. How could anyone see them as righteous?

Then there was the time they murdered the beloved queen Jezebel and her entire family for her crime of being a powerful independent woman and a priestess of Astarte and Baal. She is a real historical figure but there is no truth to their slander of her as a "harlot." Yet her name to this day is synonymous with an evil temptress. Isn't it time to stop telling these old lies?

While the old religion was all about the fecundity of nature, the new one was all about moral laws and punishment. The old religion believed in reincarnation and regeneration, death as a portal back to the womb: graves were uterus-shaped. The new religion, on the other hand, invented hell.[699] In Indo-European myths you traveled on a river or a chariot to the cold and swampy underworld. There was no return to the mother for rebirth.

But the goddess of death lived on as Baltic Ragana, Polish Jedza, Basque ari, Irish Morrigan, and Russian Baba Yaga. When the Indo-European takeover of Europe was complete, the goddess was demonized into a witch, but she kept her ancient symbols of death: toad, frog, hedgehog, and fish.[700] Patriarchy appropriated the bull, serpent and spiral, but it didn't want these.

It seems that the origins of hell and heaven, as well as judgement day, revelation, and angels and demons, go back to Zoroastrianism in Iran. This was the first monotheistic, male god religion, with the possible exception of when Egyptian pharaoh Akhenaten attempted to impose one. (He was hated for it and it didn't catch on.) It's interesting that Zoroastrianism comes from the same region as the Maykop, the first known patriarchal people. Funny how good and evil are reversed between this Persian religion and their Indian cousins, who see the *daevas* (angels) as good and *ahuras* (demons) as evil. It seems wherever these winged angels or Watchers show up, bad things happen.

294

These new monotheistic, hellfire religions were all about the father. Graves states, "The revolutionary institution of fatherhood, imported into Europe from the East, brought with it the institution of individual marriage." Before this revolution, paternity was irrelevant. Afterwards, the social status of women took a nosedive. Men took over the sacred practices which had once been the sole province of women. They became heads of the households, though, for a while, property still passed from mother to daughter. This second stage, the Olympian stage of classical Greece, required a new myth: the Thunder-child who castrated the Star-sun and killed the serpent. Then he became the father god or thunder god, married his mom, and had kids with her. Nice.

Even after the new institution of fatherhood became the norm, the old tradition of the mother's brother survived in myth. Recall from previous chapters that the uncle played an important role in children's lives. This role is well attested in Latvian and Lithuanian folklore, two remote places that patriarchy barely penetrated until recently.[701]

With father as head of the family and of the cosmos, the mother-goddess got demoted to wife. Her male consort/son/brother merged with the storm god to become a creator god, who usurped the power of creation and fertility. And yet, for thousands of years, the Great Goddess continued to be worshiped. The Assyrian archaeologists state that she remained the main deity in all of the cities of the Near East for two thousand years, as Aphrodite, Artemis, Eleithyia, Hera, Venus, Mylitta (Assyrian), Astarte, and Asherah.[702] As late as the 8th century BCE, the heroes of Homer's *Odyssey* encountered powerful women everywhere they sailed.

The Greeks, the Celts, and the Hebrews all had similar myths because they all conquered and absorbed the same people, the Pelasgian goddess worshipers of the Aegean. Graves claims that this is still relevant today, because modern Catholicism's popularity is due to the old Aegean mother-and-son religion to which it has slowly reverted, not to the Indo-European religion superimposed on top. Mary with baby Jesus is the most frequent image seen in Catholic homes today, especially in Latin America.[703]

The first Indo-Europeans to invade Greece, around 1900 BCE, were the Achaeans. They worshiped the male trinity of gods Zeus, Poseidon and Hades, originally known by Vedic Indian names Mitra, Varuna and Indra. Perhaps the Mitanni kingdom of Syria was the bridge between India and Greece. Slowly the Achaeans conquered the semi-matriarchal Pelasgians all over Greece, but in some places the two cultures merged: their gods were known as the sons of the old goddesses and they accepted matrilineal succession. By then this was a mixed population of long-headed Indo-Europeans and broad-headed Pelasgians.[704]

But where the indigenous were not so lucky, they fled the invaders. They escaped to the islands of Lesbos, Chios and Cnidos; others founded cities in Thrace (Bulgaria), the Troad (northwest Turkey), and the North Aegean.[705] These would be the matriarchal strongholds that would send Amazon warriors to bring down the empires.

One Greek myth that referred to these battles was the Gigantomachy, a fight between the giant sons of Gaea and Uranus, and the Olympian gods attempting to be the new rulers of the cosmos. This particular battle was to subdue the Magnesian tribe for the crime of sex outside of the new patriarchal marriage contract. The Magnesians have gone down in mythology as sexual fanatics. Myth is written by the victors.

SHE GOT DEMOTED AND RE-BRANDED

Little by little, the gods stole almost all of the powers that belonged to the Great Goddess, the only power in the cosmos for countless millennia. The Greek myth of the Three Muses features the Goddess in her poetic aspect. She's courted by the thunder god, who Graves calls "a rebellious Star-son infected by Eastern patriarchalism". She bears twins by him, known in the Welsh epics as Merddin and Olwen. She still reigns over incantations, but forfeits to the thunder god her dominion over laws and oaths, and grants the power of poetic enchantment to her twins. Then she splits into a council of nine lesser goddesses of inspiration, the Muses, who finally became ladies-in-waiting to her son

Apollo. This is an example of how the Great Goddess got slowly demoted, step by step.[706] The sun gods replaced the moon goddesses.

There was a stage in which men appropriated female power through their dress, or through castration rituals where they bled in imitation of women. Men took over female mysteries. There's a story in Tierra del Fuego that the men rebelled against the moon goddess by slaying her priestesses, only allowing the uninitiated girls to survive.[707] In Indian coronation rituals, the king sits on a throne that represents the womb.[708]

The final stage, thousands of years later, was purely patriarchal — no goddesses at all. This stage wasn't reached until the Abrahamic religions: Christianity, Islam and Judaism. Even after that, the Virgin and Son (in the words of Robert Graves) "took over the rites and honours of the Moon-woman and her Star-son — were of greater religious importance than God the Father." This persisted in England until the 17th century, fifty years longer in Wales, and still does in Ireland.[709]

The Gnostics, one of the earliest sects of Christianity in the 1st century BCE, saw the Holy Spirit as female; the Hebrew word was feminine.[710] Wherever Christianity spread, Jesus was seen as the latest version of their pagan sacred year king. Pagan gods and goddesses became Christian saints. For example, St. Bridgit kept a sacred fire going perpetually in a monastery at Kildare. The heathen festivals got re-branded as Christian.[711]

When Christianity came to Latin America with colonization, the old goddesses got Christian names. For example, earth mother Pachamama became the Virgin Mary.

Dobeiba was the main deity in Colombia. The Kogi of Colombia "believe that the world was created by the great mother Gauteovan who created the sun from her own menstrual blood, and who is also the origin of everything else in the world..."[712]

Latin American myths speak of the original primacy of the goddess, and of a past where women were independent and powerful. Amazonian peoples tell of Women-Living-Alone, Women-Without-Husbands, Masterful-Women. The male takeover is a theme in many mythologies.

297

The Chamacoco say that this overthrow of women killed the *ajnábsero*, or spirits.[713]

The Chibcha people tell of the goddess who challenged the new patriarchal order: "The goddess Huitaca appeared in this new situation that gave men more power, a beautiful woman of great resplendence who preached her rebellion against patriarchy and the necessity of a broad life, open, full of games, pleasure and drunkenness."[714]

In Europe, too, reverence for women and female spirits survived throughout the millennia. Baltic people retained fifty animist powers, such as Mother Fire, Mother Sea, and Mother Forest. The Livonians of Latvia still honor the sea mother *mjer-ämä* as their greatest deity. Estonians sing to the mother of the forest.[715]

It's only now, in the last few generations, that the last vestiges of the most ancient myths of all are disappearing into the miasma of modernity.

CHAPTER THIRTEEN

CONCLUSIONS AND SOLUTIONS

I hope that you are convinced that our predecessors lived in egalitarian, peaceful societies for long periods.

There's no smoking gun in any single academic discipline, but it's irrefutable when you consider all the details: the DNA evidence for matrilineal people before the arrival of the steppe nomads; the similarities between the hundreds of matrist cultures that survived into the historical era; the survival of goddess worship, matrilineal customs and confident sexy females in the areas that were previously matrist strongholds; the battles over patrilineal succession in the Bronze Age; the correspondence between history and mythology ... all this taken together tells the tale.

It's the tale of the civilizations of Mesopotamia, the Middle East, India, and Europe: they are hybrids. The men from primitive patrist cultures, possibly the first ever, colonized the women from the much more advanced ancient matrist cultures. The men imposed themselves as overlords and appropriated the cultures as their own.

This is not a pretty story. It's not politically convenient. The winners of history, the conquerors, want you to think civilization was their idea. With all the rape and genocide, it's not a nice origin story. But it needs to be told. We deserve to understand our origins. Science should be about facts, not feelings. Don't we tell the story of the European colonization of the Americas, and the hybrid cultures that resulted? It's eerily similar, though far more indigenous male DNA survived this later invasion.

No one in the relevant fields would attempt to deny these things. They just fail to mention them. It's less risky and more "objective" to limit oneself to a mind-numbingly dull litany of dates, dig sites, and pottery styles than to speculate about the human beings behind them. Perhaps that's one reason they hated Marija Gimbutas so much. She was a multidisciplinary thinker who dared make inferences about the data, which she was well-qualified to do, after 50 years of research. The public deserves more than pottery shards. That's why I slog through the dry papers and draw conclusions. With no professional reputation to defend, I can afford to do so.

However, as we have seen, some academics have no qualms about making sweeping statements about the inevitability of inequality, despite a total lack of evidence. But for those who care about evidence, the real debate is whether patriarchy arose only once and then spread through contact, or did it arise more than once, naturally, due to local processes?

The latter is an assumption of many, so let's examine it. One popular theory is that patriarchy arose with agriculture. This is obviously wrong, given that there were many thousands of years between the first farmers and war. Another theory is that it arose with the use of the plow, which requires male strength. This seems reasonable. Yet another is that it arose with the increase in population. This too seems reasonable, but the book *The Dawn of Everything* gives many examples of large egalitarian populations. One more theory points to the drying of the climate, which favored a shift from farming to pastoralism, promoting male skills. This is also a reasonable hypothesis.

However, none of these can be proven. What we *do* know for sure is that hierarchy and violence appeared in the archaeological record alongside signs of the steppe people: rope designs and solar symbolism on pottery, barrow graves, tall long-headed skeletons, horses, and different kinds of dwellings. If this is a coincidence, it's a big one.

In the words of J.P Mallory, archaeologist and Indo-Europeanist:

> One cannot ignore that a substantial number of leading East European archaeologists acknowledge an expansion from the Pontic-Caspian to be a major factor in effecting this transformation of society and, in general, they identify these intruders as the earliest Indo-Europeans. It is difficult to deny that there is evidence for intrusions unless one's preoccupation with explaining all cultural change purely through local cultural processes precludes this concept.[716]

As we have seen, politics can often override truth in academia. No one wanted to believe that the ancestors whose languages we speak raped and pillaged their way across Eurasia. But the evidence is overwhelming. Mallory speaks of the "embarrassment one associates with long-ridiculed invasion hypothesis. We are always wary of suggesting models of expansion that will be caricaturized as hordes of frenzied Aryans bursting out of the Russian steppe [...]"[717]

But this "long-ridiculed invasion" was in fact the truth. The evidence lies in the abandoned cities and genocides. It wasn't always that simple; some cultures on the frontier between Old Europe and the steppes co-existed for long periods of time. It's fascinating to imagine three very different cultures in the Balkan region: Indo-Europeans, Old European farmers, and hunter-gatherers, trading copper artifacts and sometimes mates. Perhaps for them, cultural change was more of an infiltration than a sudden invasion. But we can say for sure that the imposition of Indo-European and Semitic languages was disastrous to the indigenous peoples of western Eurasia, and often violent.

This wasn't due to a fundamental flaw of Indo-European and Semitic peoples. They, too, had an egalitarian past. Germanic and Scandinavian people stayed egalitarian until the Iron Age. It was traumatic climate change to blame, combined with a pastoral lifestyle that made limited

301

resources easy to hoard. Groups on every continent, of every ethnic type, have become warlike with contact.

And with war came racism, paternity, marriage, monogamy, sex shaming, body shaming, trauma, authoritarianism, income disparity, mental illness, and environmental destruction.

This package also leads to many related cultural traits, such as: the military-industrial complex, the caste system, boastfulness, circumcision, and bad sex. I could go on and on. The patriarchal psyche is a mess of tensions, fears, and conflicts.

If we accept the lie that civilization can't exist without this package, we are doomed. A bleak desert planet is the world that our post-traumatic psyches are the best suited for. Our post-traumatic psychology leads us to hate and fear what we have not been allowed. If we lack a joyful connection to nature and a robust sex life, how can we tolerate that for others? If striving for status through the pursuit of money and meaningless sex is the only value we've been taught, why would we value nature for its own sake?

The long-awaited sequel to the movie *Avatar* that's capturing public imagination in 2022 is about all these themes. I believe this movie resonates because it portrays events buried in our cultural memories: the first colonization of Eurasia starting 5000 years ago, and the colonization of the Americas, Asia and Africa starting 500 years ago.

The audience identifies with the colonized alien, even though the colonizers are us. I believe that's because most people are decent at heart. The psychopaths rise to the top in dominator societies, but most of us are along for the ride. We don't see any alternative to the system, so, like the scientist in *Avatar* who participates in the rape of the planet because it funds his research, we go along. The system self-perpetuates. But unlike the psychopaths at the top, who enjoy it, most of us cheer for the other side. During the colonization of America, some settlers defected from their culture to join the natives — never the other way around. Just like in Avatar.

The movie portrays so beautifully how you can have a pure body that's either alien or human, or mixed, but either an indigenous soul or a colonizer soul. The hybrids of the Indo-European invaders and the indigenous farmers would have taken after both parents. Maybe one child looked more like the invaders but related more strongly to his mother's culture, or vice versa. Perhaps we identify so strongly with the colonized aliens in *Avatar* because most of us have the blood of both the colonizers and colonized running in our veins.

Any mind from any culture can be colonized and become a colonizer. It's a virus that passes from host to host and then needs new continents, maybe new planets, to devour and infect. It's more than just a greedy resource grab. There's an unconscious desire to destroy the intact connection with nature and our bodies that we have been denied, as the great teacher Martín Prechtel would say.

Now that we understand that trauma and easily hoarded limited resources are at the root of the colonizer virus, we can change the world. We have the technology to provide for everybody, once we get rid of the system of greed and corruption that allows most of the resources to be hoarded by the .01% at the top of the hierarchy. We can create a just society. It's not a zero-sum game.

One thing that would help is a collective acknowledgment of what has happened. Do you remember the apology from Vietnam veterans who begged for forgiveness from Native American elders, at Standing Rock in 2016? I shed tears just thinking about it. What If something like this can happen, an acknowledgment of the crimes against women over the past 5000 years? Might this help the collective healing? I use the word "acknowledgment", not "apology", as most men today have nothing to apologize for: they didn't create this situation. Most men in the past were sexist because that was the norm at the time, but most men today are decent, even if some can't quite put themselves in women's shoes.

Of course, there are a minority of douchebags, the Andrew Tates of the world; most women who have worked in male-dominated fields know at least one guy who made their lives miserable because he doesn't want to work side by side with women, or especially, with a female boss. But these guys are rare.

It's not about revenge. We don't have to even the score by marginalizing men. It's much better now, at least in the West, but there are still many ways in which we are dehumanized, sexualized, treated as inferior. We can heal this through bringing awareness. We can gently ask our friends not to make sexist remarks. We can raise our daughters to believe they can do anything. We can give women a chance to prove themselves.

It's fashionable to cite studies that say that boys prefer trucks and girls prefer dolls no matter how hard we try to push gender-neutral toys, and to claim that this means these preferences are biologically innate. But people don't realize how much conditioning has already taken place by age three; gender stereotypes have already formed. How can we truly treat male and female babies equally?

Now that feminist activists have changed sexist laws, and society is legally fair for both sexes, the biggest obstacle we have still to overcome are attitudes and assumptions that boys are more capable, and girls are only valued for their sexuality and service. We can't force people to change their views. All we can do is to provide information showing how women have excelled in every field. The more we understand our past, the more things will continue to shift.

We need to forgive each other, and forgive ourselves, too, for all the ways in which we have dominated others, exerted our power to impose our will over another person. The more we stay alert, and watch our own behavior, the less we give in to the temptation to play the oppressor, and the more we put others' needs on par with our own.

There has been a lot of talk about "toxic masculinity" lately. Some people act confused, like it means that *all* masculinity is toxic. That makes no sense; the whole point is to distinguish "toxic masculinity" from masculinity in general. No one can agree on what masculinity really is. I believe that patriarchy is so ubiquitous and invisible that we don't know which gender roles are natural and which are patriarchal conditioning. Most of the ideas we associate with masculinity and femininity aren't actually biology, but culture.

Personally, I associate masculinity with physical prowess and athleticism. I define "toxic masculinity" as the worst side of patriarchal male conditioning: suppressing emotions and empathy; being tough; dominating women. This is the extreme of how men are taught to behave in patrist societies. I define "toxic femininity" as the worst side of patriarchal female conditioning: competition, malicious gossip, manipulative behavior. These are the ways women are conditioned to behave, to keep them apart from each other through competition. Female "wiles", or manipulation, was the only form of power women were allowed until the feminist revolutions changed things. Toxic femininity has had more of an impact on my life personally, with the envy other women have projected on me. But at least it doesn't involve war and genocide.

CYCLES OF PROGRESS AND BACKLASH

Western civilization has made enormous strides over the past hundred years, partly thanks to feminists who endured violence and humiliation to bring more matrist values into the center of our culture. Non-violent activists like the suffragettes, Martin Luther King, and Gandhi created enormous social change. Women in the West now have much more control over their financial, sexual and reproductive choices. They can inherit property, choose their own mates, divorce, have rights over their children, and live independent lives. Children of unwed mothers are no longer starved to death in institutions.[718]

Yet, we have a long way to go in the United States. Rape, human trafficking, and domestic violence are epidemics. Men still hold most government positions and run most companies. Women still face discrimination, ageism, misogyny, and double standards in sex and housework. Online, women face threats, stalking, and harassment.[719]

Of course, women of ethnic backgrounds have it worse, and women in much of the world have it much worse than Western women. They still do the majority of unpaid labor and make less than men, everywhere.

As always, movements forward are accompanied by backlashes. In the past twenty years, there's been a regression in women's participation in the labor force.[720] If you look at Figure 13.1 showing the ratio of female to male labor force participation rates, you'll see that women participate far less in the labor force in the region of Saharasia, the desert at the heart of the world.

Figure 13-1: Women's participation in the labor force is much less in the central desert region.[721]

To this day, the central desert area still plays a part in world politics. The parts of China closest to Saharasia are the most authoritarian. After the fall of the Soviet Union, the new states closest to it ended up in chaos or dictatorships, while the ones furthest away transitioned to democracy.[722]

The Swat Valley in Saharasia is a tragic example of how patriarchy kills the world. This picturesque region is a place of great natural beauty and an early center of Buddhism, but because of its strategic location as a pass where the steppes of Central Asia drop down into India, it has been fought over for millennia. The steppe people used it as a bridge to enter India. War leads to deforestation and destruction. Poverty leads to more deforestation. The patrist mandate to have many children leads to more overpopulation and deforestation. The more that women are independent and educated, and can choose whether to have children and how many to have, the higher the quality of life. Having children is a beautiful choice, but I believe it should be chosen carefully and whole-heartedly ... not done because it's the only role open to women, or the only way for a woman to gain respect.

This desert, which passes through many continents and ethnicities, is still the heart of patriarchy. In some places there, slavery wasn't abolished until 1970.[723]

Of course, there are cultures in Saharasia who have proudly held on to equality, and every culture has beautiful customs and people. But, still, in these areas we see more suffering. It begs the question of the nature of evil and free will. If people are more brutal because of their brutal upbringings, is it really their fault? How can these traditions change?

Again, it's not about men. Everybody has been raised to maintain the institution of patriarchy and its cultural traditions. In the most brutal cultures, women are enthusiastic stone-throwers, genital mutilators, and shamers of those who don't conform. We need to understand the role that mothers play, as well as fathers, hospitals and schools. Men commit most of the violence, but women play a huge role as the ones who inculcate the children.[724]

For the left-wing, liberation of women is a trivial issue to be addressed, if at all, once all men are liberated and we've solved the more "important" issues.[725] They don't understand the connection between women's rights and the rights of all people and the environment.

FAMILY LIFE

Some on the right may romanticize the period when women were subservient, in the society referred to as "traditional", with a working father and housewife mother. It was hardly traditional, as it existed for only about a decade in the 1950's. What *was* truly traditional was the matrilineal clan, which lasted for at least 20,000 years, and likely far more!

Like Malinowski, when he made anthropology irrelevant by insisting that the nuclear family was universal simply because he wanted it to be, some conservatives claim a sacred role for the family and accuse feminists of attacking it. They're not entirely wrong about that. Feminists *did* contribute to the demise of the patriarchal nuclear family by liberating women to play a part in public life. But it was inevitable: one income can't sustain a family anymore.

The problem with the modern patriarchal family model is that it's very risky for the woman. If you don't develop an income stream, and your husband dies or leaves you for a younger woman as is commonly the case, it will be too late to start a career. Unless you're independently wealthy, relying upon a relationship that's based on love and sex leaves you vulnerable.

Of course, that's why courts award alimony, but I'm not sure if that's something you can depend on, and in some cases it's unfair to the man. In the United States where we have no safety net, it's not safe to put all your eggs in one man's basket. Even if he doesn't die or leave you, you may lose your desire for him, but feel obligated to have sex with him due to economic dependency.

I think obligated sex is a terrible thing. Marriage is a form of exchange for the sake of privilege, bloodline, wealth and property. The patriarchal nuclear family is the economic unit of the patriarchal empire or state. Until recently, female desire and romantic love had to be sacrificed on that altar. In recent times, men too have been expected to be monogamous, although with a little more wiggle room than women.

It's only very recently that divorce has lost its stigma. Since then, love and sex have been the basis of marriage instead of economic exchange and family alliance. Given the high divorce rates, we can see that love isn't a stable situation, either. When sexual desire fades, lives are ripped apart. Children are uprooted and traumatized.

Perhaps we can take a page from the Mosuo people who live in the truly traditional way, in the large maternal family house. They tried the marriage thing under pressure from the Chinese, and hated it. In their system, there's no reason to fight. There's no reason to have obligatory sex. They only have sex when they feel like it, as nature intended. If a couple doesn't feel like having sex, or they don't get along, they simply part ways. The house and the children aren't affected.

In this traditional way, women didn't need men to support them and their children. They chose their partners for attraction alone. I believe this leads to more attractive men, because male attractiveness is selected for. The images of ancient Egyptian and Minoan men prove my point: they were hot.

Picture 13-1: Minoan wrestlers. Photo of museum reproduction, by author.

By contrast, men in patriarchy don't have to be sexy; they attract women with their camel or their car. In extreme patrist societies, they don't have to attract women: they just purchase them. Or rape them. This leads to a population of males selected for aggressive genes, not attractive ones. In patriarchy there are alpha men and beta men; the alphas are too cocky, and the betas lack confidence. This is probably why so many women today complain about the lack of attractive guys.

When I imagine a post-patriarchal world, I imagine more hot guys. Still, some will be hotter than others. If monogamy and marriage were no longer a thing, and heterosexual women chose sex partners based on attraction alone, some guys would get more action than others.

309

This is the bargain for men with monogamous marriage: most men can count on getting access to at least one woman. If a guy is successful, he may have access to more, through affairs, or by trading in his wife for a younger one. I think men fear that if women didn't need men for financial support anymore, and we weren't monogamous, that many men would get left out: hot men would get multiple women and unattractive men would get none.

I believe this fear is what lies behind the anger of "incels", the "involuntary celibates". They believe that all men deserve to have women allotted to them. But women really aren't that choosy about looks; if men try a little harder, and focus on their attractiveness the way women do, they can all get laid. If they exercise, do a little yoga, learn to dance, and upgrade their wardrobes, they will all do fine.

Of course, they need to choose women who are in their league of age and intelligence. Many men assume they're entitled to women who are younger and hotter than they are: this is the essence of male privilege. They feel entitled to their pick of women without improving themselves. For much of patriarchy, women had to settle for men less intelligent and attractive, because they were dependent on men for protection and support and paternity.

Now that women don't need men for those things, they hold out for men who are a match for them. But after thousands of years of being trapped at home, many women are highly motivated to educate and improve themselves. Many men, on the other hand, after thousands of years of having to be the sole providers and warriors, just want to chill. So the women are striving for perfection and don't want to settle for just any guy, while some men are resentful that they actually have to improve themselves to measure up. I believe that if they put in a bit of effort, they'll be better off for it.

Women aren't going back to being helpless pawns in a male world, forced to have sex with whoever wants them.

To be fair, I understand if men are mad at the kind of women who want to have it both ways: to be independent when they want to, and to be taken care of and paid for when they want to. That isn't fair. I advocate for fairness across the board.

Men's Rights Activists are angry about a lot of things. They have a long list of talking points that are disturbingly popular: reasons why feminism is wrong and why they hate women. They do have one point that is actually true: that women get shorter sentences for the same crimes, though I believe this is only for mothers of small children out of necessity.

But most of their gripes are, ironically, the fault of patriarchy, not feminism. For example, what they call "hypergamy" — the ability of women to marry into a higher social class if she's attractive. And, the fact that men are more likely to be homeless, to be lonely, and to commit suicide. These are all results of patriarchal conditioning which don't encourage men to prioritize social networks and self-care.

Similarly, most of the things *women* are mad about, that *they* blame on men, stem from patriarchy! Rather than play the blame game, I'd like to see us join forces, since the system has such negative impacts on us all! Let's stand together, all of us, against the system!

OUR POST-PATRIARCHAL FUTURE: SEX AND FAMILIES

People often ask me: when we no longer live in a patriarchy, what will be different? Here's what I imagine.

At the family level, I see a gradual phasing out of the nuclear family model. Children will of course take the mother's name, which makes the most sense. Wealth and property will pass to a daughter by default, unless she doesn't want children and her brother does. It's a good idea to support daughters by default anyway, since they earn less than men, as their talents are not as compensated by society.

So then, without the nuclear family, who will raise the children? In the previous chapters I described how, before patriarchy, children were raised by matrilineal clans with the brother taking the main male role. Many of you women are probably thinking, "No thank you, I don't want to raise children with my brother!" That's a fair point. You might not want to live with your brother, but he could send you checks every month. He could financially support *your* kids instead of his wife's kids. At least he can be sure the children are genetically related to him.

So, a woman's family could help her with childcare. But if she doesn't live near them, or doesn't like them, she could form an intentional family instead. The ideal would be to do it with a man she knows well. They could create a legal contract where each person commits the number of hours and dollars they can offer each month, for 18 years. If it adds up to enough, and they share the same goals and values for child-rearing, and they're compatible housemates, they can go for it.

There's no reason they can't be attracted to each other, or even in love, as long as they're realistic about weathering heartbreak, or transitioning to platonic co-parenting, if the passion fades ... as it so often does.

This man can, of course, have as a requirement that the children be his biological offspring. Now that we have paternity tests, monogamy and sexual jealousy are not required for paternity. If we got into the habit of requesting routine paternity tests, there would be no stigma around it. It wouldn't mean he didn't trust her or was accusing her of being a slut. It would be a routine way to determine a child's father without having to control a woman's sexuality.

Of course, it's also fine to have monogamy as a requirement to be sexual with someone. We can make any rules we want. But I advocate thinking it through, to make sure we don't choose monogamy out of default thinking, past trauma, or patriarchal conditioning.

In any case, a decision to limit our sex partner to one at a time is a valid and beautiful choice, but should be separate from parenting decisions. In this sane future I imagine, people will co-parent consciously, with a solid plan for what will happen if desire fades or if they desire other people. Their relationship agreements will be separate from their co-parenting agreements, as these are very different things.

Because a child needs a stable home. Before patriarchy, every child had a stable home in her clan. No child was ever illegitimate. That's my manifesto for the new world: Every human being is legitimate!

In the post-patriarchal world, the words "bastard" and "illegitimate" will become outdated and forgotten, and sound as old-fashioned as "betwixt".

If a woman really wants a child and can't find a lover who's compatible in these ways, and doesn't have a brother, she can choose anybody, or a group, to co-parent with. For example: two friends each pitch in 10 hours a week for childcare, while her brother offers financial support, and her uncle takes the kids on weekends. Maybe the mother is the breadwinner and works full time while her best friend stays at home with the child. Any combination can work, so long as everyone agrees and commits.

Again, the co-parents would talk through their needs and values, and create a contract that is legally binding. You could download a sample contract to help you think through all the issues. A child is a serious commitment for life. In our future it will be undertaken with full consciousness, intention and commitment.

This way, no sexual contracts are required. Sexuality is a mysterious force that resists obligation and definition.

It's amazing if a couple raises their biological children together and stays in love and has great sex forever and doesn't want anyone else. This is the ideal in our modern society, but it's a recent idea. People in the past coupled for the sake of family and didn't really expect great sex for life. We're conditioned to want this through fairy tales and romantic comedies where people live happily ever after. I have nothing against that. It can happen, but it's like winning the jackpot. The traditional patriarchal dream of forever love and monogamous co-parenting is still an option, it's just not the *only* option.

Serial monogamy seems to be natural for most people. I read somewhere that men unconsciously look away from an attractive woman if he's in the infatuation phase of commitment. Nature wants us

313

to commit for as long as it takes to conceive and raise a child to the age it can play with the other kids, and then move on. And yet. Romantics, don't despair. Lifelong love can happen.

Since it's so rare for this to work out, co-parents will agree on a Plan B *before* the relationship breaks down. No more broken homes or single mothers. No more children uprooted because mommy or daddy had sex with someone else.

With equality between men and women at the core level of family, equality will trickle up to all parts of society. Everything will change within a generation when children grow up seeing their parents fairly negotiate agreements and choose how to live, instead of being bound to patriarchal gender roles.

Of course, this is already happening. The percentage of nuclear family households dropped from 45% to 23.5% percent since the seventies. After all, why does marriage need to be a legal issue? If it's so natural to humans, then why does the law need to be involved? And why are so many opting out?[726]

I know many people who are forming alternative families. But most children I know have parents who started as couples and ended up as co-parents. Why not plan on co-parenting from the start, and make that more important than love and sex? Love and sex come and go, but a child is forever. Couples who start as co-parents spare the children so much drama and trauma. Sex could be the icing on the cake. If they wanted to, they could bring in other lovers, but they would remain co-parents.

So that's what I see for post-patriarchal family life. At the *community* level I see more people focusing on finding a clan or community, to meet their needs for belonging. These intentional communities could rent mansions or build large homes on a piece of land.

Even if we don't live with them, having a tribe to belong to will free many from the desperation to find a mate. Our couple-centric society is oppressive to those who can't, or don't want to, mate.

314

In my post-patriarchy world, we won't think of people as "singles" or "couples", but as humans. We won't need sex to have a family. Then the only reason to have sex is because you meet someone who makes you wet, or hard. That's number two in my post-patriarchal manifesto: Sex only when wet! And of course, everyone should orgasm if they want to!

Once a couple who can conceive a child realizes they have chemistry, they could write down their intentions before making love. If they don't agree to raise a child together, they would decide who is managing contraception, and what to do if it fails: she could decide to abort, or to raise the child without his input.

In this future world, abortion is free and easy to obtain before the fourth month. With adequate sexual education, no woman will be unaware she is pregnant after four months. She will have the education and self-respect to make responsible decisions, not needing a baby to complete her or to offer her status in society. So while the fetus is still too small to feel pain, she will have time to decide if she's in a position to do it. If there isn't enough support, or if she isn't mature and emotionally stable, her friends and family will try to talk her out of having the child. All people considering co-parenting will be encouraged to spend *at least* a week taking care of kids before deciding! I know many people who thought they wanted to become parents until they spent long periods of time around children.

Imagine a world where every child is enthusiastically wanted, by fully prepared families! Where children are welcomed by an extended family or village! Where children are conceived consciously!

That's number three on the manifesto: every child enthusiastically wanted! Every person is legitimate! Every sex act wet!

Imagine children conceived in hot Tantric intentional rituals broadcast live as positive porn! Professional porn will go out of business with all the amateurs lovingly acting out the whole Kama Sutra.

When a child is born, let's greet her singing in a beautiful place, not in an antiseptic, anti-mammal room with bright lights. She will be

315

breastfed and carried on the body whenever possible. She'll be given gentle discipline, and plenty of love and physical affection.

Her boundaries will be respected. Her gifts will be nurtured. If she shows signs of mental illness or neurological difference, she will be taught how to manage it. If she exhibits antisocial behavior like bullying or selfishness, her friends and family will stage an innovation to gently but firmly let her know it's not okay. Physical punishment and shaming will never be used.

I advocate for explicit relationship agreements not only about co-parenting, but about all things. If it works best to have the man work at an office and in return the woman cares for the children, they can agree to that, but explicitly, not because it's expected. If it works best to switch those roles because the woman has abilities that are better rewarded financially, and the man is more nurturing, they can choose that too, without shame. Maybe they want to mix it up month by month! Being up front about roles can save a relationship from the usual resentment where one or both people feel like they are doing too much.

OUR POST-PATRIARCHAL FUTURE: SOCIETIES

At the societal level, we'll put the effort we now put into war into studying how to be healthy and happy. We'll place high financial value on caring careers like teaching, nursing, and caregiving. We'll read our children stories about good people doing beautiful things, not about kidnapped maidens or wicked witches. As Riane Eisler predicts in her great work *The Chalice and the Blade* … we'll learn how to prevent illness instead of creating incentives to keep people medicated.[727]

From what I've seen, the best model for governance are nested communities ruled by council. Each community elects leaders to their council, and then those leaders represent at a larger council that includes all the communities around, and so on. I've seen villages like this in Asia, and this was how the Neolithic cities of Cucuteni in Ukraine were organized. It allows small local villages to scale up to collectives of villages.

In our post-patriarchal future, since women excel at diplomacy, they will hold at least half of the leadership positions at every level of society. Studies show that companies led by women have not only happier, more productive employees, but better profits as well.[728] This is not because women are better than men, but because men have been conditioned to lead for selfish reasons, whereas women have been conditioned to serve. When we've healed from patriarchy and learned how to channel testosterone in a positive way, the leader's sex will cease to matter.

I'm not advocating for electing women just because they are women, if they're unqualified. I'm advocating for choosing qualified women, and all other things being equal, wherever women are underrepresented. When women make decisions cooperatively with each other, there is more chance they will consider the needs of future generations, since they are more tuned-in to children than some men who may be more tempted by ego and power.

Nowadays, of course, most women who rise to the highest positions of power do so by playing the dominance game. That's why most women leaders have been the toxic dominator type. Only when we consciously choose leaders who lead from responsibility rather than from power will we see a change. When women are not the tiny minority but a large block, things will really change. A lone woman surrounded by mostly men must play by male rules of aggressive assertiveness to be respected. Also, young women are driven by their hormones almost as much as young men. I believe that's why older women had the power in traditional societies. Once they go through menopause and are free from sexual temptations and reproductive drives, there is much more clarity. Many grandmothers truly do make decisions for the good of the children, rather than for their own selfish status.

While we can criticize these Margaret Thatcher-type leaders as being warlike, we can't claim they were ineffective leaders, or too emotional, as some have suggested. Sex scandals, financial corruption, and violence are all overwhelmingly male. [729] While women aren't immune to corruption such as embezzling, it happens much less often, even accounting for the lack of opportunity. [730] Women are used to collaborating with each other, hence female leaders often try hard to find a compromise across the political aisle.[731] More female mayors than male are willing to admit problems and discuss changes.[732] The more women there are in a country's parliament, the less corrupt the country.[733] So it's reasonable to think that once at least half of leadership positions are held by ordinary women, not the most aggressive Margaret Thatcher types, wars will be less frequent.

Isn't it absurd to think that slaughtering innocent people is the way modern nations solve disagreements? In the future, wars will be prevented through negotiation. If a war can't be prevented by diplomacy, the country with the most money and the best military tactical skills are likely to win it. In the post-patriarchy, we'll play a computer simulation of a war, instead of committing atrocities and destroying buildings, infrastructure, and land. Each side's wealth and territory will get entered into the program, and the two sides will play a video game to decide the conflict.

If a nation, or a tribal nation, refuses to abide by the rules, the rest of the nations will join forces to kick their ass, but not by taking it out on innocent people or trees. They will kill the *leaders* who refuse to play by the rules.

Think of all the money we will save on horrific wars. *The cost of developing one intercontinental ballistic missile could feed 50 million children and build a hundred sixty thousand schools.*[734]

I also advocate for taking money from billionaires; leaving each billionaire two billion for himself, two for his wife and two for each child. That's more money than anyone can ever need, and still an enormous amount left over to provide for everybody else.

With that money we can buy farmland from commercial agriculture farms and turn it into intentional communities for people who are unemployed or unable to work or just don't want to participate in a meaningless job. The village members will be required to work 20 hours a week on tasks they don't mind doing: farming, cooking, cleaning, teaching, caring for children or elderly, building, fixing, landscaping.

Heide Goettner-Abendroth describes in detail how modern people can create egalitarian intentional communities using the political and social techniques of matrilineal people. I highly recommend her paper.

I realize all this sounds a lot like communism. So why didn't that work? Maybe it worked in Cuba, at a small scale. In Russia and China, the revolutionaries didn't first come up with a plan for leadership before chopping off heads, so power-hungry psychopaths rushed in to fill the power vacuum. Plus, these movements were co-opted by powerful figures. Also: equality cannot be forced. It needs to be adopted voluntarily. Otherwise, it's totalitarianism, as the previous communist societies have been.

We need to have our leaders in place *first* before dismantling the current system: a council of leaders, more than half female at first, who don't want to rule but are willing to take responsibility. Let's make those jobs low-paid and low-status so men won't want them, and women will feel deserving!

In patriarchy, traditionally male jobs are better-compensated, by design. When a job changes from being mostly male to mostly female, or vice versa, there's a corresponding shift in salary. For example, in Russia the medical profession changed from being mostly male to mostly female, at which time the average salary plummeted.

I think there are more men interested in science and technology and construction than women, statistically speaking. Post-patriarchy, we'll see more women in those fields than we do now, but there may still be still more men. Not everything will be exactly equal. I advocate for equal opportunity, and equal pay for the same levels of skill and experience.

The only statistical evidence I've seen for sex differences in personality is that men are more interested in things and women in people. This is often quoted. But this came from a study by Simon Baron-Cohen that showed that only a small number of baby boys looked at mobiles longer than they looked at faces. It's very difficult to

319

know whether tendencies for women to be more interested in people than in things is due to different conditioning and expectations. Expectations play a huge role in performance. It's called the "stereotype threat" effect. If a person is told that people of their kind perform poorly on a task, they will perform worse than controls.[735]

So who knows whether we'd see sex differences if everyone were treated the same from birth. The overlap is larger than the difference. But I might personally lean toward the idea that men would have more interest in and aptitude for construction and technical tasks than women, and the opposite for language skills and social sciences.

If that turns out to be the case, in our post-patriarchal world we will still see more men in construction and engineering (but still more women than we see now). If it's true that women are more truly biologically more drawn to careers involving people even without the different upbringing, we'll see more of them as leaders, teachers, and psychologists. But again, we'll judge each individual on merits.

It's interesting that there are no sex differences seen across all cultures, suggesting that differences are culturally determined. See the book *Inferior* by Angela Saini for a deep dive into this research. A study in a different book shows that in traditional cultures with strong gender roles, in families without girls who gave boys tasks usually given to girls, like cleaning and infant care, those boys showed less aggression and more altruism.[736] We may see that treating boys and girls as equally competent and showing them the same care and attention will close the gap in abilities.

Getting back to the societal level of our post-patriarchal society: I'm proposing a hybrid model between capitalism and socialism. Those who want to have more money by working in the rat race can do that. Those who want to create their own communities, or live in tax-supported national ones, can do that. We can offer our skills to our tribe, receive what we need, and belong to a family.

In the future, we will intentionally choose how to spend our time, who to spend it with, and whether to create new life. We will grow ourselves consciously, cultivating selflessness and service. We will live consciously, mate consciously, and then, finally, die consciously.

There you have it. That's my prediction for how things will look in the post-patriarchy. It's not some pie-in-the-sky utopian fantasy. It's normal. It's just what the world would look like if it wasn't ruled by psychopathic douchebags.

If you hadn't been raised in this twisted society, you wouldn't see the way things are now as normal. Because when you think about it, none of it makes sense. Why should a human being be illegitimate just because her father didn't have a legal contract from the government when he ejaculated inside her mother? It's absurd. It's insane what kind of nonsense humans can get other humans to believe.

Riane Eisler describes our post-patriarchy future: "Virtues of dominance and conquest will be seen for what they are: the barbaric aberrations of a species turned against itself."

Before we can transition to the post-patriarchy, we need to fix our beliefs. That's the purpose of this book: to point out how absurd they are.

Then, because scarcity of resources leads to patriarchy, we use permaculture farming techniques to make sure all people have access to food. Once we stop spending all our money on war, and take the extra from mega-billionaires, it will be easy to feed everyone.

HEALING TRAUMA

But first, we need to heal the trauma from the last 5000 years.

Trauma happens when an event occurs that's beyond our ability to process at the time. We might freeze like a deer in the headlights. When it's over, and we're safe, the natural urge is to shake off the experience. That's usually done through shaking. A deer who escapes a predator will shake until all the stress is gone. Then it's perfectly fine.

But patriarchal cultures actively suppress this instinct, perhaps because traumatized people are more easily controlled. So we're walking around with all this un-processed trauma stuck in our muscles and tissues. This makes us breathe shallowly and renders us incapable of experiencing great joy.

Bruce Garrard calls the shaking off of a traumatic event the "discharge", a normal part of life we have all forgotten. It can happen through shaking, crying, or laughing; angry shouting and vigorous movement with warm perspiration (tantrum); or live, interested talking, or even yawning.[737]

When a traumatic event gets discharged, there will be no permanent negative effects (unless, of course, there's permanent *physical* injury). The process needs enough time to finish fully. It works better if there is someone to actively witness, but a person can do it alone, too.

When discharge doesn't happen because the culture doesn't allow for it, the traumatic event gets stored in the body, and anti-rational beliefs get stored in the mind. Then, when a similar situation occurs, the beliefs will be triggered out of proportion to the situation at hand. For example, in an adult relationship, a person might get upset and blame their partner if the situation reminds them of something their parent did, especially if the partner is the same sex as the parent.

The layers of trauma pile on.

I release trauma through a regular practice of discharge through trance. The trance state is associated with the theta brain state: a non-verbal, deep, relaxed state of flow. This technology is both shamanic and scientific. We can enter this state by synchronizing rhythmic movements with breath, or with drums or chanting; it's the rhythm that's important. A 1-2, 1-2 rhythm is best, which is why Kundalini yoga is ideal. It's important to avoid speaking or thinking in words, as language takes us into a different brain state. Bright lights, machine noises, and electronics also interfere.

With this practice I have not only healed my childhood trauma but also accessed my intuitive wisdom for creative inspiration and problem solving. I've tried it with about fifty friends and clients; all but three got into a deeper state from which they could approach their issues with more peace and clarity.

All we need to change the world is to understand the truth about our past and our true nature, release our trauma, and get rid of the psychopaths in power.

There is hope. People can change. During World War II, the Japanese were brutal, and now, they arrange their shoes nicely outside refugee shelters. The Germans were monsters back then too, and now they're polite, self-deprecating people with the best environmental record in the world. In a generation, things can change.

Also, traumatic climate change has not always led to oppression. Some of our ancient ancestors turned to cooperation when things got tough. Drama makes good stories, so we rarely talk about the times things went well. A 2023 study found that many ancient cultures navigated climate change by peacefully adapting, and that egalitarian cultures fared much better than ones with rigid status hierarchies.[738]

New archaeological discoveries like this are emerging daily, questioning our assumptions that competition is more common than cooperation. New articles appear monthly about ancient egalitarian civilizations, matrist cultures, women warriors and the like. The blinders are coming off. The truth is being revealed. It's an exciting time to be alive. Check my website, BeforeWar.com, for news, for extra content, and full online references.

As the authors of *The Dawn of Everything* say:

> What other kind of world could we create, if we stop telling ourselves this is the only one possible?[739]

<u>N</u>otes

Chapter 1: The Patriarchy Package

[1] Garrard, Bruce. *The Ancient Problem with Men*. Unique Publications, 2011, iii.

[2] Ibid.

[3] Eisler, Riane. *The Chalice and The Blade*. Harper & Row, 1987, 66.

[4] David Graeber and David Wengrow, *The Dawn of Everything*. Farrar, Straus and Giroux, 2021, 433-4

[5] Martín Prechtel lecture.

[6] "Majority of Trafficking Victims are Girls and Women." *UN.org*.

[7] Darina, L. "Shocking Male vs Female CEO Statistics 2022." *Leftronic*, January 23, 2022.

[8] Sun, Rebecca. "Men Out-Talk Women Almost Three to One in the Movies, Study Finds." *The Hollywood Reporter*, March 7, 2023.

[9] Smith, Anna. "'Patriarchy has no gender. It doesn't break down like that': film-maker Nina Menkes dissects the male gaze." *The Guardian*, April 21, 2023.

[10] Laura June, "Mothers Feel More Judged Than Fathers." *The Cut*, June 2016.

[11] Kim Parker and Cary Funk, "Gender discrimination comes in many forms for today's working women." Pew Research, 2017.

[12] de Waal Frans. *Different: Gender through the Eyes of a Primatologist*. W. W. Norton & Company, 2022, 256.

[13] Saini, Angela. *Inferior: How Science Got Women Wrong - and the New Research That's Rewriting the Story*. Beacon Press, 2017, 6.

[14] Merritt, Stephanie. "The Authority Gap by Mary Ann Sieghart review – mocked, patronised and still paid less than men." *The Guardian*, July 5, 2021.

[15] Big Think. "Male inequality, explained by an expert | Richard Reeves." *YouTube*, Jan 4, 2023.

[16] Garrard, 27.

[17] "Family portrait, 1905" by Whitehead, F. is licensed under CC BY-SA 3.0.

[18] DeMeo, *Saharasia*, 54.

[19] Goettner-Abendroth, Heide. "The Way into an Egalitarian Society: Principles and Practice of a Matriarchal Politics." *HAGIA*, 2007, 3.

[20] Ibid., 7.

[21] Ibid., 8.

[22] Sliwa, Jim. "Self-Esteem Gender Gap More Pronounced in Western Countries." *American Psychological Association*, 2016.

[23] Mallory, J.P. *In Search of the Indo-Europeans.* Thames & Hudson, 1991.

[24] Manco, Jean. *Ancestral Journeys: The Peopling of Europe from the First Venturers to the Vikings.* Thames & Hudson, 2013, 207.

[25] Martín Prechtel in his classes talks about waves of invaders who get soft from the civilizing influence of those they conquer, and are then conquered by a hungrier more brutal wave of long-lost cousins coming in. He doesn't talk about gender.

[26] Gerda. *The Creation of Patriarchy.* Oxford University Press, 1986, 9.

[27] Ibid., 22.

[28] DeMeo, James. *Saharasia.* Natural Energy Works, 1998, 209.

[29] Ibid., 99.

[30] Ibid., 88.

[31] Ibid., 167.

[32] Ibid., 104.

[33] Ibid., 4.

[34] Ibid., 7.

[35] Ibid., 9.

[36] Ibid., 8.

[37] Ibid., 52.

[38] Turchin, Peter et al. "War, space, and the evolution of Old World complex societies." *Proc Natl Acad Sci USA,* October 2013.

[39] Graeber and Wengrow, 298.

[40] DeMeo, *Saharasia,* 18.

[41] Graeber and Wengrow, 508.

[42] DeMeo, *Saharasia,* 22.

[43] Ibid., 25.

[44] Ibid., 33.

[45] Ibid., 60.

[46] Ibid., 61.

[47] Ibid., 65.

48 Ibid., 334.

49 Ibid., 160.

50 Lerner, 219.

51 Sky, Michael. *Beyond the Dominator Virus*. Bear & Co, 1993, xix.

Chapter 2: The Real History of Western Civilization

52 Garrard, 37.

53 Graeber and Wengrow, 248.

54 Ibid., 314-315.

55 Ibid., 314.

56 Roebroeks, Wil et al. "Use of red ochre by early Neandertals." Anthropology, October 2012.

57 This list comes from decades of looking for Neolithic figures both in my travels, visiting museums, and searching online.

58 Lerner.

59 Eisler, 100.

60 Cline, Eric H. *1177 B.C.: The Year Civilization Collapsed*. Princeton University Press, 2021.

61 *War of the Gods: The Conflict Between Matriarchy and Patriarchy During the Greek Dark Age*. Black's Academy Limited, 2019.

62 Ibid., 58.

63 Eisler, 78.

64 Ibid., 130.

65 Ibid., 89.

66 Walker, Barbara G. "How local wise-women who carried on ancient traditions were exterminated by Christianity."

67 Ibid.

68 Quilligan, Maureen. *When Women Ruled the World: Making the Renaissance in Europe*. Liverright, 2021.

69 Eisler, 144.

Chapter 3: Anthropology

[70] DeMeo, *Saharasia*, 47.

[71] Ibid., 48.

[72] Ibid., 49.

[73] Ibid., 50.

[74] Graeber and Wengrow, 42.

[75] Sein, Daw Mya. "The Women of Burma: A Tradition of Hard Work and Independence." *The Atlantic*, February 1958.

[76] Ibid.

[77] "Mosuo people" by Goddess Sherry is licensed under CC BY 2.0.

[78] Namu, Erche Yang & Christine Mathieu. *Leaving Mother Lake: A Girlhood at the Edge of the World.* Little, Brown and Company, 2003, 16.

[79] Namu, 16.

[80] "Matriarchal societies." *Heliotricity.com*.

[81] Namu, 17.

[82] Ibid., 17.

[83] Ibid., 31.

[84] Ibid., 35.

[85] Ibid., 36.

[86] Ibid., 69.

[87] "Men Live Better Where Women Are in Charge." *Spiegel.de*, May 28, 2009.

[88] Namu, 177.

[89] Hua, Cai. *A Society Without Fathers or Husbands: The Na of China.* Princeton University Press, 2008, 99.

[90] Ibid., 185.

[91] Ibid., 189.

[92] Ibid., 196.

[93] Ibid., 211.

[94] Ibid., 202.

[95] Ibid., 121.

[96] Ibid., 212.

[97] Ibid., 214.

98 Ibid., 220.

99 Ibid., 224.

100 Ibid., 388.

101 Ryan, Christopher and Jethá, Cacilda. *Sex at Dawn: How We Mate, Why We Stray, and What It Means for Modern Relationships.* Harper Perennial, 2011, 129.

102 Hua, 386.

103 Ibid., 387.

104 Ibid., 401.

105 Ibid.

106 Goettner-Abendroth, Heide. *Matriarchal Societies: Studies on Indigenous Cultures Across the Globe.* Peter Lang Inc., 2013.

107 "Khasi Girls" by Bogman from April 9, 2010 is licensed under CC BY-SA 3.0.

108 "Matriarchal Societies." Heliotricity.com.

34 Ibid.

110 Ibid.

111 Ibid.

112 Ibid.

113 Ibid.

114 DeMeo, *Saharasia*, 174.

115 "Dahomey Amazons" by unknown author is in the public domain.

116 "Matriarchal Societies." Heliotricity.com.

117 Ibid.

118 Styles, Ruth. "Inside the world's original free love community: Islanders change spouses whenever they want, have dedicated 'love huts' and settle their differences over a game of cricket." *The Daily Mail,* May 14, 2014.

119 Diamond, Milton Ph.D. "Sexual Behavior in Pre Contact Hawai'i: A Sexological Ethnography." Pukui, Haertig, and Lee, 1972, 79.

120 "Matriarchal Societies." Heliotricity.com.

121 In Robert Briffault's *The Mothers: The Matriarchal Theory of Social Origins* (qtd. In Garrard, 153).

122 "Miskito people." Wikipedia.

123 Ibid.

124 "Taíno." Wikipedia.

[125] Lewis, Jerome. "Peaceful and Egalitarian Rain Forest Living Hunter and Gatherers." *Matriarchies of Today and the Past.*

[126] Garrard, 152.

[127] Holden, Clare Janaki and Ruth Mace. "Spread of cattle led to the loss of matrilineal descent in Africa: a coevolutionary analysis." *Department of Anthropology, University College London,* 2003.

[128] Lowes, Sara. "Kinship Systems, Gender Norms, and Household Bargaining: Evidence from the Matrilineal Belt." October 2016, 3.

[129] Ibid., 15.

[130] Ibid., 38.

[131] Ibid., 51.

[132] Knight, Chris. "Revisiting Matrilineal Priority." Radical Anthropology Group, 12.

[133] Ibid., 13.

[134] Meyerowitz, Eva L. E. "The Akan of Ghana: their ancient beliefs." Cambridge University Press, December 24, 2009.

[135] DeMeo, *Saharasia*, 59.

[136] *Ryan and Jetha*, 193.

[137] Ibid., 198.

[138] Ibid., 185.

[139] Ibid., 31.

[140] Ibid., 22.

[141] Ibid., 116.

[142] DeMeo, *Saharasia*, 141.

[143] Ibid., 146.

[144] Ibid., 135.

[145] Ibid., 133.

[146] Ibid., 111.

[147] "The Matriarchs of Papua New Guinea Shutting Down Land Developers." IWDA.

Chapter 4: Where do Europeans Come From?

[148] Anthony, David. *The Horse, The Wheel, and Language: How Bronze-Age Riders from the Eurasian Steppes Shaped the Modern World.* Princeton University Press, 2007, kindle location 1551.

149 "Indo-European language family tree based on 'Ancestry-constrained phylogenetic analysis of Indo-European languages'" by Chang et al. is licensed under CC BY-SA 4.0.

150 Documentary *Signs Out of Time: The Story of Archaeologist Marija Gimbutas*. Produced by Kino Lorber films, 2008.

151 "Prof. Dr. Marija Gimbutas im Frauenmuseum Wiesbaden 1993" by Monica Boirar licensed under CC BY-SA 3.0. "Portable Antiquities Scheme from London, England" is licensed under CC BY 2.0.

152 Ibid.

153 From a lecture Gimbutas gave in 1991 for the release of *Civilization of the Goddess*.

154 Ibid.

155 Documentary *Signs Out of Time*.

156 Ibid.

157 Ibid.

158 Ibid.

159 Spretnak, Charlene. "Anatomy of a Backlash: Concerning the Work of Marija Gimbutas." *The Journal of Archeomythology*, vol. 7 (2011), 30.

160 "Indo-European migrations" based on Anthony (2007), Nordqvist & Heyd (2020) is licensed under GNU Free Documentation License.

161 Ibid., 31.

162 Ibid., 32.

163 Ibid., 34.

164 Graeber and Wengrow, 217-8.

165 Lydia Pyne. "Researcher Makes Controversial Allegation of Archaeological Fraud at Renowned Turkish Site." *Hyperallergic*, March 23, 2018.

166 Lord Renfrew lecture to the Oriental Institute of the University of Chicago. *YouTube*, March 14, 2018.

167 Hodder Ian. "Women and Men at Çatalhöyük." *Scientific American*, January 1, 2005.

Chapter 5: The Story of a Story: How Politics Trumps Truth

168 In Lewis Morgan's *Ancient Society* (qtd. in Garrard, 17).

169 Ibid., 19.

170 In Lewis Morgan's *Houses and House-Life of the American Aborigines* (qtd. in Knight, Chris, "Early Human Kinship Was Matrilineal", in N. J. Allen, H. Callan, R. Dunbar and W. James (eds.), "Early Human Kinship." Blackwell, 2008, 67).

171 In Lewis Morgan's *Ancient Society* (qtd. in Knight, "Early Human Kinship Was Matrilineal.")

172 Garrard, 42.

173 Morgan, Lewis. *Houses and House-Life of the American Aborigines.* 1881, 122.

174 Knight, Chris. "Revisiting Matrilineal Priority." University of East London, January 2007, 2.

175 Bachofen, Johann Jacob. *Myth, Religion, and Mother Right.* Princeton University Press, 1967, 70.

176 Ibid., 135-6.

177 Ibid., 71.

178 Ibid., 135-6.

179 Knight, Chris. "Revisiting Matrilineal Priority", 13.

180 In J.F. McLellan's *Primitive Marriage* (qtd. in Knight, "Revisiting Matrilineal Priority", 3).

181 Knight, "Revisiting Matrilineal Priority," 1.

182 Knight, "Early Human Kinship was Matrilineal," 8.

183 Engels, Friedrich. *Origin of the Family, Private Property, and the State.* 1884, 17.

184 Lerner, 21-22.

185 Engels, 17.

186 In Karl Marx and Friedrich Engels' *The German Ideology* (qtd. in Knight, "Early Kinship was Matrilineal," 68).

187 Ibid., 69.

188 Knight, "Early Kinship was Matrilineal," 69.

189 Ibid., 70.

190 Engels, 18.

191 Ibid., 21.

192 In a radio broadcast by Malinowski from 1956 (qtd. in Knight, "Early Human Kinship was Matrilineal," 70).

193 Knight, "Early Human Kinship was Matrilineal," 70.

194 Peter Myers, "Bronislaw Malinowski on the Anthropology of Marriage."

195 Knight, "Early Human Kinship was Matrilineal", 74.

196 Knight, Chris. "Family Ideology and the Crisis in Twentieth Century Kinship Theory." University of East London, 1978, 1.

197 Knight, "Early Human Kinship was Matrilineal," 79.

198 Saini, *The Patriarchs*, 116.

199 Ryan, Christopher. "Pinker's Dirty War on Prehistoric Peace." *Huffpost.com*, January 9, 2012.

200 Wengrow, David. "Everything We Think We Know About Early Human History is Wrong." *YouTube*, Novara Media channel. Uploaded December 4, 2022.

201 Ibid., 342.

202 Lalueza-Fox, Carles. *Inequality: A Genetic History*. The MIT Press, 2022, 47-8.

203 "Prehistory of Iran." *Wikipedia*.

204 Kantor, Helene J. "Chogha Mish." *oi.uchicgo.edu*, 29.

205 DeMeo, *Saharasia*.

206 Kohler, Timothy A. et al. "Greater Post-Neolithic Wealth Disparities in Eurasia than in North and Mesoamerica." *Nature*, November 30, 2017.

207 Ibid, vi.

208 Lalueza-Fox, Carles and David Reich. "Carles Laleuza-Fox discusses *Inequality: A Genetic History* with David Reich. *YouTube*, uploaded by Harvard Bookstore, March 1, 2022.

209 Lalueza-Fox, 32.

210 Lalueza-Fox, 12-3.

Chapter 6: Zoology

211 "No, Your Dog Doesn't Think You're the Alpha." *YouTube*, Jul 13, 2020.

212 Saini, Angela. *Inferior: How Science Got Women Wrong - and the New Research That's Rewriting the Story*. Beacon Press, 2017, 200-204.

213 Ibid., 224.

214 "Primatologist Explains the 1% Difference Between Humans & Apes." *YouTube*, uploaded by Jordan Peterson, 12 January 2023.

215 Sapolsky, Robert. "Peace Among Primates." *Society*, September 2007.

216 Ryan and Jetha, 178.

217 Ibid., 70.

218 Konner, Melvin. *Women After All: Sex, Evolution, and the End of Male Supremacy*. W. W. Norton & Company, 2015, 114.

219 Ibid.,71.

220 De Waal, Frans. *Different: Gender Through the Eyes of a Primatologist.* W.W Northon & Company, 2022, 121.

221 Ibid., 127.

222 Ibid., 198.

223 Ibid., 118.

224 Ibid., 118.

225 Ibid., 206.

226 Ibid., 141.

227 Ryan and Jetha, 102.

228 De Waal, 140-1.

229 Ryan and Jetha, 187.

230 Hamilton, Jon. "Some Generous Apes May Help Explain the Evolution of Human Kindness." *npr.org,* March 2021.

231 Ryan and Jetha, 188.

232 Ibid., 189.

233 Power, Margaret. *The Egalitarians: Human and Chimpanzee.* Cambridge University Press, 1991.

234 Ryan and Jetha, 353.

Chapter 7: Sexology

235 Ibid., 222.

236 Simmons, Leigh W. and García-González, Francisco. "Evolutionary Reduction in Testes Size and Competitive Fertilization Success in Response to the Experimental Removal of Sexual Selection in Dung Beatles." *Evolution: International Journal of Organic Evolution,* Oct 1, 2008.

237 Dutton, Edward, et al. "Europeans Have Larger Testes than Sub-Saharan Africans but Lower Testosterone Levels." *The Mankind Quarterly,* March 2022.

238 Leivers, Samantha et al. "Sperm Competition in Humans: Mate Guarding Behavior Negatively Correlates with Ejaculate Quality." *PLoS One,* 2014; 9(9): e108099.

239 Ibid., 234.

240 Ibid., 242.

241 Ibid., 222.

242 Ibid., 266.

243 O'Malley, Katie. "Men Swipe Right on Tinder More Than Women, Study Confirms." *elle.com*, July 2016.

244 Ryan and Jetha, 56.

245 Ibid., 60.

246 Ibid., 50.

247 Ibid., 57.

248 Knight, "Early Human Kinship Was Matrilineal," 76.

249 "World's oldest nuclear family unearthed in Germany." *The Guardian*, Nov 17, 2008.

250 Ryan and Jetha, 5.

251 Bolster, W. Jeffrey. "Little Ship of Horrors." *New York Times*, Dec 7, 2003.

252 Scelza, B.A. "High rate of extrapair paternity in a human population demonstrates diversity in human reproductive strategies." *ScienceAdvances*, Feb 19, 2020.

253 Starkweather, Katherine E., and Raymond Hames. "A survey of non-classical polyandry." *Human Nature*, June 2012.

254 Dreger, Alice. "When Taking Multiple Husbands Makes Sense." *The Atlantic*, Feb 1, 2013.

255 Broude, Gwen and Greene, Sarah J. "Sexual Attitudes and Practices." World Cultures eJournal, 1986.

256 Ibid., 145.

257 Ibid., 120.

258 Shaffir, Jonathan. "The Hymen's Tale: Myths and facts about the hymen." *Ohio State Health and Discovery*.

259 Ryan and Jetha, 96.

260 Knight, "Early Human Kinship was Matrilineal." 64-5.

261 Ryan and Jetha, 38.

262 DeMeo, *Saharasia*, 158,

263 Ibid., 139.

264 Ryan and Jetha, 37.

265 Knight, "Early Human Kinship was Matrilineal," 77.

266 Bergner, Daniel. *What Do Women Want: Adventures in the Science of Female Desire.* Harper Collins, 2013, 25.

267 Ibid., 94.

268 Gorbett, Zaria. "Why Billionaires have more Sons." *bbc.com*, October 2017.

269 DeMeo, *Saharasia*, 122.

270 Ryan and Jetha, 286.

271 DeMeo, *Saharasia*, 131.

272 Bergner, 9.

273 Ryan and Jetha, 115.

274 Ibid., 96.

275 Ibid., 309.

276 Ibid., 313.

277 Ibid., 5.

278 Ibid., 2.

279 Bergner, 179.

280 Ibid., 179.

281 Edwards, Erika. "Drug to increase women's sex drive wins FDA approval." *nbcnews.com*, June 2019.

282 DeMeo, *Saharasia*, 149.

283 Ibid., 182,

284 Ibid., 183.

285 Ibid., 85.

286 Ibid., 102.

287 Ibid., 191.

288 Ibid., 193.

289 Ryan and Jetha, 221.

290 Ibid., 249.

291 "Hysteria." Wikipedia.

292 Ryan and Jetha, 247.

293 Ibid., 80.

294 Ibid., 25.

295 DeMeo, *Saharasia*, 152.

296 Bergner, 9.

297 Ryan and Jetha, 195.

[298] Mintz, Laurie PhD. "The Orgasm Gap: Simple Truth & Sexual Solutions." *Psychologytoday.com*, October 4, 2015.

[299] Ryan and Jetha, 1-2.

[300] Saxon, Lynn. *Sex at Dusk*. 2012, 173.

[301] Ibid., 234.

[302] Walker, Robert S. et al. "Evolutionary History of Hunter-Gatherer Marriage Practices." *PloS One*, April 27, 2011.

[303] Ibid, 144.

[304] Ibid., 142.

[305] Ibid., 219.

[306] Ibid., 174.

[307] Ibid., 103.

[308] Ibid., 249.

[309] Ibid., 259.

[310] Gorman, James. "Ancient Bones That Tell a Story of Compassion." *New York Times*, Dec 17, 2012.

Chapter 8: Linguistics

[311] Harbeck, James. "Can language slow down time?" *bbc.com*, August 3, 2018.

[312] "Linguistic relativity." *Wikipedia*.

[313] Anthony, *The Horse, The Wheel, and Language*, 840.

[314] Ibid., 849.

[315] Thompson, Helen. "Teenage Girls Have Led Language Innovation for Centuries." *Smithsonian Magazine*, August 10, 2015.

[316] Naik, Gautam. "The Mother of all Languages." *The Wall Street Journal*, April 15, 2011.

[317] Ibid., 27.

[318] "Nostratic Languages - Reconstruction of Proto-Nostratic - Lexicon - Other Words".

[319] Bomhard, 25.

[320] Olsen, Birgit Annette. "Aspects of family structure among Indo-Europeans," in *Tracing the Indo-European,*. Oxbow Books, 2019, 148-9.

[321] Ibid., 150-1.

322 Ibid., 151.

323 Stetsyuk, Valentyn. "Ethnicity of the Neolithic and Chalcolithic cultures of Eastern Europe," Nehring Alfons, 1968, 402.

324 Ibid.

325 "Are Ergative Languages A Sign Of An Ancient And Now Diminished Language Family?" *Dispatches from Turtle Island,* April 25, 2017.

326 Prewitt-Freilino, Jennifer L. et al. "The Gendering of Language: A Comparison of Gender Equality in Countries with Gendered, Natural Gender, and Genderless Languages." Sex Roles 66(3-4), February 2011.

327 Ulatus. "Does Gendered Language Influence the Way We Think?" *Ulatus,* June 30, 2017.

328 Luraghi, Silvia. "The origin of the Proto-Indo-European gender system: Typological considerations." *Folia Linguistica* 45(2), October 2011.

329 Toth, Dr. Alfred. "Are all agglutinative languages related to one another?". *Mikes International,* 2007.

330 Kavtaradze, Giorgi. "Some Problems of the Interrelation of Caucasian and Anatolian Bronze Age Cultures." *Quaderni di Archeologia Università di Messina* 1 (1), 2000.

331 Anthony, *The Horse, The Wheel and Language*, Kindle location 70.

332 Kavtaradze.

333 Anthony, *The Horse, The Wheel and Language*, Kindle location 641.

334 "Centum Satem map" by Dbachmann licensed under GNU Free Documentation License.

335 Ibid., 530.

336 Ibid., 44.

337 "Minoan language blog," August 2010.

338 David Anthony, and Don Ringe. "The Indo-European Homeland from Linguistic and Archaeological Perspectives". *Annual Review of Linguistics* 1(1):199-219, January 2015.

339 Mosenkis, Iurii. "Formation of the Greeks, their language and writing, 4600-2200 BCE." *academia.edu.*

340 Zvelebil, Marek. "The agricultural transition and the origins of Neolithic society in Europe." *Documenta Praehistorica* 28:1-26, December 2001.

341 Anthony, *The Horse, the Wheel and Language*, Kindle location 507.

342 Ibid., 421.

343 Gimbutas, Marija. *Civilization of the Goddess: The World of Old Europe.* HarperSanFrancisco, 1991, 396.

344 Anthony, *The Horse, the Wheel and Language*, Kindle location 616.

345 "Statuette Mehrgarh" by unknown author licensed under CC BY-SA 1.0.

346 "The Whiteness Myth." *NPR.org*, February 9, 2023.

340 Ibid.

348 Wang, Penglin. "Indo-European Loanwords in Altaic." *Sino-Platonic Papers 65*, February 1995.

349 Martin Prechtel from a lecture about a culture being intact, in touch with its indigenous spirit.

350 Anthony, *The Horse, The Wheel and Language*, Kindle location 140-1.

351 Gimbutas, *Civilization of the Goddess*, 396.

Chapter 9: Genetics

345 Zhang, Sarah. "Ancient DNA Is Rewriting Human (and Neanderthal) History." *The Atlantic*, March 2018.

353 Altinisik, N. Ezgi et al. "A genomic snapshot of demographic and cultural dynamism in Upper Mesopotamia during the Neolithic Transition." *Science Advances*, November 2022.

354 "Genetic studies of the inhabitants of one of the world`s oldest cities - Çatalhöyük", *Science in Poland*, May 2019.

355 David, Ariel. "Mysterious 6,500-year-old Culture in Israel Was Brought by Migrants, Researchers Say." *haaretz.com*, August 20, 2018.

356 Sánchez-Quinto, Federico et al. "Megalithic tombs in western and northern Neolithic Europe were linked to a kindred society." *Anthropology*, March 2019.

357 Ariel David, "DNA Study Reveals Family Values of Neolithic People in Britain. But Where Are the Daughters?" *haaretz.com*, December 21, 2021.

358 Bonn-Muller, Eti. "Dynasty of Priestesses." *Archaeology*, March 1, 2010.

359 Boyd, Donna, Terry Melton, et al. "Bioarchaeological evidence for matrilineal descent in a 13th century Native American village". *The Digital Archaeological Record*, 2015.

360 Dong, Yu et al. "Low Mitochondrial DNA Diversity in an Ancient Population from China: Insight into Social Organization at the Fujia Site." *Human Biology* Vol. 87, No. 1, Winter 2015.

361 Max Planck Society. "Ancient DNA reveals the multiethnic structure of Mongolia's first nomadic empire." *Phys.org*, April 14, 2023.

362 Knight, Chris and C. Power. "Grandmothers, politics, and getting back to science." In E. Voland, A. Chasiotis et al. (eds.), *Grandmotherhood: The evolutionary significance of the second half of female life.* Rutgers, 2005, 81-98.

363 Kennett, Douglas J. "Archaeogenomic evidence reveals prehistoric matrilineal dynasty." *Nature Communications*, 8, Article number: 14115, 2017.

364 Saini, *The Patriarchs*, 357.

365 Zeng, Tian Chenet al;. "Cultural hitchhiking and competition between patrilineal kin groups explain the post-Neolithic Y-chromosome bottleneck." *Nature Communications* volume 9, Article number: 2077, 2018.

366 Ibid.

367 Harvey, Ian. "Blond hair originated during the last Ice Age, some 11,000 years ago." *thevintagenews*, September 2016.

368 Cavalli-sforza, L.L. *The History and Geography of Human Genes.* Princeton University Press, 1994.

369 Jacobson, Roni. "New Evidence Fuels Debate over the Origin of Modern Languages." *Scientific American*, March 2018.

370 "When modern Eurasia was born: Genetics yield clues to origins of Eurasians." *ancient-origins.net*, June 2015.

371 Narasimhan, Vagheesh M. et al. "The Formation of Human Populations in South and Central Asia." *Science*, October 2019.

372 Furtwängler, Anja et al. "Ancient genomes reveal social and genetic structure of Late Neolithic Switzerland." *Nature Communications*, April 20, 2020.

373 Haak, Wolfgang et al. "Ancient DNA from European Early Neolithic Farmers Reveals Their Near Eastern Affinities." *PLOS Biology*, March 2010.

374 "Starčevo–Kőrös–Criş culture (c. 6200-4500 BCE)". *Eupedia.com.*

375 Kavtaradze.

376 New Scientist. "David Reich: The truth about us, and where we come from." *YouTube.* June 17, 2020.

377 "Haplogroup J2 Y-DNA." *Eupedia.com.*

378 Ibid.

379 Ibid.

380 Lazaridis, Mittnik et al. "Genetic origins of the Minoans and Myceaneans." *Nature*, August 2017.

381 Quiles, Carlos. "Sea peoples behind Philistines were Aegeans, including R1b-M269 lineages." *indo-european.eu*, July 4, 2019.

382 Majumnar, R.C. *The Vedic Age*, 1951.

383 "Proto-Indo-European_society." *Wikipedia.*

384 "Haplogroups of Bronze Age Proto-Indo-Europeans." *Eupedia.com.*

385 Lalueza-Fox, Carles and David Reich. "Carles Laleuza-Fox discusses "Inequality: A Genetic History" with David Reich. *YouTube,* uploaded by Harvard Bookstore, March 1, 2022.

386 Blakemore, Erin. "Surprising DNA found in ancient people from southern Europe." *National Geographic,* March 14, 2019.

387 Woolf, Chris. "DNA solves mysteries of ancient Ireland." *The World,* December 30, 2015.

388 Gelabert, Pere et al. "Genomes from Verteba cave suggest diversity within the Trypillians in Ukraine." *Sci Rep,* May 2022.

389 Immel, Alexander et al. "Gene-flow from steppe individuals into Cucuteni-Trypillia associated populations indicates long-standing contacts and gradual admixture." *Sci Rep,* 2020.

390 Keys, David. "Britain's prehistoric catastrophe revealed: How 90% of the neolithic population vanished in just 300 years." *Independent,* February 21, 2018.

391 "Bell Beaker Culture." *Wikipedia.*

392 Blakemore.

393 Jacobson, Roni. "New Evidence Fuels Debate over the Origin of Modern Languages." *Scientific American,* March 1, 2018.

394 "Haplogroups of Bronze Age Proto-Indo-europeans". *Eupedia.com.*

395 "Sintashta Culture." *Wikipedia.*

396 Friese, Kai. "4500-year-old DNA from Rakhigarhi reveals evidence that will unsettle Hindutva nationalists." *India Today,* September 10, 2018.

397 Shinde, Vasant et al. "An Ancient Harappan Genome Lacks Ancestry from Steppe Pastoralists or Iranian Farmers." *Cell,* September 5, 2019.

398 Moorjani, Priya. "Genetic Evidence for Recent Population Mixture in India." *National Library of Medicine,* September 5, 2013.

399 Sweety, Aiswariya. "Who are the Dravidians?", *Medium.com,* July 2020.

400 Saju, M.T. "Centre stopped Keezhadi dig due to place's secular culture." *Times of India,* November 2, 2017.

Chapter 10: Archaeology

401 Lundin, Elizabeth. "Cahokia Not as Male-Dominated as Previously Thought, New Archaeology Shows." *History Things,* August 11, 2022.

[402] Solly, Meilan. "Her 3,000-Year-Old Bones Showed Unusual Signs of Wear. It Turns Out, She Was a Master Ceramicist." *Smithsonian*, September 2018.

[403] Wells, Sarah. "Actually Ancient Big Game Hunters were Women." *Inverse*, November 4, 2020.

[404] Garrard, 103.

[405] DeMeo, James. "Update on Saharasia New Findings Since the First Printing." January 2006.

[406] Garrard, 116.

[407] Gimbutas, Marija. *The Living Goddesses*. University of California Press, 1999, 43.

[408] Yirka, Bob. "Archeologist suggests much of Paleolithic cave art was done by women." *Phys.org*, October 2013.

[409] "Despite Male Image, Stone Toolmaking Also Done by Women, University of Florida Scientists Say." *Science Daily*, April 7, 2003.

[410] Eisler, 13.

[411] "Maidanetske 3D model" by K. Rassmann et al is licensed under CC BY-SA 1.0.

[412] Gooch, Stan. *Cities of Dreams*. Aulis Publishers, 1989, Kindle Location 241.

[413] "Trepanated skull of a woman" by Rama and one more author is licensed under CC BY-SA 3.0 fr.

[414] Garrard, 24.

[415] "Linear Pottery culture." *Wikipedia*.

[416] "'Spanish Stonehenge' dating back to 5,000 BC has emerged from a drought-hit dam." *Yahoo news*, August 19, 2022.

[417] Handwerk, Brian. "An Ancient, Brutal Massacre May Be the Earliest Evidence of War." *Smithsonian*, January 20, 2016.

[418] DeMeo, "Update on Saharasia: New Findings Since the First Printing".

[419] Eisler, 14.

[420] "Settlements of the Cucuteni–Trypillia culture." *Wikipedia*.

[421] Chapman et al.

[422] "Venus figures from the Stone Age arranged in Chronological Order." *Don's Maps*.

[423] "Venus of Willendorf" by Mattias Kabel is licensed under CC BY-SA 2.5.

[424] "The Berekhat Ram Venus." *Don's Maps*.

[425] Eisler, 14.

[426] Gimbutas, *The Civilization of the Goddess*, 123.

427 Eisler, 20-21.

428 "The sanctuary at Keros: Questions of materiality and monumentality." Albert Reckitt Archaeological Lecture, *Journal of the British Academy*, 1, 187–212, December 2013.

429 "Venus figurines of Mal'ta." Wikipedia.

430 Garrard, 165.

431 Grosman, Leore et al. "A 12,000-year-old Shaman burial from the southern Levant (Israel)." *PNAS*, November 18, 2008.

432 Curry, Andrew. "9,000 years ago, two people were buried in Germany with hundreds of ritual objects—who were they?" *Archaeology*. March/April 2023.

433 Gimbutas, *The Living Goddesses*, 46.

434 Gimbutas, *Civilization of the Goddess*, viii.

435 Eisler, 11.

436 Garrard, 64-5.

437 Bolger, Diane. "The Dynamics of Gender in Early Agricultural Societies of the Near East." In *Signs*, Vol. 35, No. 2 (Winter 2010), 503-531.

438 Gimbutas, *Living Goddesses*, 116.

439 Gimbutas, *Civilization of the Goddess*, 8.

440 Ibid.

433 Ibid., 33-4.

442 Ibid., 338.

443 Gimbutas, *The Living Goddesses*, 68.

444 Ibid., 66.

445 Gimbutas, *Civilization of the Goddess*, 269.

446 Ibid., 276.

447 Ibid., 117.

448 Chapman, John et al. "The Origins of Trypillia Megasites." *Fronteirs in Digital Humanities*, 2019.

449 "Trypillia culture." *Wikipedia.*

450 Koftun, Valeria. "Cucuteni-Trypillia: Eastern Europe's lost civilisation." *BBC*, August 6, 2021.

451 Ibid., 77-103.

452 Gimbutas, *The Living Goddesses*, 68.

453 "Photo Ellis Hal Salflieni" by Richard Ellis is in the public domain.

454 Bolger, "The Dynamics of Gender in Early Agricultural Societies of the Near East".

455 Left: "Seated Woman of Çatalhöyük accompanied by lionesses, c. 6,000 BC" by Nevit Dilmen is licensed under CC BY-SA 3.0. Right: "Cybele enthroned, with lion, cornucopia, and mural crown" by Marshall Astor is licensed under CC BY-SA 2.0.

456 Devlin, Hannah. "Amateur archaeologist uncovers ice age 'writing' system." *The Guardian*, Jan 5, 2023

457 De Benoist, 143.

458 Ibid., 319-320.

459 Anthony, *The Horse, the Wheel, and Language*, Kindle location 231-2.

460 DeMeo, "Update on Saharasia New Findings Since the First Printing".

461 DeMeo, *Saharasia*, 299.

462 Anthony, *The Horse, The Wheel and Language*, Kindle location 355.

463 Ibid., 317.

464 Ibid., 538.

465 Shilov, Yuri. *Ancient History of Aratta-Ukraine (20,000 BCE - 1,000 CE)*. CreateSpace Independent Publishing Platform, 2015.

466 "Ancient DNA Offers New Insights into the Origins and Spread of Languages and Populations Across the Southern Arc." Howard Hughes Medical Institute, September 2, 2022.

467 Ibid.

468 "Maykop culture" by Joostik is licensed under CC BY-SA 3.0.

469 "The Caucasus: Complex interplay of genes and cultures." *Science Daily*, Feb 4, 2019.

470 "Maykop." *Wikipedia*.

471 Kessler, Peter. "Ancient Mesopotamia Samarra Culture." *History Files*, January 6, 2008.

472 "Kurgan hypothesis." *Wikipedia*.

473 Ibid.

474 Iversen, Rune. "On the emergence of Corded Ware societies in northern Europe: Reconsidering the migration hypothesis." In *Tracing the Indo-Europeans*, 80.

475 Ibid., 76.

476 DeMeo, *Saharasia*, 167.

477 Anthony, *The Horse, The Wheel and Language*, Kindle location 365.

478 de Benoit, 94-95.

479 Ibid., 100.

480 Ibid., 134.

481 Ibid., 134-6.

482 DeMeo, *Saharasia*, 285.

483 Anthony, *The Horse, The Wheel and Language*, Kindle location 319.

484 Iversen, 81.

485 Anthony, David and Ringe, Don. "The Indo-European Homeland from Linguistic and Archaeological Perspectives. *Annual Review of Linguistics*, January 2015.

486 Cycladic Museum, Athens, Greece.

487 Kavtaradze.

488 Wilde, Lyn Webster. *On the Trail of the Women Warriors: The Amazons in Myth and History*. Thomas Dunne Books, 2000, 139.

489 DeMeo, *Saharasia*, 297.

490 Wilde, 34.

491 Anthony, *The Horse, The Wheel and Language*, Kindle location 619.

492 DeMeo, *Saharasia*, 285.

493 Heraklion Archaeological Museum, Heraklion, Crete, Greece.

494 Diepenbrock, George. "Art, Religious Artifacts Support Idea of Minoan Matriarchy on Ancient Crete, Researcher Says." *The University of Kansas*, June 2017.

495 Eisler, 32.

496 Garrard, 90.

497 Eisler, 32.

498 DeMeo, *Saharasia*, 290.

499 Diepenbrock.

500 Eisler, 36.

501 DeMeo, *Saharasia*, 293.

502 Graeber and Wengrow, 438.

503 Garrard, 87.

504 Heraklion Archaeological Museum.

505 *War of the Gods*, 18.

506 Alexiou, 68.

[507] Ibid., 72.

[508] Gimbutas, *Civilization of the Goddess*, 249.

[509] Wilde, 47.

[510] Ibid., 48.

[511] Ibid., 57.

[512] Ibid., 61.

[513] "2,500-year-old DNA Confirms Existence of Amazon Warrior Women." *Forensic*, July 29, 2020.

[514] DeMeo, *Saharasia*, 231.

[515] Ibid., 261.

[516] Thomas, Ryan. "Goddess Worship in Ancient Israel (or Evidence for the Mother God from Archaeology and the Bible)." *Rational Faiths*, March 2013.

[517] Geggel, Laura. "Largest Neolithic Settlement in Israel Uncovered. Up to 3,000 People May Have Lived There." *Live Science*, July 17, 2019.

[518] Sloat, Sarah. "Bodies in 5000 Year-Old Cemetery Reveal Ancient Egalitarian Society." *Inverse.com*, 10 January 2023.

[519] The Leakey Foundation. "Massive Monumental Cemetery Discovered in Kenya." *The Leakey Foundation*, August 22, 2018.

[520] DeMeo, *Saharasia*, 287.

[521] "List of Inventions and Discoveries of the Indus Valley Civilisation." *The Archaeologist.org*, December 26, 2022.

[522] Ibid., 289.

[523] Ibid., 323.

[524] Ibid., 324.

[525] Ibid., 328.

[526] Ibid., 347.

[527] Ibid., 348.

[528] DeMeo, "Update on Saharasia New Findings Since the First Printing."

[529] DeMeo, *Saharasia*, 379.

[530] Ibid., 373.

[531] Ibid., 372.

[532] Graeber and Wengrow, 452.

[533] Ibid., 39.

534 Ibid., 371.

535 Ibid., 374.

536 "Calakmul." *Wikipedia.*

537 Graeber and Wengrow, 386.

538 Ibid., 378.

539 "Caral." Wikipedia.

Chapter 11: History

540 Ibid.

541 Ibid., 445.

542 Broyles, Shawn. "Hittite Kingship." *Oklahoma State University*, 2011, 15.

543 Blasweiler, Joost. "The bloodline of the Tawananna and the offering to the ancestors in the kingdom of Hatti." *Arnhem (NL) Bronze Age*, 2016.

544 Lerner, 155.

545 Wilde, 126.

546 Blasweiler.

547 Lerner, 155.

548 Ibid., 156.

549 Wilde, 130.

550 Lerner, 156.

551 Wilde, 121.

552 Ibid., 138.

553 Eisler, 64.

554 Graeber and Wengrow, 306.

555 Near East Kingdoms: Ancient Persia and the East. *Historyfiles.co.uk.*

556 Ibid.

557 Ibid., 65.

558 Lerner, 67.

559 Ibid.

560 Ibid., 68.

561 Ibid., 63.

562 Ibid., 87.

563 Ibid.

564 Ibid., 109.

565 Ibid., 114.

566 Ibid., 127.

567 Ibid., 132.

568 Ibid., 134-5.

569 Pitai, Raphael. *The Hebrew Goddess.* Wayne University Press, 1967, 47.

570 Lerner, 168.

571 DeMeo, *Saharasia,* 266.

572 Ibid., 250.

573 Ibid., 270.

574 Ibid., 170.

575 Lerner, 10.

576 Petra Museum, Petra, Jordan.

577 Day, Joel. "Archaeologists stunned by worship of female god in Petra 'long before Islam'." *UK Express,* December 2021.

578 "Matriarchal Societies." *Heliotricity.com.*

579 Wilde, 99.

580 DeMeo, *Saharasia,* 308.

581 Ibid., 165.

582 Ibid., 124.

583 Ibid., 298.

584 *War of the Gods,* 9.

585 Ibid., 6.

586 Ibid., 8.

587 Ibid., 12.

588 Ibid., 20.

589 Eisler, 106.

590 Ibid.

591 Blasweiler, 38.

[592] Eisler, 108.

[593] Ibid., 112.

[594] Wilde, 19.

[595] Ibid., 20.

[596] *War of the Gods*, 58.

[597] Ibid., 58.

[598] Ibid., 63.

[599] Ibid., 58.

[600] Bateman, Jessica. "The discovery of the ancient Greek city of Tenea." *bbc* September 16, 2019.

[601] Wilde, 12.

[602] Ibid., 28.

[603] Ibid., 26.

[604] Ibid., 34.

[605] Ibid., 41.

[606] Learn, Joshua Rapp. "The Forgotten History of Amazon Warrior Women of Ancient Scythia." *Discover Magazine,* July 23, 2021.

[607] "Burial of an Ancient Female Warrior Discovered in Armenia." *Archaeology,* November 28, 2019.

[608] Ibid., 178.

[609] Gimbutas, *Civilization of the Goddess,* 344.

[610] Ibid.

[611] Roller, Duane W. "Feminist Geography: The Empowered Women of Strabo." *Society for Classical Studies.*

[612] Bachofen, Johann Jacob. *Myth, Religion, and Mother Right.* Princeton University Press, 1967, 145.

[613] Ibid.

[614] Morgan, Louis H. *Ancient Society,* 1877.

[615] DeMeo, *Saharasia,* 236.

[616] Herodotus, *Histories.*

[617] "Biography of Artemisia I, Warrior Queen of Halicarnassus." *ThoughtCo.*

[618] Lerner, 18.

[619] Eisler, 116.

[620] Lerner, 76.

[621] Lerner, 22.

[622] Gimbutas, *Civilization of the Goddess*, 346-7.

[623] "Cecrops I." *Wikipedia*.

[624] DeMeo, *Saharasia*, 236.

[625] Ibid., 239.

[626] Ibid., 242.

[627] Gimbutas, *Civilization of the Goddess*, 347-8.

[628] DeMeo, *Saharasia*, 304.

[629] Ibid., 202.

[630] Gimbutas, *Civilization of the Goddess*, 348.

[631] Wilde, 128.

[632] Ryan and Jetha, 94.

[633] Gimbutas, *Civilization of the Goddess*, 348.

[634] DeMeo, *Saharasia*, 242.

[635] Eisler, 130.

[636] DeMeo, *Saharasia*, 310.

[637] Ibid., 307.

[638] Ibid., 310.

[639] Ibid., 244.

[640] Ibid., 245.

[641] Ibid., 333.

[642] Ibid., 316.

[643] Ibid., 332.

[644] Ibid., 334.

[645] Ibid., 338.

[646] Ibid., 335.

[647] Ibid., 315.

[648] Ibid., 339.

[649] Eisler, 139.

650 Ibid., 143.

651 Ibid., 154.

652 Ibid., 148.

653 Russo, Francine. "Viking Textiles Show Women Had Tremendous Power." *Scientific American*, October 2022.

654 DeMeo, *Saharasia*, 313.

655 Eisler, 140.

656 DeMeo, *Saharasia*, 313.

657 Eisler, 150.

658 Ibid., 153.

659 DeMeo, *Saharasia*, 356.

660 Snow, Justine T. "The Spider's Web. Goddesses of Light and Loom: Examining the Evidence for the Indo-European Origin of Two Ancient Chinese Deities." *Sino-Platonic Papers*, Number 118, June 2002.

661 DeMeo, *Saharasia*, 356.

662 Ibid., 357.

663 Namu.

664 "Bottle Woman: The Great Goddess in America". *DNAConsultants.com*, February 4, 2022.

665 Graeber and Wengrow, 348.

666 Santana, Daniel. "Indigenous Masculinities and the Tarascan Borderlands in Sixteenth-Century Michoacán." *University of Texas at El Paso*, January 2019.

667 Darling, Juanita. "The Women Who Run Juchitan : Matriarchy flourishes in this Mexican town where wives and mothers dominate economic and family life." *Los Angeles Times*, March 31, 1995.

668 Elbein, Saul. "Ancient Mexican city reveals social roots of democracy." *The Hill*, March 8, 2022.

669 Chinas, Beverly Newbold. *The Isthmus Zapotecs: A Matrifocal Culture of Mexico.* Harcourt Brace Jovanich, 1992, 9.

670 Ibid., 14.

671 Ibid., 47.

672 Ibid., 113.

673 Ibid., 50.

674 Ibid., 115.

Chapter 12: Mythology

675 *War of the Gods*, 2.

676 Eisler, 64.

677 *War of the Gods*, 14.

678 "History of Shaktism." *Wikipedia.*

679 Gimbutas, *The Living Goddesses*, 46.

680 Gimbutas. *Civilization of the Goddess*, 225.

681 Ibid., 69.

682 Eisler, 69.

683 Graves, 58.

684 Ibid., 61-62.

685 Ibid., 404.

686 Gimbutas, *Civilization of the Goddess*, 343.

687 Castleman, Michael M.A. "Orgies Through the Ages." *Psychology Today*, September 4, 2018.

688 Graves, 226.

689 Ibid., 226.

690 Ibid., 316.

691 Ibid., 64.

692 Ibid., 64-65.

693 Ibid., 371.

694 *War of the Gods*, 75.

695 Doniger, Wendy. *Women, Androgynes and Other Mythical Beasts.* University of Chicago Press, 1982, 211-212.

696 Brown, Dorcas and David W. Anthony. "Late Bronze Age midwinter dog sacrifices and warrior initiations at Krasnosamarskoe, Russia." in *Tracing the Indo-Europeans.*

697 Olsen, Birgit A, et al. "Tracing the Indo-Europeans: An Introduction", in *Tracing the Indo-Europeans.*

698 Eisler, 69.

699 *War of the Gods*, 14.

700 Gimbutas, *The Civilization of the Goddess*, 243.

701 Ibid., 349.

702 Lerner, 159.

703 Graves, 61.

704 Ibid., 62.

705 Ibid., 62.

706 Ibid., 93.

707 Neumann, Erich. *The Great Mother*. Princeton University Press, 1970, 290.

708 Ibid., 160.

709 Graves, 389.

710 Ibid., 157.

711 Ibid., 143.

712 Dashu, Max. "Female Divinity in South America." *Suppressed Histories*.

713 Ibid.

714 Ibid.

715 Dashu, Max. "Icons of the Matrix." *Suppressed Histories*.

Chapter 13: Conclusions and Solutions

716 Mallory, 242.

717 Ibid., 259.

718 Ryan and Jetha, 111.

719 Chemally, Soraya. "There's No Comparing Male and Female Harassment Online." *Time*, September 2014.

720 Marcelo, Sheila Lirio. "Eight numbers to keep in mind on International Women's Day." *Quartz*, March 8, 2019.

721 Ortiz-Ospina, Esteban, and Sandra Tzvetkova. "Working women: Key facts and trends in female labor force participation." *Our World in Data*, October 2017.

722 DeMeo, *Saharasia*, 341.

723 Ibid., 174.

724 Ibid., 401.

725 Eisler, 168.

726 Ryan and Jetha, 9.

727 Eisler, 195.

[728] Kapin, Allyson. "10 Stats That Build the Case for Investing in Women-Led Startups." *Forbes*, January 2019.

[729] Konner, 8.

[730] Ibid., 270.

[731] Ibid., 282.

[732] Ibid., 283.

[733] Ibid., 290.

[734] Eisler, 195.

[735] Rippon, Gina. *Gender and Our Brains*. Penguin Random House, 2019, 138.

736 Konner, 203.

737 Garrard, 111.

[738] Yoder, Kate. "What 5,000-year-old skeletons tell us about living with climate change." *Grist.com*, January 23, 2023.

[739] Graeber and Wengrow, 525.

BIBLIOGRAPHY

(See BeforeWar.com/Sources for online sources)

Altinisik, N. Ezgi et al., "A genomic snapshot of demographic and cultural dynamism in Upper Mesopotamia during the Neolithic Transition," *Science Advances*, November 2022.

"Ancient DNA Offers New Insights into the Origins and Spread of Languages and Populations Across the Southern Arc." *Howard Hughes Medical Institute*, September 2, 2022.

Ancient Origins. "When modern Eurasia was born: Genetics yield clues to origins of Eurasians." *Ancient-origins.net,* June 2015.

Anthony, David and Don Ringe. "The Indo-European Homeland from Linguistic and Archaeological Perspectives.""*Annual Review of Linguistic*s 1(1):199-219, January 2015.

Anthony, David. *The Horse, The Wheel, and Language: How Bronze-Age Riders from the Eurasian Steppes Shaped the Modern World.* Princeton University Press, 2007.

Archaeology World Team. "Burial of an Ancient Female Warrior Discovered in Armenia." *Archaeology*, November 28, 2019.

Bachofen, Johann Jacob. *Myth, Religion, and Mother Right.* Princeton University Press, 1967.

Bateman, Jessica, "The discovery of the ancient Greek city of Tenea", *bbc*, September 16, 2019.

Bergner, Daniel. *What Do Women Want: Adventures in the Science of Female Desire.* Harper Collins, 2013.

Blakemore, Erin. "Surprising DNA found in ancient people from southern Europe." *National Geographic*, March 14, 2019.

Blasweiler, Joost. "The bloodline of the Tawananna and the offering to the ancestors in the kingdom of Hatti." Arnhem (NL) Bronze Age, 2016.

Bolger, Diane. "The Dynamics of Gender in Early Agricultural Societies of the Near East", in *Signs*, Vol. 35, No. 2 (Winter 2010), pp. 503-531.

Bomhard, Allan. "Bomhard - Indo-European and the Nostratic Hypothesis", *academia.edu*, 1995.

Bonn-Muller, Eti. "Dynasty of Priestesses", *Archaeology*, March 2010.

Boyd, Donna et al, "Bioarchaeological evidence for matrilineal descent in a 13th century Native American village." *The Digital Archaeological Record*, 2015.

Briffault, Robert. *The Mothers: The Matriarchal Theory of Social Origins.* Macmillan, 1931.

Broyles, Shawn. "Hittite Kingship." Oklahoma State University, 2011.

David Cameron. "Genetics Proves Indian Population Mixture." Harvard Medical School, August 8, 2013.

Chapman, John et al., "The Origins of Trypillia Megasites." *Fronteirs in Digital Humanities*, 2019.

Chemally, Soraya. "There's No Comparing Male and Female Harassment Online." *Time*, September 2014.

Chinas, Beverly Newbold, *The Isthmus Zapotecs: A Matrifocal Culture of Mexico*. Harcourt Brace Jovanich: 1992.

Cline, Eric H, *1177 B.C.: The Year Civilization Collapsed.* Princeton University Press, 2021.

Darina L., "Shocking Male vs Female CEO Statistics 2022." *Leftronic*, January 23, 2022.

Darling, Juanita. "The Women Who Run Juchitan : Matriarchy flourishes in this Mexican town where wives and mothers dominate economic and family life". *Los Angeles Times*, March 31, 1995.

Dashu, Max. "Female Divinity in South America." *Suppressed Histories.*

David, Ariel. "DNA Study Reveals Family Values of Neolithic People in Britain. But Where Are the Daughters?" *Haaretz.com*, December 21, 2021.

David, Ariel. "Mysterious 6,500-year-old Culture in Israel Was Brought by Migrants, Researchers Say." *haaretz.com*, August 20, 2018.

Day, Joel, "Archaeologists stunned by worship of female god in Petra 'long before Islam'", *UK Express*, December 2021.

De Benoit, Alain. *The Indo-Europeans: In Search of the Homeland.* rktos Media Ltd, 2016)

DeMeo, James. *Saharasia.* atural Energy Works, 1998.

DeMeo, James. "Update on Saharasia New Findings Since the First Printing", January 2006.

De Waal, Frans. *Different: Gender Through the Eyes of a Primatologist.* New York: W.W Northon & Company, 2022.

Diamond, Milton Ph.D. "Sexual Behavior in Pre Contact Hawai'i: A Sexological Ethnography." *Revista Española del Pacifico,* 2004.

Diepenbrock, George. "Art, Religious Artifacts Support Idea of Minoan Matriarchy on Ancient Crete, Researcher Says." The University of Kansas, June 2017.

Dong, Yu et al. "Low Mitochondrial DNA Diversity in an Ancient Population from China: Insight into Social Organization at the Fujia Site", *Human Biology* Vol. 87, No. 1 (Winter 2015).

Doniger, Wendy. *Women, Androgynes and Other Mythical Beasts* (Chicago: University of Chicago Press, 1982).

Driessen, Jan. "A Prepalatial Matrilinear Society." *Proceedings of the Leuven Conference,* January 2011.

Edwards, Erika. "Drug to increase women's sex drive wins FDA approval." *NBCnews.com,* June 2019.

Elbein, Saul , "Ancient Mexican city reveals social roots of democracy." *The Hill,* March 8, 2022.

Eisler, Riane. *The Chalice and the Blade: Our History, Our Future.* Harper & Row, 1987.

Engels, Friedrich. *Origin of the Family, Private Property, and the State. 1884.*

Friese, Kai. "4500-year-old DNA from Rakhigarhi reveals evidence that will unsettle Hindutva nationalists." *India Today,* September 10, 2018.

Furtwängler,Anja et al. "Ancient genomes reveal social and genetic structure of Late Neolithic Switzerland." *Nature Communications,* April 20, 2020.

Gelabert, Pere, et al. "Genomes from Verteba cave suggest diversity within the Trypillians in Ukraine." *Sci Rep,* May 2022.

Gerrard, Bruce. *The Ancient Problem with Men: The Prehistoric Origins of Patriarchy.*

Gimbutas, Marija. The Living Goddesses, (Berkeley: University of California Press, 1999).

Gorbett, Zaria. "Why Billionaires have more Sons", *bbc.com,* October 2017.

Graeber, David and David Wengrow. *The Dawn of Everything* (New York: Farrar, Straus and Giroux, 2021)

Geggel, Laura. "Largest Neolithic Settlement in Israel Uncovered. Up to 3,000 People May Have Lived There." *Live Science,* July 17, 2019.

Gooch, Stan. *Cities of Dreams.* Aulis Publishers, 1989.

Graves, Robert, *The White Goddess: A Historical and Poetical Myth.* Farrar, Straus and Giroux, 1997.

Grosman, Leore et al. "A 12,000-year-old Shaman burial from the southern Levant (Israel)", *PNAS,* November 18, 2008.

Haak, Wolfgang et al. "Ancient DNA from European Early Neolithic Farmers Reveals Their Near Eastern Affinities." *PLOS Biology,* March 2010.

Hamilton, Jon. "Some Generous Apes May Help Explain the Evolution of Human Kindness." *npr.org,* March 2021.

Harbeck, James. "Can language slow down time?" *bbc.com,* August 2018.

355

Harvey, Ian. "Blond hair originated during the last Ice Age, some 11,000 years ago." The Vintage News, September 2016.

Heliotricity.com. "Matriarchal Societies".

Herodotus, *Histories*.

Holden, Clare Janaki and Ruth Mace. "Spread of cattle led to the loss of matrilineal descent in Africa: a coevolutionary analysis." Department of Anthropology, University College London, 2003.

Hua, Cai. *A Society Without Fathers or Husbands: The Na of China.* Princeton University Press, 2008.

Immel, Alexander et al." Gene-flow from steppe individuals into Cucuteni-Trypillia associated populations indicates long-standing contacts and gradual admixture." *Sci Rep*, 2020.

Jacobson, Roni. "New Evidence Fuels Debate over the Origin of Modern Languages." *Scientific American*, March 1, 2018.

Kapin, Allyson. "10 Stats That Build the Case for Investing in Women-Led Startups." *Forbes*, January 2019.

Kavtaradze, Giorgi. "Some Problems of the Interrelation of Caucasian and Anatolian Bronze Age Cultures."*Quaderni di Archeologia Università di Messina* 1 (1), 2000.

Kennett, Douglas J. "Archaeogenomic evidence reveals prehistoric matrilineal dynasty." *Nature Communications*, 8, Article number: 14115, 2017.

Keys, David. "Britain's prehistoric catastrophe revealed: How 90% of the neolithic population vanished in just 300 years." *Independent*, February 21, 2018.

Knight, Chris. "Early Human Kinship Was Matrilineal". Edited by N. J. Allen, H. Callan, R. Dunbar and W. James, *Early Human Kinship.* Blackwell, 2008.

Knight, Chris. "Revisiting Matrilineal Priority." University of East London: January 2007.

Knight, Chris and C. Power. "Grandmothers, politics, and getting back to science". Editors E. Voland et al, *Grandmotherhood: The evolutionary significance of the second half of female life.* New Brunswick: Rutgers, 2005.

Konner, Melvin. *Women After All: Sex, Evolution, and the End of Male Supremacy.* W. W. Norton & Company, 2015

Lalueza-Fox, Carles, *Inequality: A Genetic History*. The MIT Press, 2022.

Lavalli-sforza, L.L. The History and Geography of Human Genes. Princeton University Press, 1994.

Lazaridis, Mittnik et al. "Genetic origins of the Minoans and Myceaneans." *Nature*, August 2017.

Learn, Joshua Rapp. "The Forgotten History of Amazon Warrior Women of Ancient Scythia." "*iscover Magazine*, July 23, 2021.

Lerner, Gerda. *The Creation of Patriarchy*. Oxford University Press, 1986.

Lowes, Sara. "Kinship Systems, Gender Norms, and Household Bargaining: Evidence from the Matrilineal Belt." *NBER*, October 2016.

Lundin, Elizabeth. "Cahokia Not as Male-Dominated as Previously Thought, New Archaeology Shows." *History Things*, August 11, 2022.

Luraghi, Silvia. "The origin of the Proto-Indo-European gender system: Typological considerations", *Folia Linguistica* 45(2), October 2011.

356

Mallory, J.P. *In Search of the Indo-Europeans.* Thames & Hudson, 1991.

Majumnar, R.C. *The Vedic Age,* 1951.

Manco, Jean. *Ancestral Journeys: The Peopling of Europe from the First Venturers to the Vikings.* Thames & Hudson, 2013.

Marcelo, Sheila Lirio. "Eight numbers to keep in mind on International Women's Day." *Quartz.*

Meyerowitz, Eva L. E. "The Akan of Ghana: their ancient beliefs." Cambridge University Press: 2009.

Mintz. Laurie PhD. "The Orgasm Gap: Simple Truth & Sexual Solutions." P*sychologytoday.com*, October 4, 2015.

Moorjani, Priya. "Genetic Evidence for Recent Population Mixture in India." *National Library of Medicine*, September 2013.

Morgan, Lewis. *Ancient Society,* 1877.

Morgan, Lewis. *Houses and House-Life of the American Aborigines,* 1881.

Mosenkis, Iurii. "Formation of the Greeks, their language and writing, 4600-2200 BCE." *academia.edu.*

Namu, Yang Erche & Christine Mathieu. *Leaving Mother Lake: A Girlhood at the Edge of the World.* Little, Brown and Company, 2003.

Neumann, Erich. *The Great Mother.* Princeton University Press, 1970.

Olalde, Iñigo et al. "The Beaker Phenomenon and the Genomic Transformation of Northwest Europe." *Nature*, March 8, 2018.

Olsen, Birgit et al. "Tracing the Indo-Europeans: An Introduction", in *Tracing the Indo-Europeans*: *New evidence from archaeology and historical linguistics. Oxbow* Books, 2019.

Ortiz-Ospina, Esteban and Sandra Tzvetkova. "Working women: Key facts and trends in female labor force participation." *Our World in Data.*

Narasimhan, Vagheesh M. et al. "The Formation of Human Populations in South and Central Asia." Science, October 2019.

Patowary, Kaushik. "Venus of Berekhat Ram: The World's Oldest Piece of Art That Predates Humans." *Amusing Planet*, Oct 13, 2016.

Pitai, Raphael. *The Hebrew Goddess.* Wayne University Press, 1967.

Power, Margaret. *The Egalitarians: Human and Chimpanzee.* Cambridge University Press, 1991.

Quiles, Carlos, "Sea peoples behind Philistines were Aegeans, including R1b-M269 lineages." *indo-european.eu,* July 4, 2019.

Reckitt, Albert. Archaeological Lecture "The sanctuary at Keros: Questions of materiality and monumentality." *Journal of the British Academy,* 1, 187–212, December 2013.

Rippon, Gina. *Gender and Our Brains.* Penguin Random House, 2019.

Robb, David, "Female Leads a Hollywood Rarity, Study Finds", *Deadline.com,* February 9, 2015.

Roller, Duane W. "Feminist Geography: The Empowered Women of Strabo.""*Society for Classical Studies.*

Russo, Francine. "Viking Textiles Show Women Had Tremendous Power." *Scientific American*, October 2022.

Ryan, Christopher and Cacilda Jetha. *Sex at Dawn: How We Mate, Why We Stray, and What It Means for Modern Relationships.* Harper Perennial, 2011.

Sánchez-Quinto, Federico et al. "Megalithic tombs in western and northern Neolithic Europe were linked to a kindred society."Anthropology, March 2019.

Santana, Daniel, "Indigenous Masculinities and the Tarascan Borderlands in Sixteenth-Century Michoacán." *University of Texas at El Paso,* January 2019.

Saini, Angela, et al., *Inferior: How Science Got Women Wrong - and the New Research That's Rewriting the Story.* Beacon Press: 2017.

Sapolsky, Robert. "Peace Among Primates." *Society*, September 2007.

Shaffir, Jonathan. "The Hymen's Tale: Myths and facts about the hymen", *Ohio State Health and Discovery.*

Shilov, Yuri. Ancient History of Aratta-Ukraine (20,000 BCE - 1,000 CE). CreateSpace Independent Publishing Platform, 2015.

Shinde, Vasant et al. "An Ancient Harappan Genome Lacks Ancestry from Steppe Pastoralists or Iranian Farmers." *Cell*, September 5, 2019.

Sky, Michael. *Beyond the Dominator Virus.* Santa Fe: Bear & Co, 1993.

Solly, Meilan. "Her 3,000-Year-Old Bones Showed Unusual Signs of Wear. It Turns Out, She Was a Master Ceramicist". *Smithsonian*, September 2018.

Spretnak, Charlene. "Anatomy of a Backlash: Concerning the Work of Marija Gimbutas." *The Journal of Archeomythology*, vol. 7, 2011

Stetsyuk, Valentyn. "Ethnicity of the Neolithic and Chalcolithic cultures of Eastern Europe."

Styles, Ruth. "Inside the world's original free love community: Islanders change spouses whenever they want, have dedicated 'love huts' and settle their differences over a game of cricket." *The Daily Mail*, May 14, 2014.

Sweety, Aiswariya. "Who are the Dravidians?", *Medium.com*, July 2020.

Thomas, Ryan. "Goddess Worship in Ancient Israel (or Evidence for the Mother God from Archaeology and the Bible)."*Rational Faiths*, March 2013.

Toth, Alfred. "Are all agglutinative languages related to one another?" *Pikes International*, 2007.

Wade, Nicholas. "What We All Spoke When the World was Young." *New York Times*, 2000.

Wang, Penglin. "Indo-European Loanwords in Altaic." *Sino-Platonic Papers* 65, February 1995.

War of the Gods: The Conflict Between Matriarchy and Patriarchy During the Greek Dark Age. Black's Academy Limited, 2019.

Wells, Sarah. "Actually Ancient Big Game Hunters were Women." *Inverse*, November 4 2020.

Wilde, Lyn Webster. *On the Trail of the Women Warriors: The Amazons in Myth and History.* Thomas Dunne Books, 2000.

Wilford, John Noble. "Mummies, Textiles Offer Evidence of Europeans in Far East." *New York Times*, May 1996.

Woolf, Chris. "DNA solves mysteries of ancient Ireland." *The World*, December 30, 2015.

Yoder, Kate, "What 5,000-year-old skeletons tell us about living with climate change." *Grist.org,* January 23, 2023.

Zdzieblowski, Szymon. "Genetic studies of the inhabitants of one of the world's oldest cities - Çatalhöyük." Science in Poland, May 2019.

Zeng, Tian Chen et al. "Cultural hitchhiking and competition between patrilineal kin groups explain the post-Neolithic Y-chromosome bottleneck". *Nature Communications* volume 9, Article number: 2077, 2018.

Zhang, Sarah. "Ancient DNA Is Rewriting Human (and Neanderthal) History." *The Atlantic*, March 2018.

Zvelebil, Marek. "The agricultural transition and the origins of Neolithic society in Europe." *Documenta Praehistorica* 28:1-26, December 2001.